Integrating the Individual and the Organization

Integrating

the Individual

and the Organization

CHRIS ARGYRIS

Professor, Department of Industrial Administration

Yale University

John Wiley & Sons, Inc.

New York · London · Sydney

Copyright © 1964 by John Wiley & Sons, Inc.

All Rights Reserved
This book or any part thereof
must not be reproduced in any form
without the written permission of the publisher.

20 19 18 17 16 15 14 13 12 11

Library of Congress Catalog Card Number: 64-13209
Printed in the United States of America

ISBN 0 471 03315 4

To my grandmother

Δ. Π.

This book is dedicated to the only grandmother I have ever known;
a warm, loving person with a deep concern for human beings.

Preface

About a decade ago I wrote *Personality and Organization* whose theme was that implicit in the traditional organizational theory and practice were factors that led to unintended consequences with negative effects on the organization and the individual.

The intervening years have been spent in conducting research which hopefully has helped to expand the knowledge of the problems as well as to refine the theoretical framework. However, along with the need for this research activity, there developed the need to conduct research to test out possible solutions to the problems.

This need turned out to be extremely difficult to begin to satisfy for three reasons. First, I lacked a sound philosophical orientation with which to deal with the knotty value issues involved in attempting to integrate the individual and the organization. Second, there was a dearth of research findings on which to draw. Apparently few researchers are interested in developing solutions to the problems that research has raised. Third, there was the absence of a model or theoretical framework that could help to provide some guideposts to this activity.

During the past three years I have been striving to decrease some of these deficiencies by reading studies that even remotely related to the problem, by theorizing with fellow social scientists and with executives as to how organizations might be modified, and, finally, by striving to develop a systematic framework from which to develop solutions that can be tested.

As a result of a conference sponsored by the National Institute of Mental Health and directed by Dr. Raymond F. Gould, I became encouraged to publish my extremely tentative theories with the hope that colleagues would raise objections, point out gaps and inconsistencies, and suggest more effective ways of conceptualizing the problem. Once all this added knowledge and experience was digested, it was hoped we could refine the theoretical framework once more and then begin to conduct empirical research.

The primary objective of this book, therefore, is to present my *preliminary thinking* and *theorizing* about how organizations might be redesigned to take into account—more fully than has been possible up to this date—the energies and competences that human beings have to offer. Unfortunately, only the broad outlines can be presented because the specific details must await systematic empirical research.

Many of the readers of the earlier manuscript noted a difficulty in following the suggestions about how to change organizations because they were not up to date on my thinking about the causes of these problems. They suggested that a full statement of the problem be included before the discussion of the possible solutions. In effect, this meant a summary of the framework presented in my previous books.

Rather than present such a summary, I decided to take another tack. The early version of *Personality and Organization* needed revision, so why could not such a revision serve as an up-to-date introduction to the main theme of this book? Following a brief introductory chapter, therefore, are four chapters which present a revised view of *Personaltiy and Organization.*

Anyone who attempts to develop a theoretical framework may be said to be responsible for constantly comparing it with his own and other's empirical research and theorizing, modifying the framework whenever appropriate, and developing new research whose successful completion would enlarge and deepen the framework. Each of my recent major publications attempts in a small way to contribute something toward each of these objectives.

One of the problems involved in publishing such research (as is illustrated by the readers' comments cited earlier) is the necessity to include the original framework in order to remind the reader of the previous work and to make clear what is to be tested. The reader who is primarily interested in the ideas of the framework and who, therefore, does not focus on the empirical evidence developed for each study may experience a feeling that "I have read this before."

This feeling of repetitiveness could be especially strong in Chapters 2 through 5. With the exceptions to be noted hereafter, the theoretical views in these chapters are not new. However, with the minor exception of the discussion of the foreman, *the empirical data cited to support the position is new in the sense that it has never been quoted with this objective in mind.* In short, it is hoped that the reader interested in the empirical dimensions of a theoretical framework will not find these four chapters repetitive.

The first part also contains some innovations. First, there has been developed (what I hope is) a more effective way of conceptualizing the individual as a participant in the organization. Instead of conceiving the individual in terms of "mature" and "immature" (as was true in the early version), I speak of "psychological energy" and how the amount of this energy can be increased in the service of the organization and individual effectiveness.

Second, two questions are explored that were not discussed in the early work. First, I discuss the relation between the environment (especially social class) and the internal behavior of the organization. Second, I attempt to defend the position that the concept of individual positive mental health used in this book is not simply a middle-class value.

Beginning with Part II (Chapter 6) is a discussion of organizational effectiveness and ineffectiveness. In Chapter 7 the theoretical point of view of the dimensions that must be taken into account to integrate the individual and the organization is described, whereas in Chapter 8 relevant literature that indirectly illustrates our point of view is introduced.

In Part III some theorizing is developed as to how organizations might be redesigned. This includes a discussion of "organizational structures" (Chapter 9), "organizational staffing and job design" (Chapter 10), "managerial controls, rewards and penalties, and incentive systems" (Chapter 11), "evaluating, hiring, and terminating employees" (Chapter 12), and an overall summary (Chapter 13). *None of these is meant to be an exhaustive analysis.* The hope is to present some of the major issues and the major policies involved.

In Part IV two further topics are investigated: "integrating the sociological and psychological levels of analysis" (Chapter 14) and relating "organizational pseudo-effectiveness and individual pseudo-health" (Chapter 15).

I should like to acknowledge my indebtedness to the National Institute of Mental Health. It is their generous financial support (3M-9128) that made the review as well as the preliminary exploratory study possible. Dr. Raymond Gould of N.I.M.H. provided important scholarly and administrative assistance.

Many individuals have given generously of their time and efforts to help me to clarify my thoughts, correct my errors, and enlarge my horizons. In this connection, I especially wish to thank Clayton Alderfer, Wilfred Brown, Professors Warren Bennis, Vernon Buck, Robert Dubin, Roger Harrison, Morris Janowitz, Robert Kahn, Daniel Levinson, Howard Perlmutter, Edward Schein, Charles Summer, Donald W. Taylor, James Thompson, Stanley Udy, and Goodwin Watson. Needless to say, I alone am responsible for the interpretations presented herein.

Miss Sally Marchessault, Miss Julie Merkt, and Mrs. Alice Galper were especially helpful in typing the manuscript and preparing it for the printer.

Chris Argyris

New Haven, Connecticut
December 1963

Contents

Part Four

PART I

Chapter 1 ☒☒☒☒☒☒☒☒☒☒☒☒☒☒☒☒☒☒☒☒☒☒☒☒☒☒☒☒☒☒☒☒☒☒☒☒☒☒☒

Introduction to Individual and Organizational Effectiveness

One of the main themes of this book is that the problem of integrating the individual and the organization is one in which both have to "give a little" to profit from each other. One of the major issues is how much should each "give"? Is it possible to maximize these relationships? I doubt it. Nor does an optimal integration seem likely in the near future. Borrowing from March and Simon,[1] it is suggested that the best that can be offered in this book are some suggestions as to how to "satisfice" the relationships between the individual and the organization. Unlike optimizing, where a set of criteria exists that permits all alternatives to be compared and the alternative in question is preferred by these criteria, a "satisfactory" solution occurs when a set of criteria exists that describes minimally satisfactory alternatives, and the alternatives meet or exceed all these criteria.

Our objective is to do better than minimally satisfice, but we expect to be far short of optimizing. Some of the reasons for suggesting that this level of aspiration may be realistic follow.

The notion of *effectiveness* at any level of analysis is an extremely elusive concept. For some time the measure of business organization effectiveness could be discussed in one word, profit. During the last

[1] James March and Herbert Simon, *Organizations*, Wiley, New York, 1958, pp. 140–141.

decade, it has almost become a fad to discuss the multi-objective business firm. Recently many organizational theorists have pointed out that measures of effectiveness should take into consideration numerous intervening variables such as personality, traditions, cognitive orientations, perceptions, and others.

The moment one speaks of organizations that take the individual more into account, images are evoked ranging from organizations striving to make people happy, reduce work, treat them with kid gloves, to organizations that skillfully and covertly manipulate individuals so that they think they are happy when "we've got them all the time."

We are interested in developing neither an overpowering manipulative organization nor organizations that will "keep people happy." Happiness, morale, and satisfaction are not going to be highly relevant guides in our discussion. Individual competence, commitment, self-responsibility, fully functioning individuals, and active, viable, vital organizations will be the kinds of criteria that we will keep foremost in our minds. As we shall see, the former can be "painful" to the individual and the latter "painful" to the organization. But if these "pains" are necessary for increasing individual and organizational effectiveness, they will be included in our considerations.

In all fairness it should be pointed out that this trend away from "keeping people happy" has a long but, until recently, not carefully examined history. According to Erikson, even Freud emphasized, in addition to love, the importance of work in being a healthy person.[2] Experimental evidence has been presented by Barker, Dembo, and Lewin showing that a certain amount of tension and frustration actually increases creativity in some children.[3] Goldstein suggested that happiness can be akin to psychological death.[4] Allport questioned the theory that the only basic need of man was to reduce tension. He pointed out that tension enhancement can be characteristic of healthy individuals.[5] Lewin et al.[6] showed experimentally that man has the capacity to develop realistic levels of aspiration which lead to a life of continually in-

[2] Erik H. Erikson, "Identity and the Life Cycle," *Psychological Issues*, Vol. 1, No. 1, 1959, International University Press, p. 96.

[3] Roger Barker, Tamara Dembo, and Kurt Lewin, *Frustration and Regression*, University of Iowa Studies in Child Welfare, Vol. XVIII, No. 1, 1941.

[4] Kurt Goldstein, *Human Nature*, Harvard University Press, 1951.

[5] Gordon W. Allport, "The Trend in Motivational Theory," *American Journal of Orthopsychiatry*, Vol. XXIII, No. 1, January 1953, pp. 107–119.

[6] Kurt Lewin, Tamara Dembo, Leon Festinger, and Pauline Sears, "Level of Aspiration," in J. M. V. Hunt (Ed.), *Personality and the Behavior Disorders*, Ronald Press, New York, 1944, pp. 333–378.

creasing (realistically) challenges. Maslow [7] emphasized the importance of self-actualization; Rogers,[8] the importance of striving to function fully; Allport,[9] the importance of, and responsibilities involved in, "becoming"; White,[10] the basic need to be competent and deal with one's world effectively; Bruner,[11] the intrinsic value of growth strivings. Fromm [12] has suggested that modern man's concept of freedom is one of being free *from* responsibilities. He argues that this concept must be changed to freedom *to be more responsible.*

Interestingly, some of the most eloquent and cogent arguments for the new emphasis have recently come from psychiatrists and others who lived through the horror of the German concentration camps. Bettelheim,[13] for example, raises some serious questions concerning the value of psychoanalysis under extreme conditions and for developing effective "normal" relationships. Frankl further suggests that without responsibility to something outside of himself man is not able to be free. Responsibility is the criterion of freedom.[14] In a more recent statement, Frankl writes: [15]

To be sure, man's search for meaning and values may arouse inner tension rather than inner equilibrium. However, this is precisely that which is an indispensable prerequisite of mental health. There is nothing in the world, I venture to say, that would so effectively help one to survive even the worst conditions, as the knowledge that there is a meaning in his life. There is much wisdom in the words of Nietzsche: "He who has a *why* to live for can bear almost any *how.*" I see in these words a motto which holds true for any psychotherapy. In the concentration camps one could witness what was later confirmed by American psychiatrists both in Japan and Korea, that those who

[7] Abraham Maslow, *Motivation and Personality,* Harper, New York, 1954.

[8] For example, Carl Rogers, "A Theory of Therapy, Personality, and Interpersonal Relationships, as Developed in the Client-Centered Framework," in Sigmund Koch (Ed.), *Psychology: A Study of a Science,* Vol. III, McGraw-Hill, New York, 1959, pp. 184–256.

[9] Gordon Allport, "The Open System in Personality Theory," *Journal of Abnormal and Social Psychology,* Vol. 61, No. 3, 1960, pp. 301–310.

[10] Robert White, "Motivation Reconsidered: The Concept of Competence," *Psychological Review,* Vol. LXVI, 1959, pp. 297–333.

[11] Jerome Bruner, "The Act of Discovery," *Harvard Educational Review,* Vol. 31, No. 1, Winter 1961, pp. 26–28.

[12] Eric Fromm, *The Art of Loving,* Harper, New York, 1956.

[13] Bruno Bettelheim, *The Informed Heart,* Free Press, Glencoe, Ill., 1960.

[14] Viktor E. Frankl, *From Death Camp to Existentialism,* Beacon Press, Boston, 1959.

[15] Viktor E. Frankl, "Basic Concepts of Logotherapy," *Journal of Existential Psychiatry,* Vol. 3, No. 9, 1962, pp. 113–114.

knew that there was a task waiting for them to fulfill were most apt to survive.

Thus, it can be seen that mental health is based on a certain degree of tension, the tension between what one has already achieved and what he still ought to accomplish, or the gap between what he is and what he should become. Such a tension is inherent in the human being and therefore is indispensable to mental well being. We should not, then, be hesitant about challenging man with meaning potentialities for him to actualize, thus evoking his will to meaning out of its latency. I consider it a dangerous misconception of mental hygiene to assume that what man needs in the first place, is equilibrium or, as it is called in biology, "homeostasis," i.e., a tension-less state. What man actually needs is not a tension-less state but rather the striving and struggling for some goal worthy of him. What he needs is not the discharge of tension at any cost, but the call of a potential meaning waiting to be fulfilled by him.

Recently Wolf has asked that we consider if we are not making our society "too full" of security and too prevalent with dependence.[16] Szasz has even gone so far as to hypothesize that our society encourages mental illness by overprotecting the individual who, because he behaves as if he is ill, is assumed to be ill.[17]

Leighton [18] has suggested that social psychiatry's primary responsibility is to society or a subgroup within a society. He cites examples in combat, at court, and within organizations where the group's need must be kept in mind even though it may appear to be done at the expense of the individual. Leighton is careful to emphasize that this point of view does not relegate the individual to the background. It places greater emphasis on the individual's contribution to society as well as the society's capacity to provide a milieu in which psychologically healthy individuals can be developed. In short, it is the study of relatively healthy individuals that resulted in the new emphasis on man's responsibilities and commitments.

Turning closer to organizations, Herzberg [19] has suggested, and Schwartz, Jenusaitis, and Stark [20] have confirmed, that the healthy in-

[16] William Wolf, "Wider Horizons in Psychotherapy," *American Journal of Psychotherapy*, Vol. XVI, No. 1, January 1962, pp. 124–149.

[17] Thomas S. Szasz, *The Myth of Mental Illness*, Hoeber-Harper, New York, 1961.

[18] Alexander Leighton, *An Introduction to Social Psychiatry*, Thomas, Springfield, Ill., 1960, pp. 17–23.

[19] Frederick Herzberg and Roy M. Hamlen, "A Motivation-Hygiene Concept of Mental Health," *Mental Hygiene*, Vol. 45, No. 3, July 1961, pp. 394–401.

[20] Milton M. Schwartz, Edmund Jenusaitis, Harry Stark, "Motivational Factors among Supervisors in the Utility Industry," *Personnel Psychology*, Vol. 16, No. 1, Spring 1963, pp. 45–53.

dividuals look for responsibility, develop commitments, and establish challenges. Vroom also found that workers who were highly involved in their jobs tended to obtain satisfactions from opportunities for self-expression.[21] Haire [22] has asked why man's responsibilities and authority must be equal, noting that responsibilities assigned to people seem to be much greater than the authority given to them. Perhaps the attempt to balance them may lead to increased costs for the organization and the individual. Henry [23] has recently suggested that the more competent executives were, the more they were in conflict and preoccupied. Cartwright,[24] in a cogent inquiry into Whyte's *Organization Man*, suggests that there is "productive conformity."

It is in keeping, therefore, with a long and fine tradition to attempt to create a world in which man focuses on challenges that test and develop his self. *It is our hypothesis that the incongruence between the individual and the organization can provide the basis for a continued challenge which, as it is fulfilled, will tend to help man to enhance his own growth and to develop organizations that will tend to be viable and effective.* The incongruence between the individual and the organization can be the foundation for increasing the degree of effectiveness of both.

Historical Perspective

The problem of integrating the individual and the organization is not a new one. Scholars beginning with the ancient Greeks have made references to the impact of the organization on the individual. Apparently, Henri Saint-Simon was one of the first sociologically oriented thinkers to note the rise of modern organizational patterns. He predicted that organizations would play an increasingly important role in society. Comte, on the other hand, tended to suppress the positive aspects of formal organization. Comte was convinced that "spontaneous

[21] Victor H. Vroom, "Ego-Involvement, Job Satisfaction, and Job Performance," *Personnel Psychology*, Vol. 15, No. 2, 1962, pp. 159–178.
[22] Mason Haire, "The Concept of Power and the Concept of Man," in George B. Strother (Ed.), *Social Science Approaches to Business Behavior*, Dorsey-Irwin Press, Homewood, Ill., 1962, pp. 171.
[23] William E. Henry, "Conflict, Age, and the Executive," *Business Topics*, Michigan State University, Vol. 9, No. 2, Spring 1961, pp. 15–25.
[24] Dorwin Cartwright, "Productive Conformity and the Organization," Research Center for Group Dynamics, mimeographed, University of Michigan.

organization" was superior to planned organization.[25] Weber, like Comte, feared that organizations could begin to destroy individual personality and subject it to a "dehumanizing regimentation." [26] The alarm concerning the impact on the individual of the formal industrial organization and its unilateral authority system was further reinforced by the work of Mayo and Roethlisberger. They and others disagreed with the apparent deemphasis of the human side of organization on the part of the "molecular approach" of men like Taylor [27] and with the work of the more traditional administrative theorists.[28, 29] The concern caused a great flurry of writing, some research, and much admonition about the importance of "human relations" and the informal organization versus the formal organization. The pendulum was swinging toward emphasis "spontaneity" and "human satisfaction." [30]

Bakke, one of the first to question the dichotomy between people and organizations, did so on two levels.[31] First, he questioned whether the informal system (the main area of interest of human-relations researchers at that time) was indeed separable from the formal organization. He pointed out that authority in organizations was not unilateral; organizations had directive and representative authority. Later, he extended the representative aspects of the organization to the other organizational processes.[32] Gouldner,[33] still later, suggested that organizations have a "punishment-centered" and "representative bureaucracy." About the same time Whyte also began to question the informal-formal dichotomy. More recently, some evidence has been presented suggesting that the informal system can have as much a "negative" impact on mental health as does the formal organization.[34]

Although these dichotomies still are being questioned, it does not

[25] Alvin W. Gouldner, "Organizational Analysis," in Robert K. Merton, Leonard Broom, and Leonard S. Cottrell (Eds.), *Sociology Today*, Basic Books, New York, 1959, pp. 400–401.

[26] *Ibid.*, p. 402.

[27] James March and Herbert Simon, *Organizations*, Wiley, New York, 1958, Chap. I.

[28] Warren Bennis, "Leadership Theory and Administrative Behavior: The Problem of Authority" *Administrative Science Quarterly*, Vol. 4, 1959, pp. 259–301.

[29] Chris Argyris, *Personality and Organization*, Harper, New York, 1957, Chap. III.

[30] Chris Argyris, *The Pesent State of Human Relations Research*, Labor and Management Center, Yale University, 1953.

[31] E. W. Bakke, *Bonds of Organization*, Harper, New York, 1950.

[32] E. W. Bakke, *The Individual and the Organization*, Labor and Management Center, Yale University, 1951.

[33] Alvin W. Gouldner, *Patterns of Industrial Democracy*, Antioch Press, Yellow Springs, O., 1954, especially pp. 15–29 and Chap. 10.

[34] Chris Argyris, "Individual Actualization in Complex Organizations," *Mental Hygiene*, Vol. 44, No. 2, April 1960, pp. 226–237.

follow that they are completely incorrect. The validity, for example, of the separation of the formal-informal systems depends on the point of view one takes. The point of view, in turn, typically depends on the problems in which one is interested. A plant may contain a manufacturing, sales, engineering, and finance component. If one is interested in studying these parts of the company, then these are perfectly valid components. On the other hand, if one wants to focus on the organization as a whole, then it does not make much sense to speak only in terms of manufacturing, sales, or finance. The interrelationships among these components must be understood. Similarly, biologists caution us that the boundary between the body and the environment is extremely difficult to establish. They disparage the dichotomy of body-environment. However, this dichotomy is an extremely important one for a soldier aiming at an oncoming enemy soldier.

The same may be said for organizations. If one views the organization as a unity then the formal-informal dichotomy may be of little value. However, if one is interested in the parts, then categories such as these have positive value.

Blau and Scott give these concepts an important place in their theoretical framework. They believe that "in every formal organization there arise informal organizations" and that the "roots of these informal systems are embedded in the formal organization itself and nurtured by the very formality of its arrangements." [35] Dubin also believes that some form of differentiation of the whole is necessary. He contributes a fourfold classification of "behavior systems," namely, technological, formal, nonformal, and informal. The technological behavior system is the system that comprises the job or task activities. The informal activities as used here are differentiated by Dubin into nonformal and informal. The former is behavior that modifies the technical behavior system within the allowable limits of the formal system. Finally, the informal behavior system covers the area of direct interpersonal relations of a voluntary character. [36]

Brown, on the other hand, believes a more useful categorization is the *manifest* organization, the one that is seen on the "organization chart' and is formally displayed; the *assumed* organization, the one that individuals perceive as the organization (were they asked to draw their view of the way things work); the *extant* organization, the situation as revealed through systematic investigation; and the *requisite* organiza-

---

[35] Peter Blau and Richard W. Scott, *Formal Organizations*, Chandler, San Francisco, 1962, pp. 6–7.
[36] Robert Dubin, *The World of Work*, Prentice-Hall, Englewood Cliffs, N.J., 1958, pp. 61–73.

tion, the situation as it would be if it were "in accord with the real properties of the field in which it exists." [37]

We believe that it is a matter of empirical research, however, to determine which of these sets of categories is helpful. Our hypothesis is that since all the schemes presently used are manipulations of the same conceptual universe, the empirical tests will show that they each will serve differential purposes. There are some scholars, however, who probably would not agree. For example, Thompson believes that the formal-informal dichotomy may not cope with the phenomenon of "tradition" within the organization.[38]

To return to our main theme, the early dichotomies, although probably necessary at their time, are beginning to be questioned. The organization is not all bad, nor are the human relations aspects all good. Selznick attempted to conceptualize the theme of integration by differentiating between "organizations" and "institutions" and placing the integrative possibilities within the "institution." [39] The most recent voices to be heard that emphasize the necessity for an integration of points of view are Katzell [40] and Thompson.[41] They attempt to specify some changes in present organization which may integrate aspects of the formal organizational and human relations' views. Scott suggests that classical and human relations theories may be special cases of a more inclusive "system theory." [42]

Before we turn away from the historical perspective, it seems useful to emphasize that the more recent critics of traditional formal organizational theory have not emphasized adequately, as Thompson and Gouldner suggest, the values of the traditional approach. For example, Gouldner differentiates two ideal types or models of organizations, the "rational" and the "natural." He suggests that those who have focused primarily on the natural model have missed or underemphasized several

[37] Wilfred Brown, *Exploration in Management*, Heinemann, London, 1960, p. 24.
[38] Personal communication. It is my view that tradition can be coped with by conceptualizing it in terms of the effect it has upon the present. For a detailed discussion, see Kurt Lewin's concept of "contemporaneity," *Principles of Topological Psychology*, McGraw-Hill, 1936.
[39] Philip Selznick, *Leadership in Administration*, Row, Peterson, Evanston, Ill., 1957, pp. 5–22.
[40] Raymond A. Katzell, "Contrasting Systems of Work Organization," Pres. Address, A. P. A., September 4, 1961, mimeographed, Department of Psychology, New York University.
[41] Victor A. Thompson, *Modern Organization*, Knopf, New York, 1961, see especially pp. 187–197.
[42] William G. Scott, "Organizational Theory: An Overview and an Appraisal," *Journal of the Academy of Management*, April 1961, pp. 7–26.

important aspects of the rational model.[43] They are (1) the significance of rationally organized structures for planned growth and adaptation; (2) the importance of formalized codes, division of labor, and so forth, on the growth of the organization; (3) the crucial role of rationality in human affairs; (4) the value of organizational constraints that are conducive to the *realization* of democratic values; and (5) the variations in degrees of interdependence among units.[44] Hutte expands the last point and presents an insightful analysis of the meaning of "interdependence of parts." [45]

In the writer's opinion, Gouldner's criticism is valid. There are important values to the formal rational model, which have been deemphasized in the past by the adherents (including the writer) to the natural model. An objective of this work is to describe a way to integrate both models.

Complexity of Organizational Life

Organizations are extremely complex systems. As one observes them they seem to be composed of human activities on many different levels of analysis. Personalities, small groups, intergroups, norms, values, attitudes all seem to exist in an extremely complex multidimensional pattern. The complexity seems at times almost beyond comprehension. Yet it is this very complexity that is, on one hand, the basis for understanding organizational phenomena, and on the other, that makes life difficult for an administrator.

As much as we aspire to respect complexity, we will have to simplify it somewhat. One of the critical problems that we will face is how much to simplify. The answer depends on the theoretical scheme that we develop, which will guide us as to what factors are relevant, and which, in turn, depends on the problems being studied.

Our problem is to understand the changes that the organization (and the individual) will have to make if it is to obtain the most possible

---

[43] Alvin W. Gouldner, "Organizational Analysis," *op. cit.*
[44] For example, on point five see, Henry Landsberger, "The Horizontal Dimension in Bureaucracy," paper given at American Sociological Association meeting, September 1957, Washington D.C.; Melville Dalton, *Men Who Manage*, Wiley, New York, 1959; Frank Jasinski, "Use and Misuse of Efficiency Controls," *Harvard Business Review*, July–August 1956, pp. 105–112; Chris Argyris and Frank Miller, "The Impact of Budgets upon People," Controllers Foundation, 1957, and the work of Robert Blake on Inter-Group Rivalry cited in detail in this chapter.
[45] H. A. Hutte, "Experiences in Studying Social Psychological Structures in Industry," *Human Relations*, Vol. XI, No. 2, April 1949, pp. 185–195.

human energy for productive effort. Consequently, our organizations are going to be described as a patterning, including such factors as (1) individual needs, attitudes, values, and feelings; (2) group attractiveness, goals, processes, and norms; (3) organizational activities and policies related to power, rewards, penalties, communication, and work flows; and (4) informal activities such as goldbricking, apathy, indifference, interdepartmental conflict, conformity, and mistrust.

We do *not* maintain that these factors account for all of organizational life. We simply maintain that they are the relevant (but not necessarily the sufficient) factors to understand the problem of integrating the individual and the organization.

Organization: Open System

The traditional methods of depicting organizations tend to be inadequate when one is interested in conceptualizing the actual behavioral patterns of an organization. What is now needed are concepts that will permit us to conceptualize as one integrated behavioral system all these multidimensional parts (formal, informal, individual, small group, etc.).

One way to cope with this problem is to conceive of organizations as "open systems" imbedded in, but constantly influencing and being influenced, by the environment.[46] Consequently, one cannot predict completely the future of an organization by knowing only its present state.[47] Another characteristic of an open system is that the output [48] does not necessarily vary systematically with any known input.[49] Thus, if input is increased or decreased, the output may not necessarily vary systematically with changes in the input. Nor is there a fixed constant relationship between output and input.

As Katz and Kahn suggest: [50]

[46] William K. Kapp, *Toward a Science of Man in Society*, Martinuso Nyhoff, The Hague, 1961.

[47] Ludwig Bertallanfy, "Problems of General System Theory," *Human Biology*, Vol. 23, No. 4, December 1951, pp. 302–312.

[48] Output is the desired product of the system plus other relevant consequences of functioning.

[49] Input is anything put into the system which affects the output. (See John D. Trimmer, *Response of Physical Systems*, Wiley, New York, 1950, Chap. 1.) These definitions are stated by John B. Knox, "Productivity and Human Relations: Some Basic Principles," *Proceedings of the 16th Congress*, International Institute of Sociology, Beaune, France, September 19–26, 1954.

[50] Robert L. Kahn and Daniel Katz, "Concept of Objective Organization," in J. R. P. French et al. (Eds.), *The Industrial Environment and Mental Health, Journal of Social Issues*, Vol. XVIII, No. 3, 1962, mimeographed, p. 35.

We begin by defining the organization as an open dynamic system; that is, it is characterized by a continuing process of input, transformation, and output. Organizational input characteristically includes people, materials, and energy; organizational output is typically in the form of products or services, although it may consist mainly of direct psychological return to members. The openness of the organization as a system means that it is eternally dependent upon its environment for the absorption of its products and services, and for providing the necessary input which activates the organizational processes of transformation and thereby maintains the organization in existence.

In short, conceiving of an organization as an open system tends to lead to a different way of describing organizational behavior. As Kahn and Katz point out, "as an open social system, the organization is defined and its boundaries set by the relationships and the patterns of behavior which carry out the continuing cycles of input-transformation-output." [51] We will discuss this further in Chapter 5.

The Relation of Personality to Organization

Understanding the human personality is an extremely complex task. It is not possible to do justice in this work to the richness of data and concepts that are available. If we are to get on with the primary objective of understanding organizations, we will have to sacrifice an extended discussion of personality and select only those factors that seem to be most relevant. The personality factors chosen are those that (1) help to "cause" or to create and maintain the organization, (2) that could operate to ignore the organization's coerciveness, and (3) that could destroy the organization. In order to do this, we will attempt to understand individual needs, abilities, levels of aspiration, and self-concepts as they arise in and influence the system.

To put this another way, we believe that organizations and personalities are discrete units with their own laws, which make them amenable to study as separate units. However, we also believe that important parts of each unit's existence depend on their connectedness with the other. We hypothesize that one cannot fully understand the individual without understanding the organization in which he is embedded and vice versa. We are not negating the value of studying individuals *or* organizations. Our primary interest is at the boundaries of both—at the points where they overlap and are interrelated.

[51] *Ibid.*

How can one develop a theoretical framework that draws upon the psychological and sociological levels of analysis in order to help us understand the interrelationships between the two? One possibility that we suggest is to hypothesize that "in the beginning" (the creation) of an organization there must have been people and a set of complex specifications (objectives, roles, policies, etc.) called formal organization. Knowing as we do some of the basic properties of each, can we begin to spin a web of interconnections between the individual and the formal organization that would eventually approximate the complexity of organizations as they exist in real life?

From the literature on scientific management, industrial economics, and public administration, we learned about the properties of formal organization. From the literature in clinical, social, child, and adolescent psychology, we learned much about the human personality. Putting together our two pictures of personality (in our culture) and formal organizations, we developed some propositions which became our first attempt at a theoretical framework.

Understanding Formal Organizations

Defining the underlying nature of *formal* organizations is not very difficult. Formal organizations are based on certain principles such as "task specialization," "chain of command," "unity of direction," "rationality," and others. These are the basic "genes" that are supported by, and at times modified in varying degrees by the technology, the kinds of managerial controls, and the patterns of leadership used in the organization.

This is not to imply that all organizations are the same. They are not. Clearly there are differences according to size, technology used, objectives and stage of development, and so on. Moreover, organizations manifest a wide range of differences in their internal make-up. Thus, the nature of the departments within one organization may vary more than two different organizations. For example, we found that the difference between the bookkeeping and auditing department of a bank on the one hand and the remainder of the bank was greater than the difference between those departments included in the remainder of the bank and most departments in investment firms and insurance home offices. The sales departments in insurance firms, in turn, differed significantly from their parent organizations. Goffman,[52] on the other

[52] Irving Goffman, "The Characteristics of Total Institutions," *Symposium on*

hand, has shown that orphanages, sanitoriums, mental hospitals, prisons, army barracks, ships, boarding schools, abbeys, and monasteries seem to have certain basic characteristics which are typical of "total institutions." By "total institutions" he means those institutions that place a barrier to social intercourse with the outside world.

It is our working hypothesis, however, that even though formal organizations manifest large differences among and within themselves, those differences can be ignored *at the beginning* in order to produce a general theory of organization.

However, as we have documented elsewhere,[53] if one attempts to predict the behavior of a particular organization, one will have to add the unique properties of the organization to the more general ones being considered here. Thus, our theory may tell us something about complex organization, but it will require supplementation of a more specific organizational theory in order to understand the individual case. It is our hypothesis that banks, insurance firms, automobile plants, churches, governmental bureaus, trade unions, schools, and so on, can have only a part (we believe an important part) of their behavior explained by our theoretical framework. The remainder will require the construction of more narrow and specialized models that can be integrated with (and hopefully some day derived from) the general theory.

The Importance of the Environment

Most scholars readily admit that reasonable limits or boundaries must be placed around research activity for it to be manageable by one individual. The writer has placed this admittedly arbitrary boundary around the "skin" of the organization. Everything within the organization is part of the problem. Much (not all) of what is outside is arbitrarily set aside until the first job is completed or until other scholars who are more interested in the environment develop conceptual schemes with which to relate the organization to it.

However, this does not deny the importance of the influence of the cultural environment on the "inside" of the organization. Such studies as the one by French, Israel, and As,[54] who attempted to replicate in a

Preventive and Social Psychiatry, April 15–17, 1957, Walter Reed Army Institute of Research, Washington, D.C.

[53] Chris Argyris, *Understanding Organizational Behavior*, Dorsey Press, Homewood, Ill., 1960.

[54] John R. P. French, Joachum Israel, and Dagfinn As, "An Experiment on Participation in a Norwegian Factory," *Human Relations*, Vol. 13, No. 1, pp. 1–19.

Norwegian firm an experiment on "participation, decision making, and productivity" previously carried out in this country, illustrate clearly the importance of cultural factors. Although they found some of their original data replicated, they uncovered some major differences. Apparently, workers in Norway were brought up with different feelings about participation than those in the United States. The Norwegian workers did not believe that participation was as legitimate an activity as did the American workers. Consequently, the effects of participation in Norway were significantly different. Also there are the studies by Harbison and Burgess [55] who have cited case material supporting the conclusion that participation may not be valued by employees in Europe. Whyte [56] has done the same in South America.[57]

Another example of how the environment may influence the internal activities (in this case the leadership pattern) is provided by Hartmann's work on the German executive. Hartmann suggests that many high level executives grow up in a culture where they learn that their power and authority to govern is almost a God-given right. Holding such views leads them to behave differently than their American counterpart. For example, they tend to be more directive and authoritarian, and at the same time they tend to feel much less defensive about it.[58]

Harbison and Burgess have also shown that the culture may influence the organization in terms of the values inculcated into the managerial class, who in turn influence the organization. American managers tend to be hard working, driving, and organization centered. The European manager, on the other hand, although hard working, comes from an elite background and schooling. He typically sees the organization as an adjunct to his family and as subordinate to leisure.

Moreover, "American management usually thinks of greater productivity as increased output and consequent lower unit cost, whereas European management normally struggles to reduce unit cost while

[55] Frederick Harbison and Eugene Burgess, "Modern Management in Western Europe," *American Journal of Sociology*, Vol. 60, No. 1, July 1954, pp. 15–23.
[56] William F. Whyte and A. R. Holmberg (Eds.), *Human Organization*, Vol. 15, No. 3, Fall 1956.
[57] There are some who would interpret these results to suggest that the European and South American workers are less healthy. Although there is no evidence to support such a conclusion, the present policy of such organizations as the World Health Organization suggests that this interpretation may be worth testing. They have issued reports which imply that the psychological lot of the workers in South America is not as good as that of workers in this country.
[58] Heinz Hartmann, *Authority and Organization in General Management*, Princeton University Press, 1959.

rigidly limiting output. The latter emphasize such things as saving materials, elimination of waste, and improvement of quality, whereas comparable American plants would aim at increasing production." [59]

Another empirical study that illustrates the impact of the environment on the organization is related to an analysis diagnosing the factors that shape industrialization and, consequently, organizational birth, survival, and growth. The authors found five important factors in the environment that influence industrialization. They are (1) the level of technology in the most advanced countries and the level of technology in the particular country; (2) the known natural resources of the country; (3) the educational development as it affects the skill, training, and experience of workers, and the skill, organizing ability, and competence of the managerial and professional groups and government personnel; (4) the level of population, its age distribution, and the rate at which the population is increasing; and (5) the capacity to borrow funds or to secure grants.[60]

There is another dimension of the problem that is not included in this discussion. It is the impact of the organization on the environment. We note for example that sociologists beginning with Warner and Low have shown that the industrial organization significantly alters the social relations in the environment. For example, the mechanization of shoe production completely changed the skill hierarchy and the age-grade system that accompanied it. The skill of workers was significantly altered and the occupational structure similarly so. Smith and Nyman,[61] and Form and Miller [62] support this view in describing their individual cases. James Thompson and his associates are developing a theory of the impact of occupational structure upon the society. They differentiate types of work in terms of jobs that are "occupation-centered or "profession-centered" such as engineering, social work, nursing, and jobs that are organization-centered. Occupation-centered jobs tend to be taught outside the organization while organization-centered jobs tend to be taught within the organization. Jobs can also be differentiated in terms of those that are closed (limited advancement) and those that are open (unlimited advancement). They point out that work within the firm is increasingly being dominated first by open-ceiling jobs and second by

[59] Frederick H. Harbison and Eugene W. Burgess, *loc. cit.*

[60] Clark Kerr, J. T. Dunlop, F. Harbison, C. A. Meyers, *Industrialism and Industrial Man*, Harvard University Press, 1960, p. 100.

[61] Elliot D. Smith and R. C. Nyman, *Technology and Labor*, Yale University Press, 1939.

[62] W. H. Form and D. C. Miller, *Industry, Labor, and Community*, Harper, New York, 1960, pp. 50–53.

closed-ceiling jobs, both of which are occupation-centered. This is a new trend since organizations in the past have been primarily organized around jobs that are organization-centered.[63]

As the new occupational structure takes form, and as its occupants who are primarily "cosmopolitans" (that is, their reference group is a professional group outside the organization) become more important, the nature of the values presently implied on the organizational structure, managerial controls, and leadership will tend to become modified. This upheaval has already begun. It is seen in the numerous changes being considered for industrial laboratory organizations. Interestingly, most of the changes today have been in terms of personnel matters (wages, benefits, etc.). It may be that management is reacting to this new problem in the same way it has reacted to the others. Instead of focusing on the basic causes the trend seems to be more in terms of "making up" for the difficulties through material rewards, status symbols, and superb working facilities.

Studies such as these are extremely important and eventually their results must be systematically integrated if the conceptual scheme that we are proposing is to have increased power. Until this is done, however, these studies to remind us of the limits to the present framework presented by the culture.[64]

[63] J. D. Thompson, R. W. Avery, and R. O. Carlson, "Occupations, Personnel, and Careers," Administrative Science Center, University of Pittsburgh, mimeographed, July 1962.

[64] Dill * and Whyte † have concluded that the best way to study the impact of the environment on the organization is to focus at the point where it impinges on the the organization. For example, Dill suggests that we need to know how *information* "enters" the organization and is recorded or stored for its use. This involves an analysis of the kinds of information to which an organization is exposed, its readiness to deal with the information, and its strategies to search for information.‡ Environmental information, suggests Dill, can influence the organization by providing (a) "triggers" to action; (b) sources of information about goals; (c) sources of information about means to achieve goals; (d) sources of information about constraints; and (e) sources of evaluation and judgments on organizational performance.

Dill distinguishes between influences of the environment on the organization when it is just established and the continuing problem of organizational learning. He suggests the following hypotheses which warrant further study.

1. An environment that gives members of a new organization the feeling that they must spell out their structure and their operating rules in detail and to justify the appropriateness of these rules to existing conditions is likely to enhance the organization's chances for immediate survival at the expense of long term adaptability.

2. An environment that creates pressures on members to publicize goals and policies and to differentiate them sharply from the goals and policies of other organizations will increase the costs of later changes in objectives.

Although, we do not discuss in detail these important dimensions, we do attempt to study some environmental factors that "enter into" the system. Thus, although social class and status will not be discussed as societal phenomena in their own right, they will be discussed in terms of how they affect the organization and how the organization affects them. We will, for example, attempt to deal with the fact that the lower working classes tend to be exposed to different social values than the upper-upper classes. Also, we are aware that trade unions do exist and we present an hypothesis regarding how they arise. However, we do not intend to go into detail regarding their own problems or the problems involved in labor-management relations. Both of these areas are important and, as we expect to show briefly, are potentially partially manageable within the theoretical framework being evolved.

---

3. Organizations that are established under unstable environmental conditions will have poorer chances for short-run survival but better chances for long-run survival than those that are established under stable conditions.
4. Organizations that are induced by technological factors and other external conditions to seek personnel who do not feel threatened by change, who have high levels of aspiration, and who are easily dissatisfied will be better able to adapt than organizations who seek other kinds of personnel. §

* William R. Dill, "The Impact of Environment on Organizational Development," in S. Mailuk and E. Van Ness (Eds.), *Readings in Administrative Behavior*, Prentice-Hall, Englewood Cliffs, N.J., 1961.
† W. F. Whyte, "Framework for the Analysis of Industrial Relations: Two Views," *Industrial and Labor Relations Review*, Vol. 3, No. 3, April 1950, pp. 393–401.
‡ Dill, *op. cit.*, pp. 5–6.
§ *Ibid.*, pp. 13–14.

Chapter 2 🙰🙰🙰🙰🙰🙰🙰🙰🙰🙰🙰🙰🙰🙰🙰🙰🙰🙰🙰🙰🙰🙰🙰🙰🙰🙰🙰🙰

The Input

The task before us is to examine the internal make-up of formal organizations to see what factors inhibit and what facilitate organizational effectiveness. Organizations, we suggested in the first chapter, are open systems with inputs, internal make-up, outputs, and corrective feedback mechanisms. The analysis in this chapter begins by examining the nature of the inputs and their relationship to organizational effectiveness.

Organizations have many different kinds of energy inputs. There are, for example, mechanical, electrical, physiological, and psychological energies that may act as inputs. For the sake of convenience and manageability, our analysis shall be limited to the energy that human beings contribute. In limiting the analysis to this type of input, we also limit the generalizability of the analysis. A general theory requires that all the energy inputs be included. Consequently, this analysis eventually must be integrated with analyses from other fields that deal with the other available energy inputs.

Human energy may be categorized as being primarily physiological or psychological. Physiological energy is best understood in terms of the physiology and biochemistry of the body. This extremely important type of energy has been studied for many years by those in the "life" sciences as well as physiological psychologists. We will not be concerned with physiological energy other than to acknowledge that it is intimately related to psychological energy and that ultimately the two must be interrelated if the framework is to be complete.

Before we continue, it is important to emphasize that the study of personality is a complex field, full of its share of theories and its internal conflicts and disagreements. It is neither our objective nor desire to review the field in any complete manner. Our role will be one of selecting some concepts from the many available and presenting only those aspects of personality theory that seem necessary to help us to understand the problems on which we intend to focus. The result will no doubt be oversimplified and incomplete. Indeed, the personality theorist may conclude that the analysis glosses over subtle but important points. If this is the case, it is hoped that the injustices are neither grave nor injurious to a valid presentation. We believe that the views we have selected are represented in a simplified, but adequate manner.[1]

The central focus of this analysis is on psychological energy. Psychological energy is postulated to exist in order to help explain observable human behavior that is not adequately explained by physiological energy. For example, it is not uncommon for individuals to sleep for many hours only to wake up and report that they are tired. College students become tired by playing tennis all day, but seem to become rejuvenated if an unexpected date is offered to them. Executives report that they feel "good" after a hard day's work, yet can report that they are tired if the day has been "dull and quiet." College students have remained awake by taking sugar pills, thinking they were benzedrine, while others have fallen asleep because they assumed that the benzedrine tablets they took were only sugar pills.

The theme underlying all these examples is that the human being seems to have available or to lose energy that cannot be explained (at this time) on physiological grounds, and this seems to be related to psychological factors. In order to help us understand these phenomena,

---

[1] Carl R. Rogers, "A Theory of Therapy, Personality, and Interpersonal Relationships, as Developed in the Client-Centered Framework," in Sigmund Koch (Ed.), *Psychology: A Study of a Science*, Vol. III, McGraw-Hill, New York, 1959. Robert White, *Lives in Progress*, Dryden Press, New York, 1952. Kurt Lewin, *A Dynamic Theory of Personality*, McGraw-Hill, New York, 1935. Gordon W. Allport, *Basic Considerations for a Psychology of Personality*, Yale University Press, 1954. George Kelly, *The Psychology of Personal Constructs*, Vol. I, Norton, New York, 1955. Rollo May, Ernest Angel, and Henri R. Ellenberger, *Existence*, Basic Books, New York, 1958. Erich Fromm, *The Sane Society*, Holt, Rinehart, and Winston, New York, 1955. Lawrence S. Kubie, *Neurotic Distortion of the Creative Process*, University of Kansas Press, 1958.

psychologists postulate that psychological energy exists.[2] In doing so, they have created a construct whose existence does not depend on its being located in the empirical world (as may be the case for physiological energy). The acceptance of the contruct of psychological energy will be a function of its (1) logical validity, which, in turn, is a function of its internal consistency as well as its relevance in a conceptual scheme and (2) its power to help explain human behavior.

Psychological energy is assumed to exist "in" the needs of individuals. Needs are viewed as parts of the human personality which, when activated, are "in tension." Activated needs are alway in tension in relation to some objective or goal in the environment. It is this tension that is supposed to motivate behavior. Human beings are seen as constantly striving to reduce the tension in the need by striving to achieve the goal to which the need is related. In doing so, they must behave, and it is this behavior that is apparently explained by saying "it (the behavior) is caused by the need in tension in relation to such and such goal." A psychological need may therefore be defined as a part postulated (1) to exist "in" personality of the individual; (2) is related to the other needs, and (3) to a goal in the environment; and (4) initiates and guides behavior until the goal is reached, which destroys the tension, or until the tension is released in some other way. It should be added that tension reduction is not the only basic activity of life. As Allport has shown, many people actually increase their internal tension, and, in this process, behavior is created.

For our purposes, it is important to point out that psychological energy is postulated thus: [3]

1. It exists in all individuals.
2. Its expression cannot be blocked permanently. If a barrier is placed on its expression, it will find a way to overcome the barrier or to get around it.

[2] There is an increasing trend to view man's actions in terms of cognitive information theory. I believe that both will lead to similar conclusions, while the psychological-energy view is presently able to account for certain human behavior that information theory is not able to explain—for example, a "lazy" man who is utilizing much energy and the individual who feels tired when he reports "rested." For some excellent examples of the information-theory approach, see Donald W. Taylor, "Toward an Information Processing Theory of Motivation," in M. R. Jones (Ed.), *Nebraska Symposium on Motivation*, University of Nebraska Press, 1960, pp. 51–79. George Kelly, *The Psychology of Personal Constructs*, Vol. I, Norton, New York, 1955.

[3] J. Reusch and G. Bateson, *Communication: The Social Matrix of Psychiatry*, Norton, New York, 1957, pp. 248–249. David Rappaport and Morton Gell, "The

3. Its amount varies with the "state of mind" of the individual. The amount is not fixed nor is it limited.

The Self [4]

In order to make explicit the implications of the foregoing properties as well as to define some of them more accurately (for example, "state of mind"), we need to explore several other concepts.

Human beings may be said to develop needs, values, and abilities, of which some will be peripheral and some will be central. The degree of centrality will be a function of the individual's growth pattern, his present degree of fulfillment of needs, and factors in his environment.

The socio-cultural matrix in which the individual is embedded has an important influence on the development of these factors. Through the parents, the child begins to learn about the norms of the culture. The specific needs, values, and abilities that he develops will be highly influenced by these cultural norms. Also, we shall see, the social class in which his family exists plays a major role in defining the nature as well as the rate of his development. Indeed, one may predict that not only the component parts, but the very organization of the parts of the youngster's personality is highly influenced by the culture. The culture has much to say as to which needs will tend to be central and which will tend to be peripheral.

The unique integration of these needs or values and abilities into an organized pattern that is fuctionally meaningful for the individual represents the individual's personality or *self*. The self includes all aspects of the person whether conscious or unconscious. The individual's *self-concept* includes those aspects of the self of which the individual is aware. The more the individual enlarges his self-concept to include more aspects of his self, the greater the potential for the individual to understand and ultimately control his own behavior. There is also the *ideal self* which includes those values and needs to which the individual aspires, but which he has not achieved. These ideals are culturally rooted. They represent the "societal conscience" that the parents have been able to inculcate in the child.

Points of View and Assumptions of Metapsychology," *International Journal of Psycho-Analysis*, Vol. XL, Parts III–IV, 1959, pp. 1–10.

[4] Carl Rogers, "A Theory of Therapy, Personality, and Interpersonal Relations as Developed in the Client-Centered Framework," in Sigmund Koch (Ed.), *Psychology: A Study For Science*. Vol. 3, McGraw-Hill, New York, 1959.

Competence and the Self

Following White, we postulate that all human beings need to feel a sense of competence.[5] They strive to deal with their environment as competently as possible. Competence may be defined as the solving of problems by developing those solutions that prevent their recurrence, and doing so with minimum utilization of energy.

Competence may be hypothesized to increase (1) as one's awareness of problems increases; (2) as the problems are solved in such a way that they remain solved; and (3) with minimal expenditure of energy and disruption to the problem-solving process (within or between individuals).

An hypothesis such as this raises questions as to the meaning of "awareness," "problems," "minimal expenditure of energy," and nonrecurrence of problems. These are extremely complex issues. The field of perceptual psychology is centrally concerned with these issues, and much research has been conducted that is much too voluminous to be discussed here. The best we are able to do at this time is to scratch the surface of these issues deeply enough to permit the main theme to continue.[6]

For analytical convenience only, we may differentiate between intellectual cognitive competence and interpersonal competence. Having made this admittedly arbitrary differentiation, we may now state that our objective is to ascertain how interpersonal competence influences the intellectual cognitive competence of the members in the organization. To put this another way, we are interested in ascertaining the effect that a given amount of interpersonal competence has on the cognitive problem-solving activities within the organization.

Self-Awareness

A basic requirement for interpersonal competence is self-awareness. This awareness influences the individual's stability and effectiveness because, once it is formed, the self influences what the individual is able

[5] Robert W. White, "Motivation Reconsidered: The Concept of Competence," *Psychological Review*, Vol. 66, 1959, pp. 297–333.

[6] A more detailed discussion of human competence will be found in the writer's *Explorations in Human Competence: (Individual, Small Group, and Organizational)*, mimeographed, Dept. of Industrial Administration, Yale University, 1963.

to "see" in the environment, how he evaluates it, and how he deals with it. If what he is experiencing "out there" is consonant with his self-concept, then he will tend to "see" it in an undistorted manner. If what he is experiencing is antagonistic to his self, it is a threat. The greater the discrepancy between the self and what it is experiencing, the greater the threat. He may respond to a threat by attempting to integrate it with his self. This means that he must change his self, which, in turn, may mean that he will engage in a long and differentially painful process. Another alternative is to protect or "defend" the self from having to change, by "not seeing," distorting, or rejecting what is "out there." In rejecting what is "out there," the individual may be defending his self, thereby, in fact, also refusing to see "what is inside," that is, those aspects of his self requiring denial of reality.

Thus, to reiterate, competence requires self-awareness. But how does an individual become more aware of his self? One way is to receive feedback (or information) from others as to how they see his self and how he affects them. In this sense, self-awareness requires the help of others.

But, in order to be able to receive the information from others, the individual must be able to accept it. By acceptance, we mean that he must receive the message as it is sent with minimum distortion. The individual can minimize the distortion by not being easily threatened by the message. In order not to be easily threatened, the individual must have a relatively high degree of self-awareness and *self-esteem*. He must value himself enough so that possibly threatening messages are received with minimum distortion.

Before we outline a view of how self-esteem may be developed, it is important to point out that another way to maximize the learning to be received from others is to minimize the defensiveness of others, because the more defensive they are, the more their messages will tend to be distorted. The defensiveness of others can be a function of their own personality defenses and the impact that others have on them. The former type of defensiveness may be beyond our control, but the second is not.

The operational criterion of self-acceptance is the ability to send and receive information to and from others with minimum distortion. In everyday life, this can be accomplished through increasing self-esteem and the esteem of others. The greater the self-steem, the less the tendency for distortion that is "internally created." The greater the esteem of others, the less the tendency to create defensive conditions that lead to distortion within others.

Here again the environment plays a crucial role. Society may have norms that tend to prescribe how much self-awareness is permissible.

In some societies the child is greatly restricted, by the societal norms, as to what aspects of his self he can explore and modify. In other societies the opposite tends to be true. Societal factors may also influence greatly what the individuals will tend to consider "appropriate" exposure as well as "appropriate" feedback. Thus the nature, scope, and depth of competence that the individual may develop is partially influenced by the environment in which he is embedded.

Self-Esteem

To manifest self-esteem is to value one's self.[7] Manifestations of self-esteem are the predispositions to enlarge the awareness of one's self and others and to enlarge the acceptance of self and others. In other words, we are assuming that the individual's self-esteem is not independent of the self-esteem of others. If a man desires to grow, others around him must also desire to grow and be willing to help him to grow.

How is self-esteem developed? Our hypothesis is that self-esteem is developed by dealing with the world competently in such a way that a person can assign the solution of the problems to himself, to his abilities, to his efforts, to his work. This means that solving problems per se is not enough. The individual must experience a connection between his own part in the solution and the actual solution of the problem.

How may this be accomplished? We shall hypothesize that the probability for increasing self-esteem for a given individual increases in a situation as the following factors increase.

1. He is able to define his own goals.
2. The goals are related to his central needs or values.
3. He is able to define the paths to these goals.
4. The achievement of these goals represents a realistic level of aspiration for the individual. A goal is "realistic" when it represents a challenge or a risk that requires hitherto unused, untested effort to overcome which the individual can make available to himself. A goal that is too difficult or one that is below his present level of achievement will not lead to success—indeed it may lead to failure and a lowering of his self-esteem.

These conditions for increasing self-esteem are identical to the ones developed by Lewin and his associates in their experiments on "psycho-

---

[7] One may esteem some aspects of his self and not others. In the discussion above we are using the term self-esteem in the global sense.

logical success and failure." Psychological success is therefore hypothesized to be the mechanism for increasing self-esteem. Psychological failure is hypothesized to be the mechanism for decreasing self-esteem.

If we examine the nature of psychological success, it seems clear that an individual seeking it will need a world in which he can experience a significant degree of (1) self-responsibility and self-control (for example, in order to define his own goals, paths to goals, etc.); (2) commitment (to persevere to achieve the goals); (3) productiveness and work (to achieve the goals); and (4) utilization of his more important abilities.[8]

The theoretical viewpoint that we hold implies that there are some unique problems in measuring self-esteem. If perceptions of ourselves increase in accuracy as our self-esteem increases, then to ascertain an individual's true self-esteem by asking him to fill a questionnaire or to respond in an interview giving his evaluations of his competence is to subject the results to the same (conscious and unconscious) errors to which the individual is constantly subjecting himself. The lower the self-esteem, the greater the probability of distortion. The higher the self-esteem, the lower the probability of distortion.

One way to overcome this problem is to ascertain self-esteem by how an individual behaves toward self and others. The more his behavior provides opportunities for others to enhance their self-esteem, the higher his self-esteem. The logic is as follows.

1. The higher the self-esteem, the more the individual values himself (true by definition).
2. The more the individual values himself, the greater the need to become more aware of self in order to realize his unused potential as well as the limits of his abilities.
3. Increased self-awareness requires nondistorted feedback from the environment.
4. The probability for nondistorted feedback from the environment increases as the defensiveness of those in the environment giving the feedback decreases.
5. The more an individual behaves to minimize others' defensiveness, the greater the probability that the others will provide minimally distorted feedback. (Or, if the feedback is distorted, it is caused by external factors existing before the relationship.)
6. As an individual's internal conflict decreases, his awareness and acceptance of self increases, and the greater the probability that he will

---

[a] Kurt Lewin, Tamara Dembo, Leon Festinger, and Pauline Sears, "Level of Aspiration," in J. M. V. Hunt (Ed.), *Personality and the Behavior Disorders*, The Ronald Press, New York, 1944, pp. 333–378.

be able to help others to minimize their defensiveness and thereby increase the probability that he and others can give and receive minimally distorted feedback.

Therefore, the individual who behaves in a way *not* to decrease others' or his own self-esteem (that is, not to make others defensive) must have a relatively high sense of self-esteem.

Confirmation

The final aspect of human personality to be discussed, at this point, is what Buber has called the process of *confirmation*. Buber believes confirmation is a basic need and activity in human life. He writes, "The basis of man's life with man is twofold, and it is one—the wish of every man to be confirmed as what he is, even as what he can become, by men; and the innate capacity in man to confirm his fellowmen in this way." [9]

In the writer's opinion, the need for confirmation may be shown to stem from the nature of the human personality as discussed earlier. Man perceives the world (of human problems and activities) through his self-concept. This means that he can never know (this aspect of) his world objectively. He will see what his self "encourages" or "permits" him to see. As he gains experience, he learns that his perceptions are constantly subject to error—*his* error. Since all men are subject to this "flaw," then the possibility for error is enhanced because others may also perceive the world incorrectly. The awareness of the potentiality for error tends to create a basic posture of uncertainty and self-doubt and a predisposition to constant inquiry into the accuracy of his perception of his world. Hence the need for confirmation.

If his view and evaluation of self, others, environment, is confirmed by others, then an individual's confidence in his present evaluations of his competence should tend to increase. The feelings of confidence will tend to be strengthened especially when he is receiving confirmation from those he values. It is important to emphasize that it is the feelings of confidence that are hypothesized to increase directly as a result of confirmation. Self-esteem and competence are not directly increased by experiencing confirmation. Self-esteem is increased by experiencing

[9] Martin Buber, "Distance and Relation," *Psychiatry*, Vol. 20, May 1957, pp. 101–103; and Maurice Friedman, *Martin Buber, The Life of Dialogue*, Chicago, University of Chicago Press, 1950, p. 81.

psychological success, and competence is enhanced as psychological success increases.

Confirmation, however, may act to validate, for the individual, his present level of self-esteem; it may increase the individual's confidence in his view of his self and his capacity to perceive the world accurately.

An individual with a relatively high sense of self-confidence may be able to understand and tolerate much defensive behavior in others because he "knows" (from previous confirmatory experiences) that he tends to perceive himself and the world quite accurately. To put this another way, if A's esteem is high and experience with confirmation is low, while B's self-esteem is equally high and confirmatory experiences are high, then B will be more able than A to resist becoming or making others defensive (when others are acting defensively). This, in turn, may tend to decrease the probability that either indvidual's self-esteem will be lowered.[10]

The Proper State of Mind

We are now ready to define the "proper state of mind" to which we related the degree of psychological energy that an individual has available with which to work.

The *potential energy* an individual has available to him will be a function of the degree of self-esteem: the higher the self-esteem, the greater the *potential energy*. The *actual* energy an individual has will be a function of the degree to which he can experience psychological success. Psychological success (and its derivatives of self-esteem, etc.) is therefore defined as the condition for creating the proper state of mind.

According to the researchers, it is also true that once an individual has achieved a level of aspiration that has led to psychological success, his tendency will be to define a new level of aspiration which is realistic and higher. Once this is achieved, still another goal which is realistic and higher will be defined. In other words, we may infer that there is no inherent limit to man's psychological energy. This is why we say the amount of energy varies with the individual's state of mind.

Again, we must not forget that the individual's state of mind can also be influenced by societal factors. Not only the frequency of psychological success and failure, but the nature and scope of each of these experiences, can be influenced by the environment.

For example, societal factors can influence what goals will tend to be

[10] Confirmation will be discussed further in Chapter 11.

available for the individual, as well as the goals that he will tend to consider realistic. We have already seen that the same is true for the needs and abilities that the individual tends to develop. The levels of aspiration that may be considered by the individual as realistic and unrealistic, as appropriate and inappropriate, will also be influenced by the process of acculturation or socialization that he experiences. We will see that the lower-class norms tend to sanction certain values such as a low level of aspiration and indifference. Middle-class values tend to be oriented toward high levels of aspiration toward work and goals of service and success. The reader may recall the study, cited in the previous chapter, in which Norwegian employees tend to feel that it is less legitimate for them to request greater control over, and participation in, their work, than do American employees.

Moreover, the societal norms also influence the make-up of the environment and thus the probabilities that the individual will tend to be offered opportunities to fulfill his aspirations. In some cultures, risk-taking opportunities are created by the adults for the child, while in others the children are greatly overprotected.

The individual also exists in several subsocieties and cultures. One important such subsociety for our purposes is the organization in which a person seeks to earn his living. The organization, as a subsociety, may influence (1) what the individual will tend to desire, (2) the probability of achieving it, and (3) the meaning of the success or failure. For example, the technology may offer different (in number and in kind) opportunities for psychological success and failure. A refinery with its continuous flow of work, an assembly line with its fractionized, highly paced work, the craft work of blowing a crystal bowl or creating a sterling silver candelabrum, all provide different opportunities for psychological success. The same may be true for the nature and "tightness" of managerial controls. An organization administered by financial systems that control every move of a worker tend to create a different world from that created by the organization that is much less tightly run. The same is true for the leadership styles of management. The more directive, "production-centered," "structure-oriented" the manager, the less the probabilities of his creating opportunities for his subordinates to experience psychological success.

The importance of the quality of the work can also be a factor influencing the degree of psychological success that is possible. Thus, the stress for high-quality control in the production of a drug may be more accepted by the employees working for a drug manufacturer than the same high standards would be accepted by the employees in a toy factory. Indeed, in the latter case, the individuals may gain some psycho-

logical success by breaking production rules even if it may mean a reduction in the quality of the output.

The degree of trust and respect between management and employees
are also very important factors. As we shall see, when the climate of
trust is low, the employees may gain part of their success by aspiring
to break various management rules and "get away with it." Under conditions of low trust (and high frustration) the employee may express
his aggression by setting very low or very unrealistically high levels of
aspiration. In either case, the goals will probably never be achieved.
Depending on the employee's involvement in his work (and the degree
to which his decision to develop unreal levels of aspiration is conscious),
he may be affected by the lack of goal achievement. We may hazard a
guess that, all other factors being equal, the greater the involvement
and the less the conscious awareness of one's motives to adapt, the
greater the probability of psychological failure.

However, under a climate of trust, the individuals may increase their
opportunities for psychological success. With trust, the management
may tend to feel less a need to develop tight control mechanisms, thereby
creating greater opportunity for psychological success. However, also
under a climate of mutual trust, the employees may be more willing
to see the legitimate needs of the organization. For example, there is
always the need for the administrators to balance the many conflicting
demands in order to develop some meaningful plan for the overall organization. The concept of psychological success may naturally lead to
sales goals being developed by the individual. However, since by the
very notion of psychological success they may be raised increasingly, the
organization would have difficulty in planning the work for manufacturing, engineering, and so on. Thus, the organization's need to limit the
probabilities for psychological success may be understood by employees
where a climate of trust exists. The same may be true when the financial health of the organization is not good. An organization that is having problems to survive may legitimately call on the participants for
sacrifices.

A final dimension that may act to decrease the legitimization of psychological success in work is the legal one.[11] There are certain jobs, in
banks and insurance firms, for example, whose content is defined in detail by the law. These laws are designed to protect the customer and
do not permit alteration of the work. For example, it may be that the
auditing function in a bank could be the responsibility of those being

[11] Some of the legal barriers may be temporary. We do not mean to imply that we
are not willing to consider changes that will lead to more effective organizations if
they are beyond the present statement of the law.

audited. Such a notion would not only violate present auditing practice, but also legal rules regarding internal bank auditing.

Societies can also influence the psychological growth of individuals by their state of development. We may hypothesize that the more un- derdeveloped the society, the less the number of opportunities that it may offer for psychological success in an organizational setting.

Another characteristic of underdeveloped countries may be that they offer opportunity for individual psychological success along a limited set of needs. Using an oversimplified model of Maslow's concept of hierarchy of needs, let us postulate the existence of physiological, se- curity, and self-actualization needs.[12] Maslow suggests that the first needs that must be fulfilled are the physiological needs (food, sex, etc.). Next are the security, and, finally, the self-actualization needs. At the risk of oversimplifying, we say that the former needs are related to the pro- tection of one's self and the latter to the full expression of the individ- ual's present potential and the striving to expand it. Maslow also states that the individual will not tend to aspire to fulfill the next higher level of needs (in the hierarchy of needs) until he has achieved a certain degree of fulfillment of the lower-level needs. Also, a need that is rela- tively fulfilled does not tend to motivate behavior.

In a modern industrial society, to the extent that the physiological and security needs have been relatively fulfilled,[13] they will no longer tend to provide strong motivation for behavior. The self-actualizing needs will tend to be the source for human energy. Thus, what will provide psy- chological success in an underdeveloped society may not be relevant in the more economically advanced societies.

In modern industrial life, it may be that we are offering opportunities for the fulfillment of the physiological and security needs, but because of the nature of the industrial world that we have created, the modern industrial society is not able to offer fulfillment of the self-actualizing needs. Ironically, modern industrial life may solve the physiological and security needs of man through a social mechanism (of organization) which, by its present nature, is unable to provide expression for the next level of needs for most of its participants. Unless these needs are ex- pressed, the society may eventually lose much of its available source of energy for work.

We end by returning to the concept of competence. Hopefully, it is now clear that understanding the meaning of "awareness," "problems," and "energy consumption" is extremely difficult.

[12] A. H. Maslow, *Motivation and Personality*, Harper, New York, 1954.
[13] This is *not* to imply that much more does not need to be done in these societies to eliminate hunger and poverty.

However, we do wish to emphasize that the proposed view of competence is not a simple theory of efficiency. For example, we might argue that competent problem solving in art may not require minimal use of energy. Also, in some situations human beings may wish to have certain problems recur because they are satisfying. The reply depends on one's conceptions of satisfaction as well as the needs to be fulfilled. For example, if we conceive the artist as fulfilling some need grossly labeled here as "painting," then our view would indeed seem limited. However, if we hypothesize that the artist paints because he strives for psychological success and increased self-esteem (to mention only two), then our view becomes more compatible with understanding his behavior. Thus "minimal use of energy" refers to what is necessary to gain psychological success and increase self-esteem. One artist might conceivably achieve this state of affairs in one day and another in three weeks.

Also, the need for problems to recur is consistent with the concept of psychological success. The reader may recall that the concept suggests that once a realistic level of aspiration is achieved, a new and higher level is aspired. We would argue, however, that a painting of, let us say, a barn at one time is not psychologically the same problem if the artist decided to paint the barn again and if he were striving to experience further psychological success (because he would have raised his level of aspiration for the second painting.)

"Minimal use of energy," therefore, does not mean the objective minimal use of energy. It means the utilization of all the energy necessary to achieve psychological success *and* the minimization of energy utilized in experiencing psychological failure.

Summary

Organizations have many sources of energy. We are able to focus on only one of these—the psychological energy of individuals. This energy is hypothesized to increase as the individuals' experiences of psychological success increase, and to decrease with psychological failure. In order to experience psychological success, three requirements are essential. The individuals must value themselves and aspire to experience an increasing sense of competence. This, in turn, requires that they strive continuously to find and to create opportunities in which they can increase the awareness and acceptance of their selves and others.

The second requirement is an organization that provides opportunities for work in which the individual is able to define his immediate goals, define his own paths to these goals, relate these to the goals of the organization, evaluate his own effectiveness, and constantly increase the degree of challenge at work.

Finally, the society and culture in which he is embedded can influence the individual and the organization. It can influence the individual, through the process of acculturation, to place a high or low value on self-esteem and competence. The process of acculturation, in turn, is a function of the society's norms and values as well as its economic development.

This book focuses primarily on the first two factors. As has been said before, the societal and cultural factors are extremely important and eventually must be integrated with the first two.

The Organizational Dilemma

Organizations are usually created to achieve objectives that can best be met collectively. This means that the sequences of activity necessary to achieve the objectives are too much for one individual and they must be cut up into "sequential units" that are manageable by human beings. At the individual level the units are roles; at the group level the units are departments These units are integrated or organized in a particular sequence or pattern designed to achieve the objectives, and the resulting pattern constitutes the organizational structure. Organizations, therefore, have an *initial* or *intended* structure which is simply a static picture of the pattern of the units as planned by the creators in order for people to achieve the objectives.[1]

Most organizations today have had their initial structure designed by architects of a school which has been called "scientific management." These architects tend to hold some assumptions about the best way in which to design work that human beings are to perform. Elsewhere, it was suggested that these assumptions tended to create organizations with built-in unintended consequences.[2] It was concluded that the initial or-

---

[1] For one of the first systematic discussions of the concept of people as agents of the organization known to the writer, see E. W. Bakke, *Bonds of Organization*, Harper, New York, 1950.

[2] Chris Argyris, *Personality and Organization*, Harper, New York, 1957.

ganizational structure tended to create work situations having requirements counter to those for psychological success and self-esteem. In an attempt to adapt to these work situations, individuals tended to modify the organizational structure. They added to the intended or initial structure an *unintended* structure. This unintended structure, although antagonistic to the intended or initial structure, actually dovetailed with it in order to guarantee the maintenance of the intended structure. This was suggested as one explanation why most organizations manifest unintended or "informal" activities that tend to make organizations much more complex and different from the original design.

The point is that the organization as a going, living system has many "parts" that do not appear on the drawing board; that indeed may not be recognized by the top administrations; that may, however, keep the total organization viable and operating. In other words, we attempt to account for the unintended parts by showing that the initial structure is incongruent with the nature of individuals who strive for psychological success. Therefore, they create the unintended activities in order to perform the intended ones and to obtain a minimum amount of psychological return.

It may be argued that organizations in "real" life are not populated by people who aspire for psychological success. We would only agree and add that indeed people will tend to aspire for different amounts of psychological success. The amount and kind of psychological success that any given individual may desire is highly influenced by early-life psychological factors such as the impact of his parents, siblings, and adolescent friends. We have already pointed out how the society can influence the level of aspiration of individuals.

To put this another way, we acknowledge the existence of individual differences and the impact of the society on the need for psychological success. However, in order not to be immobilized by the enormous number of possible combinations, we have to begin somewhere. We do so by simply asking what would happen if people who aspire for psychological success populated organizations. In doing so, we are *not* attempting to eliminate individual differences. We will discuss, for example, the impact of the organization on individuals who do not aspire for psychological success. The impact that may occur along the continuum between these two extremes is a matter for empirical research. Our model can provide the basis for such research. But we will not explore this in detail in this book.

However, our selection of the individual who aspires toward psychological success is not an arbitrary one. As we shall see, there is an increasing number of psychologists who believe that self-esteem, self-acceptance, and psychological success are some of the most central factors that constitute individual mental health in our culture.[3] If we are able to understand better how one may enhance the opportunity for individual psychological success, we believe that this will contribute toward individual mental health.

Nor is this the only reason for our selection. Indeed, from the point of view of theory building, it is not even the more important reason. We have selected as our personality model the individual who aspires for psychological success because, by doing so, we will be able to "derive" and predict certain informal or unintended consequences of organizations which are supported by existing studies as well as independent theorizing. We are not satisfied with the amount of support provided by either source, but as we will show, the empirical research is increasing. If informal activities can be "derived" by postulating a different concept of personality, this theoretical framework will have to be seriously questioned.

Returning to the discussion of the unintended parts, we suggest that their nature varies with the level of the hierarchy of the organization. This is true because the organization tends to make different requirements of individuals at different levels of the organizational hierarchy. Workers on the assembly line, for example, tend to experience different work requirements than do their executives. The latter have a much greater opportunity for psychological success.

The Organizational Activities at the Lowest Level

Elsewhere we have attempted to describe, in some detail, the working world of the lower-level employee.[4] We have suggested that the worker finds himself in a work world whose technology, managerial controls (for example, budgets, incentive systems, etc.), and the directive leadership tend to create the following conditions.

1. Work is highly specialized and fractionized; it is broken down to the simplest possible motions. The assumption is that the easier the work,
   (a) the more the productivity; (b) the less the training time needed;
   (c) the greater the flexibility for interchangeability of the worker;
   (d) the greater the satisfaction of the employee because the less the frustration and/or responsibility that he will tend to experience.
2. Responsibility for the planning of work, for defining production rates, for maintaining control over speed, is placed in the hands of manage-

---

[3] For example, Allport, Rogers, Maslow, Miller, and Sullivan.
[4] Chris Argyris, *op. cit.*, Chap. III.

ment and not in the hands of those doing the actual producing of the product.

3. Responsibility for issuing orders, changing work, shifting employees, indeed for most of the important changes in the workers' world is also invested in top management.

4. Responsibility for evaluating performance, for developing and disbursing rewards and penalties lies primarily in the hands of management.

5. Responsibility for deciding who may remain, who must leave, and when these decisions shall be made is also vested in the management of the organization.

The exact degree to which these assumptions or premises are followed in any given organization varies with the organization. However, we may hypothesize that, to the extent that organizations attempt to follow the consequences of these premises, they will tend to create a work world for the lower-level employee in which:

1. Few of his abilities will be used. Those abilities that will be used will tend to be the ones that provide more limited potential (in our culture) for psychological success (such as finger dexterity and other motor or "doing" abilities). The abilities more central to self-expression and psychological success such as the cognitive (intellectual) and the interpersonal abilities will tend to be utilized minimally.

2. The worker will tend to experience a sense of dependence and submissiveness toward his superior because the decisions of whether or not he works, how much he shall be paid, and so on, will be largely under his superior's control. In short, the worker will tend to feel that he has little control over such crucial decisions about his organizational life as the activity that he will be required to perform, the rewards and penalties, and his membership.

In stating this generalization we are aware of seeming exceptions. For example, Mechanic has shown that under certain conditions the lower-level employee can act to make his superior dependent upon him. He hypothesizes that this will tend to occur when (other factors remaining constant) (a) the individual's access to persons, information, and instrumentalities increases; (b) the individual has expert knowledge not available to high-ranking participants; (c) he is difficult to replace; and (d) the superiors are not highly motivated to work.[5] Let us examine each of these briefly. It is our view that the pyramidal

[5] David Mechanic, "Sources of Power of Lower Participants in Complex Organizations," *Administrative Science Quarterly*, Vol. 7, No. 3, December 1962, pp. 350–364.

structure is a strategy designed to give the greatest influence over persons, information, and instrumentalities to the higher-level positions. It may not always work out this way, as Mechanic suggests. However, it is our hypothesis that if we conducted an empirical study, we would find that it works more frequently in the intended direction of the strategy than the unintended direction. Thus we would hypothesize that the major control over people, information, and instrumentalities increases as the individual goes up the line. However, if the opposite were true, we would predict that, if the subordinates needed to be relatively independent (and they were), the consequences to be cited later would *not* tend to occur.

The second condition that Mechanic cites is one in which the subordinate has expert knowledge not available to the superior. Again, we agree with his conclusion, up to a point. It is our observation (discussed in the next chapter) that many situations exist in which subordinates do have expert knowledge and whose sense of dependence is still quite high. The reason is that the superior controls the rewards and penalties as well as the possibility of remaining or leaving the organization.

This leads to the third condition, namely, the difficulty to replace the subordinate. This too has to be tempered by the psychological and social "difficulties" involved in moving and dislocation as well as the probability of the next situation being any better. It has been our observation that an expert scientist or engineer may remain in a situation that he does not like, not because of the absence of new jobs, but because of the expectation that another situation will not tend to be much different and/or that the dislocation will carry "costs" to himself and family that he is unwilling to pay.

Finally, we also agree that the foregoing predictions would not tend to be operative if the superiors were not highly committed to their work. These conditions are not consonant to the values implicit in the pyramidal structure. Indeed, we may speculate that when the subordinates run the organization because the leaders are not willing to put in the effort necessary, the pyramidal structure is no longer operating.

3. The worker will tend to experience a decreasing sense of self-responsibility and self-control. This will tend to be true because he notes that someone else will tell him what to do, how well he ought to do it and when, how much he ought to perform, whether he has performed adequately, and so on.

If we compare these (psychological) requirements with those necessary for psychological success and self-esteem, we find that they are not consonant. Indeed, they all tend to emphasize the conditions for psychological failure. The reader may recall that the conditions for psychological success were to experience (*a*) self-responsibility and self-control, (*b*) internal commitment to work that was meaningful and that (*c*) utilized the employees' important abilities.

In addition to psychological failure, these conditions should also tend to *frustrate* those employees aspiring for psychological success, and this frustration should lead to feelings of *conflict*. (Should they leave this work and risk unemployment or a worse job?)

The foregoing may be summarized in the form of three propositions:

Proposition I. There is a lack of congruency between the needs of individuals aspiring for psychological success and the demands of the (initial) formal organization.

Corollary 1. The disturbance will vary in proportion to the degree of incongruency between the needs of the individuals and the requirements of the formal organization.

Proposition II. The resultants of this disturbance are frustration, failure, short-time perspective, and conflict.

If the participants in the organization desire psychological success:

1. They will tend to experience frustration because their self-expression will be blocked.
2. They will tend to experience failure because they will not be permitted to define their own goals in relation to central needs, the paths to these goals, and so on.
3. They will tend to experience short-time perspective because they will have no control over the clarity and stability of their future.
4. They will tend to experience conflict because, as healthy agents, they will dislike frustration, failure, and short-time perspective which is characteristic of the present job. However, if they leave they may not find a new job easily, and/or even if a new job is found, it may not be different.

Proposition III. Under certain conditions the degree of frustration, failure, short-time perspective, and conflict will tend to increase.

The resultants of the disturbance in the organization will tend to increase in degree:

1. As the individual agents increase in degree of desire for psychological success.
2. As the degree of dependence, subordination, passivity, and so on, increases. This tends to occur (*a*) as one goes down the chain of command; (*b*) as directive leadership increases; (*c*) as management

controls are increased; and (*d*) as human relations programs are undertaken but improperly implemented.
3. As the jobs become more specialized.
4. As the exactness with which the traditional formal principles are used increases.

Before we describe how the employees may adapt to failure, frustration, and conflict, it is important to remember that, as we pointed out earlier, such conditions will *not* tend to be highly frustrating to individuals in countries where the physiological needs and security needs are difficult to fulfill; where for some social or legal reasons, the work must be accepted as being of this character; when the organization's survival is in question; when the individual is "taught" by his culture's norms; where for personal psychological reasons, the individual has decided not to aspire toward psychological success; where it is a cultural norm not to be involved in work.[6]

In a more fully economically developed country, the major conditions under which the frustration, failure, and conflict will tend to decrease will probably be related to the reasons mentioned last (that is, the culture has "taught" them or they have decided not to become involved in their work.) These possibilities will be discussed more fully later.

It seems appropriate to emphasize again that we have chosen to illustrate our viewpoint with the case of (1) the individual striving for psychological success; (2) holding a job that, because of the technology, has been designed to be highly specialized and (3) because of the managerial controls and directive leadership provides minimum opportunity for psychological success. We realize that we have probably made our case much more "black" and "white" than is the situation in real life. *We are aware that jobs vary greatly in terms of the degree of psychological success they will tend to permit, and individuals vary greatly in terms of their need for psychological success.* We should also emphasize that up to this point we are speaking of the formal or intended organization. These will be discussed in a subsequent section.

However, it is our hypothesis that if we select a given formal organization, we will tend to find that, on the average, due to the organizational structure, managerial controls, and directive leadership, the gap or conflict between the individual needs and the organizational requirements tends to become worse as one goes down the chain of command and as the job exerts more control over the individual. The gap or con-

[6] Robert Blauner, *Alienation and Freedom*, Department of Sociology, University of Chicago, 1962, mimeographed, p. 167.

flict decreases as one goes up the chain of command and as the individual is able to control the requirements made of him by the job. This proposition, along with generalizing about what we should find in organizations "in general," permits the exceptions to exist. Thus, it may be that due to an extremely authoritarian president, a given vice-president may have less control over his job than a foreman or, indeed, even a janitor. Also it may help to account for the scientist or staff specialist who may not be very high in the hierarchical structure, but who is permitted a substantial degree of control over the design and definition of his work.

Some Empirical Illustrations of Parts of Our Viewpoint

We should like to present some empirical research that illustrates parts of our viewpoint. None of these studies was available when the theoretical framework was originally stated. With the exception of the first study, none was specifically designed to test Propositions I, II, and III stated earlier. Consequently, they do *not* constitute a "test" of the propositions. However, they do constitute an illustration of some of the consequences predicted by the hypotheses as well as the conditions under which these consequences are expected to be found.

Example I

Farris has tested aspects of Propositions I, II, and III in a questionnaire study of 513 scientists from eleven university, industrial, and governmental laboratories.[7] The study focused on the following eight questions.

1. To what extent is there an incongruency between the motives of the scientists and the provisions by their organizations for satisfying these motives?
2. Do the individuals with the greatest incongruency tend to experience more disturbance, frustration, failure, and short-time perspective? Do they tend to avoid taking risks?
3. Do incongruency and its resultants increase as one goes down the chain of command?

[7] George F. Farris, "Congruency of Scientists' Motives with their Organizations' Provisions for Satisfying Them: Its Relationship to Motivation, Affective Job Experiences, Styles of Work, and Performance," Department of Psychology, University of Michigan, mimeographed, November 1962. I draw heavily from his report.

4. Is there any relationship between the degree of congruency and scientific performance?
5. Is total motive congruency the best predictor in Questions 2, 3, and 4, or does a different pattern of congruency and its resultants emerge for different motives?
6. Do different patterns of congruency and its resultants emerge for doctoral and nondoctoral scientists?
7. Do different patterns of congruency and its resultants emerge for scientists in departments emphasizing research and scientists in departments emphasizing development?
8. Do different patterns of congruency and its resultants emerge for scientists in departments that are relatively coordinated in selection of work goals and relationships with colleagues and for scientists in departments that are relatively autonomous in these respects?

Quantitative indices of "motive for self-actualization," "motive for status," "provision for self-actualization," and "provision for status" were developed. Also developed were measures of "perceived congruency" (subtracting the individual's motive from his perception of his organization's provisions for satisfying that motive) and ".objective congruency" (subtracting the individual's motive from the mean of the provisions for that motive perceived by all members of his department in a "similar job situation.") In addition, measures of total perceived congruency and total objective congruency were determined by summing the congruency scores of each of the three factors after weighting them according to their variances. A total of eight measures of congruency were available. These were perceived and objective measures of self-actualization congruency, status congruency, social congruency, and total congruency.

The dependent measures developed are related to the degree of perceived (experienced) "disturbance," "frustration," "failure," "time perspective," "motive to avoid taking risks," and five indices of performance.

The results may be summarized as follows.

Question 1. To what extent is there an incongruency between the motives of the scientists and the provisions by their organizations for satisfaction of these motives?

More than 60 per cent of the scientists preferred to have more opportunities for satisfying their motives for self-actualization and status than their organizations provided, and over 30 per cent reported an incongruency on the social motive. These findings held true whether perceived or objective measures of congruency were used.

Question 2. Do the individuals with the greatest incongruency tend to experience more disturbance, frustration, failure, short-time perspective? Do they tend to avoid taking risks?

Disturbance. Items reflecting involvement, interest, identification, and importance were combined to form an index of intensity of motivation, and a high score on this index was assumed to be indicative of little "disturbance." If Proposition II is correct, positive correlations between congruency and intensity of motivation may be expected. The data show that this was so when perceived measures of congruency were used: the more the scientist perceived his motives as being potentially satisfied in his organization, the greater his motivation and the less his disturbance. Objective measures of congruency showed no such relationships: in fact, with the self-actualization motive, the more the actual provision exceeded the individual's motive, the less his reported motivation.

Frustration. Proposition II states that individuals will tend to experience frustration *because their self-actualization is blocked.* It is predicted, therefore, that a negative relationship occurs between self-actualization congruency and the measure of frustration (the ratio of the difficulties of the job to the respondent's abilities to cope with them), and that no particular relationship exists between other types of congruency and frustration. The findings strongly confirm this prediction.

Failure. According to Proposition II, respondents are expected to report less failure or a greater rate of progress when they reported higher congruency. The data show no strong evidence favoring or opposing this expectation.

Time Perspective. With certain exceptions a negative relationship occurs between congruency measures and short-time perspective, as expected from Proposition II. Objective measures of congruency show stronger relationships, and status congruency shows the strongest relationships of all. No particular relationship occurs between congruency and long-range time perspective although Proposition II predicts a positive one.

Motive to Avoid Risks. A clear negative relationship between all measures of congruency and the motive to avoid risks is shown. The relationship is highly significant in all but one case. Thus, the more a scientist's motives are potentially satisfied by his organization, the more willing he is to take risks in his work.

Question 3. Do incongruency and its resultants increase as one goes down the chain of command? (Proposition III, 2a.)

This proposition received substantial support. With one exception, the eight measures of congruency were positively correlated with the index of status in the organization (*p* of .05 or less). With increasing status, motivation tended to increase, feelings of failure tended to decrease, and risks were more apt to be taken. No clear relationships were found between status and frustration or time perspective.

Question 4. Is there any relationship between the degree of congruency and scientific performance?

A definite tendency was found for scientists who reported high congruency to be rated high in scientific contribution and usefulness to their organizations. With all measures of perceived congruency, and objective measures of total congruency and social congruency, the relationships were significant at better than the .05 level. No general relationships occurred between congruency and output of patents, papers, or unpublished reports. An overall pattern cannot be expected, since different types of laboratories stress different types of output; however, positive correlations might be expected to occur for patents in development departments and for papers in research departments. It was found that for the groups of scientists in development departments, 20 of 31 correlation coefficients between designated measures of congruency and patents were positive, 5 being significant at the .05 level. Also, 11 of 16 correlations between congruency and papers were positive for scientists in research, none of them being statistically significant. No trends seemed likely for the various groups of scientists in the relationships between measures of congruency and unpublished reports; the data show that none were found, although positive correlations generally occurred.

Question 5. Is total motive congruency the best predictor in Questions 2, 3, and 4, or does a different pattern of congruency and its resultants emerge for different motives?

In order to answer this question with reference to Question 2, it was necessary to summarize the correlations between each measure of congruency and the six dependent measures of Proposition II for all six groups of scientists. A summary of the number of positive, negative, and significant correlations was made and points were assigned. Despite the arbitrary assumptions made, certain pronounced tendencies were discovered. Except for the social motive, the perceived measures of congruency showed stronger relationships in the expected direction than the objective measures. Status congruency and self-actualization congruency generally showed stronger relationships than social congruency.

All measures of congruency, except objective self-actualization congruency, showed strong positive relationships to the scientist's position in the chain of command. All the perceived measures showed strong relationships in the expected direction to judgments of contribution and usefulness, while of the objective measures only total congruency and social congruency showed significant relationships. No overall summary was made for the three measures of output, since the directions of the relationships were considered unpredictable in these cases. Thus, although the perceived and objective measures of total congruency were very good predictors of Questions 2, 3, and 4, a different pattern of congruency and its resultants did emerge for different motives.

Question 6. Do different patterns of congruency and its resultants emerge for doctoral and nondoctoral scientists?

The data showed a slight tendency for stronger relationships to occur for the nondoctoral scientists when Proposition II was tested, and a pronounced tendency for stronger relationships in the nondoctoral groups when judgments of performance were used. The greatest difference occurred in the relationships between self-actualization congruency and judgments of performance, which tended to be stronger for nondoctoral scientists.

Question 7. Do different patterns of congruency and its resultants emerge for scientists in departments emphasizing research and scientists in departments emphasizing development?

In general, stronger relationships were found in the development departments. The greatest differences occurred for Proposition II when the total congruency and self-actualization congruency measures were used. Status and social congruency showed the greatest differences for the judgments of performance.

Question 8. Do different patterns of congruency and its resultants emerge for scientists in departments that are relatively coordinated in selection of work goals and relationships with colleagues and for scientists in departments that are relatively autonomous in these respects?

The data indicated that stronger relationships were found in coordinated departments using the measures of Proposition II, the overall difference being due almost entirely to differences when the self-actualization measures of congruency were used. Strong positive relationships between self-actualization congruency and the measures of Proposition II occurred for scientists in coordinated departments, but strong relationships in both the expected and unexpected directions occurred for the scientists in autonomous departments. Little difference was found between autonomous and coordinated departments when the relationships between measures of congruency and judgments of performance were examined.

Example II

The second study to be cited also deals with the managerial levels. It is our position that the probability to experience a sense of self-esteem, autonomy, and self-actualization tends to increase as one goes up the line and tends to decrease as one goes down the line. It would follow that if we were to measure the degree of fulfillment of these needs we would find that the degree of deficiency fulfillment (a) should increase as one goes down the administrative hierarchy, (b) should be greatest with the needs for self-actualization and autonomy. The first is related to opportunities for psychological success and the second to the opportunity for self-control. We have hypothesized that the opportunities to express these two needs increases as one goes up the line.

Porter's [8] study illustrates these expectations. He received 1916 usable responses from five levels of management (ranging from the presidential level to the level of first- and second-level supervisors) representing manufacturing (66 per cent), transportation and public utilities (7 per cent), finance and insurance (7 per cent), wholesale and retail trade (5 per cent), and the remaining 15 per cent from other kinds of organizations.

The degree of perceived deficiency in fulfillment for each respondent on each questionnaire item was obtained by subtracting the answer to Part a of an item ("How much of the characteristic is *now connected* with your position?") from Part b of the item ("How much of the characteristic do you think *should be connected* with your position?"). The assumption was that the larger the difference—a subtracted from b—the larger the degree of dissatisfaction or the smaller the degree of satisfaction.

Porter believes that this method of measurement has two advantages. The first is that the subject is not asked directly about his satis-

[8] Lyman W. Porter, "Job Attitudes in Management: I. Perceived Deficiencies in Need Fulfillment as a Function of Job Level," *Journal of Applied Psychology*, Vol. 46, No. 6, December 1962, pp. 375–384.

faction. Therefore, the tendency for a simple "response set" is reduced. The second advantage is that this method of measuring need fulfillment is a more conservative measure than would be a single question concerning simple obtained satisfaction.

Porter found, as predicted, that need-fulfillment deficiencies for most items definitely tended to increase at each successive lower level of the management hierarchy. This occurred with all four age groups (with education being constant). The second major finding was, as predicted,

Table 3-1. Number of Changes in Size of Mean Deficiencies from Higher to Lower Levels of Management within Four Age Groups

Need Category	Item	Age Group												Total Sample		
		20–34			35–44			45–54			55+					
		+	0	−	+	0	−	+	0	−	+	0	−	+	0	−
Security	I-1	1	0	2	2	0	2	2	1	0	2	0	1	7	1	5
Social	II-1	1	1	1	2	0	2	1	1	1	1	2	0	5	4	4
	II-2	0	1	2	2	1	1	1	0	2	1	1	1	4	3	6
Category total		1	2	3	4	1	3	2	1	3	2	3	1	9	7	10
Esteem	III-1	3	0	0	3	1	0	2	1	0	1	2	0	9	4	0 **
	III-2	3	0	0	4	0	0	2	1	0	3	0	0	12	1	0 **
	III-3	2	0	1	2	2	0	1	1	1	0	2	1	5	5	3
Category total		8	0	1	9	3	0	5	3	1	4	4	1	26	10	3 **
Autonomy	IV-1	2	1	0	3	1	0	2	0	1	2	1	0	9	3	1 *
	IV-2	3	0	0	4	0	0	3	0	0	3	0	0	13	0	0 **
	IV-3	3	0	0	4	0	0	2	1	0	3	0	0	12	1	0 **
	IV-4	2	1	0	3	0	1	3	0	0	3	0	0	11	1	1 **
Category total		10	2	0	14	1	1	10	1	1	11	1	0	45	5	2 **
Self-actualization	V-1	2	1	0	4	0	0	2	1	0	2	0	1	10	2	1 *
	V-2	3	0	0	4	0	0	2	0	1	1	2	0	10	2	1 *
	V-3	3	0	0	2	1	1	2	1	0	1	2	0	8	4	1 a
Category total		8	1	0	10	1	1	6	2	1	4	4	1	28	8	3 **
Total for all items		28	5	6	39	6	7	25	8	6	23	12	4	115	31	23 **

a Approaches significance ($p = .10$).
* $p = .05$.
** $p = .01$.

that the largest deficiencies were found in the needs for autonomy and self-actualization.[9]

Table 3-1 illustrates these findings. It presents data on the number of changes in size of mean deficiencies from the higher to the lower levels of management. We note that need-fulfillment deficiencies progressively increased from the top to the bottom of the management hierarchy for three of the five need categories—esteem, autonomy, and self-actualization. Eight of the ten specific items in these three categories showed significant trends of increase in deficiencies at or exceeding the .05 level of confidence (by a sign test); one item showed a trend significant at the .10 level of confidence; and only one of the ten items failed to produce a trend approaching statistical significance.[10]

It is interesting to note that the two needs of security and social satisfaction show no difference among levels. These findings are understandable and do not contradict our point of view. Neither need is related to psychological success and self-esteem. They reflect the fact that executives tend to feel they have secure positions and that they obtain about the same degree of social satisfaction on the job.[11]

In closing, it is interesting to note that Porter states that the overall findings were supported with regularity in each of the four age groups, showing that these trends are not merely a function of higher-level managers being older, on the average, than lower-level managers. Age differences among managerial levels clearly do not explain the differences in perceived need-fulfillment deficiencies that occurred among the levels.[12]

Example III

The main theme of Propositions I, II, and III is that, all other things being equal, the lower one goes down the chain of command, the less

[9] In a subsequent study Porter obtained these findings even when the size of the company is controlled. In the same study Porter found that, at lower levels of management, small-company managers were more satisfied than large-company managers, but at higher levels of management, large-company managers were more satisfied than small-company managers. Lyman W. Porter, "Job Attitude in Management: IV. Perceived Deficiencies in Need Fulfillment as a Function of Size of Company," manuscript, University of California, 1963.

[10] *Ibid.*, p. 380.

[11] Many of these findings are valid for different cultures. M. Haire, E. E. Ghiselli, and Lyman W. Porter, "Cultural Patterns in the Role of the Manager," *Industrial Relations*, Vol. 2, No. 2, February 1963, pp. 95–118.

[12] Lyman W. Porter, *op. cit.*, Part IV, p. 381. In a subsequent study, Porter found

opportunity to use one's abilities, to have responsibility, to guarantee one's membership in the organization, and to block interruptions by others in one's work; in short, the less control one has over his work activities, rewards and penalties, and membership.

In a recent study by staff members of the Opinion Research Corporation, the unfulfilled needs of managers were studied by examining questionnaire returns from over 1000 managers from five organizations (a manufacturer of auto supplies, one of household parts, one of metals, one of household products, and an insurance firm).[13] They found that the pressure of *unfulfilled* needs increases as one goes down the chain of command and is greatest at the lower levels. In Table 3-2 the responses are categorized in terms of "top," "middle," and "lower" level managers. We note that the lower one goes down the organization, the greater the "wish my job had more of" (1) "making the most of my capacities," (2) "chance to learn new things," (3) "chance for greater responsibility," (4) "feeling I am getting somewhere," (5) "recognition when I do a good job," (6) "a chance to earn more money," and (7) "to feel really secure in my job."

These findings are consonant with the expectations discussed in Propositions I, II, and part of III. The lower one goes down the chain of command, the greater the unfulfilled opportunities for using one's abilities, learning new things, control over one's work, membership in the organization, and long-term security.

Example IV

During the past several years, there have been various empirical reviews of the literature on employee satisfaction. It seems useful to attempt to relate their findings to our point of view, so we have developed the following reasoning.

If it is true that people strive for (varying degrees of) psychological success, and if it is true that the potential amount available tends to vary with the position on the hierarchy, then we should expect studies

that higher-level managers placed relatively more emphasis on self-actualization and autonomy needs than did lower-level managers. For each of the other three types of needs, however, there were no differences between responses from higher-level or lower-level managers. Lyman Porter, "Job Attitudes in Management: II. Perceived Importance of Needs as a Function of Job Level," *Journal of Applied Psychology*, in press, 1963.

[13] Primary responsibility for the study was in the hands of Stanley E. Carnarius, *Motivating Managers*, Opinion Research Corporation, August 1962.

Table 3-2. Unfulfilled Needs of Managers

Opportunity Cluster [a]	Top Managers	Middle Managers	Supervisors
Making the most of my capacities.	39%	47%	49%
Chance to learn new things.	34%	33%	50%
Chance for greater responsibility.	27%	46%	48%
Feeling I am getting somewhere.	20%	47%	55%
Recognition Cluster			
Recognition when I do a good job.	32%	46%	52%
Good relations with my superior.	14%	22%	25%
Orderliness Cluster			
Efficient arrangement of the flow of work.	43%	47%	55%
Having things go along smoothly.	39%	52%	59%
Compensation Cluster			
A chance to earn more money.	25%	56%	69%
Suitable provisions for my retirement.	16%	34%	46%
Security Cluster			
Feeling really secure in my job.	5%	21%	42%
Congenial Work-Group Cluster			
Doing things socially with associates.	11%	17%	27%

[a] Stanley E. Carnarius, *Motivating Managers*, Opinion Research Corporation, August 1962, p. 12.

of employee satisfaction to find that, on the average, the individuals at the upper levels of organizations should be most satisfied, and that the degree of satisfaction should tend to decrease as one goes down the hierarchy and as individuals are controlled by their job.

Put in another way, our prediction is that if we ask people to state how satisfied they are with their work, their answers will tend to increase in positiveness as the individual is performing work over which he has increasing control. In terms of our scheme, the frequency of such jobs should increase as one goes up the organizational hierarchy.[14]

[14] This hypothesis is stated to account for the majority of the cases. There are, we realize, many individual differences which we cannot take into account at this point.

The work of Kahn and Weiss,[15] Gurin et al.,[16] Rosen,[17] Blauner,[18] Kornhauser,[19] Inkeles,[20] and Baldamus,[21] representing several European countries, illustrates this prediction. Karsh, in his review of the literature, confirms this trend. His conclusions are representative. He states that work satisfaction is bound up with the degree to which the worker can exercise his judgment on his job and thus have some control over how he spends his time and effort.[22] Blauner concludes, "It is possible to generalize on the basis of evidence that the greater the degree of control that a worker has (either in a single dimension or as a total composite) the greater his job satisfaction."[23] Later he writes,

. . . the marked occupational differences in work attitudes and the great significance which workers impute to being, at least to some extent, masters of their destiny in the work process, along with the fact that surrender of such control seems to be the most important condition of *strong* dissatisfaction are findings at least as important as the overall one of general satisfaction. Perhaps the need for autonomy and independence may be a more deep-seated human motive than is recognized by those who characterize our society in terms of crowdlike conformity and the decline of individualism.[24]

Gurin, Veroff, and Feld, as a result of a study based on a national sample, provide further supportive evidence. They report,

Also, we are aware that studies such as the one by Robert Hoppack report that most employees are satisfied with their work. Our predictions are not related to employees "in general" but to the different occupational levels in an organization.

[15] Robert Kahn and Robert Weiss, "The Evaluation of Work by American Men," University of Michigan, 1955, mimeographed.

[16] Gerald Gurin, Joseph Veroff, and Sheila Feld, *Americans View Their Mental Health*, Basic Books, New York, 1960, Chap. VI.

[17] Hjalmar Rosen, "Desirable Attributes of Work: Four Levels of Management Describe Their Job Environment," *Journal of Applied Psychology*, Vol. 45, No. 3, 1961, pp. 156–160.

[18] Robert Blauner, "Work Satisfaction and Industrial Trends in Modern Society," in Walter Galenson and Seymour M. Lipset (Eds.), *Labor and Trade Unionism: An Interdisciplinary Reader*, Wiley, New York, 1960, pp. 339–360.

[19] Arthur Kornhauser, "Mental Health of Employees," Foundation for Research in Behavior, November 1961.

[20] Alex Inkeles, "Industrial Man: The Relation of Status to Experience, Perception, and Values," *American Journal of Sociology*, Vol. LXVI, No. 1, July 1960, pp. 1–31.

[21] W. Baldamus, *Efficiency and Effort*, Tavistock Publications, London, 1961.

[22] Bernard Karsh, "The Meaning of Work in an Age of Automation," *Current Economic Comment*, August 1957, pp. 3–13.

[23] Robert Blauner, *op. cit.*, p. 346.

[24] *Ibid.*, pp. 352–353.

A very strong relationship [exists] between the social status of the occupation and the tendency to find ego gratification in the work. Whereas 80% of the professional group reported exclusively ego satisfaction in the work, this type of satisfaction was the exclusive source of gratification for only 29% of the unskilled workers, with the other occupations tending to fall into a consistent progression between the two extremes." [25] [The one exception was the clerical group.]

More germane to our position are the findings in Table 3-3. They indicate that, in general, reported job satisfaction declines with occupa-

Table 3-3. Relationship between Occupational Status and Job Satisfaction among Employed Men [a]

	Occupational Status							
Job Satisfaction	Professional Technician	Managerial Proprietor	Clerical Workers	Sales Workers	Skilled Workers	Semiskilled Workers	Unskilled Workers	Farmers
Very satisfied	42%	38%	22%	24%	22%	27%	13%	22%
Satisfied	41	42	39	44	54	48	52	58
Neutral	1	6	9	5	6	9	6	4
Ambivalent	10	6	13	9	10	9	13	9
Dissatisfied	3	6	17	16	7	6	16	7
Not ascertained	3	2	...	2	1	1	...	...
Total	100%	100%	100%	100%	100%	100%	100%	100%
Number of cases	119	127	46	55	202	152	84	77

[a] From Gerald Gurin, Joseph Veroff, and Sheila Feld, *Americans View Their Mental Health*, Basic Books, New York, 1960, p. 163.

tional level.[26] (However, the clerical and sales persons do report a low level of satisfaction.)

From these studies, we can infer that the higher up the organizational ladder and/or the greater the professionalization, the higher the probability that people will report intrinsic work satisfaction. The lower one goes down the organizational ladder and the less skilled the work, the lower the probability that people will report intrinsic work satisfaction.

[25] Gerald Gurin, Joseph Veroff, and Sheila Feld, *op. cit.*, p. 160.
[26] *Ibid.*, p. 163.

Incidentally, it is our view that the decline of "individualism" thesis and Blauner's findings are integrable. It is our hypothesis that employees tend to have a need for autonomy. However, after years of work they suppress these needs and conform in order to "get by." It may be that the satisfaction studies tap the employees' suppressed desire and the "loss of individualism" studies tap the observable behavior.

Example V

Let us assume for the moment that the foregoing findings are representative of our blue- and white-collar work population (which as yet they are not). We may then conjecture what would tend to happen to employees who have to suppress their desire for control, autonomy, and independence. One hypothesis may be that such a work world may, after many years, influence the employees' view of himself, his esteem of his self, his degree of tension, satisfaction in life, and indeed his values about the meaning of work.

Recently, a study was completed that tapped all these factors from a group of lower-level employees. The objective of the study was to shed light on employee "mental health." The definition of mental health that was used suggested to us that the study might serve to illustrate (or to refute) our position. Kornhauser [27] developed an index of mental health, which was validated by an independent check with clinical psychologists and psychiatrists, and which included the following dimensions:

1. An index of anxiety and emotional tension.
2. An index of hostility.
3. An index of social participation and friendly attitudes (versus withdrawal).
4. An index of self-esteem, favorable self-feedings.
5. An index of personal morale (versus anomie, social alienation, etc.).
6. An index of overall satisfaction with life.

If our view of organization is valid, then we would expect that the "mental health" of the employee should decrease as one goes down the chain of command and where the job controls the individual. "Mental health" should tend to increase as one goes up the chain of command and as the individual has greater control over the job (for example, higher skilled work).

[27] Arthur Kornhauser, "Mental Health of Factory Workers: A Detroit Study," *Human Organization*, Vol. 21, No. 1, Spring 1962, pp. 43–46.

Kornhauser's findings illustrate our expectations. He concludes that when workers are classified by skill level and variety of work operations, mental-health scores do show consistent correlation with occupational hierarchy. The higher the occupational level, the better the mental health. He writes:

One simple set of figures will suffice to make this more concrete. Let us compare occupations by the percentage of workers enjoying "good" mental health—i.e., having "high" mental health scores (the cutting point for "high" is of course arbitrary.) We have two age groups—men in their 20s and those in their 40s. For the middle-age group—approximately 300 men —the results are as follows:

Skilled workers	56%	"good" mental health
High semi-skilled	41%	" " "
Ordinary semi-skilled	38%	" " "
Repetitive semi-skilled	26%	" " "
(Repetitive, machine-paced only)	16%	" " "

For the young group—109 men in their 20s—the percentages run:

Skilled and high semi-skilled	58%	"good" mental health [28]
Ordinary semi-skilled	35%	" " "
Repetitive semi-skilled	10%	" " "
(Repetitive, machine-paced only)	7%	" " "

Amount of schooling, then, affords one good test of the *selection* explanation of occupational mental health differences. Since substantial educational differences do occur between occupations and since education is also associated with better mental health, the possibility has to be examined whether this association is sufficient to produce the obtained results. Conversely, do occupational mental health differences persist apart from the influence of education—i.e., when only persons of like amounts of education are compared? Our findings strongly suggest that the latter is true. Proportions of workers having good mental health consistently decrease from higher to lower level occupations *for each of three educational categories separately.* Moreover, the magnitude of the differences is very nearly the same as when education is not controlled but is permitted to add to its influence.

For the middle-age group (in which the n is large enough to permit more adequate analysis) occupation and education show a small additive effect on mental health. Thus, mental health is best among those high in education *and* occupation, poorest for those low in both education and occupation. This is contrary, of course, to the psychologically plausible hypothesis that mental health is adversely affected by lack of congruency between educational status and occupational status—the view that poorest mental health occurs among

[28] *Ibid.*, pp. 44–45.

persons of better education in low-level jobs (and perhaps also among those low education in high-level jobs). This hypothesis receives no support at all from our data. In fact, the percentage of "good" mental health in lower-level jobs is *greater* for persons having more schooling.[29]

The next question is whether these occupational differences are due to *effects of the jobs* or to the *selection of certain kinds of persons* who go into these jobs. Kornhauser says that

the analysis of our data as a whole leads to the conclusions that educational differences, either by themselves or in interaction with job level, do not account for the observed mental health variations by occupation. . . . [We could conclude] that the influences determining occupational mental health differences among factory workers are to be found in the jobs themselves and their associated life conditions.

Kornhauser concludes:

. . . the indications from our present data are: (a) that mental health (as here assessed) is poorer among factory workers as we move from more skilled, responsible, varied types of work to jobs lower in these respects, and (b) that the relationship is not due in any large degree to differences of prejob background or personality of the men who enter and remain in the several types of work. The relationship of mental health to occupation, in other words, appears to be "genuine"; mental health is dependent on factors associated with the job.[30]

Example VI

This example is also taken from a study designed to understand various aspects of the mental health of employees. One of the variables studied was the degree of stress employees tend to experience. It is our hypothesis that, on the average, stress should tend to be experienced at its greatest strength among the lower-level nonskilled employees, and it should decrease in the more skilled jobs where greater control over the work is permitted and more use of one's abilities is possible.

Kasl and French, in a carefully executed study in two plants (more than 6000 employees), attempted to relate illness as recorded in dispensary visits (and as categorized in 35 diagnostic categories) to stresses of the job. After correcting for age and distance from the employee's work location to the dispensary, they found that skill level was inversely related to dispensary visits. In Company H the low-skilled employees

[29] *Ibid.*, pp. 44–45.
[30] *Ibid.*, pp. 44 and 45.

had 73 more medical cards than the high-skill employees ($p < .0001$). Similar results were found in Company B. Finally, it was found that self-esteem was inversely related to medical visits. Perceived monotony and dullness of one's job correlated (in both companies) .59 with frequency of dispensary visits. The number of dispensary visits in both plants was significantly correlated (.61 and .79) with decreasing skill required by the job.[31]

In terms of our theory, if we hypothesize that the stress was due to the lack of congruence between the individual's needs and the demands made by the organization, then the foregoing data are consonant with our point of view. This hypothesis seems warranted by the fact that Kasl and French found that the lower the self-esteem, the greater the job stress and the more frequent the dispensary visits. We have already presented data suggesting that lower-level employees tend to have a lower sense of self-esteem. The positive correlation, already cited, between monotonous and dull jobs on the one hand and dispensary visits on the other, would also tend to support our view.

Also in line with our view were the findings (in Company A) that the foremen supervising low-skill craft jobs had 37 per cent more cards than those supervising high-skill craft jobs ($p < .0001$). In Company B the foremen of low-skill craft work had 146 per cent more visits than those who supervised higher-skilled work ($p < .0001$).[32] The apparent contradiction in these findings may be explained when it is noted that foremen are at the bottom of the managerial hierarchy and as such reported the greatest degree of tension and pressure (in the managerial system).

Example VII

Finally, the least direct but still relevant data come from a study by Mann and Williams. According to our conceptual scheme, employees, on the average, are capable, indeed are probably desirous, of more complex challenging work than tends to be available to them. If this is true, we may develop the following hypothesis.

In a situation in which the work has been significantly enlarged, we should find that the employees speak positively of the opportunity for a greater sense of challenge and self-responsibility. We also predict that, for a specified time, they should be uncomfortable with the risk and tension associated with psychological success (since presumably in their old jobs they had not experienced psychological success).

[31] Stanislav Kasl, and John R. P. French, Jr., "The Effects of Occupational Status on Physical and Mental Health," *Journal of Social Issues*, Vol. XVIII, No. 3, 1962, Chap. III.
[32] *Ibid.*, pp. 20 and 23.

Mann and Williams [33] report such results in a study of the impact of data-processing equipment on job requirements. We focus on two populations of employees for whom matched data "before" and "after" (the introduction of the equipment) were available. They report that significantly more of the occupants in higher jobs, in contrast with those in less enlarged jobs, reported greater satisfaction with the increased amount of job responsibility, more variety and change in their jobs, greater opportunity to learn, and felt these jobs were more important *and* that their work was now more demanding, more risky, and more tension producing. In our terms, the employees found their new and enlarged jobs more challenging and meaningful, yet, at the same time, more tense. This suggests that employees are able to respond to the new challenging work even though their satisfaction with the new job is not necessarily greater than with the old one. Indeed, it suggests a hypothesis that we intend to explore further; namely, that need fulfillment and happiness are not necessarily related.

Summary

Although most of the studies do not provide direct support of our viewpoint, all together they do lend some support to our view of the basic dilemma between the needs of individuals aspiring for psychological success and self-esteem and the demands of the pyramidal structure. At the risk of oversimplification, our view may be stated as follows. The formal organization (which *includes* the technology) and the administrative control system typically used in complex formal organizations may be viewed as part of a grand strategy to organize human effort to achieve specific objectives, and this strategy is based on such "principles" of administration as specialization of work, chain of command, unity of direction, and span of control. The strategy creates a complex of organizational demands that tend to require individuals to experience dependence and submissiveness and to utilize few of their relatively peripheral abilities. The degree of dependency, submissiveness, and so on, tends to increase as one goes down the chain of command and as the job requirements and managerial controls direct the individual; they decrease as one goes up the chain of command and as the individual is able to control the job requirements.

[33] Floyd C. Mann and Lawrence K. Williams, "Some Effects of the Changing Work Environment in the Office," in Sven Lundstedt (Ed.), *Mental Health and the Work Environment,* Foundation for Research on Human Behavior, 1962, mimeographed, pp. 16–30.

The Nature of the System:
The Lower Levels

Employees are living organisms capable of adapting to their environment. Part of the adaptation may take the form, as we saw in Chapter 3, of "accepting" the environment and the concomitant dissatisfactions, stress, and lower mental health that may be associated with it. However, employees are also capable of modifying their working world so that they can express some of their frustrations, decrease them, or partially avoid them.

Adaptive activities arise that are unintended by the original designers, but are necessary (from our viewpoint) if the employees are to make the original design work. These adaptive activities vary greatly in the degree of antagonism that they manifest with the original design.

We may hypothesize that the more rigidity, specialization, tight control, and directive leadership the worker experiences, the more he will tend to create antagonistic adaptive activities. However, limits are placed on the employees in creating adaptive activities that are antagonistic to the system. They are, after all, subject to dismissal or reprimand. Consequently, they increase their risks as the adaptive activities become more antagonistic. One way to resolve these activities is to institutionalize some of them by developing a new organization that has equal power—a trade union, for example. Another way to resolve the issue is to withdraw psychologically so that the frustration and stress are not too incapacitating. The exact solution will probably vary in each organization and within each organization at different states of development.

The probable forms of the informal activities have been discussed in more detail elsewhere.[1] Here we examine them briefly and pause only to cite relevant literature that has developed since the first statement was published.

The first mode of adaptation cited in the earlier work was *absenteeism* and *turnover*. Kornhauser, in the study mentioned earlier, found that mentally healthy workers report considerably less absence from work and that company records confirm this.[2] Some recent research suggests that people who have a high absentee rate tend to be frustrated on the job by poor supervision and nonchallenging routine work. Fleishman and Harris relate turnover as well as grievance rates to leadership behavior. The more the leader structures, directs, and controls, the greater the probability of turnover.[3] Directive leadership which, like the pyramidal structure, also creates dependency and subordination, has been related to absenteeism [4] and to an unfavorable job adjustment,[5] where need fulfillment was found to be difficult.

Paterson has presented detailed evidence from one factory over an extended period of time to show that absenteeism and accidents are related to the "arbitrary" pressures that the employees perceive management creates in order (again from their view) "to whip them into line." Indeed Paterson's data indicate that even accidents may increase as the employees' feelings of dependence, submissiveness, and frustration increase.[6]

The next mode of adaptation is *aggression* against those who the employees feel are causing the frustration, conflict, and so on. In industrial organizations, this tends to be the management. The aggression can be expressed in varying degrees and in a number of ways. The degree

[1] Chris Argyris, *Personality and Organization*, Harper, New York, Chap. IV.
[2] Arthur Kornhauser, *Mental Health of the Industrial Worker: A Detroit Study*, Department of Psychology, Wayne State University, mimeographed, 1962, Chap. 3, p. 10.
[3] Edwin A. Fleishman and Edwin F. Harris, "Patterns of Leadership Behavior Related to Employee Grievances and Turnover," Department of Industrial Administration, Yale University, mimeographed, 1961.
[4] Michael Argyle, Godfrey Gardner, and Frank Coffee, "Supervisory Methods Related to Productivity, Absenteeism and Labor Turnover," *Human Relations*, Vol. XI, No. 1, 1958, pp. 23–40.
[5] A. Lindquist, "Absenteeism and Job Turnover as Consequences of Unfavorable Job Adjustment," *Acta Social*, Vol. 3, Nos. 2 and 3, 1958, pp. 119–131.
[6] T. T. Paterson, *Glasgow Limited*, Cambridge University Press, 1960, pp. 198ff.

of aggression will probably be a function of the degree of frustration, conflict, and failure as well as the freedom (from within the organization and permitted by the internal culture and society) to be aggressive. There are numerous examples in the literature of quota restrictions, goldbricking, slowdowns, and rate setting that serve as examples of aggressive activities used by employees.[7] Stealing, cheating (on production records), causing waste, and errors reducing quality of work are also frequently used.

If these activities are not adequate to help them adapt to the frustration and conflict, the employees may take other action. One step is to attempt to decrease the degree of personal and institutional dependency and submissiveness that they feel toward management. This may be done by bringing in a *trade union* which will not only represent their interest and back them up with appropriate weapons (for example, strikes), but will tend to ask for some voice in such practices as job rates, job changes, layoffs, discharges, and so on.

The irony of this mode of adaptation is that the union also organizes itself by using the pyramidal structure. Now, the worker may become doubly dependent and subordinate. In terms of our viewpoint, there is very little, or should be a decreasing, difference between a union and a management *organizational structure* if the union does not exploit and strengthen its elective-representative structure. When unions lose their democratic potential, the employee may have jumped from the frying pan into the fire.[8] This is not said to suggest an anti-union bias. We are simply attempting to follow our theoretical "nose" wherever it takes us. In the earlier version we noted several studies that suggested that some trade unions had a long way to go to fully utilize their potentiality.

In a more recent study, Joel Seidman analyzed the constitutions of

---

[7] These studies are summarized in Chris Argyris, *Personality and Organization, op. cit.,* Chap. IV.

[8] This does not mean that the workers will necessarily dislike the union. Indeed, as Purcell has shown, workers are perfectly capable of liking their union and their management. (Theodore V. Purcell, *The Worker Speaks His Mind: On Company and Union,* Harvard University Press, 1954). Moreover, up to the publication of this book, the majority of trade unions have done very little to remedy the causes that influence the deterioration of human dignity due to the nature of the work, organizational structure, etc. The early union organizers did well in raising wages, benefits, and bettering working hours and working conditions. There are now laws plus industrial, union, and governmental agencies that watch over these aspects. But very few trade unions apparently are thinking in terms of, and fewer yet, taking positive actions in terms of the dimensions that, according to this theory, are crucial.

93 unions reporting memberships of 25,000 or more in 1957 in an effort "to see to what extent they encouraged or discouraged rights of members that many would consider essential to the effective functioning of union democracy." He uses three criteria of democracy in his analysis: "(1) the right to form and finance political groupings within the union, (2) the use of official journals for political purposes, and (3) the right to communicate through other channels."

Seidman concludes: "This review of union constitutional clauses indicates that it is a rare union that recognizes, in its basic legal document, the right of an opposition group to form, to raise the necessary funds, and to reach the membership with its program of action." He credits the Labor-Management Reporting and Disclosure Act of 1959 with helping many unions move "in the direction of greater membership participation and democratic rights." [9]

The findings of Tannenbaum and Kahn suggest that the opposite is also possible. In a study of control and power they cite some unions that have less restrictive control curves than those that have been plotted in any management organizations.[10]

Some readers may be concerned with the implication that such an important societal institution as trade unionism is classed as a "mere" adaptive activity. They may see trade unionism as explained in terms of economic, political, and social forces much larger and more comprehensive than the internal workings of an organization.

We too would be concerned if the foregoing were interpreted as *the* cause of unionism in a modern society. Just as is true of most societal institutions, unions are created by a constellation of forces. However, as the framework suggests, we do mean to imply that a major factor for the rise in trade unionism is related to the frustration an employee experiences within the organization. It is difficult to provide evidence for this view with data from a society such as ours which has a long history of trade unionism. However, if our view is correct, then the potency of the "internal organizational" factors in giving rise to trade unions ought to be more easily observed in a much less industrialized society where trade unionism is not fully integrated in the life of the workers.

Sinha and Sarma present such data from a study conducted in India.

[9] Joel Scidman, "Political Controls and Member Rights: An Analysis of Union Constitutions," *Essays on Industrial Relations Research—Problems and Prospects*, Institute of Labor and Industrial Relations, University of Michigan-Wayne State University, 1961.
[10] A. S. Tannenbaum and R. L. Kahn, *Participation in Union Locals*, Row, Peterson. Evanston, Ill., 1958.

They report a negative relationship between job satisfaction and union attitude.[11] A worker possessing favorable attitudes toward the union tended to have unfavorable attitudes toward work.[12]

The authors attempt to explain the statistical relationship in the following manner.

One of the chief reasons [for the union is] that it has served as a channel for the expression of workers' needs and demands and as a vehicle of their dissatisfaction. There is a polarization between the management and the union and the accepted *norm* of the union is usually one of hostility and dissatisfied attitudes. Therefore workers possessing a favorable attitude toward the union indicated a degree of identification with its norms and viewed the job situation in an unfavorable light.[13]

Another possible mode of adaptation is *to ask for increasing compensation for the degree of dissatisfaction, tension, and stress experienced.* The employee's logic may be described as, "if I am going to be frustrated, and if it is true that management cannot do much about it, *then* they ought to at least pay me for it." The greater the dissatisfaction, the greater should be the reward. Under these conditions, the nature of wage and salary administration would be significantly altered because, along with productivity, the employer would be paying increased wages for the degree of dissatisfaction that the employee experiences.

One study that indirectly illustrates this point was conducted by Herzberg, Mausner, and Snyderman, who found that they could differentiate between employees who placed emphasis on self-actualization and those who did not. Those who did desire self-actualization were not highly motivated by increased increments of money or benefits. They preferred opportunities for challenge and satisfaction while at work.[14] However, those employees who tended to deemphasize self-actualization placed a greater emphasis on money, benefits, and good working conditions.

From two other studies comes supporting evidence for the hypothesis

[11] Duragnand Sinha and Kishab C. Sarma, "Union Attitudes and Job Satisfaction in Indian Workers," *Journal of Applied Psychology*, Vol. 46, No. 4, August 1962, pp. 247–251.
[12] *Ibid.*, p. 250.
[13] *Ibid.*, p. 251.
[14] They were already earning adequate wages so that their physiological and security needs were probably fulfilled. Frederick Herzberg, Bernard Mausner, and Barbara Snyderman, *The Motivation to Work*, 2nd ed., New York, Wiley, 1959.

that those who value self-actualization highly do not tend to value money and material benefits as much. Rim [15] found that those who score low on neuroticism ranked "opportunity to learn new skills" as having greater importance than did the high scorers. Those scoring high on neuroticism ranked "good salary" as more important than low scorers. Rosenberg,[16] in a study of a national sample of college students, found that those who chose money and security as being important tended to reject the value of self-expression.

These data should not be interpreted to suggest that there is some-thing neurotic about desiring to earn money. We mean to hypothesize that given the probable or actual fulfillment of basic physiological needs, those individuals who tend to value self-actualization do not tend to value money as highly as those who do not value self-actualiza-tion.

If we now hypothesize that the lower one goes down the chain of command, the less the probability that one can significantly alter one's working world, then the lower-level employee is left with little op-portunity for self-actualization. Under these conditions, the employee may eventually suppress his desire for self-expression while at work. He may indeed eventually experience little conscious need for it. Under these conditions, the meaning of work focuses primarily on earning a living as well as the psychological satisfaction that comes from being at work.

Focusing on the latter point for the moment, Weiss and Kahn [17] and Zweig [18] found in a national sample that, although many employees re-ported little satisfaction in their work, they also reported that they pre-ferred to continue to work even if they could afford not to. Doing nothing apparently violates the culturally learned role of what it means to be a working individual. Employees prefer to work in a job with minimum satisfaction rather than not to work.

If this finding is valid, it is understandable why workers are eventually coerced into placing an increasing emphasis on monetary and other material rewards and decreasing emphasis on human satisfaction while

---

[15] Y. Rim, "Dimensions of Job Incentives and Personality," *Acta Psychology*, Vol. XVIII, No. 5, 1961, pp. 332–336.
[16] Morris Rosenberg, *Occupations and Values*, The Free Press, Glencoe, Ill., 1957.
[17] Robert S. Weiss and Robert L. Kahn, "On the Evaluation of Work among American Men," Institute for Social Research, University of Michigan, mimeo-graphed, April 21, 1959.
[18] F. Zweig, *The Worker in an Affluent Society*, The Free Press, Glencoe, Ill., 1961, p. 77.

at work. This emphasis is reported in one study [19] and is illustrated by a retired worker who replied as follows:

Q: Was there anything you liked about the job?
A: No, I can't think of anything. It was hard, hard work and I wouldn't go through it again.
Wife: Come now, honey, you couldn't have worked there all those years and not found something you liked.
A: There is nothing I can think of—only the money—I couldn't think of anything else.[20]

Next we consider *alienation*. There is some very preliminary support for Weber's [21] and Fromm's [22] hypotheses that participants will tend to feel a sense of powerlessness and helplessness, two conditions that lead to alienation of the individual from himself and others.[23] Friedman has summarized much of the evidence indicating alienation may exist among the workers. He suggests that alienation is related to the depersonalization of work, which eventually leads the worker to believe that in management's eyes he is an "interchangeable" unit. "Thus, he gets the sense of being anonymous, a mere cypher among a mass of other workers. This feeling is reinforced by the absence of any real participation in the business." [24] Another dimension of alienation, namely, valuing a sense of disconnectedness in relationships, is illustrated in a study of two plants where the majority of the employees described their company as "friendly." When asked to describe how "friendly" people behave, over 90 per cent said, in effect, "Friendly people are people who leave you alone and who you hardly ever see."

Pearlin [25] has reported alienation among staff members in a large

[19] Chris Argyris, *Understanding Organizational Behavior*, Dorsey Press, Homewood, Ill., 1961.

[20] Eugene Friedman and Robert J. Havighurst, *The Meaning of Work and Retirement*, Chicago, University of Chicago Press, 1954, p. 27.

[21] Hans W. Gerth and C. Wright Mills, *From Weber: Essays in Sociology*, Oxford University Press, 1946, p. 50.

[22] Erich Fromm, *Escape from Freedom*, Harper, New York, 1958, p. 185.

[23] For an interesting discussion on empirical problems of measuring alienation, see the work of Melvin Seeman, "On the Meaning of Alienation," *American Sociological Review*, Vol. 24, December 1959, pp. 783–791; and Dwight C. Dean, "Alienation: Its Meaning and Measurement," *American Sociological Review*, Vol. 26, October 1961, pp. 753–758.

[24] Georges Friedman, *The Anatomy of Work*, The Free Press, Glencoe, Ill., 1961, pp. 139–140.

[25] Leonard I. Pearlin, "Alienation from Work," *American Sociological Review*, Vol. 27, No. 3, June 1962, pp. 314–326.

mental hospital. He found that alienation (a feeling of powerlessness over one's own affairs) exists (*a*) where authority figures and their subjects stand in great positional disparity, and (*b*) where authority is communicated in such a way as to prevent or discourage exchange of influence. Both of these conditions are inherent in the pyramidal structure.

Blauner [26] has presented data to show that the degree of blue-collar alienation may vary as a function of the industry in which the employee works. He defines alienation as including feelings of powerlessness, meaninglessness, normlessness, isolation, and self-estrangement. He then differentiates along each of these continua the degree of alienation that employees tend to experience. Regarding powerlessness, employees in the craft industries experience a great deal of control over their work. The freedom and control over work enjoyed by workers in machine industries, however, is much less. In the assembly-line technology the workers' control over his immediate work process is reduced to the most minimal level. In the automated, continuous processes, however, when the operations are going smoothly, the work atmosphere is extremely relaxed. Workers are free to do their routine monitoring tasks at their own pace. Automation also may increase the employees' feeling of responsibility.

A similar trend seems to occur, by and large, for the dimension of meaninglessness. The craft jobs permit a high degree of meaningfulness in work, while the semi- and low-skilled work does not. On automated work (for example, a continuous chemical process) the work coerces the employee to transfer his attention from the individual job to the process of production. Also, the worker's role changes from being an *able* to a *reliable* employee. Similarly, normlessness and self-estrangement are greatest in assembly-line operations and least in skilled operations in relatively small plants as well as in the continuous-process operation. The most striking characteristics of the latter type of work are its variety and unpredictability. There are periods of routine activity, waiting and relaxing activity, and intense activity.

Finally, there is some evidence to suggest that some employees adapt by withdrawing from work and showing a *lack of involvement*. It may be manifested in apathy and lack of an interest in work, which is the next adaptive activity to be considered. As we have shown elsewhere, Dubin, Remnik, and Argyris suggest that employees do not tend to see their work as a central life interest. It may be that they have learned through work experience and/or through their early socialization not to expect

[26] Robert Blauner, *Alienation and Freedom: The Manual Workers in Industry*, Department of Sociology, University of Chicago, mimeographed, 1962.

much by way of self-expression. The less the possibility to influence those in power to change the conditions, the less the probability for aggressive modes of adaptation. Another hypothesis may be that apathy itself breeds inaction. If this continues long enough, the individual may withdraw from his work situation but increase his demands for higher wages, benefits, and greater job security.

The Exceptions to the Rule

Let us pause to make it clear that *we are not suggesting that all organizations suppress individuals' self-expression nor that all individuals desire psychological success. The basic hypothesis is that the organization will tend to develop unintended consequences when there is a lack of congruency between individual needs and organizational demands.* Although we have focused on the incongruency between the need for psychological success and the requirements of the lower levels of organization, this is not the only possible incongruency. *We predict that the same unintended consequences will tend to occur if the individual does not desire to experience psychological success and the organization requires an individual to do so.*

On the other hand, the unintended adaptive activities already discussed should *not* tend to exist where there is a significant degree of congruency between individual needs and organizational demands—for example, if the individual does need to experience psychological success and the organization requires it, and if the individual does not desire to experience psychological success and the organization makes it difficult to do so.[26a]

We are emphasizing that this is a theoretical framework that predicts the adaptive activities as unintended consequences when there is some degree of incongruency between individual needs and organizational demands. If it can be shown that the adaptive activities are related to a congruency between individual needs and organizational demands, then this viewpoint may be untenable.

Some have attempted to criticize this framework on the grounds that parts of it do not tend to fit empirical reality. Thus, Bennis [27] notes

[26a] An interesting example of a researcher who has not misunderstood our viewpoint came to my attention too late to discuss in detail. Alexander M. Gottesman, *Fusion Concept in Classroom Teaching*, Dept. of Education, George Peabody College for Teachers, Nashville, Tenn., 1963.

[27] Warren Bennis, "The Revisionist Theory of Leadership," *Harvard Business Review*, January–February 1951, pp. 26–28, 34ff.

that the forest ranger's predispositions tend to be consonant with the demands of the job and not necessarily consonant with the growth demands that we have postulated. For example, Kaufman [28] reports that many forest rangers seem to want to be alone, do not aspire continually for higher jobs, and so on. The fact that the ranger's predispositions are not similar to ours is not a test of the framework. The test of the framework is *if* the predispositions are consonant with the organization's demands *then* informal activities such as absenteeism, trade unionization, apathy, hostility toward management, and so on, should *not* tend to be found. Kaufman's findings are in accordance with our prediction.

Another example is the work by Grusky,[29] who hypothesized that inmates will tend to be more accepting of the prison's demands, other things being equal, if their personalities predispose them toward being dependent and submissive. On the assumption that the F scale measures the individual's willingness to submit to strong authority, he hypothesized that those with high F ratings should cooperate most with the institution and find it of value. His data illustrate his hypothesis. For example, of the eleven inmates who evidenced the most favorable adaptation, eight were high authoritarians.[30] Moreover, Grusky found that a slightly greater proportion of high authoritarians than low authoritarians were likely to participate in prison activities. Also, the higher authoritarians expressed more positive attitudes about the officials, the camp, and the program of treatment. Finally, he found that the high authoritarians received a higher rating by the guards for their degree of adjustment.

In the previously cited study of alienation by Pearlin, it is interesting that alienation was not found to exist in those workers "who have an obeisant regard for the honorific aspects of status." [31] In other words, when the needs of the individual are consonant with the requirements of the organization, then the adaptive activity (in this case alienation) does not tend to appear.

Still another illustration of the same phenomenon comes from the writer's work. In a study of two plants, it was found that the needs of the individuals and the demands of the organization were highly congruent. For example, the most important predispositions of the high- and low-skilled employees were high wages, high job security, minimal

[28] Herbert Kaufman, *The Forest Ranger*, Johns Hopkins Press, Baltimore, 1960.
[29] Oscar Grusky, "Authoritarianism and Effective Indoctrination: A Case Study," *Administrative Science Quarterly*, Vol. 7, No. 1, June 1962, pp. 79–95.
[30] *Ibid.*, pp. 91–93.
[31] Leonard I. Pearlin, *op. cit.*, p. 325.

management pressure, and to be left alone by fellow employees. In both plants, the organization was able to fulfill these needs. The high degree of congruence between the needs of the employees and the demands of the organization was seen as a major factor in the relatively high productivity, low turnover, low absenteeism, and low grievance rates.

Recently, Zweig has published a most interesting study on the relation between the workers' plant and home life.[32] In it, he presents some data that seem to contradict our viewpoint. He suggests that the process of "de-humanizing human beings by the impact of industrial machinery is partly offset by the process of humanizing the machine itself, as the factory pays an ever greater attention to the personal and human needs of its workers." [33] Moreover, Zweig concludes that unhappiness in work may "have been a fact in the past and it may still occur here and there, but there is very little of it in modern, well-organized and well-run industrial establishments." [34]

It is difficult to understand how Zweig arrives at his conclusions from the data that he presents. For example, he notes that in the motor industries the majority of the employees report that work "gives only money, nothing else." [35] He also states that in the steelworks most workers responded in the opposite direction, reporting that work does offer more than money. When asked what it is that work offers them (other than money), they responded, "you learn something," "passing the time," "pleasure to earn your own living," or "interest." Unfortunately, Zweig gives us no quantitative figures to understand how many workers made each response.

However, even a cursory examination of the quotations cited would hardly lead one to infer that work has suddenly provided man with an opportunity for self-expression and dignity. What is it that the man is learning? What does he mean when he responds "interest"? In our experience when workers are pushed to fill in these statements they are unable to do so. The statements slowly emerge as attitudes that help them to maintain some semblance of what Zweig later on has called "homeostasis." As far as the writer can tell, Zweig is referring to a "self-regulating" tendency that helps man to adapt to his world. Thus Zweig cites that the man who is on a night shift eventually develops a reason why the night shift is not "too bad." The worker who describes

[32] F. Zweig, *op. cit.*
[33] *Ibid.*, p. 80.
[34] *Ibid.*, p. 79.
[35] *Ibid.*, p. 76

his job as heavy, dirty, and very uncomfortable, eventually also adds that his job is interesting.[36]

The difficulty with this view is that it tells us little about the impact of this "homeostatic principle" on the individual. For example, it is possible to account for these attitudes in a different way by using the "imbalance theories" of Heider or Festinger. Thus we might hypothesize that the worker prevents himself from experiencing continual internal imbalance or dissonance created by his impoverished work by developing these attitudes. If this is the case, then Zweig is incorrectly using these attitudes as evidence that work is being viewed as a "blessing."

We are not stating categorically that the positive findings reported by Zweig are definitely rationalizations to reduce internal dissonance. But we maintain that this *may* be the case, and conclusions such as those just cited have to be delayed until this question can be answered.

This caution seems to be supported by cues that can be obtained from Zweig's own data. We note, for example, that he asked the workers to respond to the following question. "Some people enjoy work, others tolerate it, still others endure it, what is your experience?" [37] Zweig then states, "What came out was the general conclusion that although work is mainly for money, it *has to be* [38] enjoyed and it can be enjoyed."

Why must work have to be enjoyed? One man quoted in the book responded, "If I didn't enjoy it, I would be miserable." Another, "If I didn't enjoy it, I would change my job," and finally, "It helps you if you enjoy it." [39]

None of these statements seem to confirm Zweig's view that work is increasingly being humanized. We could argue that the workers are saying (1) "I must enjoy it in order to live with myself" (thereby reducing the potentiality for dissonance); (2) "I must enjoy it or else I have to go through the extremely difficult task of finding another job" (thereby again reducing the probability of his own unhappiness and discomfort); and (3) "One way to live with the job is to enjoy it."

Later, Zweig reports that "only a small minority" agreed with the saying that "Work lends dignity to man." [40] Apparently, "most men regarded this saying as far-fetched or untrue." Still later the workers reported that they hardly ever talked about work matters at home. "Work," continues Zweig, "means tension, and home is for relaxation."

[36] *Ibid.*, p. 189.
[37] *Ibid.*, p. 77.
[38] The italics are mine.
[39] *Ibid.*, p. 77.
[40] *Ibid.*, p. 78.

He quotes one worker as saying "I never mention work at home, otherwise I would never relax."

It may help if we differentiate between satisfaction and morale on the one hand and opportunities for psychological success on the other. It may well be that Zweig has interviewed workers whose lot has changed for the better in recent years. The positive attitudes therefore could be related to the change for the better. Zweig reports:

Many more are now satisfied with their work and working conditions than before the war. Many men whom I interviewed referred to their bad past. "I enjoy my work now, but if you had asked me the same question before the war I would have said definitely not." Or, "Compared with now the prewar days were slavery." [41]

Such positive attitudes may also be related to the trend of decreasing authoritarianism in industry cited by Zweig and earlier by McGregor.[42] If this is true, then these positive attitudes are more related to our view that people do not desire positions of dependency and subordination. The point we are suggesting is that the attitudes are more closely related to satisfaction than they are to psychological success.

The Turner and Miclette [43] results are somewhat more puzzling to understand, partially because the report, being in article form, does not include as detailed data as does the one by Zweig. Turner and Miclette report that almost half of 400 assembly-line operators found their work to be intrinsically satisfying and interesting.

The first and more minor problem with these results is that they were obtained by asking the employee, "What do you like most about your job?" This seems like a loaded question because it asks the employee to comment only on what he likes about his job. Perhaps such a question can be viewed by the employee as restricting him to report only the positive side of life. Unfortunately, there is no report as to whether the authors asked the opposite question.

More important, however, is the fact that the authors attempt to explain their results by utilizing Baldamus's interesting concept of "traction." [44] Traction, according to Baldamus, is the opposite of "distraction." It is a feeling of being pulled along by the inertia inherent in

---

[41] *Ibid.*, pp. 68 and 69.
[42] Douglas McGregor, *The Human Side of Enterprise*, McGraw-Hill, New York, 1960.
[43] Arthur N. Turner and Amelia L. Miclette, "Sources of Satisfaction in Repetitive Work," *Occupational Psychology*, Vol. 36, No. 4, October 1962, pp. 215–231.
[44] W. Baldamus, *Efficiency and Effort: An Analysis of Industrial Administration*, Tavistock Publications, London, 1961, p. 59.

a particular activity. Baldamus continues, "the experience is pleasant and may therefore function as a *relief from tedium*." (The italics are mine.)

According to this definition, the satisfactions related to traction must be different from those to which we and others have referred, because they are adaptations to tedium. Turner and Miclette, therefore, may be tapping the workers' attempts to develop some positive satisfactions about their jobs precisely because they are tedious. This hypothesis gains further plausibility when we note that traction is associated "with a mild, *noninvolved*, positive feeling about the work." [45] (The italics are mine.)

The authors also point out that these satisfactions were found in a situation in which the product was crucial to the national defense and that it necessitated a greater than normal emphasis on quality. These findings are reminiscent of the studies conducted during the World War II when it was found that monotony and boredom were suppressed in the national interest.

In summary, it may be fair to conclude that the authors are reporting a different or more "skin-surface" level of satisfaction which employees develop when the work is tedious but offers a more than normal challenge in quality output and identification with an important national cause.

Administrative Reactions to the Adaptive Activities

Returning to our main theme we find that those informal activities that tend to be antagonistic to those valued by the administrators are often diagnosed by them as being "bad." Interestingly, their attempts to resolve these problems are consonant with the formal organizations' values of directiveness, selective rewards and penalties, and control, and the expectation that employees will behave "logically" (that is, suppress their feelings). For example, in recent years there has been a huge number of "human relations" and "communications" programs. These programs are based on the assumption that the employees' adaptive behavior is easily influenced by clearly presented mass communications. Consequently, the behavior can be modified and combatted by programs designed to persuade employees into giving up or minimizing their adaptive activities by (1) convincing them of the "wrongness" of

[45] Turner and Miclette, *op. cit.*, p. 217.

these activities, (2) persuading the employees that their management likes them and is concerned about fulfilling their material needs, and (3) introducing possible punitive action if the adaptive activities do not decrease and certain punitive action if they do increase.[46]

In addition to these programs there may also be an increase of managerial controls to check and hopefully curb absenteeism, turnover, goldbricking, apathy, poor quality of work, and so on. If the situation is perceived as dangerous by the top management, they may also develop various kinds of "cost-reduction drives" to pressure the organization into becoming more efficient.

Historically, employees have tended to perceive these strategies as increasing the pressures on them from above. This, in turn, creates feelings of decreasing control over their immediate work world, increasing feelings of dependence and submissiveness, and increasing concern for the "safety" of the adaptive activities. Depending on the degree of trust between the administrators and the employees as well as the latter's freedom to communicate upward and resolve adequately their concerns, the employees tend to react in ways which defend, strengthen, and further entrench their adaptive activities. These actions, in turn, make the management defensive. A closed loop is now developed in which each side intends to correct the situation but actually only makes it more difficult.

Other Modes for Adaptation

It is legitimate to ask if employees cannot adapt by leaving. They could "leave" by working their way up the organizational ladder into positions providing them greater self-determination. Or it may be possible that individuals at the lower levels of the organization, or those who cannot be promoted, may learn to express their needs outside the organization. If so, this would have important effects on the internal activities of the organization.

Let us first consider the activity of leaving the jobs at the lower levels and climbing into the management levels. This alternative is not a realistic one for most factory workers or probably for most employees in other organizations. The number of promotions into management is small.[47] Moreover, as technological improvement and automation in-

---

[46] Chris Argyris, *Personality and Organization*, Harper, New York, 1957, Chap. V.
[47] Robert Weiss and David Reisman, "Social Problems and Disorganizations in the World of Work," in Robert Merton and Robert A. Nisbet (Eds.), *Contemporary Social Problems*, Harcourt, Brace, New York, 1961, p. 486.

creasingly dominate the industrial scene, the first-line manager will need so much technical knowledge that engineers will increasingly be required in these first-line jobs. In two unpublished studies conducted by some large oil companies, the employees with little education found it almost impossible to advance. Engineers were being brought into the organization directly from college to fill first-line supervisory positions.

Guest [48] found that among automobile workers one foreman's job became vacant for every 120 workers per year. Chinoy's findings were even more pessimistic. He suggested that there were only ten or twelve openings per year for 6000 workers.[49] Berger's findings corroborated the trend. Ninety-four per cent reported that they considered their jobs as "permanent" jobs. Only 3 per cent were upwardly mobile.[50] It should not be inferred that the men did not have some aspiration for advancement. Thus, 32 per cent said that they would like to be foremen, but only 21 per cent thought these aspirations were realistic. Berger suggested even this number was high and that the workers were probably responding ideologically rather than realistically.

The worker learns, therefore, to lower his level of aspiration whether he likes it or not. Berger quotes an employee as saying, "If I found something better, I'd take it, but you can bet that this job is permanent." [51] Lipset and Bendix add that the problem becomes compounded over time. If an individual comes from a working-class family, he will typically receive little education or vocational advice while he attends school. His job plans for the future will be vague, and when he leaves school he is likely to take the first available job that he can find. Thus, the poverty, lack of education, absence of personal "contacts," lack of planning, and failure to explore fully the available job opportunities that characterize the working-class family are handed down from generation to generation.[52] Chinoy [53] confirms the lowering of aspirations. Of the sixty-two workers interviewed, thirty-one said that they had "never thought of becoming a foreman . . ." One out of six wanted to become foreman and felt that they had a good chance to do

[48] R. H. Guest, "Work Careers and Aspirations of Automobile Workers," *Administrative Science Review*, Vol. 19, 1954, pp. 155–163.

[49] E. Chinoy, *Automobile Workers and the American Dream*, Doubleday, New York, 1955, p. 44.

[50] Bennett Berger, *Working-Class Suburb*, University of California Press, 1960, p. 16.

[51] *Ibid.*

[52] S. M. Lipset and Reinhard Bendix, *Social Mobility in Industrial Society*, University of California Press, 1959, pp. 197–198.

[53] E. Chinoy, *op. cit.*, p. 49.

so. These results are consonant with those reported by Bakke,[54] Blum,[55] Guest,[56] and Schneider.[57]

Form and Geschwender, as a result of an intensive analysis of 545 interviews with manual workers, conclude (1) it is the *normal*[58] thing for most manual workers not to expect great upward mobility and (2) not to internalize strongly the ideology of opportunity. Many of them use their families as "reference groups" with which to compare their degree of success in work. "The greater the amount of mobility a worker has experienced relative to these social references, the more job satisfaction he will feel." Interestingly, working-class males who become imbued with middle-class values of upward mobility and are not able to find such opportunities become increasingly dissatisfied. "Thus it appears that limited occupational mobility is a self-defeating process for the manual worker who is imbued with the middle class ideology of opportunity and who is faced with the relatively rigid barrier which exists between the manual and white collar worker.[59]

Herzberg also suggests that employees may become dissatisfied after they experience work. The results of 17 out of 23 studies suggest that morale is high when people start their first jobs; it goes down during the next few years and remains at a relatively low level; when workers are in their late twenties or early thirties, morale begins to rise. This rise continues through the remainder of the working career in most cases.[60]

The explanation suggested by the writers is that the drop in morale is due to the monotonous, dissatisfying nature of the first job. The lack of clear understanding of the extremely low advancement possibilities and the feelings of insecurity are also important. The rising morale in older workers is related to the probability that they have become resigned to the work situation and, therefore, it troubles them much less. In our terms, they have become less involved and more withdrawn.

---

[54] E. W. Bakke, *Bonds of Organization*, Harper, New York, 1950.
[55] F. H. Blum, *Toward a Democratic Work Process*, Harper, New York, 1953, pp. 389–390.
[56] R. H. Guest, *loc. cit.*
[57] Eugene V. Schneider, *Industrial Sociology*, McGraw-Hill, New York, 1957, pp. 389–390.
[58] Italics are theirs.
[59] William F. Form and James A. Geschwender, "Social Reference Basis of Job Satisfaction," *American Sociology*, Vol. 27, No. 2, April 1962, pp. 228–237. (All quotations from pp. 236–237.)
[60] Frederick Herzberg, Bernard Mausner, Richard Paterson, and Doral F. Capwell, *Job Attitudes: A Review of Research and Opinion*, Psychology Service of Pittsburgh, 1957, pp. 1–12.

Consequently, the frustration and dissatisfaction is no longer as potent in their work lives as it was when they began.

We may wonder if the employees, especially at the lower levels, are not able to obtain need satisfaction *outside the work place.* One of the most comprehensive summaries of the findings on leisure is to be found in Friedman's recent study.[61] Friedman concludes that there is a relationship between the depersonalized work and leisure. First, he differentiates between time away from the job spent in performing various chores or extra work and free time for leisure. Leisure among the working class consists of "killing time," expressing bottled-up feelings through drinking, games of chance and luck, brutal amusements like "stock cars," and mass spectacles such as wrestling, speed racing, crime, and horror films.[62] Friedman agrees with Bell [63] who concludes "the worker becomes bored, absent-minded, accident-prone, or he retreats from reality, engulfed in a myriad of obsessive reveries."

In another work Bell concludes that the glamour of leisure can be substituted for the drudgery of work. "Yet the harsher aspects are present as well. These take the form of crazy racings against the clock to vary the deadly monotony." Still later, Bell writes, " 'conspicuous consumption' was the badge of a rising middle class, 'conspicuous loafing' is the hostile gesture of a tired working class." [64]

Recently, Friedman [65] continues, there has been a surge of "do-it-yourself" activities which has led to a marked development of hobbies—hobbies which, we may add, provide the opportunity to be alone. Friedman concludes

However, there are different ways of escaping during leisure hours—two opposed types of activity. At one extreme, there is the behavior called "killing time," and, at the other, genuine active leisure pursuits. "Killing time" is a general feature of behavior found among the masses in our technical civilization. The means of passive enjoyment are constantly being increased and new ways found, ever more artificial, hollow and mechanical, of "having fun," of "amusing oneself"—a range infinitely varied according to income and taste. They are all ways of forgetting oneself, one's emptiness and extreme boredom. whether one is aware of it or not, to which work dissatisfaction has greatly contributed. The mad search for "fun" may be a sign that someone is frustrated in his work and seeks compensation for it in the

---

[61] Georges Friedman, *The Anatomy of Work,* The Free Press, Glencoe, Ill., 1961, Chap. VII.

[62] *Ibid.,* p. 104.

[63] D. Bell, "Notes of Work," *Encounter,* June 1954, p. 12.

[64] D. Bell, *Work and Its Discontents,* Beacon Press, Boston, 1956, pp. 15–16.

[65] Georges Friedman, *op. cit.,* p. 113.

only ways that are *possible for him*. Let us not forget in any case that in our great industrial centres the cultural institutions available to the workers and which they are capable of using are very meagre, if not almost non-existent. We must take this fact into account when seeking to understand the way in which they spend their leisure (and still more when attempting to judge it) quite apart from any attempt to encourage popular education. Let us note in passing that in all the major languages a need has been found for an expression denoting this "killing of time," such as the French *tuer le temps*, the German *die Zeit todschlagen*, etc. In the technical societies of capitalism the "alienated" human being is unhappy. "Consumption of 'amusement' serves to repress the awareness of his unhappiness. He tries to save time and yet is eager to kill the time he has saved." Dissatisfaction with his atomized work is in my opinion one of the chief features of his alienation.

Turning to some studies published in America, we note that the lower-class individual apparently participates very little in the organized life of the community. Berger reports that 70 per cent of his respondents belong to no clubs, organizations, or associations at all; only 8 per cent belong to more than one. Moreover, the frequency of attendance at meetings is low for both men and women. Of the thirty men who reported belonging to one or more organizations, two never go to meetings, eleven go rarely, nine occasionally, and eight often. The figures are slightly higher for women. Berger [66] adds that the low degree of involvement cannot be attributed to the absence of any opportunities. Komarovsky found only 6 per cent of the unskilled male workers belonged to two or more organizations.[67]

Weiss and Reisman [68] reported that when workers were asked what they would do if they had an extra hour a day, most of them responded, "sleep." Few working-class individuals, continue these authors, spend time to educate themselves for higher vocational tasks. Few turn out to union meetings, even fewer are interested in improving the lot of the occupation group to which they belong or participating in decisions that may affect them in the future. The writers state:

In this situation most industrial workers appear to fall back on their families as the enclave within which leisure is to be spent. The long drive on Sunday, with it combination of aimlessness and togetherness, is traditional in this group. Leisure time away from the family, "with the boys," is defined as

[66] Bennett Berger, *op. cit.*, pp. 61–64.
[67] Mirra Komarovsky, "The Voluntary Associations of Urban Dwellers," *American Journal of Sociology*, Vol. 11, No. 6, 1946, Table I.
[68] Robert Weiss and David Reisman, "Some Issues in the Future of Leisure," *Social Problems*, Vol. IX, No. 1, Summer 1961, pp. 78–86.

time for blowing off steam, and is limited to what is thought to be physiologically and psychologically necessary. Of course, this is not the whole story. Many workers cultivate fairly expensive and time consuming hobbies, such as hunting. Some attend art classes for adults, and a handful may join the predominately middle class groups devoted to amateur music. A very few take part in voluntary associational activities; by and large these are staffed by the upper social strata.[69]

Turning to community and neighborhood activities, Knupfer reports that face-to-face contacts of low-skill employees are limited. Informal social activities are infrequent among them. She reports that working-class men and women seemed more suspicious of contacts with others. Two examples are: "It doesn't pay to be too friendly" and "I never chum with anyone; it's dangerous." [70] Hollingshead reports that time has little value in the daily routine beyond the demands of the job. "Since they do not participate in organized community affairs, hours spent off the job are spent . . . loafing around the neighborhood, in the downtown district, along the river, and at home. Intimate associations are limited in large measure within the class." [71] Berger also found a low informal contact rate among the working class. Although many reported that they had developed "friends" in the new suburb, a majority reported that they visit friends "rarely." Moreover, only 19 per cent reported that they were "very" friendly with their neighbors, whereas 34 per cent reported that their relationship with the two closest neighbors was one of nodding acquaintance.[72]

The Relation of Social Class to Our Viewpoint

We might argue that the gap between individual needs and organizational demands is significantly decreased by the fact that the working-class individuals tend to have lower levels of aspirations, do not expect to use their abilities and to have control over their work life. Kahl has shown, for example, that the children of working-class families "learned to an extraordinary degree to view the occupational system from their parents' perspective." If the parents believed their child

[69] *Ibid.*, pp. 81–82.
[70] Genevieve Knupfer, "Portrait of the Underdog," *Public Opinion Quarterly*, Vol. XI, Spring 1947, pp. 103–113.
[71] August B. Hollingshead, "Selected Characteristics of Class in a Middle Western Community," *American Sociological Review*, Vol. 12, No. 4, August 1947, pp. 385–395.
[72] B. Berger, *op. cit.*, pp. 68–77.

should "get ahead," the youngster tended to be motivated. If not, and this was true with the majority of the respondents, he tended to have a low level of aspiration.[73]

In another study Kahl summarizes the literature, concluding that ordinary working-class men seek to work steadily. They have no particular specialty and drift from job to job as the labor market dictates. "His basic value orientation is simply to get by." They tend to accept the unpleasantness of work in order to bring home a pay check. Work is not enjoyable nor is it supposed to be. The lower class, continues Kahl, react to their economic situation and to their degradation in the eyes of respectable people by becoming fatalistic. They feel that they are down and out and that there is no point in trying to improve, for all of the odds are against them.[74]

Since working-class employees [75] tend to have lower levels of aspiration for self-actualization and since they primarily desire money, job security, and benefits, and since these are increasingly available to them (as the writer would agree they are), then why do we suggest that the employees will find that there is a gap between their predispositions and those of the organization? [76]

It is our position that in spite of this congruency, employees with working-class values will still tend to experience frustrations and conflict for several reasons. First, the official management culture within the organization probably will not sanction such working-class behavior as "apathy," "getting by," and low levels of aspiration. Moreover, as recent research has shown, the employees live in a world in which pressure is brought upon them constantly to become less apathetic and more involved. Friedman,[77] Meyerson,[78] and Hearnshaw [79] have em-

[73] Joseph Kahl, "Educational and Occupational Aspirations of 'Common Man' Boys," *Harvard Education Review*, Vol. 23, No. 3, 1953, p. 202; also Joseph Kahl, *The American Class Structure*, Rinehart, New York, 1957, Chaps. 9 and 10.
[74] Joseph Kahl, *op. cit.*, pp. 205–215. There are several other studies that confirm this view. See, for example, R. Bendix and S. M. Lipset (Eds.), *Class, Status, and Power*, The Free Press, Glencoe, Ill., 1953, and E. Gross, *Work and Society*, Crowell, New York, 1958.
[75] See the works of Chinoy, Guest, and Kahl, cited earlier.
[76] First, let us again emphasize that in the previous analysis we were dealing with hypothetical cases at the extreme ends of the continua. We are aware that there are cases where the gap is small and therefore the informal activities are few. Indeed we will present a study of our own in Chapter 15 to support this position.
[77] Georges Friedman, *op. cit.*, pp. 107–108.
[78] I. Meyerson, "Comportment, Travail, Expériénce, Oeuvre," *L'Auneé Psychologique*, 1951, C. Hommeye á Heuré Piéron, p. 78.
[79] L. S. Hearnshaw, "Attitudes of Work," *Occupational Psychology*, July 1952, p. 132.

phasized that the worker's world is one of constant pressure, constraint, and discipline. Hearnshaw makes this point by stating that the "characteristics of constraint, obligation, and discipline" are the very essence of the meaning of work. They find, through management's actions, that their wages and security are constantly associated with their commitment to the organization.

We might argue that organizations do tend to give lower-class employees opportunity to utilize their few abilities. Thus there may be some degree of congruency between working-class needs and organizational requirements in terms of the use of the employees' skills. However, in the area of control the gap may still exist. Even though the worker may not have high levels of aspiration about his work, he may still have a need to protect the degree to which he may choose to be apathetic, indifferent, noninvolved, or aggressive and somewhat hostile.

However, since their chosen forms of adaptation are not officially sanctioned and are under attack, employees must react in such a way as to guarantee the survival of these activities as well as the survival of themselves. Thus, although lower-class workers may come into the organization with lower aspirations and few needs, the needs that they bring to the organization are not related to high productivity nor are they viewed as compatible with management philosophy. Therefore, employees do tend to experience a gap between their predispositions and the demands of the organization.

Moreover, since we hypothesize that the working-class values tend to arise as the employees adapt to the organization, it suggests that "underneath" the layers of social learning there may be strong but repressed needs and capabilities for self-actualization. Unfortunately, there are no systematic studies that have focused on this proposition. However, we can present some indirect and admittedly meager evidence that may be enough to consider the hypothesis worth testing.

Bakke, Hollingshead, Guest, and Chinoy, quoted previously, all point out that the workers learn to lower their level of aspiration once they "hit the job." For example, Bakke notes, "Many a working class family was integrated around the effort to provide children with educational and training equipment which would make it possible for them a non-working class life. This desire was shared also by the children *until they took their first job.* Very few ambitions to get out of the working class apparently survived the actual experience of having made a start as a worker." [80] Friedman similarly notes that assembly-line workers initially show some signs of restlessness and distress. After a while, however, they "settle down and refuse to run any risks or to gamble by changing

[80] E. W. Bakke, *The Unemployed Worker,* Yale University Press, 1940, pp. 20–21.

their work in the factory or looking for another more interesting and better paid job elsewhere." [81]

Chinoy states the problem very well when he cites discrepancies between tradition and reality in the workers' experience. These provide the insight we need to hypothesize the mechanisms that must be at work to cause the individuals to lower their aspiration and to develop working-class values. In every example the worker tends to experience frustration, failure, disillusionment, and discouragement. Experiencing these feelings for many years could lead to the apathy and resignation apparently so frequently found by sociologists in the working-class culture.

1. Each job should be looked upon as a step to something better. *But:* In the factory there are few clear-cut sequences of progressively more skilled, better-paid jobs.
2. The corporation provides a "pyramid of opportunities from the bottom toward the top." *But:* Executives and technicians are increasingly recruited from well-trained college and technical school graduates rather than from the ranks of factory labor. In the factory the narrow range of wage rates sets a low ceiling on possible advancement.
3. Initiative and ability inevitably lead to promotion and advancement. *But:* Carefully laid-out time-studied jobs in a highly rationalized industry provide little opportunity to display either initiative or ability.
4. Success depends primarily upon each individual's efforts and capabilities. *But:* Advancement within the factory is increasingly collective in character.[82]

Although this analysis hypothesizes that a major set of the variables creating working-class values is related to the conditions within the firm, it does not contradict the sociologists' findings that these values exist "independent" of the organization. Our hypothesis is that years of experience with varying degrees of frustration, conflict, dependence, apathy, and failure influence and become a part of the working-class culture, and are then communicated to the children. If we look at our society at the present time, the causal relationships understandably run in both directions (from society to the organization and vice versa).

Another important factor that may be limiting the direct influence of class structure within the firm is the degree to which skill in work as well as the differential in pay between high- and low-skill employees is

[81] Georges Friedman, *op. cit.*, p. 112.
[82] Edward Gross, *op. cit.*, p. 476.

constantly being decreased.[83] Consequently, it pays an employee to aspire toward some nonskilled work in which, with long production runs, he can make as much money—or nearly as much—as the high-skilled employees.

Our Concept of Personality and Social Class Values

There are some who suggest that such concepts as psychological success, self-actualization, and self-esteem are less signs of individual mental health and more middle-class values. They argue that middle-class values should not be superimposed on the lower class (or upper class) as indices of mental health.

First, let us emphasize that we agree with the critics when they point out that workers tend to live in an impoverished working world and in a social culture that values apathy, indifference, resignation, and fatalism. We have spent much time documenting this view.

However, *if* our concept of mental health includes attributes that are valued in the middle-class culture, it does not necessarily follow that they are necessarily limited to this strata of society.

Traditionally, semiskilled and unskilled employees have been classified as being part of the low status groups. The high-skilled employees have tended to be in the upper-lower or lower-middle class and, in some cases, the middle-class groups. Keeping this in mind, we recall the numerous studies cited previously showing that the degree of satisfaction with work tends to decrease as work becomes less and less skilled. We pointed out that two very crucial variables influencing the dissatisfaction were "lack of control" over one's working world and the inability to use one's abilities.

If lower-class workers truly accept lower-class values, then why should they be dissatisfied with their work? More important, if they did not have some concept of self-actualization, why should they be dissatisfied when their work permits little opportunity for self-control and expression of their abilities? As Blauner concluded from his review, the need for autonomy may be a very basic need among workers.

Banks [84] recently studied steelworkers' attitudes toward technical changes. She found that 33 per cent ($n = 278$) of the steelworkers reported higher job satisfaction after the change (51 per cent reported

[83] Clark Kerr, John Dunlop, Frederick Harbison, and Charles A. Meyers, *Industrialism and Industrial Man*, Harvard University Press, 1960, p. 208.
[84] Olive Banks, *The Attitudes of Steelworkers to Technological Change*, Liverpool University Press, 1960, pp. 24 and 25.

no change and 16 per cent a decrease in job satisfaction). The relevant findings here are that of the group who answered "better," "many of them had moved from a relatively routine job to one involving *greater interest, variety* or *responsibility*" (italics are mine). If our hypothesis that workers desire more interesting, challenging, and responsible work is a middle-class value, we would not expect the workers to describe the reason for their increased job satisfaction as being these factors. In other words, the attitudes of these men changed (but their social class did not), and this change was related to their job. To quote Banks, "This group of men clearly found pleasure and satisfaction in new skills and responsibilities. . . ." [85]

The group that answered "worse" was confined to the unskilled workers and to those whose wages had decreased as a result of the change. Interestingly, many of them complained that their new work did *not* carry with it any interest or responsibility.[86]

Recently, the Opinion Research Corporation published a study that also illustrates our point. They attempted to tap the unfulfilled needs of managers as well as those of the lower-level employees.[87] They found that as many of the lower-level employees reported unfulfilled needs related to self-actualization as did foremen through top executives. In responding to the question, "I wish my job had more of this . . ." the results shown in Table 4-1 were obtained.

Interestingly, as many employees in factors 8–13 and more in 1–7 reported unfulfilled needs related to self-actualization as did managers. For example, the employees reported needs for challenge in their work (4 and 6), opportunity to learn more (5), chance for greater responsibility (10), opportunity to make the most of their capacities (11), and a feeling of success (13).[88] In dimensions of "responsibility," "making most of their capacities," and "success," almost as many employees as managers desired more opportunity. Keeping in mind that managers include top- and middle- as well as lower-level managers, we find that upper- and middle-class people (managers) did not tend to differ significantly from lower-class individuals (hourly employees) in terms of the need for more (indices of) self-actualization.

There are, however, some interesting differences. For example, more hourly rate employees expressed a desire for work that was more "interesting" (1) and has more "variety" (2), "job being worthwhile" (3),

[85] *Ibid.*, p. 24.
[86] *Ibid.*, p. 25.
[87] Stan E. Carnarius, *Motivating Managers*, Opinion Research Corporation, December 1962, p. 13.
[88] *Ibid.*

Table 4-1. Unfulfilled Needs [a]

	Percentage Base			
		Unit K		
Opportunity Cluster	*All Managers* 1207	*Managers* 34	*Hourly Workers* 575	*Points Difference*
1. Work that is interesting.	21%	20%	46%	+26
2. Variety in the work I do.	13	12	29	+17
3. Feeling it is worthwhile to really pitch in.	31	32	44	+12
4. Chance to work with more than petty problems.	32	26	38	+12
5. Chance to learn new things.	44	44	54	+10
6. Getting a real kick out of my job.	31	35	44	+9
7. Chance to argue things out to a productive conclusion.	30	29	37	+8
8. Solving problems on my own.	22	23	25	+2
9. Making important decisions.	38	29	31	+2
10. Chance for greater responsibility.	47	41	42	+1
11. Making the most of my capacities.	48	47	45	−2
12. Feeling I am helping people.	35	41	37	−4
13. Feeling I am getting somewhere.	52	62	56	−6

[a] Stanley E. Carnarius, *Motivating Managers,* Opinion Research Corporation, December 1962, p. 13.

and an opportunity to deal with meaningful problems (10) than did managers. These differences support our view regarding the aspirations of lower-class individuals, but they do not necessarily mean that hourly employees have stronger needs for self-actualization than managers. It is our hypothesis that the differences represent the possibility that the needs for self-expression of lower-level employees tend to be less satisfied, and thus they request more.

It is also interesting to note that the greatest differences between employees and managers existed in the need for variety and challenge in work. It may well be that managers tend to believe that they obtain adequate variety and challenge on their job while the employees do not. It may also indicate that employees' responses to "I wish that I had more of this . . ." were realistic in that they were choosing those areas in which change seemed probable to them. One final point: beginning with item 8 the figures for the employees and managers become relatively the same. This suggests that as many employees as managers wish more opportunity for "making important decisions," "greater responsibility," and so on. We might wonder, however, why the gap between managers and employees found in the first seven items is not maintained in the last eight. One possibility may be that, as mentioned earlier, the managers tend to obtain more fulfillment in the area of variety and challenge than do employees. However, in the area of control (decision making and control over their work), the managers experience as much relative deprivation as do the employees. Perhaps it is worthwhile to repeat that, for our purposes, the main finding is that more lower-level employees report desire for work that has self-actualization possibilities along the first seven dimensions, and as many for the last six, as do managers (including top- and middle-, and lower-level managers).

There is one study by the writer that could be used, at first glance, as evidence to the contrary. In this study it was found, as in the foregoing cases, that the higher the skill level, the greater the desire for challenge in the work, for use of one's abilities, and the need for variety in work. However, the satisfaction with the job in the high- and low-skilled groups was found to be equally high in both groups. The reason was that for both groups their "high potency predispositions" were the same. Both were predisposed toward higher wages, job security, control over their work, noninvolvement and "togetherness," (liking someone because you hardly ever see him and when you do the relationship is superficial). [89]

In our opinion these results fit within our framework. The need for high wages and job security is high in both groups for economic reasons. Next, the fact that control over one's work world is true for both groups illustrates our view that people at the lower levels prefer some self-actualization while at work. Finally, the low desire of members in both groups for involvement and meaningful relationships illustrates again that social class may be less important than the nature of the work world that the employee experiences. The fact that both have expressed needs for noninvolvement is, in our opinion, consonant with our hypothesis that this is one way employees may manifest to adapt to their

[89] Chris Argyris, *Understanding Organizational Behavior, op. cit.*

work situation. In this specific case the type of management resulted in the high-skilled employees desiring just as much noninvolvement as the low-skill employees.

If these data are replicated, they will *not* tend to disprove that lower-class culture values apathy, indifference, and so on. We believe that the lower-class values or norms will always tend to mirror the realities of life. At the moment, it is our hypothesis that most lower-level employees do tend to work in relatively impoverished worlds. Consequently, they may internalize these cultural values in order to maintain some semblance of sanity. If all of them aspired strongly for self-actualizing work, they (and our society) would probably be in difficulty. The workers would be frustrated and if the frustration became deep and widespread, the workers could decide to take action.

However, it is our hypothesis that the lower-class worker is still capable of aspiring toward psychological success, but he has suppressed this desire. The irony is that, from our point of view, his (understandable) choice of apathy, indifference, fatalism, could also lead to decreasing individual mental health. Admittedly, this hypothesis will be extremely difficult to measure for two reasons. First, this behavior is centered toward reality, and that is one (but only one) component of mental health. Second, because it is reality-centered and culturally supported, if there are negative effects, it will take many years before they become available to measurement.

What is the natural conclusion to the argument that our concept of individual mental health is a middle-class value because it emphasizes psychological success, which is a difficult accomplishment in the workers' world? Would it not imply that a lower-class worker must accept the lower-class values *because* they are adaptive? Such a position would, in effect, create a concept of individual mental health that would be based on the acceptance of the status quo. Why should individual mental health be equated with accepting the status quo?

There is another important reason why we do not adhere to the "middle class" argument and it should be included. We have been able to develop a framework that we believe presents a plausible explanation of many organizational phenomena ranging from absenteeism to alienation, at the lower levels, and (as we shall see later on) conformity to mistrust, at the upper levels. This framework partially hinges on the hypothesis that individual mental health includes the dimensions that we have mentioned and the assumption that these dimensions are valid at all levels of our society. It may well be that the entire framework is incorrect, but this must be discovered through empirical research.

Politics and Organizational Ineffectiveness

Although our discussion will be very incomplete, we cannot resist the temptation to indicate a possible relation between the internal organizational problems just discussed and political behavior of lower-level employees. It would be interesting to conduct research on the exact relationship between the tendency for increased political apathy that has been reported,[90, 91] and the apathy reported in the plant. The research would focus not so much on which causes which (that would be like the old chicken-or-egg conflict) but on the way that each feeds back and mutually reinforces the other (that is, how industrial apathy influences political apathy and vice versa). Rosenberg, in a depth interview study of seventy respondents, suggests that the three most important areas for political apathy are (1) the threatening consequences of political activity, (2) the futility of political activity, and (3) the absence of spurs to interest and participation.[92] Rosenberg points out that people often lack a personal thrust to action. The following comments of respondents are similar to those management usually hears when it inquires why the employees are not more spontaneous in their suggestions.

"No, I wasn't asked to do anything. . . ."

"Well, I might have helped if they'd really wanted me to and if it didn't take too much time. . . . Besides, no one asked me to help out, so I didn't volunteer."

"You can probably class me as apathetic, except when it's brought right to my attention, but I think most people are the same way." [93]

The possible relationship between the internal organization and political activity is not as remote as it may sound. Work, in terms of numbers of hours spent performing it, is probably the single activity that takes up most of our waking life. If it can coerce young men to alter their values about, and their level of aspiration at, work (as we have suggested it does for the lower-level employees), then why may its influence not radiate to other areas of life?

[90] Gordon Connely and Harry Field, "The Non-Voter; Who He Is, What He Thinks," *Public Opinion Quarterly*, Vol. 8, 1944, pp. 175–187.
[91] P. F. Lazarsfeld, B. Berelson, and Hazel Gaudet, *The People's Choice*, 2nd ed., Columbia University Press, 1948, pp. 4–51.
[92] Morris Rosenberg, "Some Determinants of Political Apathy," *Public Opinion Quarterly*, Vol. XVIII, No. 4, Winter 1954–55, pp. 349–366.
[93] *Ibid.*, p. 364.

If our analysis of the lower-level employees' lives is valid, we can hypothesize that as apathy and indifference increase, feelings of resignation, noninvolvement, and alienation should increase. Presthus has concluded from a review of the literature that alienation in political and community affairs is common.[94] As alienation increases, feelings of dependence and helplessness should increase; and as these two forces increase, desire for security and surity in one's life should increase as well as fear of change and self-responsibility. The latter feelings should tend to arise if, as we have suggested, employees are learning to adapt by running away from opportunities for decisions; escaping, as Fromm suggests, from freedom. (The fact that they may have to do this in order to maintain some semblance of mental health may, in some peoples' eyes, justify their behavior, but it is not relevant to our argument. Our point is that we may be creating a world in which the only choices that we offer to employees are between two evils.)

If these conjectures are valid, we can predict that even as the satisfaction of physiological and security needs becomes increasingly assured in a society, the workers will tend to demand more benefits from the politicians and will not tend to agitate for opportunities that may lead to psychological success.[95] In this connection, it was learned recently that workers in Detroit who had been unemployed for a year or more preferred to remain on unemployment benefits—or to ask the government to give out more benefits—rather than take the opportunity to retrain themselves.[96]

Indeed, we may hypothesize that if employees are experiencing some degree of psychological failure, dependence, and perhaps alienation, they will tend to fear political freedom and responsibility. Recently, Kornhauser has published some results illustrating this hypothesis. The reader may recall that his study found that there was a correlation between mental health and the degree of skill and challenge required by work: the less the skill required, the less the challenge offered, the lower the mental health.

In the detailed publication, Kornhauser reports that economic "liberalism" of a pro-labor New Deal type is more popular among the working people with lower mental health (who at the same time manifest lower education, income, and occupation). Liberalism toward race re-

[94] Robert Presthus, *The Organizational Society*, Knopf, New York, 1962, p. 223.
[95] Robert L. Kahn points out that if the analysis is valid, one can infer that our society may be helping to eliminate some important opportunities for psychological success, but (so far) is unable to eliminate those phenomena that give us a sense of impotence (e.g., nuclear insecurity).
[96] Personal communication, Detroit Industrial Mission.

lations, international relations and anti-authoritarian attitudes is quite another matter. More liberal orientation here is associated with *higher* mental health.[97] These results, continues Kornhauser, are congruent with other studies reporting that economically and educationally limited groups are liberal on economic issues dealing with income, benefits, control of business, and so on, while being quite conservative on other issues.

Kornhauser also lists some attitudes that workers held regarding free speech and political and international responsibility. They show a surprisingly large number who seem not to support these qualities usually identified with a viable democracy. These figures are in line with the hypothesis that we suggested earlier.

	Percentage of auto workers ($n = 407$) [98]
1. Should people be allowed to speak in public against all religion?—*No.*	69%
2. What do you think ought to be done about race relations in this country, that is, between whites and Negroes?—*For segregation; against full equality.*	58%
3. The *most important* thing to teach children is absolute obedience to their parents.—*Agree.*	56%
4. Should people be allowed to speak in public against our democratic form of government?—*No.*	48%
5. What do you think should be America's position in world affairs; what should this country do about the way things are going in the rest of the world?—*Isolationist and/or emphasis on military power.*	43%
6. What do you think the United States should do about working with the United Nations?—*Not work with or serious reservations.*	37%
7. On the whole would you say your job is (3 choices): really interesting; not very interesting; dull and monotonous?—*Last two choices.*	35%
8. A few strong leaders could do more for this country than all the laws and talk.—*Agree.*	34%

[97] Arthur Kornhauser, *Mental Health of the Industrial Worker: A Detroit Study,* Department of Psychology, Wayne State University, mimeographed, 1962, Chap. 3, p. 10.
[98] *Ibid.,* Chap. 3, pp. 11–12.

*Percentage of auto
workers* ($n = 407$)

9. Do you think that it is a good thing to have colleges where people study all kinds of ideas, even if many of these are ideas that most of us believe are untrue and harmful?—*No.*   34%

10. Self-rating of "how you feel about your job" on 5-point scale.—*Rating below "well satisfied" (i.e., dissatisfied or neither satisfied nor dissatisfied).*   31%

11. Would you say your job gives you a chance to use your abilities or is the job too simple to let you use your abilities?—*No, too simple.*   29% [99]

12. Rating of family adjustment, based on entire interview.—*Unsatisfactory or questionable.*   21%

In a study of worker attitudes, Lipsitz developed a continuum of the degree of fatalism that an individual manifested while at work.[100] The continuum began with *integral fatalism* (a strong belief in the inevitability of many social phenomena, such as war, poverty, and oppression, with a strong sense of personal helplessness) to *moderate* and then *peripheral* fatalism, and finally to no fatalism.

The results are presented in Table 4-2.

Table 4-2. Degree of Fatalism among Employees (%)

	Integral	*Moderate*	*Peripheral*	*Little or None*
Unskilled	41.5(5)	41.5(5)	17.0	0
Semiskilled	12.5(2)	50.0(8)	18.75(3)	18.75(3)
Skilled	13.3(2)	33.3(5)	40.0(6)	13.3(2)

We note that the unskilled man is the most fatalistic, with the semiskilled in the middle, and the skilled the least. Since this classification

[99] On the basis of our view and Kornhauser's data, we might expect a higher percentage. One possibility is that these data do not confirm our hypothesis; another is that this figure is much lower than is actually the case. For example, we may hypothesize, as in the last chapter, that after many years of working, the employees become adapted to their environment and thus lower their level of aspirations to use their abilities toward the enhancement of their self-esteem.

[100] Lewis Lipsitz, "Mass Production and Political Attitudes," preliminary manuscript for Ph.D. degree, Department of Political Science, Yale University, 1963.

was based on the judgment of the researcher, an independent set of questions was asked of the men regarding the degree of fatalism and the probability of poverty, war, change of government, and the opportunity to plan and carry out plans. The answers to these questions were scored along a continuum from strongly fatalistic to strongly nonfatalistic. The lower the scores, the less the fatalism. The mean scores on this scale were 15.1 for the unskilled, 13.4 for the semiskilled and 10.8 for the skilled. Using the Cornell technique to test reproducibility, these questions obtained a score of .94 which indicates that the scale is one-dimensional. Using the more stringent Goodenough and Edwards test, the reproducibility score is .86, which is close to the .90 level considered desirable. The mean scores for the scores dichotomized were unskilled, 2.58, semiskilled and skilled, 1.40. The F score was 3.21. A score of 3.23 would be needed to be significant at the .05 level.

Lipsitz also presents data that agree with some of the Kornhauser data. For example, if one measures sympathy by saying that anyone is sympathetic who mentions any reason for poverty aside from the failing of the individual, the low skilled are *least* sympathetic and the high skilled the most sympathetic. Also the low skilled were found to be least tolerant of our policy to understand Russia, and least tolerant of capital punishment.

Recently, Wolf has implied that the concepts being formulated about psychological health suggest that there may be a limit to how much security and dependence an individual ought to experience in his life.[101] These questions may alarm some individuals. Are we suggesting that advanced societies ought to create anxiety and insecurity? Clearly, this is not our mention.

We mean simply to follow the implications of the way we view the nature of psychological health. There is no antagonism between paying people high wages, guaranteeing them against the strains of unemployment far beyond their control, helping them to meet their basic physiological and security needs, and soon, and psychological health. We are suggesting that if the people in a society are to remain viable, alive, and seeking change, they need to develop increasingly their sense of self-esteem and acceptance. These feelings tend to develop under conditions for psychological success. Thus, it follows from our position that, in addition to protection from uncontrollable calamities, individuals also need to be offered by their society opportunities for psychological

[101] William Wolf, "Wider Horizons in Psychotherapy," *American Journal of Psychotherapy*, Vol. XVI, No. 1, January 1962, pp. 124–149.

success. This means opportunity to define and fulfill challenges, to take risks, to experience the kind of tension and pain that Goldstein suggested was a root for human resiliency.

Planning for the fulfillment of physiological and security needs is a difficult challenge. Planning opportunities for psychological success is a challenge infinitely more complex. Its execution is especially difficult because it requires a new set of values and attitudes—those that emphasize self-actualization, psychological success, and self-responsibility.

Summary

Jobs that have been fractionized and specialized in accordance with the "scientific management" principles tend to require the employees to experience dependence and submissiveness and to use few of their relatively important abilities. To the extent that the employees may aspire toward psychological success, they will tend to experience frustration, conflict, and psychological failure. The degree to which they will experience any of these should tend to increase as one goes down the chain of command and as the job controls the individual.

In an attempt to adapt to the work environment (so that they are not discharged), the employees tend to accept part of the frustration, conflict, and failure as inevitable. However, they may also create adaptive activities to modify the environment. The exact nature and quantity of these adaptive activities will tend to vary with the individual, the organization, and within each of these, under different conditions.

The adaptive activities identified are absenteeism, turnover, quota restriction, goldbricking, slow downs, trade unions, increasing emphasis on material factors and decreasing emphasis on human factors, noninvolvement, withdrawal from work, and alienation.

Exceptions to these predictions were discussed and the influence of social class on the internal operation of the system analyzed.

The Nature of the System: Managerial Levels

The Organization at the First-Line Supervisory Level

In the previous chapter we saw that adaptive activities are created by the employees to help them adapt to their work world so that they may reasonably accomplish what is expected of them. In creating the adaptive activities, they have actually created a world with values that are different from, and often antagonistic to, those implicit in the initial design of the organization. For example, the organization sanctions values such as neatness, involvement, hard work, upward mobility, and unquestioned loyalty. The employees sanction absenteeism, turnover, noninvolvement, apathy, slowdown, rate setting, cautious loyalty, and so on.

These two worlds exist simultaneously and overlap. We may predict that difficulties will not tend to arise as long as (1) the individuals are not required to accept both worlds simultaneously, or (2) as long as they can keep the nature of one secret from the other, or (3) they openly acknowledge the incongruency and defend themselves (through a trade union, for example).

Although these alternatives may be open to the employees, they do not tend to be open to the foreman or first-line supervisor. He is conceived by the top management as being a member of both worlds. Theoretically, he provides a link between the two worlds as well as representing management's formal interests. This places the foreman in the classical situation of the *marginal man*. He is, as it is called in industry, "the man in the middle." One foreman describes the situation eloquently when he remarks:

I'll tell you one thing that you can put down in your little black book, and I want you to remember this, and that is that the supervisor is a "bumping post." That's something you can remember, he's a "bumping post" because he's in the middle; he has to take it from both ends; and those running the place don't give him any credit for it.[1]

Another foreman describes the problem as follows.

When you get right down to it, the supervisor really doesn't have very much to say. He just tries to keep everybody happy down here, but he can't say anything to management, if it's doing something that's not going to work out for the best interest of everybody concerned.[2]

On the basis of a study of 791 production foremen and assistant foremen in fourteen companies, Renck concludes:

The fact that the foremen have membership in two different and sometimes conflicting groups is not only a source of pressure for the foremen—but it is also often a source of emotional conflict. It is a source of conflict which neither the executive nor the production worker meets. The conflict stems from this source: The foreman recognizes that he doesn't have all the facts, that he is not in a position to make clear-cut judgments on the actions of his superiors. But he is in a position—a better position than anyone else—to judge the impact of these actions on himself and his work group. Because this impact is often a negative one—one of change—he is frequently frustrated in attempting to implement it with his employees. Frequently, and from time to time, he may identify more strongly with his employees than he does with management. Unlike the executive he cannot be analytical because he is not informed; more like the production worker, he can be critical in spite of the fact that he is usually willing to give management the benefit of the doubt

---

[1] Burleigh B. Gardner and William F. Whyte, "The Man in the Middle: Position and Problems of the Foreman," *Applied Anthropology*, Vol. 4, No. 2, Spring 1945, pp. 19–20.

[2] For those interested in a study of what types of activities foremen tend to engage in during the day, see, W. L. Wallace and J. V. Galleagher, *Activities and Behaviors of Production Supervisors*, PRS Report 946, Department of the Army, April 1952. Unfortunately, the study lacks any description of the psychological dimensions (e.g., do foremen frustrate or place their workers in failure) and any attempt at correlating what foremen do with some criterion. Nevertheless, it is a useful piece of work if one is interested in a description of certain nonpsychological activities of foremen.

over the long haul. And in addition, he, too, is dealing with problems of the organization; problems which he more often sees as "mistakes" of management rather than as the inevitable result of maintaining and expanding the company.[3]

Turning to the concept of the marginal man in overlapping antagonistic situations, we may hypothesize:

1. The foreman is aware that there is a difference between the employees' world and the management world. He may feel that (*a*) he belongs to neither world; (*b*) he belongs to one, but not the other; or (*c*) he belongs to both.
2. Although he is responsible for their world, the foreman may not be informed of all the employees' activities (e.g., rate setting, loafing in the washrooms, and goldbricking on the job.) Although he is a member of the management world, he may not be informed about all management's activities involving him (e.g., their evaluation of him, a possible raise, and possible long-run technological changes.)
3. The foreman is not only a marginal man, but he also tends to be uninformed about certain activities that may be crucial in the effective administration of his unit. He may be aware of certain employee or management activities and he may wish he could participate in them, but the employees and management can prevent him from participation. To the extent that these activities are highly important to him, the foreman will experience frustration. He may be permitted, and at times be asked, by the employees to sanction certain informal activities that they know are antagonistic to management. To the extent that the foreman is loyal to the management, he will tend to be in conflict. He will experience the same conflict when asked by management to support certain activities known to be antagonistic to the employees.
4. The foreman can experience conflict when the employees or management fluctuate about their decisions (e.g., the foreman may complain, "I wish management would make up its mind as to what is the policy on the union," or "Those damn employees, one day they want something, the next day they change their minds.").
5. The foreman will tend to experience conflict if he is coerced by management (*a*) to cooperate in an employee activity that the employees like (e.g., cooperate with the shop steward); (*b*) not to participate in an activity the employees like; (*c*) to coerce the employees to par-

[3] Richard Renck, "Morale in Four Key Groups in Industry," *Occasional Papers,* Industrial Relations Center, University of Chicago, November 1955, Chap. 7, p. 28.

ticipate in an activity that they do not like; and (*d*) to coerce the employees not to participate in an activity they like.

On the basis of many studies of supervision by the Survey Research Center, Kahn illustrates the foregoing analysis and enlarges on it by making the following prediction as to factors that can influence the foreman's conflict.

1. When the foreman perceives the expectations of the men as being the same as those of management, he will see his role as congruent with those expectations.
2. When the foreman perceives a conflict between the expectations of the men and those of management, his perceptions of his own role will depend upon:
   a. His sensitivity to the attitudes of the workers.
   b. His concern for the problems of persons under his supervision.
   c. His awareness of what factors are responsible for worker motivation.
   d. His perception of the job of foreman as defined by management.
   e. His perceptions of the demands of his own supervisors, and
   f. His perception of the degree of consensus among the men in their demands of him.[4]

Recent findings by Mann and Dent [5] suggest that 47 per cent of the supervisors report the conflict just discussed. A large proportion of the remaining 53 per cent do not report the conflict. They apparently are able to relate themselves to both management and the workers. It is interesting to note, however, that this "double membership" succeeds if management does *not* try to make the foreman exclusively a member of management *or* if the employees do not try to capture the foreman's complete loyalty.[6]

To summarize, although the foreman's work presumably is (potentially) more challenging than that of the lower-level employees, he tends to exist in a work world of greater tensions due to his membership in two overlapping worlds as well as the demands on him to work cooperatively with peers in other departments, many of whom are, by the nature of the organization, in competition with each other. Unlike the

[4] Robert L. Kahn, "An Analysis of Supervisory Practices and Components of Morale," in *Groups, Leadership and Men,* Carnegie Press, Pittsburgh, 1951, pp. 86–89.
[5] Floyd C. Mann and James K. Dent, "The Supervisor: Member of Two Organizational Families," *Harvard Business Review,* Vol. 32, No. 6, November–December 1954, pp. 103–112.
[6] Robert L. Kahn and Diel Katz, "Leadership Practice in Relation to Productivity and Morale," in D. Cartwright and A. Zander (Eds.), *Group Dynamics,* Row, Peterson, Evanston, Ill., 1953, pp. 612–628.

employees the foreman cannot (as easily) join a union, become apathetic, goldbrick, and so on.

It is understandable to learn that Kasl and French found that tension, stress, and dispensary visits are significantly higher among supervisors than among employees.[7]

But this does not represent all of the problems that first-line supervisors tend to face.

Selekman,[8] Roethlisberger,[9] Gross,[10] and Gardner and Whyte [11] describe the plight of the foreman when the union enters. Before the union enters the foreman is the sole formal leader. His initial reactions to unionization are inevitably related to the emotions and feelings that cluster about his original leadership position. He fears his position has deteriorated although his formal title remains the same and his responsibilities have increased tremendously. Before, he could fire and hire; he could set production standards; he could maintain his own quality control. With the entrance of the union and the emergence of the union contract as a potent policy statement, the foreman finds himself hedged in on all sides with cost standards, production standards, quality standards, specifications, regulations, rules, laws, and agreements. Most of these are formulated without his participation.

Perhaps even more threatening in the eyes of the foreman is the new human relationship between the employees and himself created by the union. He no longer feels that all the employee loyalties are focused toward the company and toward him. The union and the union officials are receiving a substantial part of employees' loyalties. Moreover, his management, still a bit dazed, tends to react to unionization with a get-tough-tighten-the-screws policy. The foreman is expected to pass this pressure on to the employees. It is not uncommon for the foreman to find himself the recipient of an unexplained order to raise production which, if he tried to put into action, could lead the "other side" to open up with a barrage of defensive reactions. The employees,

---

[7] Stanislav Kasl and John R. P. French, Jr., "The Effects of Occupational Status on Physical and Mental Health," *Journal of Social Issues*, Vol. XVIII, No. 3, 1962, pp. 20–27.

[8] Benjamin Selekman, *Labor Relations and Human Relations*, McGraw-Hill, New York, 1949, pp. 35ff.

[9] Fritz Roethlisberger, "The Foreman: Master and Victim of Double Talk," *Harvard Business Review*, Spring 1945, pp. 284ff.

[10] Ira B. Gross, Jr., "When Foremen Joined the CIO," *Personnel Journal*, 1940, p. 276.

[11] Burleigh B. Gardner and William F. Whyte, "The Man in the Middle: Position and Problems of the Foreman," *Applied Anthropology*, Vol. 4, No. 2, Spring 1945, pp. 19–20.

under their new-found protection, may thumb their noses at any speed-up. If the foreman decides to push hard he may find his pressure translated into a grievance that, because of the grievance machinery, may eventually be communicated to top management. It is not difficult to see why the foreman may easily become an anxious individual. The union looks after the employees. The employer is able to take care of himself. Who will look after the foreman?

The foreman is faced with the dilemma of being "in the middle" and losing much of his authority and status to the union. He is also greatly influenced by the impact of increased rationalization of equipment and organization. Mills [12] points out that with the coming of big industry, the foreman's function has been diminished by the new technical dictates of modern mechanization. The increasing use of semi-automatic machinery run by trained technicians diminishes the foreman's sphere of technical competence, and his skills become those of the personnel agent rather than of the master craftsman and work guide.

In short, the first-line supervisor goes from a situation in which he makes important decisions and manifests substantial control over his working world to a situation in which his "space of free movement" is greatly restricted. This results in increasing feelings of frustration, tension, conflict, and vacillation.

Pelz [13] has presented evidence showing that a restriction of the supervisor's space of free movement and of his power leads to a decrease in the degree of influence he is able to exercise over his department. This in turn will lead to a decrease in the supervisor's effectiveness. Pelz suggests that a noninfluential supervisor who attempts to help employees achieve their goals will tend to fail, not necessarily because of "poor" leadership style, but because of lack of organizational influence.[14] A supervisor soon finds himself in the difficult position of being unable to make desired changes even if he is personally capable.

The Organization at the Managerial Levels

As we climb the organizational hierarchy, we begin to leave the area of overlapping between the employee and management worlds, and enter a world that is primarily management.

[12] C. Wright Mills, *White Collar*, Oxford University Press, New York, 1953.
[13] Donald C. Pelz, "Leadership Within a Hierarchical Organization," *Journal Social Issues*, Vol. VII, No. 3, 1951, pp. 49–55.
[14] Donald C. Pelz, "Influence: Key to Supervisory Leadership," *Personnel*, Vol. 29, No. 3, November 1952, pp. 209–217.

At the lowest levels in the organization, human effectiveness, we believe, is highly influenced by the technology and control systems. The effectiveness of the first-line supervisor is also significantly influenced by the same factor plus those just discussed.[15]

However, the higher one climbs the managerial hierarchy, the less technology and controls influence behavior, and, we hypothesize, the more job objectives and interpersonal factors influence the effectiveness of the executives. In mentioning job objectives we imply that an important variable is to find men who are competent in the specialty required by the job. Although this is not an easy task, we are not going to consider this variable in detail. We will assume that the organization is able to find the professional managerial resources that it desires.

The task remains to show how the interpersonal relationships can influence the effectiveness of management.

Values about Interpersonal Effectiveness Implicit in Organizational Design

The intended design of organizations has implicit values about the effectiveness of human relationships.[16] It has been shown that these values can be internalized by those who climb the managerial hierarchy, and their behavior therefore is influenced by them.[17] Briefly, these values are:

1. The important human relationships are those that are related to achieving the organization's objective. It was found, for example, that in over 150 different types and sizes of meetings, the executives (twenty in the total sample) always tended to focus their behavior on "getting the job done." In literally thousands of units of behavior, almost none were observed where the men spent some time in analyzing and maintaining their group's effectiveness. This was true even though in many meetings the group's effectiveness "bogged down" and the objectives were not being reached due to interpersonal factors. When the executives were interviewed and asked why they did not spend some time in examining the group's operations or process, they replied that they were there to get a job done and, besides, "If

[15] For an interesting study to see how much the technology influences the foreman's behavior, see Robert H. Guest, "Foremen at Work: An Interim Report on Method," *Human Organization*, Vol. 14, No. 2, 1955, pp. 21–24.
[16] For a more detailed discussion of this section, see the author's *Interpersonal Competence and Organizational Effectiveness*, Irwin-Dorsey Press, Homewood, Ill., 1962.
[17] *Ibid.*, Chap. III.

the group isn't effective, it is up to the leader to get it back on the track by directing it."
2. The second value is the emphasis on cognitive rationality and the deemphasis on the rationality—indeed the existence—of feelings and emotions. This value influences the executives to see cognitive, intellectual discussions as "relevant," "good," "work," and so on. The emotional and interpersonal discussions tend to be viewed as "irrelevant," "immature," "not work," and so on.

As a result, when emotions and interpersonal variables become blocks to group effectiveness, all the executives reported (and were observed doing so) that they should *not* deal with them. For example, if there were an emotional disagreement, they would tell the members "to get back to facts," or "Keep personalities out of this." In other words, the value that effectiveness was primarily a cognitive dimension tended to coerce the men to suppress and deny the emotional and interpersonal variables that influenced their group's effectiveness.
3. The third value suggests that human relationships are most effectively influenced through unilateral direction, coercion, and control, as well as by reward and penalties that sanction all three values. This value of direction and control is implicit in the chain of command as well as in the elaborate managerial controls that have been developed within organizations.

We may now ask: how do these values influence the effectiveness of the executive systems as well as the remainder of the organization. For example, how do (the resulting) interpersonal relationships feed back to influence such primarily cognitive activities as decision making, problem exploration, and information transmission? How do (the resulting) interpersonal relationships influence the norms of the organization toward or against such phenomena as dependence, conformity, interexecutive trust, and internal commitment? How are such factors as organization rigidity, flexibility, and climate influenced by all the foregoing factors?

To the extent that individuals dedicate themselves to the value of intellectual rationality and "getting the job done," they will tend to be aware of and emphasize the cognitive, intellectual aspects of the interactions that exist in an organization and (consciously or unconsciously) suppress the interpersonal and emotional aspects, especially those that do not seem relevant to achieving the task.

As the interpersonal and emotional aspects of behavior become suppressed, we may hypothesize that an organizational norm will tend to arise that coerces individuals to hide their feelings. Their interpersonal difficulties will either be suppressed or disguised and brought up as cognitive, technical, intellectual problems. Receiving or giving feedback (information) about interpersonal relationships will tend to be suppressed.

Under these conditions we may hypothesize that the individuals will tend to find it very difficult to develop competence in dealing with feelings and interpersonal relationships. We may also hypothesize that, in a world where the expression of feelings is not valued, the individuals will build personal and organizational defenses to help them suppress their own feelings or inhibit others in such expression. If feelings are suppressed, the individual will tend not to permit himself to *own* his, or others to *own* their feelings. For example, the individual may say about himself, "No, I didn't mean that," or "Let me start over again. I'm confusing the facts." Equally possible is for one individual to say to another, "No, you shouldn't feel that way," or "That's not effective executive behavior," or "Let's act like mature people and keep feelings out of this."

Another way to prevent individuals from violating the organizational values and from embarrassing one another is to block out, refuse to consider (consciously or unconsciously) ideas and values which, if explored, could expose suppressed feelings. Such a defensive reaction in the organization will eventually lead to a barrier to intellectual ideas and values. The participants will tend to limit themselves to those ideas and values that are not threatening, and so not violate organizational norms. The organization will tend to decrease its capacity to be open to new ideas and values. We may hypothesize that, as the degree of openness decreases, the capacity to experiment will tend to decrease, and the fear to take risks will tend to increase. As the fear to take risks increases, the probability of experimentation may decrease, and the range or scope of openness may be decreased which, in turn, decreases risks. We have a closed circuit which could be an important cause of the loss of vitality in an organization.

To summarize, to the extent that participants are dedicated to the values implicit in the formal organization, they will tend to create a social system in which the following characteristics will tend to *decrease:*

1. receiving and giving feedback on the interpersonal level;
2. owning and permitting others to own their ideas, feelings, and values;
3. openness to new ideas, feelings, and values;
4. experimentation and risk taking with new ideas and values.

As any one of these decreases, it acts to decrease all the others and to increase the opposite situations. As with the foregoing conditions, we may hypothesize the following "outputs."

1. Members of this system of relationships will not tend to be aware of their interpersonal impact on others.
2. The members of this system of relationships will not tend to solve interpersonal problems so that they (or similar problems) will not tend to occur.

We may hypothesize that the formal organizational values, if followed, will tend to create a social system in which the members' interpersonal competence will tend to decrease (up to this point we are not hypothesizing the impact on cognitive competence, which presumably should not be, but is, affected by these values).

The Impact of Decreasing Interpersonal Competence on the Organization

We also hypothesize that, as interpersonal competence tends to decrease, the rationality and predictability necessary for effective functioning of the organization tend to decrease, and the rigidity of the organization tends to increase. Why is this so?

If individuals are in social systems in which they are unable to predict accurately their interpersonal impact on others and the impact of others on themselves, and it is important to be able to do so, they may begin to feel confused. Why are people behaving that way toward me? Why do they interpret me incorrectly? Since such questions are not sanctioned in an intellectually oriented system, no less answered, the confusion will tend to turn to frustration and feelings of failure regarding interpersonal relations. In an attempt to maintain their sense of esteem, the members may react by questioning the honesty and genuineness of the interpersonal behavior of their fellow workers. Simultaneously, they may place an even greater emphasis on the rational, technical interactions, in which they probably experience a greater degree of success. The emphasis on rationality will act to suppress the feelings even more, which, in turn, will decrease the probability that the questions of confusion and the mistrust (of self and others) will be explored.

As interpersonal mistrust increases, and as the capacity (individual and organizational) to cope with this mistrust decreases, then the members may tend to adapt by "playing it safe." The predisposition will be to say those things that cannot be misunderstood and to discuss those issues for which there exist clear organizational values and sanctions. The desire "to say the right thing" will be especially strong toward one's superiors, toward one's peers with whom one is competing, and toward one's subordinates who may be known to by-pass their superiors. The result is that conformity begins to develop within an organization. Along with conformity, the interpersonal relationships will tend to be characterized by "conditional acceptance" (as Rogers has called it) where the members will tend to feel accepted if they behave in accordance with certain organizational specifications.[18]

The Impact of Power on the Effectiveness of the Executive System [19]

Compounding these problems is the fact that the pyramidal structure is based on the control of subordinates through power and appropriate rewards and penalties. This leads to the superior becoming, whether he desires it or not, the "gatekeeper" to the success of the subordinates.

Lewin, Lippitt, and White [20] were the first to make explicit some of the dynamics of "gate keeping." Picture four managers (at any level) each of whom has certain goals that he wishes to achieve. These may be any of several goals (more money, more challenging work, promotions, etc.). The important point is that the managers have some goal(s) whose fulfillment is to occur in, and depends on factors within, their working world.

Between the managers and their goals is a gate through which they must pass to reach their goals. At the gate is a "gatekeeper" who controls when the gate will open, who will be permitted to go through, and so on. One important "gatekeeper" in most organizations is the superior. He is "told," in part, when to open and shut the gate and whom to invite in and keep out, by policies, practices, and managerial controls.[21]

The subordinates realize that in order to enhance their chances of getting through the gate they should discover the criteria that are required to open the gate and to work hard to develop themselves in terms of these criteria. They soon discover that there are at least two sets of criteria. The first is related to the professional, technical job that

---

[18] The "positive" aspects of conformity as well as the values of the pyramidal structure will be discussed later.

[19] We shall use power to include the total potentiality given to individual by the organization to influence others' behavior.

[20] Kurt Lewin, Ronald Lippitt, and Ralph K. White, "Patterns of Aggressive Behavior in Experimentally Created 'Social Climates,' " *Journal of Social Psychology*, Vol. V, No. 10, 1939, pp. 271–299.

[21] Dalton has provided an excellent account of some of the informal gatekeeper activities that executives may create. Melville Dalton, *Men Who Manage: Fusions of Feeling and Theory in Administration*, Wiley, New York, 1959.

they are asked to do. These criteria tend to be more objective and are usually defined by the job and by the organization.

The second set of criteria are much more subjective and tend to be defined by the particular superior. It is he who must do the selecting and the rewarding. Therefore, the evaluation that he makes of the subordinates is crucial. His evaluation will be partially in terms of the professional skills (if any) required of the subordinates. However, an equally (if not more) important set of criteria are the superior's view of the subordinate's "loyalty," "commitment," "cooperation," "team spirit," "proper attitude," "leadership skills," and so on. All these factors are highly subjective. The superiors judgments will tend to be affected by his own conception of himself, his leadership pattern, and his degree of organizational and psychological security.

In order to "play it safe" and increase as much as possible their chances for promotion, the subordinates will tend to become leader centered. What is he worried about? What are his prejudices, values, dislikes? In short, there is a built-in tendency for dependence on the leader and conformity to his wishes. The degree of each will tend to vary with the particular situation. If an executive "learns" to value the superior's feelings, needs, and prejudices, and to suppress his own, his own sense of self-esteem will tend to decrease. This, in turn, will tend to reinforce his dependence on the superior. We begin to see how organizations may tend to coerce, to esteem themselves less, to be more dependent, and more conforming (in the sense of suppressing their values).

A second mechanism that tends to increase the problem is interpersonal competition. As one group of executives studied put it, "You have to get used to the rules and acts of competitive warfare," and another, "It's not a dog eat dog world, but I get nibbled at a few times." These conditions of rivalry and competition, in turn, lead to interdepartmental hostilities and rivalries, mistrust and lack of confidence, and "politicking." These, in turn, may tend to coerce the subordinates to look to the superior to solve their major disagreements. This dependence on him "proves" to the leader that he is absolutely necessary and that without him the team would tend to be ineffective. Thus, we find the superior, through the nature of the organization and controls, creating a situation in which he becomes indispensable, which "confirms" in his mind that he must be strong because his subordinates tend to be weak. As a result of this "confirmation," which actually is a self-fulfilling prophecy, the superior tends to increase his control and directions and to make more explicit the requirements for effective leadership ("so that there will be no mistake and we are all clear").[22] This, in turn,

[22] Chris Argyris, *Executive Leadership*, Harper, New York, 1953.

causes the already dependent leader-centered subordinates to pattern their behavior in line with the criteria, and we have the beginning of subordinates developing in the image of their superior.

This may lead to organizational success, but it may also lead to personal failure since the individual is not defining his own goals, his own level of aspiration, and his growth. If he "succeeds" he now will "owe" it to his boss. The subordinate knows that he is mimicking someone else and that he is suppressing his feelings, values, and attitudes. One way to rationalize the "giving up of oneself" is to say that it is part of life and nothing can be done about it. Another is to require the subordinates to do the same. It is not long before the seeds have been planted for conformity,[23] decreasing self-esteem, dependence, and psychological failure throughout the entire organization.

Ward [24] found that executives prefer subordinates who make no trouble, avoid arguments, are somewhat retiring, meek, and even bashful to the more argumentative, impatient, rebellious types! As we shall see in a moment, these qualities are consonant with the values implicit in formal organization. Freeman and Taylor also report that although executives said that they looked for aggressive, energetic applicants, they personally wanted "tactful" subordinates.[25]

In another illuminating study it was found that superiors tended to list initiative and problem-solving ability as major job requirements. Their subordinates, however, did not mention these at all. A subsequent study suggested that there was more agreement between superiors and subordinates when subordinates were eager and ambitious for promotion than when they were less ambitious. It appears that ambitious subordinates are more cautious in their behavior and upward communications because they have an eye on the consequences. "Playing it safe" is a way to keep the road to advancement open.[26]

To summarize, basic to the formal strategy is power and control of

---

[23] E. J. McCormick and R. W. Middaugh, "The Development of a Tailor-made Scoring for the How-Supervise? Test," *Personnel Psychology*, Vol. IX, 1956, pp. 27–37.

[24] Lewis B. Ward, "Do You Want a Weak Subordinate?", *Harvard Business Review*, September–October 1961, pp. 6–26.

[25] G. L. Freeman and E. K. Taylor, *How to Pick Leaders*, Funk and Wagnalls, New York, 1950.

[26] Norman R. F. Maier and John J. Hayes, *Creative Management*, Wiley, New York, 1962, pp. 40–41. See original work by N. R. F. Maier, L. R. Hoffman, J. G. Hooven, and W. H. Read, *Superior-Subordinate Communications in Management*, American Management Association, 1961; and W. H. Read, *Some Factors Affecting the Accuracy of Upward Communications at Middle Management Levels in Industrial Organizations*, doctoral thesis, University of Michigan, 1959.

the subordinates by the superior. The power is especially related to the capacity to direct, reward, and penalize. If we now add the existence of mistrust and conformity to dependence, we may hypothesize that the members' commitment to the organization will tend to be external, as far as interpersonal activities are concerned. External commitment tends to exist when the source of commitment for any given individual lies in the power, rewards, and penalties that some other individual may use to influence the first individual. Internal commitment exists when the motive for a particular behavior resides from within (for example, self-realization). A certain amount of internal commitment restricted to rational activities may be possible in this system, if the rational, intellective aspects of the job are consonant with the individuals' abilities and expressed needs.

External commitment will tend to reinforce the conformity, conditional acceptance, and especially the dependence on the leader. The subordinates will tend to look for cues from the leader and will be willing to be influenced and guided by him. In fact, they may develop great skill in inducing the leader to define the problems, the range of alternatives, and so on. The subordinates will tend to operate within limits that they know to be safe. As the dependence increases, the need for the subordinates to know where they "stand" will also tend to increase.[27]

Thus, interpersonal mistrust, conformity, conditional acceptance, external commitment, and dependence tend to be "outputs" of decreasing interpersonal competence. Each of these feeds back to reinforce itself. All, in turn feed back on interpersonal competence to decrease it further or to reinforce it at its existing level.

At some point (to be empirically determined) these consequences will tend to feed back to influence the rational, intellective competence of the executives. For example, in some of the situations to be discussed later, we shall learn that mathematicians and engineers dealing with highly technical issues developed strong emotional attachments to these issues. During discussions held to resolve technical, rational issues, the emotional involvements tended to block understanding. Since the men did not tend to deal with emotions their inhibiting effects were never explored. On the contrary, they were covered up by the use of technical, rational arguments. Since these arguments were attempts by people to defend themselves or attack others, there was a tendency for the rationality of the arguments to be weak. This, in turn, troubled

[27] I am perplexed as to how many writers "prove" the importance of "merit ratings" or "evaluation" programs by citing people's need to know. These data may simply show how dependent the subordinates are and how well the programs are institutionalizing the dependence.

the receiver of the argument, who tended to attack obvious rational flaws immediately. The attack tended to increase the degree of threat experienced by the first person and he became even more defensive. Similar impacts on rational decision making were also discovered in such areas as investment decisions, purchasing policies, quality control standards, product design, and marketing planning.

Similar problems tended to occur with decisions that involved human factors in an organization. They were not explored thoroughly. Layoffs, demotions, promotions, reprimands, discipline, evaluation of ineffectiveness, are but a few examples of such decisions. Finally, there were cases on record where the organization never explored a new product or a new manufacturing process because the "powers that be wouldn't hear of it."

Another crucial area of decision making that can be influenced by interpersonal incompetence is the area of organizational change. For example, let us consider an organization that desires to go from a highly centralized to a decentralized structure. We may predict that executives operating under the conditions described earlier will not tend to explore or take adequate account of the feelings that subordinates under decentralization would have regarding decentralization. The executives will tend to "sell" decentralization by using cognitive influence largely missing such subordinates' feelings as dependence, conformity, and fear of, or ambivalence toward, authority. The subordinates in turn will tend to suppress such feelings (assuming they are even aware of them) and communicate to their superiors that they understand the meaning of decentralization and that they agree with it. However, we predict that if the superiors actually do decentralize and give the subordinates authority and responsibility, the latter will tend to seek ways to induce their superiors to make the decisions. The superiors, in turn, will tend to feel perplexed if not irritated. However, since the expression of such feelings is not sanctioned, they will tend to find indirect ways to express their disappointment and hold new meetings loaded with new cognitive reasons "selling" the importance of decentralization.

When executives perceive that their present leadership is not as effective as they wish it to be, they may take two courses of action. The first is to emphasize even more the values of the formal organizational structure. This means that they place greater emphasis on the use of rationality, direction, control, rewards, and penalties. In practice this means that they begin to check on other people's work not only to see if it is done, but also to see how it was accomplished. Another activity is to manage by questioning the executive about issues and problems that may exist at much lower levels. For example, the president might ask a personnel vice-president the price of sandwiches in one of the cafeterias in a plant away from the home office.

The result of such action on the part of the superior is to create defensiveness in the subordinate. The subordinate now finds himself constantly checking on all details lest he is "caught" by the superior. However, the activity of the organization is not carried forward with such behavior. The result is simply one of making the subordinates (and usually his subordinates) more defensive. Their response is to build up organizational defenses in order to protect themselves. For example, in one case where executives were managing by detail, the subordinates created the "j.i.c." file, which stands for "just in case" some superior asks. This file was kept up to date by several lower-level managers working full time and countless other people working part time. The j.i.c. file is an organizational defense to threat experienced by individuals at various levels.

In short, we may hypothesize that organizational defenses will be developed in an organization to protect various individuals and groups.

These organizational defenses can be expanded to the area of feelings, which we have suggested are typically out of bounds. This tends to occur when the intellectual methods fail. But since the use of feelings is deviant behavior, and since the superior or subordinates do not have much experience in their use, the tendency may be to have feelings *overdetermined*. Behavior may be said to be overdetermined when feelings tend to be much stronger than the situation warrants. Their overdeterminedness is compounded by the fact that subordinates do not tend to be accustomed to dealing with feelings.

Executives may speak of "needling the boys," "once in a while, 'raising hell' to keep them on their toes," and so on. If these conditions continue, it is not long before the "hot" decisions of the organization are administered by the use of emotions. This is the state commonly known in industry as "management by crisis."

As management by crisis increases, the subordinate's defensive reaction to these crises will tend to increase. One way to protect himself is to make certain that his area of responsibility is administered competently and that no other peer executive "throws a dead cat into his yard." The subordinate's loyalty will tend to be centered toward the interests of his department. As the department centeredness increases, the interdepartmental rivalries will tend to increase, thus decreasing the the organization's flexibility for change as well as the cooperation among departments. This decrease, in turn, will tend to be adapted to by the top management by increasing their directives which, in turn, begins to recentralize the organization.

The external commitment, conformity, interpersonal mistrust, ineffective decision making, management by crisis, and organizational rigidity will tend to feed back to reinforce each other and to decrease interpersonal competence. Moreover, each will feed upon all the others to reinforce itself.

Summary

The first-line foreman tends to be coerced into straddling two worlds with antagonistic values. He is a marginal man and tends to experience the frustrations and conflicts of being in such a situation.

If followed completely, the organizational structure, with its values about effective interpersonal relationships, would tend to create a managerial world in which there is (1) an increase in not owning, not being open, not taking risks; (2) an increase in conformity, dependence, external commitment; and (3) an increase in organizational defenses, interdepartmental rivalries, and less effective decision making.

Summary of Part I ⊞⊞⊞⊞⊞⊞⊞⊞⊞⊞⊞⊞⊞⊞⊞⊞⊞⊞⊞⊞⊞⊞⊞⊞⊞⊞⊞⊞⊞⊞⊞⊞

At all levels there is behavior that is not productive in the sense of helping the organization achieve its objective(s). For example, at the lower levels we found apathy, indifference, and noninvolvement. The first-line supervisors spent much energy coping with the problem of being "the man in the middle." At the upper levels we found conformity, mistrust, inability to accept new ideas, and fear of risk taking.

At all levels there is also behavior that is actually working against the achievement of the organization's objectives. For example, at the lower levels there was goldbricking, rate setting, slowdown, and cheating on production records. The first-line supervisor spent time protecting some of the employees' adaptive activities that restricted production in order to prevent increasing difficulties and labor grievances. Ineffective decision making, management by crisis, interdepartmental hostilities, and management by fear are some examples of antiproductive behavior at the upper levels.

We may argue that although both of these kinds of behavoir may not be essential in achieving the objectives of the organization, they are necessary to maintain the internal system. But the essentialness of this kind of maintenance behavior is more a function of the "incorrect" design of the organization. Thus to define the behavior as essential is to state a self-fulfilling prophecy. It is our hope to show that with appropriate modifications of organizational design and individual expectations many of these unintended consequences may be significantly decreased.

At all levels these unintended organizational activities which range from nonproductive to antiproductive eventually become ends in themselves. Much effort is used to maintain them as well as to keep them hidden from top management. For example, the lower levels tend to hide their goldbricking, slowdowns, and so on. The upper levels hide their difficulties with "politicking" and "private deals."

Once these activities are institutionalized, new activities are developed around them to protect and maintain them. Thus the top management may develop "j.i.c." files. The lower levels may develop several different kinds of "informal" production forms. The first-line supervisors may defend themselves by insisting that low production records are due to unfair production goals, poor production standards, time and motion men, and so on.

As these unintended activities become institutionalized, they tend to reduce the probability that accurate information will flow throughout the organization to make corrections of errors or to report accurately the effectiveness of the system. The less the truth is communicated, the more distorted facts may fill the communication channels. If this occurs, the more those who may be held responsible must protect themselves. At the lower levels the employees may depend on their union and seniority rules to protect them. The upper levels of management may depend on elaborate procedures such as keeping detailed files of memos "to the file." In short, the organizational corrective mechanisms may become "infected," which leads to decreasing awareness of problems and more defensive behavior.

As the flow of accurate information is decreased, as "noise" in the form of distorted information is increased, the organization may begin to become more rigid, less able to change as quickly as necessary, and at the same time it may add unnecessary staffs, levels of authority which protect those who fear making decisions.

As the organization begins to show these difficulties, given the values implicit in the pyramidal structure, we may hypothesize that management will tend to react with greater pressure, stronger leadership, tighter controls, and stiffer penalties. All these reactions are similar to the very causes of the problems in the first place. Consequently, they may induce a higher degree of productivity, but they will probably do so at increasing increments of cost to the organization. The defenses at all levels will be strengthened, the barriers to the facts raised, the justifications "to the file" even more detailed. Management by crisis, through fear, and by detail, will tend to increase, which will in turn increase the concomitant organizational defenses such as j.i.c. files, politicking, and rivalries. As the pressure trickles down to the lower levels, their defenses will be increased, and the cycle is now ready to be repeated.

Three characteristics about these unintended activities require emphasis.

1. All the unintended activities consume human energy. Moreover, the activities designed to protect and hide (thereby integrating) the un-

intended with the intended activities also consume much human energy.

2. The unintended activities become integrated with the rest of the organization through protective mechanisms, which give them the quality of being repetitive, compulsive, nonconstructive, and leading primarily to more difficulties. For example, apathy, indifference, and goldbricking are concealed through employees' distortion of the information fed upwards via managerial controls, as well as keeping them hidden from first-line supervisors or by making these supervisors "friends" and thereby coercing the supervisors not to report them. The top management, in turn, only knows that "things are not going as well as they desire." They tend to react by placing further pressure and increasing the controls. This only makes the situation worse, from the employees' viewpoint, and they respond by increasing (among other activities) the apathy, indifference, goldbricking, as well as hiding and distorting information and "befriending" first-line supervisors to do the same. This forms a closed loop of activity which is repetitive and compulsive; and rather than solving the underlying causes, it actually helps to deepen them.

3. Many of the unintended activities at all levels (for example, apathy, rate setting, noninvolvement at the lower levels, and conformity, mistrust, and rivalries at the upper levels) can lead to conditions that increase the probability for the experience of psychological failure, frustration, and conflict. They may also act to decrease the probability for experiencing psychological success. Recalling the nature of psychological energy, this means that the individual's state of mind will tend to be such that the activities *decrease* his energy potential for work.

In short, individuals will tend to consume much energy in unintended activities *and* decrease the potential amount of energy that they bring to their work situation.

PART II

Organizational Effectiveness and Ineffectiveness

One of the difficulties encountered in understanding organizational effectiveness is that as a result of the internal imbalances, conflicts, interdepartmental rivalries, protective mechanisms, discussed in the previous part, each group in the organization tends to develop its own concept of organizational effectiveness which is consonant with and helps to reinforce their experience, and which each group believes to be essentially correct. Indeed the members of each group base their beliefs on their experiences. So as long as experience is the major criterion, each side will continue to be, in their own eyes, correct.

Each may be in the "same" organization, but they are experiencing it significantly differently. For example, employees frequently report that they feel uncomfortable from the increasing pressure from management. The employees may even predict that the pressure will lead to real difficulties. Their management, however, may perceive the same pressure as contributing to organizational effectiveness. They feel that much more is necessary if the long range survival and growth of the plants are to be enhanced. On the other hand, the employees perceive their apathy and noninvolvement as enhancing their individual effectiveness and, therefore, the effectiveness of the organization. Management tends to diagnose the same apathy as leading—if it has not already done so—to organizational decay. They desire to change it, and they do so by acting in ways that are consistent with their view. As a result, they may develop all types of communications programs "encouraging" the employees to work harder and to be more efficient. In addition, economic education programs may be given to all employees. The logic has been that "workers are ineffective and noninvolved because (partially) they do not understand the importance of profit. If we teach them the importance of profit they will work harder."

To increase organizational effectiveness, management will also focus on the first-level supervisor. Supervisors are subjected to courses in human relations and leadership that at best teach the foreman how he should behave when management is nearby. At worst, the programs tend to widen the gap between the supervisors and the top executives because the former feel deeply misunderstood and somewhat manipulated.[1] The foremen in one situation were in precisely this position, although the management, due to research, became more careful about "solving" the problems with training courses. Once the pressure was instituted to cut costs, the management, as part of the new "push," developed several different types of training programs to make the foremen more "effective." The foremen, on the other hand, could see little relevance of the training courses to what they felt were their real problems. Unable to communicate this concern, most of them attended the courses, leaving them with attitudes ranging from indifference to frustration and mistrust. When asked to evaluate the program, most of them replied "positively," according to the foremen, in order to decrease the possibility of having more such programs. As one man put it, "If we tell them it was worthwhile, they may feel that the job is done and they'll get off our back."

To make matters more difficult, some sharp differences in viewpoint regarding organizational effectiveness tend to develop *within* the management world. Finance people, for example, tend to believe that pressure to cut costs is the key to organizational effectiveness, whereas the line (especially manufacturing and sales) perceives that the same pressure leads to difficulties. (At times line and finance agree that pressure is necessary.) Finance may believe that saving earnings and investing them for a rainy day is sound fiscal policy. Manufacturing may believe that the same funds are best used for capital outlays to decrease production costs, thereby lowering the price. Sales usually goes along with manufacturing (when the latter argues for lower prices), but, in

[1] Frank J. Jasinski, "Some Neglected Aspects of Supervisory Selection," *Personnel*, Vol. 33, No. 5, March 1957; "The Dynamics of Organizational Behavior," *Personnel*, Vol. 36, No. 2, March–April 1959. A. Zalesnik, *Foreman Training in a Growing Enterprise*, Division of Research, Harvard Business School, Boston, 1951.

turn, manufacturing may disagree with the usual philosophy of sales that manufacturing should be able to predict product needs more effectively and provide manufacturing with stable orders with minimal need for "rush orders." Research usually depends on spending the same money for further research, whereas product development commonly believes in upgrading the quality of the product to the highest possible standards.

Reactions of Top Management

Top management becomes tired, if not mistrustful, of these differences. They expect their managers to be more cooperative and loyal. They emphasize to their subordinates the importance of seeing the organization as a whole. However, from the subordinate's view, the organizational structure tends to create a world in which he focuses primarily on his part, and is oriented toward and dependent on his superior. Indeed, if he perceives the whole it may have to be more from necessity to protect his part.

This apparent narrowness and dependence by the subordinates tends to upset the top management. They react and, again, their reaction tends to be consistent with their "theory" of organizational effectiveness. For example, one executive decided it was necessary to "pressure" his subordinates. The initial impact of the directive leadership is to make the subordinates more tense and to increase their interpersonal rivalries. But since they are dependent on and centered toward their superior, they do not tend to express their feelings or feel free to explore with the executive the problem that his behavior may tend to lead to difficulties within the executive world. Rather, the subordinates take great pains to behave as if "everything is going along fine," "they are all one happy, hard-working team," "they respect their boss," and "believe he is largely responsible for the organization's success." [2]

Moreover, if confronted with an opportunity to talk about the actual problems, the subordinates not only hesitate but they actually distort the facts (as they see them) to protect their relationship with their superior.[3] If they live in such a world long enough, it is possible for difficulties to become so much a part of "the facts of life" that they no longer perceive them as problems—for example, the tension and frustration experienced by subordinates tend to become accepted. As one

[2] Chris Argyris, *Executive Leadership*, Harper, New York, 1953, pp. 47 and 95–98.
[3] *Ibid.*, pp. 65–67.

subordinate put it, "Life is tension—what else?" As a result of these constant rationalizations, an interesting development takes place. Since tension is "natural," one begins to expect it. As a supervisor builds up more and more expectation of tension, the existing tension seems less. This tends to occur because his tolerance for tension is now higher. Thus, if a supervisor senses as much tension as he is accustomed to, the existing tension has to increase. In other words, the more we expect something to occur, the less impact it may seem to have when it does occur. When people expect to be disappointed and are disappointed, the disappointment may seem less than otherwise. We now see another reason why the tension in an organization can be less noticeable to the supervisor than to an outsider.

Moreover, since tension is "natural," it no longer produces an urge on the part of the supervisors to want to change the situation. It is for these supervisors, as if they were asked to consider eliminating storms from weather. Others take on a different point of view, but one with the same effects: they suggest that tension is so prevalent, it is inconceivable to think of eliminating it. Where would one start? This resignation to tension naturally helps maintain the status quo—tension.

Resignation to tension leads to another rationalization relating to the necessity for "strong" leadership. Since the world is full of troubles, there is a need for strong leadership. Thus, an acceptable reason for strong leadership arises from the tension and conflict that is partially created by strong leadership!

It might be useful to comment on the nature of "strong" leadership. Strength, in physical education, is defined in terms of an individual's ability to *overcome* the forces of nature. For example, the number of push-ups, chin-ups, and so on, may indicate an individual's strength because it indicates how he is able to overcome forces of gravity. Utilizing the same concept of strength, we may conclude that directive, authoritarian leadership, commonly viewed as being strong, goes in the same direction as the forces of influence go in an organization due to the nature of organizational structure and managerial controls. They both tend to be authoritarian, to make people dependent. If this is true, directive leadership is not overcoming any forces; it is in line with existing forces. Directive leadership, in this sense, is weak leadership.

However, directive leadership can be accurately conceived as "strong" leadership if one focuses on the difficulties of overcoming the *expected resistance* that the subordinates will probably manifest once pressure is applied. It seems, therefore, that directive leadership in a formal organization is strong leadership *if* the people resist it. Is it possible that one reason so much resistance is unknowingly developed by directive leaders is that they need the "confirmation" of strength? Perhaps a directive leader is "strong" by creating the very resistance he denies that he desires in order not to see the possibility that he is covering up some feelings of inadequacy.

The foregoing discussion suggests that it is difficult to define organizational effectiveness by simply looking at the policies and practices of present-day organizations. Nevertheless, we wish to develop some way to understand these different views and to see how to obtain the "best" from each, *or* at the very least to develop a model that could help us to determine the "costs" in following one or some combination of these viewpoints.

The Essential Properties of Organization

The "real" or empirical world is usually understood by superimposing upon it a theoretical framework that is more abstract and that purports to mirror the relevant variables. The theoretical frameworks may exist at various levels of abstraction. The scientific-management framework, which is close to the empirical world, has been explored and found to be incomplete in helping us to understand much of (the unintended activities of) the organization. To develop our concept of organizational effectiveness we must climb to a higher level of abstraction.

Let us begin the development of the conceptual scheme with a definition of organization. This definition will serve as a "base point" from which we expect to extend our framework in many different directions.

In the literature of fields such as anthropology, psychology, biology, and political science, we find that the following kinds of propositions seem to be repeated continually and are common to biological, psychological, or social organizations. Some examples are: [4]

An organization is characterized by an *arrangement* of parts that form a unity or whole which feeds back to help maintain the parts: [5] a "part" of an organization is actually an "organic" part in that it exists by virtue of its position in the pattern that is the whole; [6] The whole, in turn, may be

---

[4] For a detailed sampling of the readings, please see my *Understanding Organizational Behavior*, Dorsey Press, Homewood, Ill., 1960, pp. 26–27.

[5] Norbert Weiner, *The Human Use of Human Beings*, Houghton Mifflin, Boston, 1950.

[6] Clyde Kluckhohn, "Anthropology," in James C. Newman (Ed.), *What Is Science?*, Simon & Schuster, New York, 1955, pp. 356–357.

differentiated from the parts along two dimensions. First, the whole has a different boundary than any given (or subset of parts.) [7] Second, the functional unity of the whole display properties only revealed in the actual process of full operation of the whole.[8]

These propositions suggest that the following properties may be essential to any living organization (pure organization): (1) a plurality of parts (2) maintaining themselves through their interrelatedness and (3) achieving specific objective(s), (4) while accomplishing 2 and 3 adapt to the external environment, thereby (5) maintaining their interrelated state of parts.[9]

Implicit in this definition of organization are three kinds of activities: (1) achieving objectives, (2) maintaining the internal system, and (3) adapting to the external environment. We shall refer to these activities as the *organizational core activities* or *core activities*. All organizations (which will concern us) will manifest them.

The reader may wonder how "goal setting" is dealt with. Goal-setting activities are viewed as being on a different level of analysis. They are part of the problem-solving process. So far, we have been dealing with the "steady state" of the organization. Goal setting and problem solving deal more with the mechanisms for change. Goal-setting and problem-solving activities "cut across" and include aspects of all three core activities. Consequently, problem-solving activities will be discussed separately later.

The second point that may be worthwhile to emphasize is that the problems discussed in Chapters 3, 4, and 5 are assumed to exist (in varying degrees) in all complex organizations. They are hypothesized to occur no matter what the specific "product" goal of the organization. Another way to conceptualize our viewpoint is to view the formal pyramidal structure as a strategy for solving problems. So far, we have been asking what kind of a "living" steady state will be developed in an organization if the pyramidal strategy is used (and if people have certain hypothesized needs).

The nature of the "steady state" requires further explication. It is conceptualized in terms of the interrelationships among the parts. On

[7] P. G. Herbst, "Situation Dynamics and the Theory of Behavior System," *Behavioral Science*, Vol. III, No. 1, January 1957, pp. 13–29; and Herbert A. Simon, "Comments on the Theory of Organization," *American Political Science Review*, Vol. XLVI, No. 4, December 1952, pp. 1130–1139.
[8] P. Kurtz, "Human Nature, Homeostasis and Value," *Philosophy and Phenomenological Research*, Vol. XVII, No. 1, September 1956, pp. 36–55.
[9] For a more detailed discussion of interdependence and the nature of the parts, see the Appendix.

the empirical level, the interrelationships are social interactions that, over time, have developed reciprocal relationships, which leads to a self-maintaining, patterned, state of affairs. Each part (social interaction) plays a function. This function may vary in degree of importance from peripheral to central when the system is in a "steady state." However, if any part, no matter how peripheral, stops functioning, it has the capacity to eventually upset the entire system. There is implicit in the system the notion that the whole is maintained through the interaction of all the parts (and not primarily by the interaction of one or a few master parts.)

In the biological literature, we find an interesting trend away from the notion of "master" parts or "governing" parts. For example, a more "minor" part such as the excretory system, if disabled long enough, can cause death. It seems then that, as long as we are dealing with living open systems, what part we judge essential is largely a function of the time span considered and what we want to consider essential in our research design. Our notions of dominant parts tend to evolve more from the way we have been studying organization than from the nature of living organizations per se. If we conduct an experiment by changing a variable systematically, the resulting domination of the variable during the experimental period may be more a function of the dominance of the experimental conditions than of the variable under consideration. Thus the scientist is in a position of never being certain about the dominance of a part. Even when a more naturalistic approach is followed, the scientist cannot be sure what impact the research process has on the "data" he is collecting. As a consequence, the scientists have tended to talk more about the essentiality of parts and less about the dominance of parts. Under the new conception, no one part is seen as being in complete control over the others.

L. K. Frank summarizes the position as follows:

When we look more intently at man's internal environment, we find a number of organ systems, each performing its specialized functions in the internal environment which is highly organized and interrelated. This internal organization, like the organization we are discovering in the rest of nature, is not a relation of dominance and submission, of a governing or dictator organ exercising control over all others, as we have long been accustomed to think. The kind of organization we find is a patterned activity in which all the specialized organ systems and functional processes constitute the organization and maintain the organized whole by the way each articulates, synchronizes, compensates and otherwise operates in relation to all others. The organization arises and is maintained, therefore, by the specialized constituent parts which, thereby, create the organized whole and this organized whole, in turn, reacts back upon the parts to keep them articulate and synchronized. This is the same kind of organization or field found in the atom, the molecule, the crystal and other orderly configurations and also in human society.[10]

It should be clear now that the "whole," which is created by the interrelationships of the parts, is therefore not conceived as some deified unity that can "do" something to all the parts as "it wishes." True, we suggest that the larger system is to be understood as the "whole" and the subsystems (parts) as bearing an instrumental relation to the "whole." As Shands has suggested, "this method of speaking, by assigning an agency to the larger system and instrumentality to the smaller, is grammatical and remains useful as long as the deification of the larger system is understood simply as a conceptual device." [11] When Cannon spoke of "organisms learning . . . ," the "organism" was used as an "apparent entity" simply serving as a formal subject for the predicate much in the same way "it" serves in "it is raining." [12]

However, this should not be interpreted to mean as Beckner suggests that the concept of organization has no place within a science. Beckner believes that there is only a "problem of organization," which he defines as the study of "systems which are highly complex." [13] Thus, Beckner dismisses organization as a concept but in the very next sentence introduces a similar concept, that is, "complex system." It is our view that systems have properties that are different from parts, that these differences reside in the interrelationship of the parts, and finally, that these differences do *not* mean that the whole is some mystical unity beyond what is included in the "interrelationship of its parts."

Finally, all organizations are assumed to be embedded in an environment that is continually changing and, thus, continually influencing the organization. A major task of any organism is to adapt to its environment either by changing its own internal arrangement and objectives or by striving to change the environment.

Exactly where the organization ends and the environment begins is a difficult question. For our purposes we will simply say that it is our task to isolate any system from its environment by trying to determine "how little" of the environment should be included in our description

[10] Lawrence K. Frank, *Nature and Human Nature: Man's New Image of Himself*, Rutgers University Press, 1951, pp. 53–54.
[11] Harvey C. Shands, *Thinking and Psychotherapy*, Harvard University Press, 1960, pp. 80–81.
[12] Walter B. Cannon, *The Wisdom of the Body*, Norton, New York, 1932.
[13] Morton Beckner, *The Biological Way of Thought*, Columbia University Press, 1959, p. 173.

to render the behavior of the system neutral to or independent of the rest of environment—that is, to determine whether the whole can be understood in terms of its parts.[14]

Organizational Effectiveness

Following open systems theory (as described in Chapter 1), we may now develop the following definition of organizational effectiveness. An organization increases in effectiveness as it obtains: (*a*) increasing outputs with constant or decreasing inputs, or (*b*) constant outputs with decreasing inputs, and (*c*) is able to accomplish this in such a way that it can continue to do so.

We have also said that an organization manifests three core activities: achieving its objectives, maintaining itself internally, and adapting to its external environment. If this is related to the foregoing definition, we may suggest that as an organization's effectiveness increases, it will be able *to accomplish its three core activities at a constant or increasing level of effectiveness with the same or decreasing increments of inputs of energy.*

What is meant by the core activities being achieved at a constant or increasing level of effectiveness? Let us take as an example the core activity of achieving the organization's objective. If the objective is making shoes, we mean that the factory is able to make the same number of shoes by using less inputs of energy (human or nonhuman), or that it can produce the same number of shoes without an increase in the level of energy expenditure.

The same criteria can be applied to the organization's internal maintenance and external adaptation activities. Their effectiveness can also be ascertained by noting the energy expenditure necessary to carry them out. As the energy required decreases, these activities may be said to be more effective.

The criterion for total organizational effectiveness, therefore, is an integration of the three effectiveness "scores," namely, the degree of energy needed to carry out the three core activities in relation to the outputs or "pay-offs." For any given organization this means that its effectiveness can be increased by an increase in any one or a combination of the three activities.

The core activities may, in turn, be categorized in a somewhat less abstract manner. To the core activity of "achieving the objective," we

[14] Hyman Levy, *The Universe of Science*, Appleton-Century, New York, 1933.

coordinate all the behavior in the organization that leads to the direct accomplishment of the objective(s) of the organization—for example, all the actual jobs or prescribed roles, the machines, the technology used, including the informal behavior that the employees have evolved and integrated with their jobs and the technology.[15] In the activity of "maintaining the internal system," we may include all the formal and informal activities of authority and controls, such as budgets, incentive systems, communications, discipline, hiring, firing, training, goldbricking, rate setting, rate busting, and noninvolvement.[16] In the activities that "help an organization to adapt to its environment," we may consider the whole range beginning with sales, public relations, community relations, legal and government relations, and some aspects of collective bargaining.

As we become more concrete we begin to realize the hundreds of variables included in each activity as well as the enormous difficulty involved in developing operational criteria for some satisfactory mix of all these factors.

Nevertheless, this is the direction in which we wish to travel. Our formulation of organizational effectiveness is therefore broader than some in that it emphasizes all three core activities—not simply achieving a goal—[17] and it focuses on the human as well as nonhuman dimensions. This broader emphasis seems necessary because it may be possible for an organization to increase or decrease its effectiveness without significantly modifying the activities that lead to achieving its goals. Thus a completely new marketing program (external) or a reorganization of the accounting and other informational processes (internal) could significantly decrease the costs of producing product X independent of whether or not more of product X is produced.

The three-dimensional definition of effectiveness may also help the diagnostician focus on the total organization in a more differentiated manner. It may be that an organization has a set of very efficient goal-achieving activities. The other two activities, however, are so inefficient that the organization could be heading for serious difficulties.

To put this another way, our view of organizational effectiveness is based on a systems model as differentiated from the traditionally more popular model of focusing on the achievement of the organizations'

---

[15] This is close to what Bakke described originally as "functional specifications" in his *Bonds of Organization*, Harper, New York, 1950, pp. 10–48.

[16] Rensis Likert has described these as "intervening variables," *New Patterns of Management*, McGraw-Hill, New York, 1961, p. 201.

[17] Theodore Caplow, "The Criteria of Organizational Success," *Sociological Forces*, Vol. 32, No. 1, October 1953, pp. 1–9.

goals. As Etzioni has stated, the system model, unlike the goal model, deals with multifunctional units.[18] It assumes a priori that a social unit ". . . that devotes all its efforts to fulfilling one functional requirement, even if it is that of performing goal activities, will undermine the fulfillment of this very functional requirement because recruitment of means, maintenance of tools, and the social integration of the unit will be neglected." [19] Our system model is an effectiveness model. It attempts to define a "pattern of interrelationships among the elements of the system which would make it most effective in the service of a given goal." [20]

Georgopoulos, Mahoney, and Jones have taken a similar point of view. They have defined effectiveness in terms of the goal as well as the path to reach the goal.[21] In another article Georgopoulos and Tannenbaum define effectiveness in terms of (*a*) productivity, (*b*) intraorganizational strain as indicated by the incidence of tension and conflict among organizational subgroups, and (*c*) organizational flexibility, defined as the ability to adjust to external or internal change.[22] Selznick has also suggested a multidimensional approach which, in addition to achieving the objectives, includes the internal system as well as its relationships to the environment. He cites five dimensions. They are (1) the security of the organization as a whole in relation to social forces in its environment, (2) the stability of the lines of authority and communication, (3) the stability of informal relations within the organization, (4) the continuity of policy and of the sources of its determination, and (5) a homogeneity of outlook with respect to the meaning and role of the organization.[23]

If this criterion for organizational effectiveness is to become operational, we need to define more clearly the three activities and spell out mechanisms by which they are interrelated. We also need an operational definition of "costs" that is much broader than the one presently in use. Up to now the accounting procedures have been based on the

[18] Amitai Etzioni, "Two Approaches to Organizational Analysis: A Critique and a Suggestion," *Administrative Science Quarterly*, Vol. 5, No. 2, September 1960, pp. 257–258.

[19] *Ibid.*, p. 261.

[20] *Ibid.*, pp. 271–272.

[21] B. S. Georgopoulos, G. M. Mahoney, and N. W. Jones, "A Path-Goal Approach to Productivity," *Journal of Applied Psychology*, Vol. 41, No. 6, December 1957, pp. 345–353.

[22] B. S. Georgopoulos and A. S. Tannenbaum, "A Study of Organizational Effectiveness," *American Sociological Review*, Vol. 22, No. 5, 1957, pp. 534–540.

[23] Philip Selznick, "Foundations of the Theory of Organization," *American Sociological Review*, Vol. 13, No. 1, 1948, pp. 25–35.

assumption that the crucial variables for the study of organizational effectiveness are nonhuman ones and that these variables are well covered by existing accounting procedures. Likert has presented data to show that these assumptions are, at times, false and always represent only part of the problems. He cites, for example, a case in which pressure on a well-established organization did increase the productivity. These increases were admirably recorded and "captured" by the financial systems. However, these same financial records failed to record and capture the additional facts that the increase in productivity was achieved by liquidating part of the investment that the company had in the human organization.[24] The point is that since the present financial procedures do not take into account the human dimensions, they do not help the executive to be sensitive to, and become aware of, the "human costs." We will need to develop accounting systems, therefore, that are able to evaluate, in addition to the goal-achieving activities, the costs of maintaining the internal system as well as the costs required to adapt to the external environment. Also, the accounting system will include ways to measure the costs of gold-bricking, rate setting, apathy, and noninvolvement, lack of openness, conformity, mutual mistrust, external commitment, and interdepartmental rivalries and hostilities. These and many other activities seriously affect the costs of achieving the three core activities.

Organizational Discomfort, Ineffectiveness, and Pseudo-effectiveness

In studying organizations, we cannot ignore the many different points of view of organizational effectiveness that may exist in an organization as well as differentiating those that "truly" signify effectiveness from those that do not. To help us categorize these various concepts, the following concepts will be used.

Organizational Ineffectiveness. This may be defined as the state of a system when it manifests increasing inputs for constant or decreasing outputs, and it does so continuously. That is, once one cycle of input, output, and feedback is finished, there not only results an output, but also a mechanism is triggered off which leads to the cycle being repeated in as ineffective or less (but no more) effective manner.

Organizational ineffectiveness implies a disorder which, in spite of

---

[24] Rensis Likert, "Measuring Organizational Performance," *Harvard Business Review*, Vol. 36, No. 2, March–April 1958, pp. 41–50.

the responses of the unit, leads to further disorder. It is important to emphasize that not all disorder is necessarily related to ineffectiveness. Some stress may enhance effectiveness. *It is the disorder or stress that compulsively and repetitively leads to further disorder or stress that implies ineffectiveness.* Indeed, one way to measure the length of an organization's "illness" may be to measure the time it takes to begin reacting in a way that corrects itself.

The degree of ineffectiveness in an organization, at a given time, is therefore assumed to be measurable. Also, each organization is hypothesized to have a measurable *tolerance* for ineffectiveness. Finally, the causes of ineffectiveness may be different for different unities or may be different for the same unity under different conditions. Moreover, ineffectiveness for one system may not be the same for another.

The definition of organizational ineffectiveness, in the final analysis, is based on the values one holds. In the "real" empirical world it may be that no organization is completely free of ineffectiveness and in perfect health. Each organization will probably develop a state of effectiveness that is "best" for its present state. The battle between effectiveness and ineffectiveness may never be won. It may well be a never-ending struggle that, at best, the organization must continually overcome. Thus, again we have a problem of *degrees* of ineffectiveness. The exact point at which ineffectiveness becomes serious varies for different organizations and for the same organization under different conditions.

Before we leave this discussion, let us explore briefly some of the conditions under which stress may lead to organizational ineffectiveness and effectiveness.

Picture an organization as a complexity of parts each performing a function and interrelated into an ongoing, pattern system of activity. Picture also parts *contributing* or supplying help to the other parts and parts "drawing from" other parts in order to perform their functions effectively. The amount that each part gives and receives varies with each part, with each organization, and within the same organization under different conditions. The amount of activity designed for each part may be called its "capacity load" or simply its "load." The initial load specifications of an organization may be modified through redesign as well as through informal activities. Thus, there are "loads" for contributing and withdrawing which initially are designed by the planners of the organization.

Organizational Stress. Stress occurs when the giving or receiving loads are forced to go beyond their design. But this concept is not complete because the original or intended designs are, as we have seen, altered as the organization ages. It seems more accurate to describe *organizational stress as a state that exists when the actual giving and receiving loads of the parts are forced to go beyond their "threshold" so that there is a disequilibrium in the relationship among the parts.*[25]

Such a stress could lead to positive or negative consequences. The consequences will tend to be positive if the stress is a challenge and if the challenge is solvable by the participants, utilizing and stretching their potentialities. This concept of "positive" stress is (meant to be) similar to the concept of psychological success on the individual level, defined previously. In both cases the emphasis is on realistic challenges that tax individuals up to a higher point than previously reached. Under these conditions, the stress becomes a setting for the system's counterpart to psychological success, which we shall call *system success*. System success is the sum of the psychological success experiences of the participants at any given moment. System success is therefore built from psychological success and then feeds back to increase the probability of further psychological success. Psychological success, in turn, increases the amount of energy available for productive work and leads individuals to seek new challenges. Thus, there is a constant feedback for greater effort, greater work, more success, and greater ability to cope with stress.

Unfortunately most of the stress that we have discussed in the previous chapters does not tend to lead to individual or system success. Stress may be said to lead to organizational ineffectiveness when (1) the giving or receiving capacities of the parts are not adequate for the actual demands of the system; (2) the nature of help given or received by each part is unexpectedly (that is, without design) altered; (3) the time available to perform the functions is too little or too much; (4) the number of resources necessary to accomplish the task has been radically increased or decreased; and (5) when new functions arise unexpectedly and spontaneously.

Let us reexamine briefly our analysis utilizing these five conditions of organizational stress.

1. As we have seen, one of the major unintended consequences of the adaptive activities is to consume much psychological energy. Consequently, the load will no longer be consonant with the original design or with the values of the top administrators. Moreover, many of the activities are not "legitimate" in the sense that they would be approved by top management. Since they are not sanctioned, it is not easy to procure or develop the new energy resources necessary to main-

[25] This definition requires an explication of "threshold" which will have to await research in actual organizations.

tain these activities. Consequently, the participants may be forced to use the existing organizational facilities as well as to take on new responsibilities which they have created to protect themselves. This could create an "overload" problem which could eventually lead to organizational difficulties.

2. To the extent that the adaptive activities are not organizationally sanctioned, the nature of the help given and expected from each part may unexpectedly change. For example, organizations patterned after the pyramidal structure desire a high degree of interdependence and interaction among departments along the flow of work. There is supposed to be maximum possible interaction and assistance along the flow of work beginning with the input of the raw materials to the point at which the final product is shipped out of the organization.

However, the same kind and quantity of interaction is not expected along authority and control lines. The parts are supposed to be concerned with controlling their own activities. If they have difficulties with the other parts, they are expected "to go through channels." If a part has problems, the other parts are expected to clear with the appropriate authorities before going to their aid.[26]

In practice, however, these barriers between departments are ignored or often reversed. Thus the parts may "fight" each other along the workflow lines because there they may have the greatest influence over each other and their superiors.[27] Departments do not tend to wish to be caught with production errors, failures, or inability to fulfill schedules. On the other hand, departments soon learn to cooperate with each other when they are in difficulties with the people "above." Indeed, it is not uncommon to break organizational rules ranging from absorbing someone else's costs to colluding to withhold facts so that they are not penalized.[28]

These activities, since they are organizationally illegal, tend to place unexpected energy requirements (in degree and in kind) on the relationships among the parts.

3. Organizational ineffectiveness may occur among the parts if the time available to perform the functions is greatly increased or decreased. Our analysis does not include examples of the former. However, a com-

---

[26] Chris Argyris, *Executive Leadership, op. cit.*; *The Impact of Budgets upon People*, Controllership Foundation, Inc., New York, 1952.

[27] For an excellent discussion on interdepartmental relations, see Henry Landsberger, "The Horizontal Dimension in Bureaucracy," School of Industrial Relation, Cornell University, mimeographed, 1961.

[28] Chris Argyris, *Interpersonal Competence and Organizational Effectiveness*, Irwin-Dorsey Press, Homewood, Ill., 1962.

mon example may be found in an organization that goes from a highly centralized to a decentralized status. During the centralization the top management spends much time controlling, checking on, and requiring reports from the subordinates. Under decentralization the close supervision should decrease. Theoretically, the subordinates are to be left alone until they ask for help or until their quarterly reports suggest that they are in trouble. It is not uncommon to find that old-line executives accustomed to the constant contact with subordinates find the new relationship required of them, as staff, to be distressing. The strain at the executive levels increases markedly.[29]

The decrease in time available to perform the functions is a more common occurrence in our analysis. One example is management through pressure and by crisis, described previously. Such practices lead to overstaffing because the departments play it safe to make certain that they achieve their objectives within the required time. Also, there is need for staff to "protect" the department to make certain no one "throws the dead cat over in our yard or, if he does, to throw it back quick." Staff is also needed to maintain the j.i.c. files; the files that protect the departments from other departments, as well as staff that is able to "scout out" and look for information about the behavior and effectiveness of other parts "just in case we get in trouble."

4. The availability of resources needed to accomplish a task can lead to strain if the task is too small or too large. We can cite many examples of organizations that develop stress when they lack manpower. Here we need only to emphasize that the increase in human resources needed to fulfill the the adaptive activities rises slowly and is carefully "hidden" in other overtly more legitimate needs.

Examples of organizations experiencing ineffectiveness because of too many resources is much more difficult to illustrate. Under these conditions the ineffectiveness results from too little rather than too much activity. Individuals have little to do: featherbedding is one result. The employees become extremely dissatisfied, the organization increasingly rigid, and the output increasingly costly.[30] Another example is the study by Walker and Richardson [31] in which they found that an organization became rigid and less effective because it had too many individuals in the managerial structure taking part in decisions. Finally,

[29] Eli Ginzberg and Ewing W. Reilley, *Effecting Change in Large Organizations*, Columbia University Press, New York, 1957, Chap. III.
[30] Paul Jacobs, *Dead Horse and the Featherbird*, Center for the Study of Democratic Institutions, Santa Barbara, Calif., 1962.
[31] Fred L. Richardson and Charles Walker, *Human Relations in an Expanding Company*, Labor and Management Center, Yale University, 1948.

there is the example of plant X, cited earlier, which for many years manifested a relatively stress-free employee world with minimal challenge and underload of work. Under stress the system had great difficulty in meeting the challenge. It did so, but with greater cost in terms of energy used.

One might wonder if we are implying that there should be speedups? When is a part underloaded? We hope to explore these crucial and delicate questions in more detail. There is, as we shall see in the next part, some interesting research suggesting that overstaffing can lead to organizational strain of the "slow·decay" variety. At this point, let us allay some fears by saying that our intention is not to suggest a world of unfair speedups.

5. Finally, the introduction of trade unions tends to develop stress within an organization at first. The inspection function was also a point of stress when it was first introduced to the workers. On another level, stress has tended to develop especially among manufacturing and engineering departments when a "product test" or "quality assurance" department has been established to check their performance. This tends to lead to interdepartmental rivalries and hostilities.

We are led to conclude, therefore, that under the conditions just discussed organizational stress can lead to ineffectiveness because (1) it creates the need for increasing increments of energy to maintain the total system and produce a constant output, and (2) most of these activities are self-reinforcing and inadequate in resolving the basic causes. If the reaction is inadequate and leads only to further stress, the organization is in difficulty. Interestingly, Selye has analyzed physiological disease in a similar fashion when he concludes that ". . . disease is (not) due . . . to the germ as such, . . . but to the inadequacy of our reactions against the germ." [32]

Organizational Discomfort. Discomfort may be defined as the negative feelings experienced by any one or group of individuals in the organization *that are beyond their desire or control.* For example, individuals may report tension, anxiety, rivalries, and frustration, all of which are states of discomfort if they are not desired or controlled by those reporting them. Discomfort does not refer, therefore, to the tension that may occur, for example, when one is striving to achieve goals. It refers to a state of negative feelings—feelings of a desire to leave the situation and all that seems to be associated with it. Another important characteristic of discomfort is that the precise causes usually are not known, although the "patient" may assign causes to it.

[32] Hans Selye, *The Stress of Life*, McGraw-Hill, New York, 1956, p. 204.

The members in each organization, each subunit, and each individual within the organization is probably capable of reporting various degrees of discomfort. It is assumed that these varying degrees of discomfort are measurable and that a discomfort index can be evolved. Further, it is hypothesized that every unity or organism has a tolerance against discomfort, which also is ascertainable.

The causes of discomfort may be different for different organizations (individual, small groups, large complex organizations) or may be different for the same organization under different conditions. Moreover, behavior that constitutes discomfort in one organization may represent quite a different situation in another.

Organizational Pseudo-effectiveness. This may be defined as a state in which no discomfort is reported but in which, upon diagnosis, ineffectiveness is found.

Under a state of pseudo-effectiveness the core activities are achieved in such a way that the underlying ineffectiveness is not evident. The cost of achieving these core activities, at any given time, seems manifestly equal or less than at an earlier time. The true costs are not discovered because the organization usually develops a compensatory mechanism that keeps the system in operation, and thus keeps the true costs hidden. However, the compensatory mechanism will eventually require increasing units of energy to keep it working so that the system may remain in balance and achieve its core activities. Therefore, sooner or later the compensatory activity will cost too much to maintain or it will influence the system in a negative way—for example, increased rigidity due to the dependence on compensatory mechanisms.

We may now develop a conclusion from the analysis with which we began this chapter.

1. *The unintended activities with their protective defenses and the resulting employee attitudes toward being productive lead to a situation in which (a) increasing increments of energy will be used nonproductively, (b) the potential energy input will decrease, and (c) the probability of resolving these problems is decreased.* These conditions, we may hypothesize, will tend to require increasing increments of input energy for a constant or decreasing output, which leads to conditions that are opposite to organizational effectiveness and approximate organizational ineffectiveness.
2. Participants will tend to experience feelings of uncomfortableness that are beyond their control to correct.
3. In order to protect the unintended activities, the participants at all levels feed up to the top information that makes the organization

look (to the top) more effective than it actually is. This will lead to organizational pseudo-effectiveness.

For example, in the pyramidal structure it may be difficult for the people in a subunit to admit it is ineffective especially if (1) the cause of the difficulty lies in its inability to deal with top-management pressure, and (2) if the top management believes that the pressure they are exerting is in the interest of the subunit. Consequently, the subunit will tend to develop a façade of health which is what we have called pseudo-effectiveness. It will act as if there is no difficulty in order to protect itself from further harassment or to prevent itself from having to face up to its own inadequacies. Moreover, it will probably select that state of pseudo-effectiveness that seems to be consonant with the state of health as envisioned by top management. As we have seen, top management's concept of organizational effectiveness traditionally has been measured primarily in terms of financial and production *outputs* or *results*. Consequently, the sick subunits respond appropriately. They feed up to the hierarchy those financial and other data (true or false) that will decrease the probability of further stress from above.

This suggests that a given subunit may find it necessary to communicate falsehoods to the top as a function of its fears of adequacy to respond to the stress from above if it communicates the truth. If this is so, we might speculate about the internal ineffectiveness of organizations in which there have been disclosures of false statements on the part of lower levels of management to the higher levels of management. Moreover, if it is considered too risky to communicate the truth at the vice-presidential level, then how helpless the lower units must feel!

This discussion also leads to a conjecture about organizational death. Hans Selye [33] has suggested that most people do not die of old age. Rather, it is the uneven use and wear of a particular part that eventually kills the individual. The same may be said of the organization. For example, we have suggested that if an organization is composed of parts, each experiencing adequate degrees of success, then their energy and competence for learning and work should tend to increase. This means that as new people are brought in to replace those who have left, they will be "caught up" with the milieu of success and soon they will be helping to maintain the high state of effectiveness. Under these conditions it is difficult to see why a unity would tend to decrease in effectiveness, no less die.

However, if the parts wear unevenly (as a function of management

[33] *Ibid.*

stress), they could cause difficulties for the entire organization. This may help to account for the often observed practice of top management putting the "heat" on a department and then leaving it alone. Unfortunately, in order to protect themselves from undergoing similar exhausting experiences, the members of the unit become even more protective of themselves and dependent on the top. Moreover, the other units, realizing that they may be next, also begin to develop protective defenses and become centered toward the top. As we have seen, this may feed back to require top management to increase its leadership pattern of applying stress from above in order to achieve the organization's objective.

Under increasing organizational ineffectiveness the parts will tend to respond defensively. Under these conditions we may hypothesize that the parts will become oversensitive. A part is oversensitive toward another part when its cues for learning and work are derived primarily from the behavior of the other part and not from a careful examination of the internal and external environment. This is a commonly observed situation in a highly centralized organization where none of the departments move without checking with the top.

The greater the degree of oversensitivity to the top, the less the probability that the system will search for (1) troubles emanating from within, (2) factors that could develop potential internal strength, and (3) problems that may develop in the future which do not emanate from the top. In short, the system's sensitivity to and ability to cope with problems other than those of interest to the top may tend to decrease.

If management is capable of learning, and if it learns that the other parts are centered around it, it may need to increase its directiveness and stress in order to keep the whole organization working. Too much stress leads to parts that, in an attempt to protect themselves, become centered toward and seek constant guidance from the top management. This, in turn, may lead the management to apply further stress.

Under these conditions the stimulus for action will tend to be stress from above. A stress-oriented system may well become even more withdrawn from reality, less concerned with maintaining the viability of its internal self, and more concerned with its survival. Its main concern may tend to be to please the top. Thus the parts of the system may wear out unevenly due to the high points of stress applied by the top. The parts will also tend to wear out at a faster rate than necessary, since little attention will tend to be paid to repairing and maintaining, and almost no attention given to developing the internal system.

Stress may be helpful or harmful to the organization. Much depends on whether the system is capable of coping with the stress effectively. We may hypothesize that the stress will tend to enhance organizational effectiveness if it is seen by the participants as being relevant, meaningful, and a realistic challenge—a challenge requiring commitment and the use of important abilities, where choices are possible and over which the organization has adequate control. If an organization experiences stress under other conditions, it will tend to be inhibited in its effectiveness.

Under the former conditions, the organization's adaptive energy does not tend to diminish, indeed, it may increase. Under the latter conditions the organization's adaptive energy will tend to decrease. Assuming for the moment that these hypotheses are validated, we might define the life span of an organization in terms of its available adaptive energy. The more the adaptive energy, the longer the life span. The shorter the adaptation energy, the shorter the life span.[34]

Another cause also contributes to pseudo-effectiveness. Management usually adheres to the indices of organizational effectiveness that are "derived from" scientific management theory. Because the theory does not focus on the total organization (especially the unintended activities) the indices may or may not indicate organizational effectiveness. For example, there is no empirical evidence, known to the writer, that absenteeism, turnover, resistance to change, low morale, and low loyalty are necessarily and always signs of organizational ineffectiveness. Neither is there any data to conclude that the opposite conditions always indicate organizational effectiveness. For example, where absenteeism, turnover, and grievance rates were low, employee loyalty and satisfaction high, the organization was found to be leaning toward ineffectiveness.[35]

The long-range objective of our research is to develop empirically validated definitions for each of the foregoing concepts so that we can differentiate among ineffectiveness, discomfort, pseudo-effectiveness, and effectiveness. This is a difficult task. However, until it is achieved, it will not be possible to train organizational diagnosticians of the caliber and with the competence that administrators are already demanding.

It may be useful to pause to answer the question that may have come into some reader's mind that we are attempting to define work for the behavioral scientists. Why, for example, cannot line managers perform the diagnosis in their own organizations?

[34] *Ibid.*
[35] Chris Argyris, *Understanding Organizational Behavior, op. cit.*

One major reason is that the constant pressure on line management to resolve technical and administrative complexities of a "here and now" quality will not tend to make them as patient with and effective in diagnosis as is desirable. Another reason is that as understanding increases and diagnostic methodologies become more effective, two new possibilities arise. First, as the diagnoses become more accurate they may tend to be able to predict potential or actual difficulty much before it comes to the surface. Such an ability could help the organization attack the problem early. It can also develop policies that may help to prevent difficulties and decrease the predisposition to management by "putting out fires." The longer the time perspective that one can develop, the less the probability that line management with its enormous day-to-day pressures will be inclined to deal with the long-range, as yet not immediately observable problems.

The second result is that the concepts and instruments used will tend to become more sophisticated and specialized. This, in turn, will tend to require more education of a professional nature. As organizational diagnosis becomes more sophisticated and professionalized, the line manager will find it difficult to conduct such diagnosis.

The increase of knowledge, however, will help the diagnostician build up an ever-increasing sophisticated manual of "first-aid" diagnoses which the manager can use. Thus, line management can become more effective in diagnosing problems, separating those that he can and cannot cope with, and actually resolving those that are within his competence and with the time available.

Problem Solving and Organizational Effectiveness

Up to this point we have been dealing primarily with the organization in a steady state. We have focused on the question of how organizations develop the internal steady states that they seem to exhibit?

Another important question is how do organizations change their internal make-up? How, for example, can they begin to rid themselves of the stresses and the causes of ineffectiveness that we have outlined? How do they become innovative? This leads us to an exploration of the problem-solving process because it is through this process that change is effected in the organization. Indeed, to Bennis [36] and Clark,[37]

---

[36] Warren G. Bennis, "Toward a 'Truly' Scientific Management: The Concept of Organizational Health," mimeographed, to be published in *General Systems Yearbook*, Anatol Rapoport (Ed.), December 1963.
[37] James V. Clark, "A Healthy Organization," Institute of Industrial Relations, University of California, Los Angeles, Reprint No. 114, pp. 17–18.

the problem-solving process is so important that they have tended to base on it their views of organizational "health." Bennis writes, "the most significant characteristic for understanding effectiveness is competence, mastery, or as the term has been used in this essay, problem-solving." Clark seems to focus on similar dimensions when he defines a "healthy" organization in terms of its "learning," "becoming," and its "transactions" with the environment, in which the give-and-take relations become more complex as it becomes more healthy.

The question arises: do any insights come from our framework that would help us to understand what is an effective problem-solving process?

Let us begin by taking our cue for a definition of effective problem solving from our definition of effective organization. *An effective problem-solving process may be said to exist when (a) problems are being solved, (b) in such a way that they remain solved (c) with minimal unnecessary expenditure of energy, and (d) with minimal damage to the continued effectiveness of the problem-solving process.*

Briefly, a "problem" for a system may be defined as any stimulus "outside or inside" that creates a chain reaction of complex events inside the system and upsets the existing steady state of the system. The "problem" is considered solved when the causes for it (that are under the control of the system) are eliminated and the system returns to its old or to a newly desired steady state. Obviously, many problems are created by factors beyond the control of a system. The effectiveness of the system's problem-solving process cannot be evaluated by testing it with problems over which it has no control.

However, according to our definition, a problem-solving process is less effective if it utilizes increasing increments of energy or if it decreases the energy potential people bring to it. Examples of the former were discussed in Chapter 4 where we saw that executives tended to create j.i.c. files, "politics," mistrust, and conformity. These kinds of behavior consumed energy without adding to the problem-solving process. An example of the latter was the psychological failure, withdrawal, and defensiveness that we suggested could be developed in a management system. These conditions inveighed against psychological success and thereby (according to our view in Chapter 2) decreased the potential energy for productive work.

Finally, a problem-solving process increases its effectiveness as it rids itself of those characteristics that prevent it from maintaining or increasing its state of effectiveness. According to our analysis in Chapter 4, management by fear, through detail, and by crisis, conformity, mistrust, tended to increase as the executives behaved primarily according to the values of the pyramidal structure (for example, focus on the objective, be rational and suppress the emotional, control, reward and penalize).

Most decision-making meetings are administered by executives who adhere to these values. Thus executives report that problem-solving meetings will tend to be effective if (1) the leader directs the discussion, keeps people on the track, and so on; (2) if there is a clear-cut objective; (3) if there is a definite agenda; (4) if "personalities are kept out of the discussion"; and (5) if the trouble makers are carefully silenced.[38]

These are the same kinds of behavior, however, that lead to the defenses, to the compulsive noneffective activity, to the interdepartmental rivalries, and to the conformity and mistrust within the organization. Thus, as in the organization, the very values that are assumed to help make it effective may actually create activities within the problem-solving process that tend to decrease its effectiveness.

As also illustrated in the previous part, these unintended and dysfunctional activities tended to be hidden from the top. Many of the participants behaved as if all was fine to avoid upsetting their superiors. A state of well-being was created which gave the superior the impression that all was well. And, as we have also suggested, much can be accomplished within these situations, especially if the group is professionally competent and if the leader remains firmly in control. However, it is our hypothesis that the dysfunctional activities will get worse and eventually inhibit the problem-solving process.[39]

In other words, we are suggesting that there are two aspects to understanding the effectiveness in problem solving. These aspects are discrete but interdependent. It is possible for a group "to solve" a particular problem so that it never occurs again. In this sense, the problem-solving process is effective. However, it is also possible that the problems do not arise, not because they are solved, but because they are hidden or transferred to more acceptable types of problems.

Moreover, if the process by which a problem is solved is dominated by the pyramidal values, it can cause, as we have seen, a reduction in potential energy, an increase in use of the available energy, and a decrease in the capacity of the members (because of defenses, hidden agendas, rivalries, and so on) to solve problems.

This analysis may provide a partial explanation for the Guetzkow and Cyr findings as well as those reported more recently by March. March suggested, on the basis of extensive observations of actual problem solving, that the behavior of the decision makers was more adaptive

[38] Chris Argyris, *Interpersonal Competence and Organizational Effectiveness, op. cit.*
[39] An example of this is found in the writer's *Interpersonal Competence and Organizational Effectiveness, op. cit.*

than it was rational. For example (1) people seemed to search primarily for those alternatives that were close to the problem, (2) conflict seemed to inhibit problem solving, and (3) uncertainty was avoided at cost to decision making.[40] Also Dubin emphasized the importance of the "political activities" in decision making. Decisions in organizations must take into account disparate and at times conflicting interests of various parts of the organization.[41] As we have suggested by the value model, it may be that these adaptive political activities arise because the pyramidal structure and controls typically used tend to create adaptive activities that lead to employees "playing it safe," "worrying about their own department," "fighting others," and so on.

Under these conditions, individuals and groups will not tend to be effective in problem solving. We conclude that not only can an organization unintentionally become ineffective, it can also "infect" the problem-solving processes so that it will be even harder to correct its difficulties.

The reader may wonder if we have any suggestions as to how the problem-solving process can be made more effective. Some suggestions arising from our analysis may merit consideration. However, before these are presented, it is important to emphasize that increasing the effectiveness of the problem-solving process is only a part of a much larger problem. The problem-solving process takes on its character from the organization in which it is embedded. Consequently, a concept of a more effective organization is required. We shall discuss this in the next chapter.

Nevertheless, on the basis of our discussion in Chapter 5, the following outline represents our hypothesis of one way to develop a problem-solving process that will approach our definition of effectiveness.

1. At problem-solving meetings, the individuals are encouraged:
   (*a*) to be candid about their ideas and feelings
   (*b*) to be open
   (*c*) to experiment
   (*d*) to help others to be candid about their ideas and feelings
   (*e*) to help others to be open

[40] James March, "Some Models of Organizational Decision Making," presented at American Psychological Association Convention, September 1961, mimeographed, Carnegie Institute of Technology, 1961.
[41] In the same paper Dubin also emphasizes the importance of the time scale in decision making. Drawing from the admittedly scarce literature, he finds that most decisions take years to consummate. Robert Dubin, "Business Behavior *Behaviorally Viewed*," in *Social Science Approaches to Business Behavior*, George B. Strother (Ed.), Dorsey-Irwin Press, Homewood, Ill., 1962, pp. 30–34.

(f) to help others to experiment
2. A group and an organization is developed in which there exist norms sanctioning factors such as:
   (a) individuality
   (b) trust
   (c) concern
   (d) internal commitment
3. And norms against factors such as:
   (a) conformity
   (b) antagonism
   (c) mistrust
4. And as the opposite conditions tend to decrease.[42]

This hypothesis may also help to answer a perennial question regarding the present conceptions of the problem-solving process. For example, Simon [43] suggests that decision making (which is similar to what we call problem solving) is composed of three interrelated activities, not necessarily existing in any given sequence. They are search or intelligence activity; design or inventing activity; and the choice or selecting a particular course activity. From this it is possible to hypothesize that effectiveness in decision making may be a function of at least the following factors: (1) degree of recognition of problems; (2) the accuracy of searching and locating relevant alternatives; (3) the accurate determination of the consequences that follow from each alternative; and (4) the choice of the most satisfactory alternative.

The question that we are left with is how does one increase the degree of recognition, the accuracy of search, and the effectiveness of the design and choice activities?

Bakke [44] hypothesizes that problem solving should increase in effectiveness as the following increase.

1. *Awareness* of the problem, which includes knowing the nature of the problem and understanding its significance to the organization.
2. *Simplification* of the problem to the point that its complexity becomes manageable within the organization so that appropriate action can be taken.

---

[42] These hypotheses are explored in detail in the writer's *Explorations in Human Competence: (Individual, Small Group, and Organizational)*, manuscript, Yale University, 1963.
[43] Herbert Simon, "Recent Advances in Organization Theory," *Research Frontiers in Politics and Government*, Brookings Institution, 1958, pp. 33–34.
[44] E. W. Bakke, "The Concept of Social Organization," in Mason Haire (Ed.), *Modern Organizational Theory*, Wiley, New York, 1959, Chap. II.

3. *Cueing* increases, which means that alternative ends-means combinations are developed.
4. *Anticipatory response*, which includes thinking through the probable consequences of various courses of action on the organization.
5. *Mobilization* of appropriate resources within the organization.
6. *Response* of the organization is adequate.
7. *Experience* is continuously checked and new directions are taken whenever they seem necessary.

The next necessary step (as in the case of Simon) is to specify how "anticipating response," "mobilization," "response," and "experience" are increased in effectiveness. In other words, both concepts of problem solving identify crucial properties of the problem-solving process, but neither provides cues as to the variables that influence their effectiveness.

The hypothesis presented in outline earlier, concerning how the problem-solving process may be made more effective, is relevant to this problem. We suggest that search, design, and choice activity and "anticipating response," "mobilization" activity can be made more effective as the foregoing conditions 1, 2, 3, and 4 exist. We realize, however, that this is speculation, and research is needed to test its validity.

Some Questions Raised by the Concepts

Before closing this chapter, we should like to indicate some questions arising from the concepts of organizational discomfort, effectiveness, ineffectiveness, and pseudo-effectiveness that may be worth serious exploration.

1. Is it possible that particular types of organizations (social systems) are prone to particular states of discomfort and ineffectiveness? Perhaps the kinds of discomfort an organization can experience and the ineffectiveness it can develop are related to various stages of development of the organization. Larger organizations may vary in terms of discomfort and ineffectiveness from smaller ones. Similarly, older organizations may differ from younger ones.

The degree of stress, length of stress, kinds of stress, make-up of employees, nature of structure, leadership, and managerial controls, the rewards and penalties, can all be explored in terms of their predisposing the organization to discomfort and ineffectiveness.

2. Are there states of discomfort related to specific states of ineffectiveness? Is it possible that specific discomforts always lead to specific

ineffectiveness? What are the processes involved in discomfort
ymptom for ineffectiveness? What are the processes involved
... ineffectiveness causing discomfort? Is it possible that the causes of
discomfort for a given unity or subunity A may lead to ineffectiveness
in another unity or subunity B? Is it possible for the configuration of
factors that lead to ineffectiveness in unity or subunity A to lead to discomfort in unity B or subunity B?

3. What kinds of prognoses can be made for different states of discomforts and ineffectiveness? Is it possible to develop specific cures for
various states of ineffectiveness? Can one think of short-range "first-aid"
cures as well as the long-range cures? When is ineffectiveness so bad
that radical surgery (such as "amputation" of departments) is needed?

4. As these questions are answered, we may then relate the results to
what is known about individual *discomfort* and *illness*.

Much research needs to be conducted on the spread of ineffectiveness and health throughout the organization. One possible direction
of research is the use of epidemiological concepts. One might, for example, consider organizations as being composed of "hosts" and "carriers" of effectiveness and ineffectiveness. A host is anyone who is receptive to the ineffectiveness, whereas a "carrier" is one who carries the
ineffectiveness around and is able to infect others.

In one study it was found that "hosts" and "carriers" could be identified by developing a "score" for each individual depicting his degree of
self-actualization in the organization.[45]

The score for self-actualization was conceived as any attempt by an
individual to actualize any of his potential. Unlike some other approaches, it assumed no specific a priori content to self-actualization.
The only assumption was that there is a basic drive to actualize one's
self and these trends can be inferred from people's behavior or reports
about themselves. The actualization can be in the direction of maturity,
as has been defined by such scholars as Erickson, Maslow, and Rogers.
(The writer, drawing from these scholars, developed such a scheme to
define several dimensions of immaturity-maturity in *Personality and
Organization.*) However, in this scheme, the actualization could be
toward apathy and alienation, as was true for many employees in plants
X and Y.[46]

[45] Chris Argyris, *The Organization of a Bank*, Labor and Management Center, Yale
University, 1954, p. 249.
[46] For an excellent theoretical discussion of the various uses of self-actualization, see
Jack Sherwood and John R. P. French, "Some Theoretical Relationships Between
the Concept of Self-actualization and Self-identity Theory," draft, Department of
Psychology, University of Michigan, May 1961.

Some of the findings were:

1. The lower the self-actualizing score a person has, the greater are the chances that he will be a carrier of the "illness" low morale, and the greater are the chances of his infecting others.

2. Every carrier of "low morale" is also a "host" for further infection of "low morale." Subsequent infection from others will tend to have a "spiraling" or "snowballing" effect that is noticeable in an individual as his morale becomes increasingly lower.

3. The degree of infection with "low morale" is not only dependent on the number of carriers carrying this disease, but it is also a function of the number of "hosts" available within the environment of the carriers. This number, in turn, is a function of a complex set of variables in the milieu of the department in which the carriers and hosts exist.

4. Another variable that influences the chances of infection is the existence of natural boundaries in the environment to prevent a carrier from coming into contact with a host.

5. Categorizing people in terms of high, medium, and low self-actualizating scores, we find that a low-score individual tends to be a carrier of the ineffectiveness. The host tends to be a medium-score individual. Apparently the high-score individual is perceived by the carrier as being immune to infection. In the few cases noted where high-score individuals have been infected, they were infected by individuals who previously had been at the medium-score range. It seems that certain critical thresholds exist which must be reached before infection can take place. Apparently the low-score individuals are not able to trigger the mechanisms that lead to infection in a high-score individual, whereas the medium-score individual is able to. Perhaps one key to understanding the process of infection between any two individuals lies in the research that is being conducted on "interpersonal influence" as well as "mass communication and influence" especially by "opinion leaders." [47] If these results are confirmed, it may be that the spread of illness can be plotted if not predicted.

Along with concepts that describe the individuals, concepts should be developed that help to describe the role of the environment in terms of facilitating or inhibiting, generating or suppressing, states of effectiveness or ineffectiveness in question. Some departments, for example, may have a milieu or culture that generates or is receptive to certain states of effectiveness or ineffectiveness. As with individuals, maps that describe the "hosts" and "carrier" potential of each subunity (department) in the organization should be developed.

[47] E. Katz and P. F. Lazarsfeld, *Personal Influence*, The Free Press, Glencoe, Ill., 1955.

Rapoport [48] suggests that some factors that may be important to consider for individuals as well as for larger unities are (1) natural immunity, (2) limitations of infectiousness, (3) immunity conferred by the illness itself, and (4) decrease of virulence in the pathogenic organism.

Summary

We are suggesting that the organization has built into itself a series of highly complex and interrelated adaptive activities that will tend to require increasing units of energy to maintain. This energy can be devoted to more productive purposes. Moreover, as the pressure from above increases, the energy available for productivity should decrease because the type of energy that we are considering, the reader may recall, is a function of the "proper" state of mind, and this in turn is defined in terms of the experience of psychological success and self-esteem. Finally, increasing units of energy will need to be expended simply to get things accomplished in the organization. The story is told that General Motors was decentralized when the chief executive officer found that it took more than a year to receive a reply to a routine memo. This organizational atrophy that we hypothesize to exist will be difficult to diagnose partially because it is slow in developing, partially because we have almost no instruments to identify it, no less measure it, and partially because, due to technological capacities, organizations can still produce their products at a respectable rate of return. As we often hear, "why tamper with a system that is successful."

However, there is an increasing awareness among administrators at all levels and in many different types of organizations about the way the internal system can "eat up" money in order to run at an acceptable speed. If we examine the McKinsey Lectures, which are given by presidents of large corporations, we will find that all of them sound the warning that a chief problem for the organization of the future is to remain viable, flexible, and vital.

The question, and it is an extremely complex one, is how can we change the forces of this slow organizational decay in order to stop the infection. All we have been able to do at this point is to conceptualize the problems, which are organizational discomfort, pseudo-effectiveness, ineffectiveness, and effectiveness. We have defined organizational

---

[48] Anatol Rapoport, *Fights, Games, and Debates*, University of Michigan Press, Ann Arbor, 1960, pp. 51–54.

effectiveness as that state in which the organizational core activities can be achieved with a decreasing or constant input, while maintaining or increasing the output of the system. Organizational ineffectiveness is the situation in which the same is being done but with increasing inputs and constant or decreasing outputs. We have explored some of the mechanisms by which organizational stress can enhance or inhibit organizational effectiveness. Finally, we have explored how the problem-solving process may be used to help the organization overcome the forces toward organizational ineffectiveness.

The "Mix" Model

We have defined organizational effectiveness as a system manifesting increasing outputs with constant or decreasing inputs or constant outputs with decreasing inputs. We have called the energy inputs "psychological energy." The problem of effectiveness is to increase the amount of psychological energy available for work.

The first step emanating from the previous part is to strive to decrease the compulsive unproductive organizational activities that we have described and thereby free the psychological energy for productive effort. One way to decrease these unproductive activities is to increase the probability that individuals will be able to experience psychological success and opportunities for self-responsibility. To do this we believe it will be necessary to modify and add to the present strategy used to design organizations.

But how much should the organization be modified for psychological success? Will not this lead to an organization that is primarily people centered? Does not the organization have some legitimate needs that are not people centered? How far is the organization supposed to go in focusing on the needs of individuals?

First, we maintain that increased opportunities for employees to experience psychological success does not mean a completely people-centered organization. Psychological success, the reader may recall, means achieving challenging goals. Self-esteem is intimately related with responsibility to something or someone outside one's self. Why cannot the organization develop challenging goals for the members to strive to achieve? Is not the organization an excellent medium for experiencing responsibility? It is our hypothesis that organizations can be modified so that they offer increasing meaningful challenges and opportunities for responsibility.

Moreover, we do *not* believe that the organization can make all of its activities challenging and full of responsibility. But this is not necessarily a detriment. As we shall see, challenging opportunities are exhausting. Some routine and less challenging opportunities can offer a needed respite. Indeed it is the individual who has a relatively high amount of psychological success in his "psychological bank" who is able to give of himself, without giving up himself, without permitting the necessary organizational limitations to frustrate him, and who therefore will best understand the requirements of the organization.

Second, we recommend that the changes in the organization toward increasing opportunity for psychological success and self-esteem be made *as long as we are able to show that they are decreasing the unproductive, compulsive activities* summarized in the previous chapter. Exactly where this point is will have to be determined empirically for each organization.

Third, we recommend that the changes in the organization that may lead toward increasing psychological success and self-esteem be continued as long as there is evidence that the changes result in the three core activities consuming less energy.

In addition to the changes in the organization, we also recommend changes in the individual. We suggest that it is not enough for organizations to be redesigned to provide greater opportunity for psychological success and self-esteem. The participants must be capable of fulfilling the challenges and accepting the responsibilities involved. They may not be frightened or threatened by the opportunity for psychological success. This is no easy requirement when we recall that the working-class culture sanctions such attitudes as fatalism, noninvolvement, and apathy. Thus, both the formal organization and the individual will need to change.

The next question that arises is how much is each to be changed? It is at this point that the writer has no a priori answer to provide. A valid reply would require the availability of a far more sophisticated theory as well as empirical data than he is aware of.

One of the important needs therefore is to conduct research to discover the possible "pay-offs" of different combinations of individual and organizational expression under different conditions. One of the objectives of the model that we present hereafter will be to help us in the development of such research.

To develop the most useful understanding of the combinations of individual and organizational needs that are possible, we need a model that helps us to conceptualize the full range of individual and organizational potentialities. In the case of the individual there is some research (admittedly all too meager) to help us conceptualize the various needs of individuals ranging along a complex set of dimensions each approximating an aspect of what psychologists call "mental illness" and "positive mental health." One end of each dimension represents the poorest possible mental health one could manifest, and at the same time perform work in an acceptable (to the administrator) manner. The other end of the continuum is positive mental health, which we should hasten to say is an ideal that no one is able to achieve. The best that we can do is to approximate the ideal.

In exploring the range of alternatives for defining organizations, the same is not true. If we are not careful, we may limit ourselves to the pyramidal type of organization because, to the writer's knowledge, this is the only one discussed in the literature. This type of organization is so common that it may escape our notice that organized life does not necessarily have to be limited to the pyramidal structure.

If there are other possibilities than the pyramidal organization, what are they? How can we find them? One possible route to explore came to the writer while reading about axiology, the science of value.

Something is good axiologically when it fulfills the definition of its concept.[1] If this is true, perhaps we can begin to understand the alternatives open to us for other kinds of organizations by asking if the pyramidal structure actually approximates the concept of organization. If it does not, what kind of an organization would? Is such an organization feasible in real life? Would human beings wish to create it?

The Nature of Organization

To answer these questions we must first ascertain the essential nature of organization at any level of analysis. It should be clear that in asking this question we have to climb to a higher order of abstraction to find the essential properties or characteristics of the concept of organization at any level of social life. In doing so, it is necessary to empha-

[1] Robert S. Hartman, "The Science of Value," in A. H. Maslow (Ed.), *New Knowledge in Human Values*, Harper, New York, 1959, pp. 13–37.

size that, in the following discussion, *when we use the term organiza-tion, we are not referring to a specific plant, a government bureau, a school, or a trade union. We are referring to the abstract construct of organization.*

The reason for climbing to the highest possible heights of abstrac-tion is to see if we can discover any essential properties about the nature of organization that are true for any "real life" organization such as a plant, a bureau, and a trade union. If we do, we might be able to develop a model that is relevant to all of these different kinds of "firms." This is not a new procedure in scientific thought—indeed, it is quite com-mon. One of the eternal challenges facing any researcher is to climb up to the highest levels of abstraction and develop constructs that cap-ture the essential properties of what he is studying. Then he returns to the empirical world to test, through research, whether these are in-deed the essential properties. He realizes that it is too much to expect to succeed during the first trip. He knows that it will require many trips, each caused by, as well as guided by, the questions that are raised by his empirical research.

Why go to all this trouble? Because if the researcher succeeds in find-ing the necessary and sufficient concepts he will have developed a much more simple model of the causal factors than he can find if he remains close to empirical reality. If his model eventually enters the "elegant" class (that is, with the fewest possible concepts or constructs he is able to explain a large range of "real" problems), he then feels that he has helped to make a small contribution to the goal of valid and compre-hensive schemes to understand the "real" world.

In our case, *the reader is being offered the results of our first trip into the abstract without the benefit of the empirical research.* Consequently, the material that follows is extremely tentative.

And now to the first step to make explicit the essential properties of the construct organization. This can be done by referring to the defini-tion of organization that we presented at the outset. This definition, the reader may recall, was developed from a review of the biological, psycho-logical, sociological, and anthropological literature. Implicit in that defi-nition are the following essential properties of social organisms.

1. The pattern of parts.
2. The whole is maintained through the interrelatedness of all the parts in the pattern. No one part (or subset of parts) completely controls or dominates the whole. The "interrelatedness of parts" refers to the mechanisms by which parts contribute or receive help from the other parts.

3. The achievement of goals or objectives.
4. The parts and their interrelationships change to cope with, and adapt to, new stimuli influencing the internal organization.
5. The organization has sufficient control over its environment to maintain its own discreteness.

Each of these essential properties of organizations implies certain conditions. For example, the first property assumes that instead of a *plurality* of parts, an organization is characterized by a *patterning* of parts. Instead of the whole being *created* or *directed by the actions of one part or subset of parts*, it is created through the *interrelationships of all the parts*.

This leads to the possibility that each property of the construct organization may be conceptualized as a dimension. One end of each dimension would be a point of maximum possible expression of one aspect of the property (for example, plurality). On the other hand would

Table 7-1. The "Mix" Model

Away from the Essential Properties	*Toward the Essential Properties*
1. One part (subset of parts) controls the whole.	The whole is created and controlled through interrelationships of all parts.
←——————————————————→	
2. Awareness of plurality of parts.	Awareness of pattern of parts.
←——————————————————→	
3. Achieving objectives related to the parts.	Achieving objectives related to the whole.
←——————————————————→	
4. Unable to influence its internally oriented core activities.	Able to influence internally oriented core activities as "it" desires.
←——————————————————→	
5. Unable to influence its externally oriented core activities.	Able to influence externally oriented activities as "it" desires.
←——————————————————→	
6. Nature of core activities influenced by the present.	Nature of core activities influenced by the past, present, and future.
←——————————————————→	

be a point of maximum possible expression of the opposite situation (for example, patterning). Another dimension would range from the organization achieving its goals through the direction of one or subset of parts.

Such a formulation might help us in two ways. First, it suggests that there are certain values implicit in the construct organization. For example, patterning over plurality and the whole maintained through the mutual interdependence of parts versus the whole maintained by one or a subset of parts. Stating this, however, implies nothing about the validity of "patterning" or "plurality" in a given empirical organization. All we are stating at this time is that every "real" organization may have its activities described in terms of the degree to which they approximate or go away from the essential properties of the construct organization. The second way such a formulation may help is that, if we define personality as an organization, it permits us to study the integration of the individual and the organization in terms of degree rather than as discrete black or white entities. We will discuss more of this later.

From the definition of the construct organizations, it seems plausible to infer six dimensions,[1a] which are outlined in Table 7-1 and discussed in more detail hereafter.

1. *From a situation in which a part (or subset of parts) directs the organizational "core activities" (achieving the objectives, maintaining the internal system, and adapting to the environment) to the point where these core activities are influenced through interrelationships of parts.*

According to our definition of organization, the whole is maintained by the interrelationships of the parts. Also, the parts have meaning primarily in terms of their contribution to the whole. A dimension may be defined, therefore, whose one end represents a state in which the whole is maintained internally and adapts to its environment as a result of the activity of one or subset of parts. The other end of this dimension represents a state in which these core activities are carried out through the interrelationship of all the parts.

This dimension assumes, as was pointed out, that in a living organi-

_____

[1a] We should reemphasize that the discussion of the essential properties is assumed to be valid for all levels of social organization. We are assuming that individuals, groups, and formal organizations such as business firms are all examples of social organisms. Thus the model is hypothesized to be valid for the three levels of analysis. We are assuming that the essential properties of an organism at the individual and organizational levels can be described by the right ends of the continua. Whether or not this is true is a question to be determined by further analysis and much empirical research.

zation each part has some influence over the core activities. Central to making this dimension operationally meaningful is the concept of inter-dependence of parts. Do we mean that all the parts have equal influence on each other and on the core activities? Clearly, we do not. We mean to suggest that the amount of influence among the parts is so distributed that no matter what it is, the discreteness of the part plus its activities of feeding on and feeding back to the other parts is not completely controlled by any other part or subset of parts. That is, each part has a degree of influence that it requires to maintain itself and perform its function in the whole. The degree of essentiality to the whole becomes the key to understanding the degree of interdependence.[2]

2. *From awareness of the organization as a (random) plurality of parts to awareness of the organization as a pattern of parts.*

The first reason for this dimension is that the model is purported to hold for the individual as well as the group and organization. Individual behavior cannot be fully understood without taking into account the personal world of each individual. As Lewin [3] has pointed out, human behavior is a function of the individual interacting with and per-ceiving (that is, being aware of) his world.

As for organizations, this dimension seems necessary when we con-sider that organizations have human beings as their agents.[4] Organiza-tional objectives would not tend to have an influence on the behavior of the agents if they (the agents) were not aware of them. The more sociologically oriented reader may question the necessity for our view that the parts be aware of the whole. For example, why should indi-viduals in departments have to be aware of the functioning of other departments and individuals? To put it in theoretical terms, if each part is clear concerning its own narrow function, why is it necessary to be aware of the whole?

If the internal mechanisms of the whole were quaranteed to operate effectively and in balance, perhaps an awareness of the whole by the parts would not be necessary. This might also be true if there were one unequivocal, dominating, super, controlling mechanism that could "see" the total organization all the time, diagnose potential problems, resolve them by issuing orders and knowing that all parts will follow them ex-actly according to play. As we have seen, most of these conditions are rarely found in an organization. We will discuss this later.

[2] See the Appendix.
[3] Kurt Lewin, *Dynamic Theory of Personality*, McGraw-Hill, New York, 1935, pp. 1–65.
[4] For an excellent discussion of the role of "agents," see E. W. Bakke, *Bonds of Organization*, Harper, New York, 1950.

3. *From a state in which the objectives being achieved are related to the parts, to a state in which the objectives being achieved are related to the whole.*

The whole is created by the interrelationship of parts, but the parts exist in a particular pattern of interrelationships to achieve the objective of the system as a whole. An organization as a whole has by definition objectives that it must achieve. To be sure, every part has formal subobjectives, but these take on their meaning by being related to the larger overall objectives. The less an organization is guided by its overall objectives and the more the objective of each part becomes paramount and is not relatable to the overall objectives, the less the firm approximates the essential characteristics of organization.

4. *From a state in which the organization is unable to influence its internally oriented activities (achieving its objectives, maintaining the internal system) to a state in which it can influence these activities as the organization desires.*

One of the most basic characteristics of an organization is the capacity to modify any of its internal activities as it becomes necessary. Unless it is able to do so, it will have difficulty in adapting in an ever-changing environment.

Implicit in this dimension is the assumption that in an organization no activity should be beyond the control of the participants of the organization. No activity that continues independent of the external stimuli and the desires of the participants becomes compulsive or rigid. Organizational activities that continue against the desires of, and are beyond the control of, the participants are compulsive activities.

The freedom to modify activities is applicable to movement in the direction away or toward the essential properties of organization. An organization, under certain conditions (for example, crisis), may need to modify its activities away from these properties and toward the unhealthy organization. The argument implies that any *compulsive* activity toward effective organization will lead to a greater rigidity. Thus, any compulsive activity will eventually tend to lead to difficulties simply because the organization must be able to control its own behavior if it is to integrate itself in the environment and survive. This implies that an organization increases its problems as it is unable to control the direction of its own activities.

5. *From a state in which the organization is unable to influence its externally oriented activities to a state in which it can influence these activities as the organization desires.*

This dimension points to the fact that all organizations are open systems in the sense that they are influenced by and they in turn influence the environment in which they are embedded. The dimension also suggests that an organization needs to be able to modify its environmentally oriented activities as the conditions require. The degree to which these modifications are necessary for any organization will tend to vary with different stages of development, and with the nature of the environment. The criterion to be kept in mind is to develop those externally oriented activities that (1) provide the opportunity for the "best" profile along the other dimension and which (2) provide the highest degree of probability possible that the objectives will be achieved.

6. *From a state in which the nature of the core activities (achieving the objectives, maintaining the internal system, and adapting to the environment) is largely determined by the present to a state in which the present core activities are continually influenced by considerations including the past history, the present and the anticipated future of the organization.*[5]

This dimension assumes that the effective organization will be able, in defining its core activities, to take into account the relevant variables from the past and in the present, as well as to anticipate correctly the relevant variable of the future.

Determining the appropriate time perspective for each organization is a matter for empirical research.[6] One theoretical criterion of the "right" time perspective may be the amount of time necessary to solve a problem while at the same time optimizing dimensions 1, 2, 3, 4, and 5. Another criterion for determining the scope of the time perspective may be the amount of time the organization needs to plan ahead to combat external stimuli.

Does an Organization Behave? Can "It" Desire?

Throughout this discussion we have referred to the organization as "controlling its activities" or as "influencing them as it desires." To what specific processes do we refer when we say that the organization controls its activities? Who specifically does the controlling? What do we mean when we say that an organization is able to influence its behavior as "it desires"? Can organizations desire?

The first point we must keep in mind is that our concept of organiza-

---

[5] The dimension could be considered a part of dimension 4. However, it is hoped that this degree of differentiation will help the model be operationally more useful.
[6] Elliot Jaques has provided some stimulating analyses regarding this problem, some of which are discussed in subsequent chapters; see his *Measurement of Responsibility*, Harvard University Press, 1956.

tion in this model may refer to the individual, to the group, or to the organization. Second, when we say that "it" is doing something or other we are summarizing a complex state of affairs within the organism in question. In psychology we learn that when we say "he is perceiving" or "he is learning to read" we are summarizing an extremely complex set of interrelated activities not as yet fully understood.

The same is true for the group and the organization. We know very little about the internal processes of each. Actually, in terms of research, we know least about the nature of the complex organization's internal activities (for example, the business firm, the hospital, the school, and the governmental bureau). Acknowledging the lack of research in the area may be facing reality but it does not help us to explain the questions that must have been raised in the reader's mind when we said that "the organization" or "it" does such and such. Consequently, the following discussion is to be viewed only as a statement of an untested view presented primarily to indicate the direction of our thinking.

We have conceptualized organization as an interrelated set of parts striving to achieve a set of objectives. Exactly what one wishes to consider as parts of the organization depends on one's conceptual biases. These biases, in turn, usually depend on the state of the science, at a given moment, as well as the problems under study. The parts could be individuals, small groups, departments, or processes such as rewards and penalty, authority, and communication. One could also include, as we have, parts from all these different levels of analysis.

At the outset we stated that, for our purposes, we intended to conceptualize the organization as an open system. The system would have inputs, an internal structure, outputs, and feedback mechanisms. The internal structure, in turn, could be conceived as being composed of a number of subopen systems interrelated to create the whole.

Elsewhere we have attempted to present, in as much detail as possible at this time, a model of such a "total" organization.[7] If we examine the model, we will see it is composed of inputs (people with psychological energy) entering either a low- or high-skill world by going through a part called the personnel department. Each world requires certain behavior from the employees and gives something in return for this behavior. The model continues by showing that the "fit" between individual needs and organizational demands is very high. The consequences of this for the remainder of the organization are then conceptualized in terms of such variables as (1) productivity, (2) loyalty, (3) quality of work, (4) the influence on the leadership of the foremen, middle,

---

[7] *Understanding Organizational Behavior, op. cit.* The word total is in quotations to emphasize that we did not succeed in conceptualizing the total relevant variables.

and top management, and (5) the development of norms at all levels of the organization.

Actually, this is an extremely oversimplified description. The components of the model include employee needs, values, attitudes, concepts, procedures, conditions, and strategies that are linked together into a self-maintaining system.

Once the organization is conceptualized as a "total" open system, we may begin to make predictions about its behavior. Earlier we made predictions about the "parts" of the system as well as predictions about the system as a whole. Examples of the former were predictions of how the low-skill or high-skill employees would react to particular stresses. We also made some predictions as to how the foremen would react to the employee reaction.

The predictions about the organization as a whole were also stated. For example, we predicted that the organization would not change itself by internal causes. We concluded, for example, that the organization was so constituted that it would be unable to modify its internal activities. If changes were to occur they would have to be brought into the system from the environment. We then hypothesized how the organization as a whole would deal with these "externally caused" pressures for change.

The point that we are making is that organizations may be said to "do" something (for example, influence its internal activities) as long as we keep in mind that this phrase refers to a complicated set of internal processes which exist simultaneously and therefore defy simple unidimensional description.

There are two implications from this that cannot be overstressed. First, the data to decide whether or not a particular organization is doing something or can do something is *not* ascertained by simply asking all its members and then summing all the replies. Obtaining the employee attitudes, aspirations, self-concepts, perceptions of productivity and effectiveness is only a first step. These data must then be related with such organizational factors as the technology, managerial controls, rewards and penalties, norms, executive leadership, and policies and practices. Organizational mechanisms must also be inferred and made explicit by which these multilevel variables are connected into a self-maintaining system.

There are at least two tests we can apply to determine whether we have included the relevant parts. Once the model has been developed, we can see whether we are able to "derive" observable behavior such as the amount of absenteeism, turnover, and productivity. Another test is to make predictions concerning the probable behavior of the system as a whole (as well as of its parts) *if* certain changes are introduced into the system.[8]

The second point that cannot be overemphasized is that the open-system models of which we speak do not need to include explicitly the models used by management or certain seemingly crucial variables such as technology.

In the case of the former, if we examine our model of the firm, described earlier, we will *not* find the pyramidal structure discussed nor is there an extensive discussion of the various departments. This does not mean we have excluded them. In the case of the former, the power (for example) of the pyramidal structure is included through the discussion of the foremen's perception of their low status, the actions that management is able to take unilaterally, and so on. In departments, we found that all low-skill and all high-skill departments could be conveniently grouped into two respective "parts" because their properties (as we conceptualized them) were the same. The criteria to judge how many department-type parts should be included are still vague and unclear. At the moment, we hypothesize that the more the requirements made by the firm (through its technology, controls, and so on), the individual needs, the norms, the "outputs," and the management reactions are the same, the greater the probability that the departments will tend to be considered as one part. The less these types of factors are the same, the more the organization will be differentiated into parts that account for the differences.

Nor will anyone find a detailed discussion of the technology per se. But again this does *not* mean it has been excluded. As in the formal organizational structure, the relevance of the technology is included in terms of the impact it has on the groups' and individuals' behavior, attitudes, and values. Thus we found that all the low-skill employees, regardless of the nature of their work, tended to have certain similar attitudes and values. The same tended to be true of high-skill employees. We conceptualized, therefore, two "parts," the high- and low-skill worlds. Each "part" had its own norms. These values, attitudes, and norms are related in the model to the nature of the technology. Once this was done, every time we spoke of these values and attitudes we were speaking of variables that are partially (but significantly) caused by the technology.

The value of this approach is that it gives the model greater power for generalization. For example, with very little modification the model became equally valid for understanding an oil company or an electronic

[8] We attempted both of these in an extremely crude fashion in the previously cited study.

firm. Indeed, it may develop to be a general model for any firm that may conveniently be labeled as "paternalistic." If so, the fact that the technology was oil or electronic, that the budgets were type *a* or type *b*, made little difference. They are phenotypes or "samples" of the more underlying or genotypic factors conceptualized in terms of the impact of technology and managerial controls on the participants.

Mutual Dependence of Dimension

Returning to the discussion of the mix model, we see that it is important to emphasize that each dimension is conceived to be mutually dependent on the other dimensions. A change in any one dimension, in any direction, under a given or subset of dimensions needs to be discovered through systematic empirical research. It may be, for example, that a change in dimension 1 going toward the essential properties of organization will influence the remaining dimensions differently, depending on their state (that is, their position on each continuum). It is important to keep in mind that these dimensions must be viewed in their interrelationship with the other dimensions. Thus we can picture a highly authoritarian organization having control over its internal activities. These activities would therefore be located close to the right end of dimension 4. However, the activities of such an organization in dimensions 1 and 2 will probably be located close to the left ends of the continua (because in an authoritarian organization a few parts control the whole). Clearly the number of possible combinations is so large and the relationships so many that much empirical research will be required to make explicit the possible combinations. As these various combinations or the "profile" of each complex organization is developed then each profile can be compared with such independent criteria as "survival," "financial effectiveness," and "productivity." As these studies develop we will then be able to state generalizations about the effectiveness of various organizations' profiles as they strive to achieve their objectives in a particular environment.

Formulating these dimensions it begins to look as if the pyramidal organization does not tend to approximate the essential properties of organization. Indeed, it actually emphasizes a strategy that is closer to the left ends of our continua. For example, the principle of chain of command tends to place control in a few parts. In combination with task specialization, it tends to create among the participants an awareness of parts, but minimizes the patterning of parts. The adaptive activities tend to create a system that is less able to influence its internally oriented core activities. The parts are designed to be oriented primarily toward their own objectives and not those of the organization as a whole. (The latter is the primary responsibility of top management.) The time perspective of the employees, especially at the lower levels, is primarily limited to the present.

This does not imply that we believe the pyramidal organization is bad. We are simply trying to point out that rather than the pyramidal structure approximating the properties of the construct, organization, it actually tends to go away from them. The implications of this for organizational effectiveness have yet to be established. It may well be that organizations that approximate the left ends of the continua tend to be more effective. We wish to emphasize that a whole range of organizational strategies may exist for experimentation that approximate more closely the essential properties of organization. It may be that these alternatives will present us with strategies that can lead to more effective organizations.

In terms of our analysis, this would give us organizations that have increased amounts of psychological energy available for productive efforts as well as organizations that are not full of the nonproductive, compulsive, energy-consuming activities outlined in the previous chapter. According to our view, increased psychological energy may be obtained by offering the employees greater opportunity for psychological success. It also has been our view that as psychological success increases, it should set the stage for a decrease in the nonproductive activities that consume much energy.

The question arises, if we were to develop new organizational strategies that tended to mirror the right ends of the continua, would they tend to lead to increased opportunity for psychological success? The answer, we believe, is in the affirmative. As the organization approximates the right ends of the continua, the individual should be in a world in which he has greater power and control over his work world (dimension 1), where he actually perceives this control (2), where the objectives that he is achieving are central ones (3), where he has a relevant influence over the internal and external activities (4 and 5) so that he is not like a helpless individual being pushed and pulled by forces that are not under his control, and where his time perspective is expanded (6).

These conditions seem to be consonant with the requirements for psychological success. For example, the individual will tend to have a greater opportunity:

1. to define goals that are central (since his work is related to important objectives, 1, 2, and 3)
2. to define the paths to these goals (4) and therefore
3. to develop a realistic level of aspiration with a long time perspective (6) which
4. should have a greater probability for achievement because of his increased control over the internal and the external factors (4 and 5) in his environment.

But these are not the only pay-offs if we are able to devise organizations that tend to approximate the essential properties of the construct organization. In addition to creating increased opportunities for psychological success, the same organization may well increase the opportunities for increased individual mental health. Such a situation would not only tend to enhance the amount of productive energy available for work but, according to some personality theorists, it could increase the flexibility and the possibilities for creative effort in the organization.

The question arises if there is any correspondence between the right ends of the continua and individual mental health? Theoretically, we would expect such a correspondence because a "good" (personality) organization is usually equated by many personality theorists to mental health.

Positive Mental Health

Mental health is an extremely complex concept that is presently undergoing serious reexamination. The views range from the idea that the concept is invalid [9] to the idea that it is akin to the overall notions such as thermodynamics.[10] It is neither within our scope nor competence to discuss the merits and demerits of each view. To progress with our position we are going to make an assumption that an earlier review of the personality literature [11] and, more important, a more recent review by Jahoda on "positive mental health" adequately represent some important dimensions of individual mental health.[12] We are *not* suggest-

---

[9] Thomas S. Szasz, "The Myth of Mental Illness," *American Psychology*, Vol. 15, No. 2, February 1960, pp. 113–118; and "The Classification of 'Mental Illness,'" *Psychiatric Quarterly*, January 1959, pp. 1–25.
[10] M. B. Smith, "Mental Health Reconsidered: A Special Case of the Problem of Values in Psychology," *American Psychology*, Vol. 16, No. 6, 1961, pp. 299–306.
[11] Chris Argyris, *Personality Fundamentals for Administrators*, Yale Labor and Management Center, 1951.
[12] Marie Jahoda, *Positive Mental Health*, Basic Books, New York, 1958.

ing that Jahoda's conception exhausts the possibilities. We are simply assuming that all of Jahoda's dimensions are necessary but may not be sufficient for understanding individual mental health. We are not implying that the dimensions have been empirically demonstrated. We are simply assuming that when such research is conducted these dimensions will not be invalidated. Admittedly, these are assumptions, but they are necessary if we are not going to be blocked from continuing.

Beginning with the writer's less authoritative review, he found that the concept of individual mental health emphasized the same or similar values as those of the essential properties of organization (that is, the right ends of the continua in our model). For example, mental health apparently includes the ability to be aware of reality that exists "out there" as well as that which exists internally. A healthy individual strives to be aware and accepting of his self (dimension 2). This includes being aware of as many parts as possible (2), that the parts are seen as being interrelated correctly with each other (1), and that the individual develops a clarity of his self-image to the point that he knows who he is and does not feel basic doubts about his inner identity (2).

Moreover, the healthy individual manifests an integration of the parts (self) so that there is a balance among the psychic forces (1). This will tend to result in flexibility and the ability to control his impulses, purposes, acts, thoughts, and feelings (3). Also, the individual is able to regulate his behavior from within (3). In other words, he is able to influence his internally and externally oriented activities as he deems necessary (3 and 4).

The individual strives continuously to face reality and to solve problems effectively (a dimension to be added in a subsequent chapter). This includes adequate searching activity which in turn is based on perceiving reality correctly and manifesting minimal distortion. Then there occurs the consideration of alternative actions, a decision is implemented. In making decisions the past and the future are considered along with the present.

In a more systematic study Jahoda presents a series of dimensions of positive mental health which are also similar to, or consonant with, the right ends of the continua in our model. For example, the individual should be aware of, and feel responsible for, his major feelings, impulses, and capacities. The self-concept should contain an image of all important aspects of the person (1 and 2). Positive mental health means a successful synthesis of who the person is, where he is, and what he wishes to be (6). His behavior is increasingly determined by his total self-concept (3). There is an integration of the parts (one example, id, ego, and superego) in such a way that the behavior is determined by a "balanced integration" of these three instead of the domination by any one (1).

The individual is concerned with the environment. He attempts to adapt to it through "giving to it" and modifying it where necessary (2). There is a wide "range" and high quality of concern for other people and "for the things of this world" (5). The individual tends to have a unifying outlook on life, a possession of long-range goals as well as an appropriate connection with the past (6).

Finally, the behavior tends to be regulated from within (4). The healthy, flexible individual has access to all the parts of his experience and of his self (1). The rational ego is not constantly in authoritarian control but at appropriate times relinquishes control to the id or super-ego—Kris's "voluntary regression" in service of the ego (1). The healthy individual functions as a totality and is controlled and created through the interrelationships of all the relevant parts of his self (4). He is aware of the pattern of parts and is able to influence his adjustment and adaptation as he finds it necessary (2 and 4). This implies that he is capable of effective problem solving. Thus the psychologically healthy individual strives to be self-responsible, self-directed, self-motivated, aspires toward excellence in problem solving, strives to decrease his defensive and compulsive behavior, to be fully functioning, and so on. Kubie,[13] Fromm,[14] and Rogers[15] believe individual mental health, not neuroticism, are the deepest sources of productivity and creativity.

Perhaps this is enough to suggest that the nature of positive mental health as seen by one group of researchers tends to be consonant with the essential properties of organization. In other words, the model that we have presented to describe the values implicit in the construct organization may also be valid for the individual level as well as for the organization.

We can now conclude that there is a greater possibility of integrating the individual and the organization so as to begin to correct the problems discussed earlier *if* the individuals aspire toward positive mental health and *if* the organization is modified to approximate more closely the right ends of the continua in what we shall henceforth identify as the "mix" model presented earlier.

We realize that there probably are limits to our view. There are limits,

[13] Lawrence Kubie, *Neurotic Distortion of the Creative Process*, University of Kansas Press, 1958.
[14] Erich Fromm, "The Creative Attitude," in Harold H. Anderson (Ed.), *Creativity and Its Cultivation*, Harper, New York, 1959, pp. 44–54.
[15] Carl R. Rogers, "Toward a Theory of Creativity," in Harold H. Anderson (Ed.), *Creativity and Its Cultivation*, Harper, New York, 1959, pp. 69–82.

for example, to the number of organizations to which an individual may belong that require that he aspire toward psychological success and individual mental health. Such aspirations are difficult to have and to fulfill. They may well tire the individual. He will need an opportunity to rest and to recoup if he is to continue. Thus if one were to develop organizations with a perfect fit between the individual needs and its demands, this would not mean that the organization would always obtain the maximum output from each individual.

However, if we understand psychological theory, frequency of necessity as well as the time necessary to recoup from psychological success tend to be much lower than the frequency and time necessary to recoup from boredom and psychological failure. As Kubie has suggested, there may be no such thing as "hard work" if it is meaningful work. Thus the degree to which an individual is able to respond appropriately to an "ideal" situation is partially a function of the quality and quantity of his participation in other organizations.

Another limitation is the degree to which organizations can approximate the essential properties of organization. As we have often said, the technology, the managerial controls, the financial status of the organization can act to limit the possibilities for redesign. We must discover these limits through research and experimentation. We will have to study various "mixes" of individual and organizational requirements and see what are the resulting "costs" to the individual and to the organization. It may well be that the organization that approximates the right ends of the continua will tend to be less effective in "real" life. We doubt this but the answer can best come from research. This is one of the values of the model that we have presented. It can be used as a basis for describing organizations and comparing their costs and outputs. For example, it might be possible to describe organizations whose "profiles" along our dimensions range from being at the extreme left end to the middle to the right end of the continua.

As results are understood and communicated, it becomes the practitioner's responsibility to decide what costs (individual and organizational) they are willing to incur. Thus we are *not* suggesting that people must develop organizations of the kind that we plan to outline in the next part. We are suggesting that if one wishes to decrease the organizational difficulties described earlier, one way to do so is to design organizations that approximate more closely the right ends of the continua in the "mix" model.

Empirical Work Illustrating
Aspects of the "Mix" Model

In the previous chapter we conceptualized what seemed to us to be some of the essential properties of the construct organization. We pointed out that the resulting model is also a construct, an analytical guess. The next requirement is to use the model in conducting research.

The model can be used in several ways. One is to study various different kinds of organizations to see where they can be placed along each of the continua in the mix model. A "profile" can be developed therefore of each organization. One interesting possibility is to compare the profiles of a business organization, a church, a jail, the Central Intelligence Agency, a trade union, a school, and so on. Are the profiles different or are they somewhat similar? Another possibility is to compare the profiles of the same type of organization. It might be found, for example, that two jails differ from each other more than a jail and a school.

Still another possibility is to construct a profile of the same organization as it exists over time. How stable are the profiles? Do changes occur frequently or infrequently? Under what conditions do profiles change? Finally, we can compare the profiles as different key changes are instituted. For example, does the profile of a firm change significantly after it has undergone decentralization? If not, why not? If so, how much? Perhaps one way to measure the degree of decentralization is to ascertain to what extent the profile moves toward the right ends of the continua.

The profiles can also be developed at several different levels. Theoretically, it is possible to construct a profile for every individual in the entire organization. Indeed, it may well be that the profiles can serve as a quantitative indicator of the degree of "fusion" of the individual and the organization. Perhaps the profiles of the individual can serve as the basis for the studies in the "organizational epidemiological studies" mentioned in the previous chapter. If so, the individual profiles can also provide valuable assistance in problems of selection, training, manning teams, and promotion.

Formal and informal groups can also be studied to develop a profile for each. The department head can then have an analysis of his group which he can compare with other groups as well as with the organization as a whole.

It should be emphasized that the profile of the organization as a whole is not constructed simply by "adding up" all the profiles of the individuals and the groups. As we pointed out in the previous chapter, the analysis of the organization as a whole includes data from individuals and groups but each proceeds along different lines. The precise differences have yet to be made explicit. This is another empirical research task suggested by the model.

Finally, the use of the mix model need not be limited to describing the "steady state" of various organizations and their subunits. The mix model can also be used to conceptualize organizational change. What kind of change processes are used in the organizations? What profiles do they have? Do the profiles of the change proccesses vary by organization, by the nature of what is being changed, by the type of management philosophy?

All these suggested studies essentially describe without evaluating the state of things.

Another way that the mix model might be used is to correlate the profile of any organization (or any of its subunits) with its output-input ratio as well as with its capacity to correct its own behavior. It may be that certain profiles tend to lead to more outputs and less inputs, or increasing outputs with constant inputs. Also, certain profiles might be correlated with the competence of the system to correct its internal behavior. These studies are also descriptive. The difference is that they strive to relate the profile to some criterion that is external to the profile. It is these kinds of studies that will yield insights into when an organization is effective, ineffective, or pseudo-effective.

Obviously, all of these studies go beyond the scope of this book. In deed, one objective of the book has been to make explicit some of the possible research directions implicit in the mix model.

There is, however, one exercise that we may attempt. We have implied that organizations will tend to be more effective, in terms of such factors as employee commitment to productivity, employee flexibility, and satisfaction, as the organization approximates the right ends of the continua of the mix model. We have not been able to present any research to confirm these hypotheses because to do so would mean the postponement of writing anything for at least a decade.

However, it is possible to see if the existing literature illustrates these hypotheses. In doing so, it should be clear that we are *not* suggesting that this provides any kind of test of the hypotheses. Only with specifically designed and controlled field or laboratory studies can we speak of testing the hypotheses. Our objective is to indicate the *plausibility* of our view. Since our objective is one of indicating plausibility, we have been "liberal" in including research ranging from carefully controlled studies to speculative but thoughtful analyses.

Another point to remember is that the mix model is supposed to be valid for the individual, group, and organizational levels of analysis. Consequently, we will draw on research and speculation from small groups as well as organizational studies.[1]

Dimension One

In dimension 1, we hypothesize that as power becomes concentrated in one or a few subsets of parts, human difficulties will tend to arise. On the other hand, positive attitudes, commitment, and the like should be correlated with a distribution of power throughout the organization that is less arbitrary and provides the subparts an increasing degree of control.

Traditional Organization Approximates Left Ends of Continuum

We saw that the parts of the organization following the principle of "scientific management" are interrelated in such a way that one or a

---

[1] The personality studies will not be repeated since they were discussed in the previous chapter.

few subsets of parts control the whole. This organizational strategy assumes that the best way to achieve the objectives of the organization is to require the workers, for example, to produce shoes and not to be concerned with maintaining the system. The responsibility for maintaining the internal system is assigned to management, which is also assigned the power to reward, penalize, and control. According to our model, this would tend to approximate the left ends of the continuum; the literature should offer evidence of unintended consequences that are in line with our framework.

First, unilateral power seems to lead to coercion. In an extensive review of the literature, Bass reports that recipients of coercion tend to react to power by becoming hostile, withdrawn, by overreacting, and becoming poor in upward communicating.[2] Unilateral power can lead to greater defensive behavior,[3] poorer group selection,[4] and decreasing effectiveness.[5] Under conditions of decreasing effectiveness, the need for unilateral leadership appears to increase. Thus the need for unilateral leadership traditionally associated with organizations may be a self-fulfilling prophecy.[6] The authority given to a manager (who represents only part of the organization) to direct and control may be more in the interests of *maintaining the strategy* selected than in achieving the core activities.

The proponents of the traditional organizational strategy have offered little advice as to how to deal with these difficulties. Although acknowledged, they are viewed as "weaknesses of man," which are best resolved by building "loyalty," "high morale," and *"esprit de corps."* In other words, although the organizational strategy focuses primarily on achieving the goals of the organization, it (probably unintentionally) creates difficult problems for internal maintenance and external adaptation of the system. Unfortunately, little attention has been placed on developing effective means for dealing with these problems. The strategy of scientific management may be weakest where it creates the most difficult problems.

[2] Bernard M. Bass, *Leadership, Psychology, and Organizational Behavior*, Harper, New York, 1960, pp. 232–235.
[3] C. A. Gibb, "An International View of the Emergency of Leadership," *American Psychology*, Vol. 9, 1954, p. 502 (abstract).
[4] R. B. Cattell, "On the Theory of Group Learning," *Journal of Social Psychology*, Vol. 37, 1953, pp. 27–52.
[5] N. Maccoby, "Research Findings on Productivity, Supervision, and Morale," in *Research on Human Relations in Administration*, Institute of Social Research, University of Michigan.
[6] Bernard M. Bass, *op. cit.*, p. 134.

Adaptive Activities Arise That Take Organizations in the Direction of the Right Ends of the Continua

Organizations, however, do survive and perform with some degree of effectiveness. It is suggested that one important reason may be that they eventually develop a new and more functional set of relationships that begin to approximate the right ends of the continua. These developments are not necessarily preplanned and rationally executed throughout the entire organization. What may happen is that subunits modify their internal make-up and relationship with those from which they draw and to which they contribute. These parts, in turn, adapt with their own modifications. Sometimes these modifications become too threatening to the pyramidal order and they are disallowed. At other times the subunits bring to bear another set of power relationships in order to institutionalize the modifications they desire (for example, a trade union). Slowly a new structure of relationship evolves which is an integrated conglomeration of the pyramidal strategy, the informal activities, and the individual needs.

For example, in one organization a "product test" department was created as the final checkpoint for the quality of the product. Its approval meant that the company assured the customer that the product met the specifications. Understandably, the engineering and production departments saw "product test" as a thorn in their side. They were in continuous argument insisting that the products were ready and that the product test people were being too picayune. Product test, in turn, denied that they were trying to be difficult and accused the other departments on various counts all amounting to an evasion of high quality. The constant bickering had been predicted by the top management. They felt that the constant competition would lead to better quality. This did tend to occur.

But it was not the only thing that occurred. As products began to pile up in product test, pressure was put on them to test quicker. The product test people felt that they could not perform an adequate job in the decreasing time allotted to them. It was not long before the people at the lowest levels began to make informal "deals" with engineering and production. For example, if production held up a particular batch, product test interpreted the standards of another troublesome batch slightly more leniently, thereby relieving production of the stigma.

Burns describes a very common example in terms of the constant battles between the sales group and those responsible for design. Each group tended to believe that its contribution was "the" major one and that if it were not for its skill the organization would probably "fold up." As a result each side believed that it rightly should command a greater share of the scarce resources available and a greater influence over changes in product as well as operating plans. The long-standing and deep-rooted division between sales and engineering served as a frontier along which divisions of opinion and rival sets of considerations tended to range themselves. To overcome these difficulties, a new department was added which acted as a "go-between" the two warring factions as well as a "product meeting" which was a coordinating committee of the two sides.[7]

Other similar examples can be found to develop between time and motion experts, employees and foremen, salesmen and production people, and so on. Indeed the entire set of informal activities described in Part I that are developed at the top and lower levels are also illustrations of this point.

Research Illustrating the Predicted Consequences of Approximating the Right Ends of the Continua

According to our model, it would help to reduce these problems if the distribution of influence and power were changed among the parts in the direction of giving more influence to the parts. This does not mean that power among parts would not exist in the effective organization. It would exist, but the difference lies in its source and distribution. Power would be more functionally related to the requirements of achieving the core activities and less to the particular strategy employed to achieve these core activities; the power that Mary Parker Follet calls the "authority of the situation." In our terms power for any given part is derived from the essentiality of that part to the whole. In other words, the authority in these relationships lies in the requirements necessary to fulfill the core activities. An individual's "authority" is a function of his contribution to fulfill the core activities.

If the interrelationships of parts are conceived in terms of feedback and interaction, research can be cited to illustrate the importance of mutual influence among the parts for the maintenance of the whole. For example, Leavitt and Mueller [8] suggest that the presence or absence of feedback affects the relationships among individuals. In communications among members "zero feedback" was accompanied by low con-

---

[7] Tom Burns, "Ends and Means in Management," Social Sciences Research Centre, University of Edinburgh, April 1962, mimeographed, pp. 8–11.

[8] H. J. Leavitt and R. A. H. Mueller, "Some Effects of Feedback on Communications," *Human Relations*, Vol. 4, 1957, pp. 401–410.

fidence and hostility; "free feedback" was accompanied by high confidence and amity. Similarly, Lazarsfeld, Berelson, and Gaudet,[9] and Katz and Lazarsfeld [10] observe that personal interaction is likely to produce more change in opinion than mass communications from "above." Their results could be interpreted as meaning that the "parts" in a community may be influenced more effectively through personal, face-to-face interaction in which a greater degree of mutuality of influence is developed.

Bass reports that change of openness occurs most effectively under conditions of group discussion and group decision where the probability for mutual interaction and influence is greatest. Bass concludes that (1) more changes occur when interaction is possible, (2) the changes occur faster, (3) interaction itself brings rewards not possible to individuals in isolation, and (4) isolated individuals are likely to reduce the variability of their behavior or withdrew from the environment if it is not stimulating.[11] Likert concludes, "employees who feel more free to set their own work pace prove to be more productive than those who lack this sense of freedom." [12] Also, "freedom in doing one's work is associated with higher productivity." [13] And, "these results demonstrate that the capacity to exert influence upward is essential if a supervisor (or manager) is to perform his supervisory functions successfully." [14] Also, "the men in the high producing departments, in contrast with the men in the low, feel that more influence is exercised at every hierarchical level." [15] Finally, Likert summarizes the findings about influence by suggesting the more multiple linkages among groups, the more influence the participants may have. The greater the influence, the stronger the cohesiveness, the loyalty, the commitment, the identification, the cooperation within and among parts of the organization.[16] Mann and Hoffman found that in a new automated power plant the new technology brought about more equality between management and the workers as a result of a greater mutual dependence on each other. Intrinsic job satisfaction and commitment were higher under these conditions.[17]

---

[9] P. F. Lazarsfeld, B. Berelson, and H. Gaudet, *The People's Choice*, Duell, Sloan and Pearce, New York, 1944.
[10] E. Katz and P. F. Lazarsfeld, *Personal Influence*, Free Press, Glencoe, Ill., 1955.
[11] Bernard M. Bass, *op. cit.*, p. 16.
[12] Rensis Likert, *New Patterns of Management*, McGraw-Hill, New York, 1961.
[13] *Ibid.*, p. 21.
[14] *Ibid.*, p. 114.
[15] *Ibid.*, p. 55.
[16] *Ibid.*, pp. 181–182.
[17] Floyd Mann and Richard Hoffman, *Automation and the Worker*, Holt, New York, 1960, pp. 79–103.

Further illustrations of the pay-off in giving the parts (in this case employees) increasing influence over the whole come from a study by Melman. In a systematic analysis and comparison of two types of managerial philosophy he concludes that the management that develops an employee decision-making structure, so that the employee can participate in important production decisions, tends to have a more efficient and effective organization. For example, production costs are lower and wages much higher than in organizations producing similar products with only a management decision-making structure.[18]

Indik, Georgopoulos, and Seashore illustrate the same point in a carefully analyzed study of individual, group, and intergroup levels in twenty-seven suborganizations, including nearly one thousand individuals. They concluded that a high level of performance was positively associated with (1) a relatively high degree of mutual understanding of others' viewpoints and problems among those that work together, (2) a relatively high degree of local influence and autonomy on work-related matters, and (3) openness of communication channels between superiors and subordinates.[19]

Recently, the management, employees, trade union officials, and social scientists have cooperated to develop within a British industrial corporation (Glacier Metal) policies and practices which have significantly increased the mutual influence of all the participants (including customers) apparently without jeopardizing (indeed by strengthening) the executive system (which, in this case, includes employees). Briefly, Glacier has developed a set of interlocking systems (in addition to the executive) called the representative, legislative, and appeals policies and procedures. Through these systems all participants are offered increased influence over, *and* responsibility for, the effectiveness of the organization.[20]

Some other examples of the possible pay-off of increasing the influence of the parts on the whole are the bomber crews in combat. The pilot is in control only under certain conditions. At times the navigator is in control on the way to the target. As the bomber approaches the target the bombardier takes control. Another example is an operating team performing surgery. Temple Burling has shown that if one observes who is actually initiating action to whom during an operation he will find that, along with the surgeons, the anesthetist and the surgical

[18] Seymour Melman, *Decision-Making and Productivity*, Wiley, New York, 1958.
[19] Bernard P. Indik, Basil S. Georgopoulos, and Stanley E. Seashore, "Superior-Subordinate Relationships and Performance," *Personnel Psychology*, Vol. XIV, No. 4, Winter 1961, p. 357.
[20] Wilfred Brown, *Explorations in Management*, Heinemann, London, 1960.

nurses are at various times in control. Finally, a leading consulting firm utilizes "teams" to solve client problems that are organized according to the potential contribution that each individual can make to the problem. It is possible for a vice president (who is a physicist) to report to a young chemist if the chemist is the man who is seen as having the primary background necessary to resolve the problem. The chemist's position may also shift, if the nature of the problem shifts.

The reader may be interested to learn of a pioneering experiment being conducted in a plant where the traditional concepts of power are being seriously questioned. In this organization, the plan is to give any individual the organizational power as a function of what he contributes to decision making, regardless of his position in the hierarchy. If he is capable of providing much help for a particular decision, the concomitant organizational power will be given to him. The amount of organizational power an individual (or department) is given varies from decision to decision depending on the role he (it) plays in that department. One of the difficulties encountered is to develop how one is to decide who is capable of helping and who is not. Apparently, the difficult issues are not related to ascertaining who is professionally or technically competent, although there are such difficulties. The biggest difficulties are related to the problem of who is to be promoted and rewarded in the organization. Everyone seems to want to participate as many decisions as possible.

In this experiment, thought is now being given to changing the financial rewards system along similar lines. In the traditional scheme organizational power is fixed and static. Mr. A is assigned a particular responsibility and given a particular scope of authority. Mr. A's wages tend to correlate with the authority and responsibility assigned to him. In the example just cited, the organization is conceived as a series of problem-solving processes, some very simple and some highly complex. Following the first, second, and third dimensions, as many parts are included in a decision as necessary. A given individual, Mr. A, receives organizational power as a function of his contribution to a particular decision. Similarly, his wages might also be computed as a function of his contribution in the decision-making process.

An important point to note is that power and control are not necessarily eliminated. The key is to provide the participants with the control over the use of power, managerial controls, and so on. A part can dominate if the participants representing the whole decide that this direction is necessary if the core activities are to be carried on effectively. The domination of a given part is controlled by the whole. (More illustrative details are given in the next chapter.)

It should also be noted, even if only in passing, that in real life the formal centralization of power is not the only way one part or subset of parts dominates the whole. Domination can occur by function. For example, in some organizations the sales department, in others, the manufacturing, and still others, research and development, dominates the organization.

Dimension Two

Traditional Organizations Approximate the Left Ends of the Continua

Few administrators seem to take the second dimension seriously.[21] Many managers, in fact, find it easier to deal with the organization as if it were a discrete set of unrelated parts. For example, they make decisions continually about one department, apparently expecting them not to affect the total organization. The philosophy of managerial controls such as budgets, incentive systems, and industrial engineering compound this practice. Budgets, for example, split an organization into a plurality of discrete parts. The unity, if it is to exist, is to be found in the office of the top official. Such situations lead to very few people in the organization being aware of, and experiencing a feeling of responsibility for, the pattern (that is, the whole organization). Moreover, if the top management performs their coordination function well, it can be shown that they will tend to inhibit the expression of the next dimension, which will be discussed later.[22]

Some Reasons and Consequences for Approximating the Right Ends of the Continua

Organizations are open systems and thus are exposed to random and unpredictable crises from the environment. In this connection, Thompson and Hawkes have presented an intriguing analysis of how communities respond to stress. Their analysis seems relevant to organizations. Under extreme stress, they suggest, resources become scarce, the parts have tremendous pressure placed on them, and competition among parts

---

[21] The literature is full of supportive examples. See the work of E. W. Bakke, Ernest Dale, Robert Dubin, Mason Haire, Robert Guest, Douglas McGregor, and William F. Whyte.

[22] Chris Argyris, "Human Problems with Budgets," *Harvard Business Review*, Vol. 31, No. 1, January–February 1953, pp. 96–110.

becomes severe for the establishing of priorities and allocating scarce resources. All these factors combine to yield more widespread and deeper conflicts among the parts than existed in the normal state.

To make matters even more difficult, the parts are usually required to increase the rate of interaction and interdependence. We may hypothesize that under these conditions an awareness of the whole by the parts would seem to be of great assistance to an organization [23] because they would be better able to plan how much and in what directions to increase their interaction rate, and at the same time predict more accurately the probable impact of these increases on the organization.

Second, as we have seen, the moment organizations use human beings as agents who aspire toward psychological success, it becomes very costly to dominate and control their behavior completely. Consequently, more individual autonomy should pay off for the organization. An awareness by the parts of the whole now becomes especially necessary. It should aid (other positive factors being present) in increasing the probability that the parts will act in the interest of the whole.

Third, research was also cited in Part I that organizations tend to have information-processing problems. The higher up one goes, the greater the probability of distortion of information. Moreover, interpersonal relations, we suggested, tend to develop among executives which tend to increase conformity, mistrust, and fears. Thus there may be structural and interpersonal factors that greatly decrease the probability that all the relevant information will be sent to he top. Finally, even if all the information could be sent to the top there is serious question whether executives, who because of their finiteness as human beings, could process all the information in time to reach proper decisions.[24] As we have indicated by the work of Miller and others, man is a finite information-processing system with clear and important limitations.

A fourth reason why it may be important for the parts to be aware of the whole is that frequently organizations are faced with distributing scarce resources. In order to make effective decisions about the share of the resources allocated to each part, knowledge must be available concerning the actual needs of the parts. Parts may define their needs partially as a function of what they know that they need and believe that they will need. However, they may be able to make more effective estimates if they are aware of the organization's needs. This requires that they become aware of the interdependence among the parts.

[23] James D. Thompson and Robert N. Hawkes, "Disaster, Community Organization and Administrative Process," University of Pittsburgh, mimeographed, 1962.
[24] It remains to be seen if our computer technology can resolve this problem.

Because of these conditions, an organization can increase its effectiveness by making certain the parts are able to make as many decisions as possible at the local level. This requires parts that have the authority and are willing to act responsibly. To act responsibly, the parts will need to be aware of their own interdependency problems, as well as those of the organization as a whole.

Being aware of the wholeness of the organization may also help to provide the participants with a manageable (conceptual) picture to use to identify with the organization. Such a manageable picture may tend to aid in increasing the employees' feelings of responsibility or commitment to the organization. At the same time, developing a picture of the uniqueness of the organization (its organizational charter), to quote Bakke, is valuable for communicating to the outside world the "personality" of the organization. Such knowledge can significantly influence the type of person attracted to the organization as an employee. It also influences customers (individual or other organizations) in deciding whether they wish to conduct business with the organization.

Dimension Three

In dimension 3 we hypothesize that (*a*) it is necessary for the parts of organizations to be required to achieve goals that are clearly related to the organization as a whole and (*b*) that such a requirement tends to give the objective a strong influence over the internal make-up of the organization.

Let us focus first on the latter hypothesis. Many writers have implied that the definition of goals is probably the crucial activity in an organization. It is in this dimension that the more traditional theorists such as Gulick, Fayol, Urwick, and Mooney (to name but a few) have made excellent contributions. Goals define the character of the organization. Selznick, discussing goals in terms of commitments, states:

The systematized commitments of an organization define its character. Day-to-day decisions, relevant to the actual problems met in the translation of policy into action, create precedents, alliances, effective symbols, and personal loyalties which transform the organization from a profane, manipulable instrument into something having a sacred status and thus resistant to treatment simply as a means to some external goal. That is why organizations are often cast aside when new goals are sought. . . .
So long as goals are given, and the impulse to act persists, there will be a

series of enforced lines of action demanded by the nature of the tools at hand. The commitment may lead to unanticipated consequences resulting in a deflection of original goals.[25]

Sells [26] has pointed out that the goals can greatly influence the behavior of the participants. For example, he notes that as long as no cure was available for paralysis the National Foundation for Infantile Paralysis had a visible goal. All its efforts were clearly directed to a particular end. However, once it looked as if this goal was to be realized, new goals had to be developed if the organization was to be maintained. Our history suggests that such organizations as colleges, birth control foundations, anti-slavery movements, youth organizations (Y.M.C.A.), and service organizations (Red Cross) have all experienced the problem of changing goals, or as Blau has called the process, "succession of goals." [27] Thus the formal organization adherents are correct in saying that without goals an organization can develop serious crises and can begin to disintegrate. An excellent example is the Red Cross, which went through a period of slow decay because its original goals were no longer relevant to the societies in which it was embedded.[28]

A large utility recently altered its goals to include more of a marketing orientation. The new emphasis was to sell more telephone service, as well as the historical goal of giving good service. This has had important impacts on the internal system. New managers had to be developed (some brought in from the outside) in order to instill the organization with the idea of selling. Programs have been started to legitimize "selling" to the employees, many of whom, even at the management level, might be described as bewildered by the change of emphasis.

Banks are another example. As soon as the objectives of banks were altered to include reaching the small-loan market, new personnel was required to deal with the new problems. Some of these workers were so different from the traditional "right type" the banks typically hired that they left. Those who chose to remain reported experiencing some strong frustrations.[29]

[25] Philip Selznick, *TVA and the Grass Roots*, University of California Press, 1949, pp. 258–259.
[26] David L. Sells, "The Succession of Goals," *The Volunteers*, Free Press, Glencoe, Ill., 1957.
[27] Peter Blau, *The Dynamics of Bureaucracy*, University of Chicago Press, 1955, p. 195.
[28] Foster R. Dulles, *The American Red Cross: A History*, Harper, New York, 1950.
[29] Chris Argyris, "Conceptualizing the Human Climate in a Bank," *Administrative Science Quarterly*, Vol. 2, No. 3, March 1958.

Cressey [30] has shown that the internal system of prisons can be significantly influenced by the goals. Typically, society assigns retribution, deterrence, and reformation as goals to prisons. Some prison managers interpret these major goals into subgoals. One group seems to believe that the task of a prison is to understand and treat prisoners. The guards attempted to be understanding, not to be immediately punitive, and to see violations as inability to conform rather than intentional violations. Another group of persons developed their goal in terms of protecting society from the prisoners. Their internal system, the behavior of the guards, the perception of the prisoners were significantly different. Thus inmates were officially viewed as dangerous, conniving men who required strict discipline and were continuously mistrusted.

Thompson and Bates suggested four other conditions under which objectives can influence the nature of the organization. They are related to the degree of concreteness of the goals and the flexibility of the technology required to achieve the goal.

1. If the product is concrete, such as mined material, and the technology unadaptable, the major organizational concerns will be the possibility that the environment may reject or dispense with the product.
2. If the product is concrete or tangible and the technology adaptable, the major concerns will be when to shift to new products and which of the possible alternate uses of the technology present the most factorable opportunities. For example, should the manufacturer shift to cosmetic jewelry, to armament mechanisms, or to still another product calling for the machinery and skills at his disposal.
3. If the product is abstract and the technology adaptable, the organization again has great adaptability to its environment, and the major problem will be achieving agreement on goals and on the appropriate application of technologies in pursuit of them.
4. If the product is abstract but the technology unadaptable, environmental redefinition of goals presents a serious threat to the organization, since the technology can be adapted to redefined goals only within limits. The administrative problem here is to "educate" or influence relevant parts of the environment to accept those products that are possible with existing technology.[31]

[30] Donald C. Cressey, "Achievement of an Unstated Organizational Goal," *Pacific Sociological Review*, Vol. I, 1958, pp. 43–49.
[31] James D. Thompson and Fredrick L. Bates, "Technology, Organization, and Administration," *Administrative Science Quarterly*, Vol. 2, No. 2, December 1957, pp. 326–343.

In formal organizations, we will find that it is often difficult to ascertain precisely the goals of the organization. In a way this is odd because, as we have pointed out, goals or objectives are considered the crucial activity in formal organizational theory, from which internal maintenance and external adaptation flow. Dent [32] has shown that the definition of objectives may vary according to several variables. The larger the organization, the greater the concern with "good product" and "effective service" as well as the greater interest in serving the community. However, there is no apparent relationship between "broader social responsibilities" and the growth of the business. Dent suggests that the larger the size, the greater the probability of public attention focusing on it. Therefore, the greater the necessity to "look good." Katona [33] found that organizations under financial stress define their objectives in terms of quick profits and liquidity. On the other hand, the well-established firm is likely to define its objectives in longer time perspective and broader responsibilities.

Traditional Organization Approximates the Left Ends of the Continua

During the discussion of the human problems at the managerial level we saw that the traditional organization tends to be designed with each part having a specific objective. Interrelating these objectives does not tend to be the responsibility of each part. Their responsibility is to be concerned about their own goals. The overall integration, if it is to occur, officially is the responsibility of the superiors.

These conditions, as we have seen, tend to lead to interpersonal and interdepartmental rivalries. These, in turn, tend to lead to each department defining appropriate defensive mechanisms to protect itself from the others and from above.

Adaptive Activities Are Developed That Begin to Approximate the Right Ends of the Continua

As we saw in the discussions of the managerial world (Part I) and dimension 1, the consequences continue to exist and become worse. However, if these activities go beyond a certain tolerance point, they

[32] James K. Dent, "Organizational Correlates of the Goals of Business Management," *Journal of Personnel Psychology*, Vol. 12, No. 3, Autumn 1959, pp. 365–393.
[33] G. Katona, *Psychological Analysis of Economic Behavior*, McGraw-Hill, New York, 1951.

will no longer be kept covert and their damage will tend to become so obvious that all concerned will suffer.

It is at this point that warring departments may begin to focus less on rivalries and competition and more on cooperation. For example, this was what happened in the case cited earlier of the Scottish electronic industry as well as the example of the product test department. In both of these cases, the rival departments got together and defined for themselves an (informal) objective which dealt with maintaining effective relationships with the whole. Under these conditions, cooperation increased, production and creativity increased, and costs decreased.

Dimension Four

The next dimension suggests that the organization as a whole should focus continuously on its internal system, constantly striving to keep it flexible enough so that it may be changed as is necessary. The traditional view has already been made explicit in the foregoing discussion. It is usually viewed as the task of management.

Research Illustrating the Predicted Consequences of Approximating the Right Ends of the Continua

Turning to the literature, we find that feedback about how well the group is performing as a system helps to increase its effectiveness. Gibb, Smith, and Roberts [34] report that knowledge of members' feelings reported to the group produced significantly less defensive feeling than did feedback about results. Lott, Schopler, and Gibb confirm the findings that group effectiveness can increase if it focuses on maintaining its internal system.[35] Bass [36] reports that a group can be kept more flexible if it maintains constant interaction among its participants. Merton,[37] in a theoretical analysis, suggests that when the organization makes discipline an end rather than a means, individuals learn to play it safe, to be careful, and do little. This, in turn, tends to increase the

[34] J. R. Gibb, E. E. Smith, and A. H. Roberts, "Effects of Positive and Negative Feedback upon Defensive Behavior in Small Problem-Solving Groups," *American Psychology*, Vol. 10, 1955, p. 335 (abstract).

[35] A. J. Lott, J. H. Schopler, and J. R. Gibb, "Effects of Feeling-Oriented and Task-Oriented Feedback upon Defensive Behavior in Small Problem Solving Groups," *American Psychology*, Vol. 10, 1955, p. 335 (abstract).

[36] Bernard M. Bass, *op. cit.*, p. 133.

[37] R. K. Merton, "Bureaucratic Structure and Personality," *Social Forces*, Vol. 16, 1939–1940, pp. 560–568.

rigidity of the internal system. In a bank study [38] the writer found that a "right type" employee tended to be hired, rewarded, and perpetuated. Yet most of the executives spoke disparagingly of the "right type." They felt that the bank's growth was greatly inhibited by lack of people who were more aggressive and had less fear of change. Nevertheless, five years passed without any change being observed or reported.

Dimension Five

To the writer's knowledge, with the possible exception of Glacier Metal (which will be discussed in the next part), there are almost no systematic empirical studies available illustrating the kinds of externally oriented activities necessary for the organization to adapt effectively to its environment. The one exception is the work of Chamberlain in the area of labor-management relations.[39] Chamberlain defines social responsibility as "the obligation to exercise one's private authority (rights, whether legal or nonlegal) in such a manner that the performance of the correlative obligations does not frustrate important rights of expectancy held by others." [40]

For this definition to be operationally meaningful in areas other than labor and management relations, studies must be developed defining "nonlegal rights," "obligations," and "expectancies."

In one recent study, Eells has attempted the first step by trying to make explicit the controversies ranging about the meaning of these terms for management. For example, Eells describes the dilemma of the modern corporation that may wish to go further than simply meeting its legal responsibilities.[41] There are strong arguments for and against an organization focusing on expanding its social responsibilities. The positions range from Friedman who believes, "If anything is certain to destroy our free society, to undermine its very foundations, it would be a widespread acceptance by management of social responsibilities in some sense other than to make as much money as possible . . ." [42] to those who insist that the organization does have broader social responsibilities and if they are not met the corporation runs the risk of losing its autonomous position in the society.

[38] Chris Argyris, "Understanding Human Behavior in Organizations," in Mason Haire (Ed.), *Modern Organization Theory*, Wiley, New York, 1959.
[39] Neil W. Chamberlain, *Social Responsibility, and Strikes*, Harper, New York, 1953.
[40] *Ibid.*, p. 11.
[41] Richard Eells, *The Meaning of Modern Business*, Columbia University Press, 1960
[42] *Ibid.*, p. 79.

After an extended analysis, Eells (understandably) side-steps the issue partially by suggesting that the nature of the relationships between the organization and the environment will vary according to the concept of the nature of the organization. He suggests that most organizations may be classified along a continuum. At one end, the business unit is regarded as an exclusively private organ operated exclusively for stockholders. Next is the organization regarded as a mixture of public-private interests. On the other end of the continuum is the organization which is exclusively a public organ. After showing how each of these kinds of organization has tended to behave, he suggests a model which he defines as the "well-tempered' organization. Unfortunately, only the broadest and most general outline is given of the nature of such an organization. Hopefully, as research and experience develops, more concreteness will tend to be possible. It is interesting to note that Eells' concept of the "well-tempered organization" is similar to the one that mirrors the right ends of the continua in our model.

Two studies were found that attempted to describe the different modes of adaptation and relate in some way the possible pay-offs each mode would have for the organization. Thompson and McEwen [43] suggest that there are fundamentally four approaches that an organization might take in relating itself to the environment. The first is competition, where each organization fights for resources, customers, and so on. It tends to prevent unilateral or arbitrary choice of organizational goals or to correct such a choice if one is made. The other three are more cooperative in nature. First is bargaining where agreements are negotiated between organizations for the exchange of goods or services. Unlike competition, bargaining values direct interaction with other organizations in the environment, rather than with a third party. Bargaining, therefore, may invade the organization's decision process. Cooptation—a concept developed by Selznick—is the process by which the organization absorbs new elements into itself as a means of averting threats to its stability or survival.[44] Cooptation makes still further inroads on the decision-making processes. Finally, there is coalition in which organizations unite for a common purpose. Coalition seems to be the extreme condition under which the environment can influence the organization. Thompson and McEwen do not provide any criteria by which an administrator may select the "proper" mode of adaptation. They suggest that an organization should move cautiously and "sound out" the environment.

[43] J. D. Thompson and W. J. McEwen, "Organizational Goals and Environment," *American Science Review*, Vol. 23, No. 1, February 1958, pp. 23–30.
[44] Philip Selznick, *op. cit.*

Other's Points of View on Organizational Effectiveness

There are several scholars who conduct research in organizations and who have developed models of effective and ineffective organizations. It seems instructive to see if there is any degree of congruence between the model that we have presented and the model presented by these scholars. For example, is there an observable degree of correspondence between the ideal types in our model and the ideal organizational types reported by these scholars? Are the concepts of organizational effectiveness and ineffectiveness supported in the work conducted by others?

In reviewing the literature we are struck with the convergence of ideas of men like Likert,[45] McGregor,[46] Shepard,[47] Bennis,[48] Blake and Mouton,[49] Burns and Stalker,[50] Barnes,[51] and Litwak.[52] Each scholar seems to have found it useful to develop at least two "ideal types" of organizations in order to categorize his data. All of them are quick to point out that these categories are not mutually exclusive nor do they exhaust all the possibilities.

Perhaps the most comprehensive differentiation of types of organization has been done by Likert.[53] He differentiates between authoritative and participative systems of organizations. Authoritative systems may be conceptualized as *exploitative, benevolent,* and *consultative.* The participative system is conceptualized as the participative group. These systems are placed on a continuum representing degree of control. The exploitative authoritarian has most unilateral control whereas the participative has more mutual shared control. Likert does not consider, in detail, the case of complete laissez faire. However, for the dimensions that he considers, he develops a highly detailed table which describes the

[45] Rensis Likert, *op. cit.*, pp. 223ff.

[46] Douglas McGregor, *The Human Side of Enterprise,* McGraw-Hill, New York, 1960, pp. 220–221.

[47] Herbert Shepard, "Organic and Mechanistic Models of Organization," presented at the Esso Laboratories, Thayer Hotel, Summer 1959.

[48] Warren Bennis, "Leadership Theory and Administrative Behavior," *Administrative Science Quarterly,* Vol. 4, No. 3, December 1959, pp. 259–301.

[49] Robert R. Blake and Jane S. Mouton, *The Managerial Grid,* HRTL Laboratory in Management Development, June 1961, Jemiz Springs, New Mexico.

[50] Tom Burns and G. M. Stalker, *The Management of Innovation,* Tavistock Publications, London, 1961, pp. 120–121.

[51] Louis B. Barnes, *Organizational Systems and Engineering Groups,* Graduate School of Business, Harvard University, 1960, Chap. VIII.

[52] Eugene Litwak, "Models of Bureacracy Which Permit Conflict," *American Journal of Sociology,* Vol. LXVII, September 1961, pp. 177–184.

[53] Rensis Likert, *op. cit.*, pp. 223ff.

organizational and performance characteristics of each system. Although Likert is aware that such tables may tend to oversimplify the situation (for example, they do not depict how each system blends with the others), he feels that there are important values to be gained.

The value of these tables, Likert suggests, lies in the observable fact that the many operating procedures and the performance characteristics of the different management systems form an orderly pattern along every horizontal and vertical dimension.[54] The orderly pattern reminds one of the periodic tables in chemistry and apparently can serve some of the same purposes. For example, one may interpolate within the table. It may be possible to derive probable patterns of leadership, organizational characteristics, and behavior which are typical of a given system of organization when it is functioning at the optimum level.

A more important value of the table, according to Likert, is to extrapolate from it the nature of a new form of organization which has not been fully developed in practice, namely, the participative groups form of organization.[55] This new form will tend to be characterized as an integrated, internally consistent management system. The overlapping group form of organization will be its primary structure. In addition to the necessary technical and managerial skills, the manager will also hold a basic philosophy of leadership that places much emphasis on effective group functioning, supportive, ego-building climate, and cooperative relationships. The degree of trust will tend to be high enough that accurate measurements will tend to be available to all who need them.[56]

Another differentiation that seems to be developing independently among several scholars is that between "mechanistic" and "organic" organizations. The former is illustrative of the pyramidal structure; the latter tends to approximate the right ends of the continua in the mix model.

Shepard, one of the first to utilize these concepts, defines the properties of mechanical systems in terms similar to those we have used for formal organization. The organic organization is characterized as a system in which (1) good management is understood to be the emergent product of adequate working relationships among the organization's members, (2) the cement of the system is mutual confidence, (3) the structure of the organization must correspond to the network of interdependence among members required by the organization's tasks, (4) the principle of multigroup membership is substituted for the

[54] *Ibid.*, p. 234.
[55] *Ibid.*
[56] *Ibid.*, pp. 237–238.

mechanical concept of supervision, and (5) the wide sharing of control and responsibility created by the foregoing leads to the principle that (6) conflicts of interests must be resolved by the use of problem solving.[57]

Another example of the differentiation between mechanistic and organic is found in the work by Burns and Stalker.[58] For example, they characterize the mechanistic organization in such terms as (1) specialized differentiation of functional tasks, (2) each task is pursued with techniques and purposes more or less distinct from those of the concern as a whole, (3) the reconciliation of these distinct performances by the superior, (4) the hierarchical structure of control, authority, and communication, (5) the location of knowledge at the top, and (6) minimum interaction among peers.

The organic organization, on the other hand, may be characterized as (1) the contributive nature of special knowledge and experience to the common task of the concerned, (2) the "realistic" nature of the individual tasks, which is seen as set by the total situation of the concern, (3) the adjustment and continual redefinition of individual tasks through interaction with others, (4) the spread of commitment to the concern beyond any technical difficulty, (5) the network structure of control, authority, and communication derive from presumed communities of interest and less from contractual relationships, and (6) omniscience no longer is imputed to the head of the concern.

Although some slight variations exist, the work of the other scholars also emphasizes (but is not necessarily limited to) these two categories. For example, "authoritarian" is used by Likert, "habit" by Bennis, "closed system" by Barnes, "bureaucratic" by Litwak, and "Theory X" by McGregor. Summarizing the major points emphasized by all these scholars, we conclude that the mechanistic organization is characterized by (1) decision making and control at the top levels of the organization, (2) an emphasis on unilateral management action, based on dependency and passive conformity, (3) the specialization of tasks so that the concern for the whole is broken down, (4) the centralization of information, rewards and penalties, membership, (5) the management being responsible for developing and maintaining the loyalty, commitment, and responsibility of all the participants on as high a level as possible, and (6) an emphasis on social status, intergroup and individ-

---

[57] Herbert A. Shepard and Robert Blake, "Changing Behavior Through Cognitive Change," 1962, mimeographed, presented at the annual meeting of the Society for Applied Anthropolgy, May 1961. Part I from which the above is quoted was written by Shepard.

[58] Tom Burns and G. M. Stalker, *loc. cit.*

ual competition and rivalry. Such an organization assumes that people inherently tend to dislike work, be irresponsible, prefer to be directed, desire a rational world where emotions are suppressed, and "fair" management means appropriate financial rewards and penalties.[59]

The organic organization is variously called "participative group" (Likert), "problem solving" (Bennis), "open system" (Barnes), "human relations" (Litwak), and "Theory Y" (McGregor). The "organic organization" is characterized by (1) decision making widely done throughout the organization, (2) an emphasis on mutual dependence and cooperation based on trust, confidence, and high technical or professional competence, (3) a constant pressure to enlarge tasks and interrelate them so that the concern for the whole is emphasized, (4) the decentralization of responsibility for and use of information, rewards and penalties, membership, (5) participants at all levels being responsible for developing and maintaining loyalty and commitment at as high a level as possible, and (6) an emphasis on status through contribution to the whole and intergroup and interindividual cooperation. Such an organization assumes that people are capable of being responsible, committed, productive, and desire a world in which the rationality of feelings and interpersonal relationship is as valued as cognitive rationality.

In examining the models developed by these scholars it is interesting to note that certain dimensions are consonant with the continua in our model. The mechanistic dimensions are consonant with the left ends of the continua, that is, away from the essential properties or organization. Organic dimensions are consonant with the right ends of the continua, that is, toward the essential properties of organization. It is interesting that all of the scholars have concluded that the organic model tends to develop greater organizational flexibility, commitment, responsibility, effectiveness in problem solving and adapting to the environment. This is precisely what we hypothesized about organizations that approximate (tend toward) the right ends of the continua (which the organic organizations do).[60]

Moreover, as also may be predicted from our model, these scholars report the mechanistic organization to be least effective in change and the development of innovative ideas. The greatest strength of the mechanistic organization, they suggest (and we would concur), is its ability to cope with routine matters and survive in an environment that is relatively stable and benign.

[59] For a discussion of assumptions, see Douglas McGregor, *op. cit.*
[60] May we again remind the reader that these conclusions do not constitute valid empirical evidence.

Finally, all the research cited suggests that self-expression and self-actualization are best achieved in the organic organization. Such conclusions agree with our model. We hypothesized, the reader may recall, that individual self-actualization is best obtained in an organization whose activities approximate (tend toward) the right ends of the continua.

This support from the research of other scholars gives us more confidence that the direction in which we are heading may indeed be a valid and useful one. Moreover, it may be possible to utilize the empirically derived categories of the scholars as operational definitions for various points along the continua of our model. This would help to make our model more operationally definable and hopefully testable. Also, such an exercise could help to make more explicit the logical interrelationship among the categories by placing them in proper relationship to one another along the continua of our model.

Developing the discussion as we have may leave the reader with the impression that we are conceptually subserving the other models to ours. This impression is only partially correct. We do *not* mean to imply that our model is developed more fully than the other models, especially those of Likert, McGregor, Burns, Stalker, and Shepard. However, we do imply that one value of the mix model, which none of the others have, is that it is developed from the essential properties of organization. For example, when we inquire into the ultimate source of the values implicit in the participative or organic organizations, the reply that their respective authors would probably have to give is that the values are related to empirical findings. Admittedly, this is one of the highest authorities scientists can cite. It is the one we hope to cite someday. However, there is, we believe, another value worth citing. It is the possibility that, in addition to the empirical references, we can relate our views to some theoretical foundation. It is at this point that we hope we have made a contribution. If the model that we propose is empirically validated, then, along with empirical verification, it will have the added value of having its dimensions related to the essential properties of the construct organization. This will tend to provide a ladder to make connections among the organizational, small-group, and individual levels. Such connections may help to contribute to the goals of "unity of knowledge." They also may tend to contribute to the objective of making a theoretical viewpoint more comprehensive. That is, it includes more parts of the universe with fewer constructs.

Finally, we shall examine two other central topics of organizational behavior to see if there exists any degree of consonance between the findings in the literature and the expectations we would have by utilizing our model of effective and ineffective organization. The topics are organizational change and labor and management relations.

Organizational Change

The findings of Guest's [61] recent study on organizational change are in accordance with our model. Briefly, Guest studied the impact of a change in management on plant Y. This organization, which had been under an old management, was in serious difficulties. Guest perceives the major reasons as:

1. The plant manager dealt with departments as individual units, ignoring the interrelationships among them. His directives ignored "the group as a group."
2. The organization was controlled and directed by one unit, namely, the general manager. It was a "one-man show."
3. The time perspective at all levels was short and it diminished as one went down the chain of command.
4. Most managers strove to protect themselves and "live for today."

Guest presents evidence that the organization was unable to influence its internal affairs as the management wished. Nor did it seem to be able to create relationships with its environment (headquarters) that were helpful to the plant or to headquarters.

All these conditions are example of conditions along the left ends of our continua. Drawing from our discussion on human motivation under these conditions, we predict that feelings of self-responsibility, commitment to the job and the organization, and involvement should be low. We also predict that the decision-making processes should tend to be ineffective, the organization should be marked with interdepartmental rivalries and rigidities, which should lead to a state in which the system is unable to modify its own internal and external relationships as it wishes.

Guest reports that all these conditions existed. He cites the extremely low morale and commitment at all levels of management and presents qualitative evidence that each manager had learned to protect himself by taking few risks, almost no initiative, showing little responsibility, and exhibiting a low degree of commitment. Guest also gives evidence that the decision-making processes were so ineffective that the organi-

[61] Robert Guest, *Organizational Change: The Effect of Successful Leadership*, Irwin-Dorsey, Homewood, Ill., 1962.

zation had reached a point where it was no longer able to change itself internally.

Guest presents evidence showing that the plant's efficiency was low. For example, plant Y's efficiency (in 1953) was the poorest among six plants; it was utilizing 16 per cent more direct labor than was called for by standards. It had the poorest quality, indirect labor performance, safety, absenteeism, and turnover records, as well as the next to worst record in labor grievances.

In 1953 a new top manager was brought in who made significant changes in the total management philosophy and practice. Guest presents evidence that, in addition to manifesting a different leadership pattern, the new leader was able to infuse the organization with the values implicit in it. Thus the changes that were instituted remained long after he left.

Briefly, Guest describes the new management philosophy and practice.

1. Achieving the goal required interdependent activity among all relevant personnel. The leader recognized his dependence on other units, and they, in turn, came to recognize theirs. The result, suggests Guest, was a new degree of integration.
2. Moreover, the leader focused on permitting the lower levels to influence the upper levels to a degree not hitherto experienced.
3. There was a significant increase in time perspective as well as an increase in the effectiveness of decision making.

The increased integration decreased interdepartmental rivalries and "protective" activities and unfroze the organization to the point where it was able once again to solve its own internal problems. The morale, commitment, feelings of responsibility, and involvement all rose significantly.

These findings are also in line with our model. The new management philosophy led to an organization that approximated more closely the organizational health ends of our continua—for example, greater mutual influence of parts, greater awareness, greater effectiveness in problem solving and in changing its internal and external activities, and a longer time perspective.

In addition, its general efficiency (in terms of direct labor costs) was superior to all the other plants. It had moved to sharing the top position for the best record of indirect costs, the third best in quality, the best in safety and in labor grievances. Its absenteeism and turnover was also reduced significantly.

It should be pointed out that all these changes occurred in a plant where the authorities above it, the plant personnel, the formal structure (for example, number of levels), and the product to be produced did not change significantly. The improvement in performance, concludes Guest, is largely due to the new internal set of relationships which approximate the right ends of the continua in the "mix" model.

Labor and Management Relations

Bakke has suggested that labor-management relationships could be viewed as two organizations sending out their representatives to bargain. These representatives form a new organization whose characteristics are different from both "back home" situations. This permits one to treat labor-relationships in terms of organizational theory.

The question then arises, are there models of effective labor-management relationships that can be conceptualized as organizations? If so, are these model(s) consonant to the one we have developed as representing the healthy organization? Also, if there are models of poor labor-management relationships, are they consonant with our view of an unhealthy organization?

Whyte [62] has presented several detailed descriptions of changes in labor relationships going from poor to better. If the model does apply, then we would hypothesize that "poor" labor relations should approximate the unhealthy ends of our dimensions. "Good" labor relations should approximate the healthy ends of the continua. This is what we tend to find. For example, the "poor" conditions were characterized by (1) one-way origination of action within management structure, (2) ignoring mutual interdependence with union, (3) keeping union in the dark about relationships (short time perspective). The union, in turn, (1) originated action for management through mass demonstrations, (2) ignored the interdependence of relationships, and (3) kept management in the dark about its strategy. The resulting relationships seemed to be that neither side could create the conditions for effective problem solving.

The conditions of "good" labor relationships, were significantly different. Whyte describes some of them as:

1. Pressures from the top down in management have eased up and subordinates are able to get action from superiors on their complaints and suggestions with a greatly increased frequency. The work

[62] William F. Whyte, *Pattern for Industrial Peace*, Harper, New York, 1951; *Men at Work*, Irwin-Dorsey Press, Homewood, Ill., 1961, Chaps. 4, 15, and 16.

of the factory is done much more on the basis of talking things over than on the basis of ordering people around.

2. The union is able to originate action for management with a greater frequency than the conflict period. For the first time management is originating action directly for the union. This happens at all levels, particularly at the top level and at the foreman level. Management is now utilizing two channels in order to get things done.

3. The foreman's position is greatly improved. He is under less pressure from above and can originate more frequently up the line. He is also easing pressures by getting action from the steward.

4. The union officers are now originating action for their subordinates with greater relative frequency than heretofore. Throughout the period of conflict, the key officers maintained an unusual stability in their position. Nevertheless, pressures felt by rank-and-file workers were so intense in the conflict period that the leaders constantly had to act in response to those pressures. They could channel and direct the activity, but often they were in a position of carrying out activities that they would have preferred not to have underway at all simply because some actions were demanded of them. This did not mean that the officers did not want to lead the fight against management. It means that they were in a position of capitalizing on activity that was springing up all over their own designs. Now, as the union officers get action from management with increasing effectiveness and thus bring back rewards for the membership, they are in a greatly improved position to plan and control the activities of the rank and file.[63]

In terms of our model we would say that the interdependence of parts by both parties was recognized, influence of the parts on the whole (labor-management system) was significantly increased, as was the time perspective. The resulting trust and openness tends to lead to more effective problem solving and, according to Whyte, effective industrial peace.

Further illustration of our hypothesis may be obtained from the series of studies on "Causes of Industrial Peace." [64] This is a series of studies of nearly thirty different firms that had experienced some high degree of effective industrial peace. The results suggest that there are economic, political, social, and organizational factors that influence the quality and duration of industrial peace.

[63] William Foote Whyte, *Pattern for Industrial Peace, op. cit.*, pp. 169, 170, 171.
[64] *Fundamentals of Labor Peace*, Case Study No. 14, National Planning Association, December 1953.

The organizational factors are the relevant ones in our discussion. It is our hypothesis that in the cases of effective peace there should tend to exist, in a given company-union relationship, factors that approximate the healthy organization.[65] In an effective relationship the factors should tend to approximate the right ends of the continua. There are data in the findings to illustrate these hypotheses and none that contradict them.

Examples of factors influencing effective relationships follows.

1. The practice of consulting foremen and union representatives on an almost unlimited range of problems, and of inviting union participation in management on a consultative basis.
2. Use of the line organization of management and the union hierarchy as effective channels of upward and downward communication, with the foremen and shop stewards as key individuals.
3. The projection downward and the wide diffusion of management responsibility.
4. The strengthening of the sense of security of individual workers by promotions largely in line with seniority, by a liberal retirement system, and by advance consultation with them in preparation for technological changes.
5. The selection of employees partly on the basis of their ability to fit into the human-relations system of the plant.
6. The avoidance of paternalism and of pat formulas and rigid rules in favor of a flexible approach to problems.
7. Administration of the contract through an effective grievance machinery and bargaining at all levels, with the principals on both sides participating and lawyers barred.[66]

We note the emphasis on the parts influencing each other, on an awareness of the integrity and uniqueness of the whole organization (which in this example is a company and a union). The constant effort is to help the participants be aware of as much of the total organization as possible. Also, there is a selection procedure to help guarantee the entrance of individuals who tolerate the values of the system. Finally, there is mutual influence between management and the unions and an effective problem-solving process (grievance procedure).

[65] The criteria of effectiveness and ineffectiveness are defined in the studies and were accepted by both management and union representatives.
[66] Consonant data were obtained in a study of eighteen organizations. *Fundamentals of Labor Peace*, Case Study No. 14, National Planning Association, December 1953.

PART III

In the previous part we emphasized the importance of constructing models to help us understand organization effectiveness as well as the need to test these models in the real world. We also attempted to show that some of the implications of the mix model could be indirectly illustrated (not tested) by empirical research.

In this part we shall take another step to connect the model with reality. The connection will be to make explicit some ideas of what a firm might look like if we were to design it to approximate the right ends of the continua. In conducting this exercise, we are not saying that all organizations ought to approximate the right ends of the continua if they are to be effective. As we pointed out in the previous chapter, such a conclusion must await many years of careful rsearch and further refinement of organizational theory.

In striving to give the reader some idea of what a firm (or a governmental bureau, or school) would look like if its profile were to approximate the right ends of the continua, our presentation must remain at a more abstract level of description than is desirable. There are two reasons for this limitation. First, the differentiations needed to depict a particular kind of organization cannot be developed without having volumes of data on that organization. Second, for the sake of showing the range of use of the model, we must purposely focus on the aspects of organizations that are general enough to cover many different kinds of "real" organizations.

Finally, the reader is asked to keep in mind that all the following material is frankly speculative and is presented to suggest directions for research.

Returning to our objective, we desire to present some very preliminary generalizations from which organizations could be designed that would tend to:

1. Decrease many of the defensive activities leading to the organizational atrophy and illness that we have described.
2. Decrease the human energy consumed in maintaining these defensive activities.
3. Increase the probability that individuals will experience more frequent opportunities for psychological success to enhance their self-esteem.
4. Increase the human energy available for effective effort within the organization.

Before presenting our suggestions, it is important to emphasize that our objective is not to dismiss outright and arbitrarily the traditional pyramidal structure. Such action would be as ineffective as supporting the traditional model and rejecting all other possibilities. A complete rejection of the pyramidal structure would be, in our opinion, as defensive and as ineffective as the rejection of authority by an adolescent. Luckily for most of them, such a strategy is only a temporary one. The adolescent becomes an adult partially because he has come to terms with authority and sees the need for many of its impositions. The same reasoning is valid for our case. An effective theory of organizational design will have to include the positive contributions of the pyramidal structure. Indeed, this is the challenge that faces the organizational architect. It is not a challenge of discarding the pyramidal structure. It is a challenge of integrating it with other kinds of structures.

For example, it may be that detailed job descriptions (which are a hallmark of the pyramidal strategy), have value if they can be accompanied by trust, openness, individuality, and flexibility, instead of the opposite characteristics (which we have suggested tend to be more the rule than the exception). Under these conditions, a detailed and accurately defined work world may lead to the boundaries among functions becoming the firm ground on which to anchor one's security (cognitive and emotional) so that one may seek new dimensions of freedom and change. This is Brown's main thesis when he speaks of "freedom within the law." [1] His view, in our opinion, seems valid, if it is accompanied

---

[1] Wilfred Brown, "What Is Work?" *Harvard Business Review*, Vol. 40, No. 5, September–October 1962, pp. 121–129.

with flexible individuals. A bounded world will not tend to be destructively restrictive if the individuals have a high degree of self-esteem and are, therefore, "unbounded" (in the sense of willing to experiment, take risks, and so on).

Another reason why we will have to maintain some of the traditional organizational strategy is related to the age-old problem of individual freedom versus organizational planning. The more an organization needs to preplan its effort, the more it will tend to make demands on individuals that will not tend to lead to as much psychological success as might otherwise be possible. For example, from our viewpoint, one may hypothesize that the greater the internal commitment to work, the more the individual will tend to work without external pressures, rewards, and penalties. Internal commitment would be especially desirable for salesmen who are out in the field and whose effort is difficult to motivate, oversee, and control. Internal commitment tends to occur under psychological success. Psychological success requires that the salesmen be permitted to set their own goals and continually alter them as they develop further experience. Such flexibility could lead to sales being extremely difficult to predict ahead of time. Consequently, the amount of work for manufacturing, purchasing, and engineering would become difficult to preplan. It would be difficult indeed to administer a huge corporation under these conditions.

In addition to the "positive" reasons for maintaining aspects of the traditional strategy, several "negative" ones must be faced. First, it may be difficult if not impossible to redesign certain kinds of work. Until the necessary knowledge is generated, the organization will have to operate with relatively narrowly defined work. Second, legal regulations may prevent certain jobs from being redesigned (for example, an internal auditor's job in a bank may not be enlarged to permit the one being audited to participate in the audit, or the top corporate positions have their authority and responsibility clearly defined in the instruments of incorporation).

But we need not remain idle or feel completely helpless under these conditions. As a first step, why cannot we openly acknowledge the "negative" effects of the traditional strategy? Why not admit that such a strategy will tend to create a work world of dependence and boredom which will tend to lead to such activities as apathy and noninvolvement? If we are able to do these things, we may, at least, decrease the tendency in organization to create a myriad of policies and practices that are designed to hide these negative factors; or to make people like them; or to "make up" for them through paternalistic personnel programs.

Our strategy will be to attempt to develop a climate in which the difficulties can be openly discussed, the employee hostility understood and accepted, and a program defined by which everyone can participate in attempting to develop new designs. Wherever this is impossible, the attempt will be made to design new work worlds that can be integrated with the old and that help the employee obtain more opportunity for psychological success. For example, we shall see that the Scanlon Plan or the Glacier Metals Representative System can begin to fulfill these specifications.

The objective, therefore, of designing an organization without the pyramidal structure is neither useful (to the solution of our problem) nor necessary. The most difficult challenge, in our opinion, is to design an organization that is able to integrate the best of the traditional with the best of the newer concepts. The need is for an organization that can put several concepts of organizational life side by side so that they form a whole that is greater than the sum of the parts.

Finally, we should like to remind the reader that human behavior, at the lower levels, is primarily influenced by technology, control systems, and organizational structure. The behavior at the upper levels is influenced much more by interpersonal relations. This implies that, in the main, the major changes at the lower levels will tend to be in the area of job design, staffing of positions, and control systems (for example, budgets, production bogeys). The upper levels will probably be more profitably altered by focusing on the interpersonal relationships. (We assume that the organization will obtain technically competent individuals.)

The discussion will begin with some thoughts on the organizational structure, then turn to leadership, job design, reward and penalty, hiring, firing, evaluating. Each section will begin with a brief introduction of present practice and some difficulties associated with that practice. Then remedies will be suggested. It cannot be too strongly emphasized that this is a very preliminary undertaking. At best, we hope to indicate directions for future exploration and research.

The Organizational Structures of the New System

How can we create a system that will tend to lead to increased outputs with decreasing or constant inputs and do this repeatedly? Such an organization will need to increase the effectiveness of its three core activities.

It is our hypothesis that as the behavior "in" the three core activities approximates the right ends of the continua of the "mix" model, the effectiveness of the organization should increase. But how far over to the right ought they go? Is it necessarily true that the more the activities approximate the right ends of the continua, the better they will be? As already suggested, we doubt it. There must be limits to how far the activities can approximate the right ends and the organization remain effective.

However, we do not know that this hypothesis is valid. A theory of organization is needed from which various mixes of the organization and the individual can be stated and the consequences (costs and pay-offs) for each mix can be determined. Research could then be conducted to see if the costs and pay-offs that are derived theoretically actually occur in the empirical world.

Unfortunately, to the writer's knowledge, neither the concepts nor the empirical research are adequately developed for such a task. One of the most urgent needs in organizational theory is the development of such concepts to cope with these phenomena as well as empirical research to test their validity.

Structure I: The Pyramidal Structure

Let us begin with a discussion of the conditions under which the pyramidal strategy may be more of a help than a hindrance to the organization.

We may hypothesize that the pyramidal strategy should be used in the following situations.

1. When time is of the essence and a decision must be made that commits the organization in a direction already accepted by the subordinates. For example, if a customer calls and asks for a rush delivery, one would not expect the participants to want to be involved in the decision in order that the request be honored. The customer could leave and go to another organization.

Another example is an emergency situation. Presumably the members of the organization are committed to its survival. Consequently, they would be willing to subordinate their needs to help guarantee the recovery and survival of the organization.

Thompson and Hawkes [1] present some hypotheses as to why a pyramidal structure may be necessary under stress. They point out that under stress attention is focused on the primary values of survival. The time perspective is simultaneously shortened, direct action predominates, and behavior becomes oriented toward the primary unit, which in the case of the organization is the individual's department. Under these conditions only those communication links that help keep the organization alive are used. Self-actualization becomes less salient, lest the organization be completely lost. The informal activities also lose their importance. At the same time, any formal organizational arrangements that might inhibit the survival also are loosened up or violated.

Under stress the organization "regresses" to a more primitive state in which job specialization and the communication of relevant information become the crucial factors around which effort is organized. Authority to coerce or influence individuals to act and controls to check on their efforts apparently are not needed because of the high internal commitment of all to overcome the disaster. Where influence and authority are observed, they are primarily related to the necessity to com-

[1] James D. Thompson and Robert W. Hawkes, "Disaster, Community Organization and Administrative Process," University of Pittsburgh, mimeographed, 1962, pp. 10–15.

municate relevant information and to define tasks in order to get the job done.

Under these conditions, it would seem plausible that the leadership could become largely, if not completely, organization centered. Consequently, the leadership might be seen as being aloof and more hierarchically oriented. Recently, it has been found that leaders who maintained aloofness and the hierarchy tended to be more effective under stress than leaders who maintained more permissiveness.[2]

However, it should also be pointed out that the relationship just described is not linear. One may hypothesize that under ultimate stress organizations may be coerced toward a state of extreme autonomy and decentralization. There is no time or energy available for the giving of orders. Two examples are field combat conditions and extreme disasters such as major floods. Under these conditions, small troop units or parts of a community are known to operate in an autonomous manner for extended periods of time.

2. The pyramidal strategy may be effective when the decision to be made clearly falls into a category which, as a result of prediscussion and agreement among the participants, has been relegated to the pyramidal structure—for example, routine orders for products, routine requests about disposition of orders, and inquiries for such matters as delivery dates. The characteristic common to these decisions is that they are easily made, routine, require little or no creative effort, and offer little challenge. Under these conditions, it is hypothesized that people would not tend to feel a strong need to be involved in making such decisions. Presumably individuals with a relatively high degree of self-esteem would tend to shun such routine decisions. They would not tend to become upset if someone (or a machine) took care of them.

3. A third function of the pyramidal structure may be observed when a decision must be made that does not significantly affect the distribution of power, reward and penalty, controls, work specialization, and centralization of information. In other words, even though decisions may not be routine or repetitive, the individuals should not tend to experience the frustrations described *if* they do not affect seriously the crucial "power," "membership," and "reward and penalty" activities in the organization.

4. The pyramidal structure may be effective when the number of people to be influenced is high relative to the space or time available to bring them together. Lower-level employees, especially on assembly

[2] Fred E. Fiedler, William Newwess, and Sophie Oonk, "An Exploratory Study of Group Creativity in Laboratory Tasks," *Acta Psychology*, Vol. XVIII, No. 2, 1961, pp. 100–119.

lines, are greatly restricted in their movements to the assembly line. Any small error could very easily block the entire line. Under these conditions, the management may increase its surveillance and control over the employees. In this connection, Faunce reports that in a highly automated plant, machine breakdowns become very serious since they are interdependent with the entire line of machines.[3] Under these conditions, line authority is necessary in order to resolve the problem within a safe period of time. Simpson's [4] study confirms this hypothesis.

5. Finally, the pyramidal structure may be more effective (than the other types of structure to be defined) if the individual participants do not seek psychological success, prefer to remain apathetic and non-involved, and dislike the organization so intently that they are constantly striving to harm it.

These conditions include primarily situations where the participants can be expected and required to be submissive without this influencing negatively their commitment to the decisions and to their development within the organization. For example, if the organization manufactures shoes, then one may assume that a committed employee will be glad to know that his firm is receiving orders or that a customer needs to be satisfied quickly. Also, one may assume that an employee's commitment is not negatively affected if decisions that he desires to be made *without* him are made without his participation. He realizes that he can be frustrated and, indeed, pressured if he is required to participate in making routine decisions, or decisions that are clearly out of his range of relevance.

There are two fundamental assumptions underlying these statements. One is that man can be expected to be, to a certain degree, both rationally competent, dependent, and submissive. And, thus, we seem to have returned to the strategy of the original scientific-management adherents. This is not incongruent with the primary thesis of this work. We have accepted the importance of, indeed the necessity for, dependence *but have limited it to specific situations.* In effect, we are suggesting that it is understandable for the organization to expect and require rationality and dependence on the part of its participants when the decision to be made is (1) to achieve the stated objective (for example, producing and selling shoes), (2) to decide on a matter within the competence of only a few employees, (3) to decide on a matter the employees feel

[3] William A. Faunce, "Automation in the Automobile Industry," *American Sociological Review*, Vol. 23, 1958, pp. 401–407.
[4] Richard L. Simpson, "Vertical and Horizontal Communication in Organization," *Administrative Science Quarterly*, Vol. 4, No. 2, September 1959, pp. 188–196.

either routine or not significantly related to those factors that affect their commitment to the organization.

Underlying these two assumptions is another. The analysis assumes that the individuals are highly committed to the organization and have a high degree of responsibility. When this assumption is valid, the emphasis on rationality to the exclusion of emotionality and the necessity for dependency will not tend to have the negative effects discussed previously. If the assumption does not hold, and if the individuals are apathetic and indifferent or aggressive and belligerent, the suggestions will not tend to be valid. A hostile employee will tend to resist any new responsibilities toward, as well as cooperating with, the organization. An apathetic, indifferent employee will not tend to resist, but the impact of dependence will tend to have the negative impacts discussed. This illustrates the assertion made at the outset that organizations aspiring to be healthier will tend to require individuals who have the same aspirations.

Structure II: The Modified Formal Organizational Structure [5]

The next organizational strategy to be considered is located, in terms of our "mix" model, somewhere more to the right (on all the dimensions) than the pyramidal structure. The exact point and the actual distance further to the right cannot be stated with any precision at this time. Much research will be required before position and distance can be ascertained more than heuristically.

Going toward the right ends assumes that we are developing an organization in which psychological success will have a greater probability of occurring than in the pyramidal structure. This means that this structure, unlike the previous one, should help to increase the amount of energy available. In the previous structure, the best one can hope to do is minimize the energy consumed by keeping the frustration and conflict at a minimum. This was done by utilizing the pyramidal structure under conditions where apathy and noninvolvement were permissible or when involvement was necessary because of emergency conditions.

Rensis Likert and his associates have been developing an organizational structure that represents a move toward the more effective organization but is partially based on the traditional formal organizational structure. The traditional chain of command is maintained for

[5] Rensis Likert, *New Patterns of Management,* McGraw-Hill, New York, 1961.

such crucial decisions as salaries, promotions, demotions, transfers, and so on. The model differs from the traditional ones in that it conceives of any given superior as a *link* between two groups. He is a *representative* of his *group's* (not only his own) view to the group containing peers and his boss. Thus the superior provides his subordinates an opportunity to voice their views on a particular matter. He then accurately represents these views to his peers and executives above him. According to Likert, this structure provides the subordinates an opportunity to experience greater satisfaction in, and deeper commitments for, the decisions, since they participated significantly.

To the writer, this structure should be especially effective in decisions requiring that the individual's actualization be taken into account. In conflict between individual and organization needs, the decision would be made in the interest of the firm. This structure would also be effective when the opinion of all participants is desired but no opportunity available to them to participate in the decision. An example of the former would be management's acceptance of a large order that may place much pressure on the organization in terms of meeting a deadline. Under these conditions, the management may decide to canvass the opinion of some of the participants in order to gage more accurately the impact of the new order. However, the actual decision to commit the organization would still be made by the management. An example of the latter case occurs when management contemplates making new changes in the production processes and wishes to obtain the views of the employees regarding the views. The management listens to all the relevant views but makes the final decision alone.

Guest's case study of "successful" organizational change is a specimen of a new executive utilizing the link-pin to structure coupled with an emphasis on the importance of interdependence among the executives along horizontal lines.[6]

Bidwell, Farrell, and Blake,[7] and Argyris [8] have shown that organizational changes can be made more lasting if the consultant utilizes the "link-pin" concept. He attempts to become a link among the clients in order to stimulate more open interpersonal and intergroup communication within the organization.

The Coch and French and the Morse and Reimer studies are excellent examples of this approach. Coch and French found that the

[6] Robert Guest, *Organizational Change: The Effect of Successful Leadership*, Irwin-Dorsey, Homewood, Ill., 1962, pp. 125–128.

[7] Alvin C. Bidwell, John J. Farrell, and Robert R. Blake, "A New Strategy: Organic On-the-Job Training," mimeographed, Esso Oil Company, New York, 1961.

[8] Chris Argyris, *Interpersonal Competence and Organizational Effectiveness*, *op. cit.*

experience participating in decisions usually reserved for management (the design of a new job, setting of the piece rates, etc.) increases the workers' effectiveness.[9] Morse and Reimer found that high control from above tends to reduce the effectiveness of work groups.[10] Recently, Bass has presented interesting evidence to suggest the value of this structure over the traditional one.[11] In situations where the traditional as well as the Likert model were simulated, the Likert model, despite its novelty and awkwardness, outproduced and outperformed the traditional formal model. For example, profits were almost five times greater, sales volume, 15 per cent greater, operating and inventory costs lower, constructive self-criticism greater, and involvement and satisfaction higher.

The Likert structure is effective under these conditions because it permits individual participation with the possibility (if it should become necessary) for the top executive to override the decision made by the group or to go ahead and make his own decision without waiting for the group to decide.

Brown's [12] description of the representative system at Glacier Metal provides a most interesting use of the executive as a representative of the employees but still in firm control.[13] Representatives are elected for all levels of the organization. Management has no control over whom the constituents decide to have represent them.

A representative is accountable to the constituent group or electoral unit that elects him. It is his responsibility (1) to make himself aware of the main interests of all in his constituency; (2) to represent the point of view of his constituents in committees and councils, even where this may mean presenting a point of view contrary to his own personal opinion or his view in his executive role; (3) to allow councils or committees to work with the greatest possible realism by judging when to state any views held by minorities within his constituency or committee; (4) to judge when reference to constituents is necessary, and when to accept responsibility for acting without such reference; (5)

[9] Lester Coch and John R. P. French, Jr., "Overcoming Resistance to Change," *Human Relations*, Vol. 1, 1948, pp. 512–532.

[10] Nancy Morse and E. Reimer, "The Experimental Change of a Major Organizational Variable," *Journal of Abnormal Social Psychology*, Vol. 52, No. 1, 1956.

[11] Bernard M. Bass, *Experimenting with Simulated Manufacturing Organizations*, Louisiana University, Research Contract N 7 ONR 35609, Office of Naval Research, Report 27, March 1961.

[12] Wilfred Brown, *Explorations in Management*, Heinemann, London, 1960, Chap. XVI, p. 201.

[13] However, as we shall see, Glacier Metal has developed a legislative and appeals procedures which influence the degree of unilateral authority of management.

to initiate proposals for change that would be in the best interests of his constituents; (6) to act as advisor to any of his constituents in cases of appeal when requested to do so.

The task of the representative, therefore, is to represent the views and needs of his constituency. The representative (the manager) cannot be discharged for saying what he believes to be the views of his group. Only the electors can discharge a person from a representative role.[14] Finally, a higher-level manager cannot instruct the representative to argue with or persuade his electors. The only courses open to the manager are either to instruct his subordinate managers to see the members of their commands, or to control and talk to them himself. If he meets for this purpose, it is an executive meeting. Brown cites an illustration of the rights of a manager.

"Your representatives want this or that, or have done this or that." Such comment is out of order; for the information that has reached him is that his people, the members of his command, want this or that. Representatives are a channel of communication; reference to them personally is, therefore, not only factually incorrect, but will sound like a threat. If criticism or argument is required, it should be directed at its sources, i.e., those on behalf of whom the representatives speak.

When a representative communicates with a manager, there is no individual name attached to that communication. The representative speaks on behalf of an unnamed person or persons. All that the manager knows is that this communication comes from the whole or part of his command. This anonymous property of all communications reaching managers from representatives is in contrast to the opposite feature of communications from the Executive System—where the manager can insist on knowing the individual source of each message. He would not be able to do his executive job without this information. The representative, on the other hand, would be unable to do his job if he had to disclose the names of those expressing particular views.[15]

To summarize, we may hypothesize that the Likert strategy may be used:

1. When the decision is not routine but does not effect significantly or permanently the distribution of power, control, information, and the specialization of work (for example, purchasing equipment, scheduling rush orders, and establishing selling prices).
2. When adequate time is not available to include all the relevant

[14] Brown, *op. cit.*, p. 203.
[15] *Ibid.*, p. 204.

individuals or explore thoroughly the relevant issues. Adequate time *does* exist, however, to provide opportunities for participation of the upper-level executives (modifying selling arrangement, promising delivery dates, modifying delivery dates, etc.).

3. When the decision to make a major change cannot be delegated to all involved. However, participation is desired (from those affected) in order to decrease resistance to change, develop the most effective processes for a lasting change within the organization, and represent more adequately the needs of the participants involved in the change.

Structure III: Power According to Functional Contribution

The third strategy takes us further in the direction of the right ends of the continua than did the first two strategies. This strategy should, therefore, be best suited for activities that can provide a greater degree of psychological success than the previous ones. Also, to the extent that the strategy is used, it should lead to an increase in the opportunity for psychological success. This, in turn, should tend to increase further the amount of energy available for work.

Under this strategy, each individual has equal opportunity to be given power, controls, information, and so on. The individual is given power as a function of his potential contribution to the problem. For example, a company has a problem of putting into production a new product. A meeting is held in manufacturing with all levels (skilled workers, foremen, general foremen, superintendents, etc.). During the meeting, it becomes apparent to the group that Skilled Worker A, Foreman B, and General Foreman C are the most capable to "engineer" the new product. They are given the authority required to complete the job. Although the group members will work "under" these three "leaders," they may at any time meet at a group to consider changes in the leadership. The power and control is, therefore, given to the individuals by the group members because they believe that the three individuals can lead the manufacturing department to its goals most effectively.

Davis's [16] description of the role of "project manager" in the electronic industry illustrates this type of manager. A project manager cuts across traditional departments. He is responsible for seeing that a particular project is completed. Assigned to that project are all the individ-

[16] Keith Davis, "A Preliminary Study of Management Patterns of Research Project Managers in Manufacturing in the Phoenix Area," Arizona State University, Department of Management, mimeographed, November 1961.

uals who are able to contribute to the project regardless of the department that they represent or the position that they hold. Davis reports that one reason the project manager concept may be effective is that it disregards "existing levels and functions in superimposing its own structure on the existing organization. It establishes a structure of its own based upon each person's ability to contribute to that specific project, regardless of his permanent organizational location." [17] Nor is there any difficulty in the men returning to their original position once the project is completed. "They freely admitted that at the end of the project they expected to return to lower levels in their firm." Many men viewed the job of project manager as an excellent challenge and a possible testing ground for eventual advancement. Also, most of the members reported a higher sense of commitment and purpose while participating as members of the project team.

Another excellent example of this structure is the Scanlon Plan. Basically, the Scanlon Plan is a method for participation by which all levels of the organization may contribute according to their capacity. The assumption is that the workers at the lowest levels are important human resources who can make important contributions. Briefly, participants at all levels are asked to develop a commitment toward making their work more productive. Individually, but more often in groups, they meet to receive, create, discuss, and evaluate any idea that might improve productivity. Departmental committees of workers and lower-level supervision are empowered to put into effect ideas appropriate at their levels. Those ideas that have broader implications are referred to higher-level committees composed of workers and managers. [18]

McGregor states: [19]

In this fashion the concept of participation is given a meaning which everyone can understand. The fact of interdependence is accepted; reliance is placed on the know-how, the ingenuity, the innovativeness of all the human resources of the organization. The mechanics of the participation are relatively unimportant; the underlying assumptions about human beings which are reflected are crucial.

Participation in Scanlon companies is greatly different from that obtained with conventional suggestion plans. There are no forms to fill out, no impersonal "suggestion boxes," no remote committees to evaluate the merits of

[17] *Ibid.*, p. 10.
[18] Frederick G. Lesieur (Ed.), *The Scanlon Plan*, The M.I.T. Press, Cambridge, Mass., 1958.
[19] Douglas McGregor, *The Human Side of Enterprise*, McGraw-Hill, New York, p. 115.

the idea in secret. The individual in his own work setting, or at a meeting of the screening committee, discusses his idea, participates in the evaluation of it, obtains recognition if it is a good idea or encouragement to work further on it if it is promising but still impractical. Moreover, he is in a situation which encourages him to seek and obtain help anywhere in the organization in developing the idea rather than one which encourages secrecy in order to prevent someone from stealing his idea and cheating him out of an award. The focus is not on competing for awards but on improving the effectiveness of the enterprise. The economic gains are shared, but the social and ego satisfactions are his alone.

In our terms a worker begins to participate in the problem-solving processes and his time perspective and his awareness of the organization as a whole are enlarged while at the same time the organization becomes increasingly influenced through the interdependency of the parts rather than by the direction of a given part. All of these conditions are consonant with our conception of healthy organization.

It should be added that all participants, with the possible exception of the very top management, are able to share in the cost-reduction savings. The organization typically develops a ratio by which these savings may be distributed equitably. Thus, although the basic system of rewards is not altered, it is, especially for the lower-level employees, significantly enlarged.

Recently a preliminary evaluation was made of six plants that had used the plan. Two of these plants had abandoned the plan after two years of experience with it. The researchers found that the plan did seem to lead to increased efficiency in four plants, brought about chiefly by employee suggestions as to how time and effort could be saved. Where the plan did not work apparently a crucial variable was management's disbelief that employee's suggestions could be worthwhile. This disbelief was based partially on false assumptions and partially on the reality that work is becoming so complex and interdependent that it is difficult for workers to make effective suggestions.[20]

As a group-incentive system, the plan had varied results. It did tend to inject teamwork into company operations and reduce normal rivalries between groups. On the other hand, it was difficult for some employees to relate their individual effort to a group incentive. The difficulties increased if labor turnover was high, worker involvement was low, and, for whatever reason, incentives were not paid over a long period of

[20] Roy Helfgott, *Group Wage Incentives: Experience with the Scanlon Plan*, Industrial Relations Counselors, Inc., New York, February 1962.

time. In closing, the single most important variable for success seemed to be the commitment on the part of both management and labor as well as the degree of trust between them.

Glacier Metal's "legislative system" seems to be an advanced example of this stage. The legislative system "comprises councils . . . in which the Executive and Representative Systems meet and by means of which every member can participate in formulating policy and in assessing the results of the implementation of that policy." [21]

Four groups are represented in the legislative system: a group of shareholders, "who elect directors to represent them, who in turn appoint the Chief Executive and set policies within which he can operate the Company," [22] a group of customers, the representative system, and the executive system. The objective of the legislative system is to deal with long-range policies and problems of change. It is not a system to which the managing director turns for sanction and support for a particular management action, unless the action is not already covered by agreed policy and unless he believes that it may meet some resistance. Brown states:

Executive Systems exist in a field controlled by three power groups, namely, shareholders, consumers and employees. These power groups invest the Executive System with authority to develop, manufacture and sell products. The Executive System thus carries responsibility for planning these operations, and the initiation of such a rate of change as is appropriate to the changes which take place in the environment in which it exists. When such changes are felt by the Chief Executive to exceed the bounds of the authority which has already been invested in his role, he must seek an extension of that authority. In order to do this, he brings into play certain social mechanisms, e.g., meetings of Boards of Directors or meetings of shareholders, testing of customers' reactions through a sales organization, meetings with representatives of employees. In so doing, he is precipitating interaction between the power groups. This interaction is legislative by nature.

I have on many occasions made statements of the following type to representatives, and I think they have helped them to regard matters more objectively.

"You can, as a body, stop any change I wish to initiate, for you have the power to do so if you avail yourself of it. If I initiate change to which you object, but which fails to arouse sufficient objection to cause you to resort to the use of your power to stop me, I have, nevertheless, reduced morale and thereby reduced the level of efficiency. As it is my task to run the Company as effectively as possible, I must do everything possible to avoid such

[21] Wilfred Brown, *op. cit.*, p. 225.
[22] *Ibid.*

situations arising. Nevertheless, shareholders and customers also possess power in the situation. They can refuse me the necessary authority to initiate change, even though you are prepared to use your power to try and push that change through. Thus I am an active initiator of new policies which, however, can be implemented only if I have sufficient authority. I will go as far in initiating change—which seems to me likely to help this Company to increase its effectiveness—as the authority which I derive from these power groups will allow me to go." [23]

In a consulting firm known to the writer, the team selected to help the client is led by the member whose professional competence is the most central one needed for the problem. That individual could be at the lowest levels of the administrative ladder. Thus a young engineer can be in charge of a team that includes a senior physicist as well as a vice president of the firm.

Other examples of the kinds of decisions that such a structure may be used for are:

1. New product development. In the development of a new product it may be wise to bring together the individuals who will have to see that it becomes a success. These include product development, engineering, manufacturing sales, and finance in order to evaluate the problems involved in the new product, including introducing it into the market, manufacturing, selling, distributing, and financing the new product.
2. Solution of problems involving more than one department or more than one individual within the department. Ways to discover new costs and error and waste reduction may be more effectively accomplished by bringing together the individuals who must actually carry out these programs.
3. Long-range policy planning. The organization's long-range policy planning activities may be more effective if they are conducted by all the participants in the organization. Not only may an organization gain from the different points of view but such participation will tend to increase the commitment the individuals will have to the long-range plans.

In short, any given subunit has the authority and responsibility to elect its own leadership and define its own controls for any given problem-solving activity. The individuals within the subunit receive their power according to the member perception of their potential contribution to the core activities (achieving the subunit's objective, maintaining itself internally, and adapting to the larger whole).[24]

If this is to be effective, it is important that each decision-making group explore the questions that it can cope with competently. For example, in considering diversification of an organization, the upper levels of management might be more effective in answering such questions as (1) will a new line increase total sales or merely transfer some of the old product sales to the new; (2) how will manufacturing and distribution costs be influenced, and (3) will resultant profits be greater or smaller than without the new line? [25]

To answer these questions accurately, other questions must be answered first. For example, (1) can existing facilities be used for the new product, (2) do existing personnel have the technical ability to develop and produce the new item, and (3) if not, what would it take to retrain them? These questions may be best handled at the lower levels.

Structure IV: Power According to Inevitable Organizational Responsibilities

Finally, we arrive at the strategy that goes furthest in the direction of the right ends of the continua. This is the structure which should be used for decisions that involve the highest degree of responsibility and are the most basic for the organization. Under this structure each individual has equal power and responsibility and *he may not relinquish it*. The power he is given is the right (through vote or other appropriate mechanisms) to influence the nature of the core activities. It may be necessary to modify this to "unless there is a consensus decision for all individuals to delegate their power and responsibility to one (or a few) individual(s)." Such a structure is used for decisions in which maximum individual productivity and maximum feelings of responsibility and commitment are desired—for example, decisions regarding promotions, salaries, or the acceptance of a departmental production objective. Under these conditions the desire is to maximize the individual's commitment to carrying out his part of the decision and to help others to do the same.

[24] This strategy was initially defined by Knickerbocker and McGregor in D. McGregor (Ed.), "The Consultant Role and Organizational Leadership: Improving Human Relations in Industry," *Journal of Social Issues*, Vol. IV, No. 3, Summer 1948, pp. 2–40.

[25] James L. Lundy, *Effective Industrial Management*, MacMillan, New York, 1957, pp. 145–146.

Other examples in which such a structure may be used are:

1. The decision significantly affects the distribution of power, control, information, and the specialization of work.
2. The decision defines the rules that specify the conditions under which any one of the structures would be used.

The appeal system of Glacier Metal Company illustrates a basic right that employees could be granted. This power is not as complete as we believe is necessary. But it goes further than anyone else has gone. Every member at Glacier has "the right to appeal against any executive decision or action of an executive superior which affects him and which he considers to be unfair or unjust; inconsistent—or not covered by (existing) policy; or contrary to the best interests of the company." [26]

"The appeal process begins with one's immediate superior. The appellant and the supervisor whose decision is the subject of appeal both have the right to appeal . . . to the next higher manager." [27] The appeals process may continue up to the managing director.

Concluding Comments

Four types of organizational structures have been discussed and some of the conditions under which they might be used in an organization have been enumerated. The structures vary in the degree to which they approximate the right ends of the continua in the "mix" model. The first strategy is furthest away; the fourth is the closest. Each strategy has been designed to be used under conditions in which the most can be obtained from the individuals by frustrating them least, as well as by offering the best possible opportunity (for the defined conditions) for psychological success.

The exact amount that each structure is used will vary for each organization and within the same organization under different conditions. There may be times when the survival of the organization will require the use of Structure I. At other times, Structure IV may be most crucial. Presumably the normal situation will require the use of all four strategies, in some balanced amount. Again, the exact point of balance must be left to further research.

We may conclude that *organizations (of the future) will tend to vary the structures that they use according to the kinds of decisions that must be made.* If one asks the individual in the organization of the fu-

[26] Wilfred Brown, *op. cit.*, p. 261.
[27] *Ibid.*

ture to see the company organizational chart, he will be asked, "For what type of decision?"

In order to accomplish this, "decision rules" will have to be defined to guide our choice of the proper structure. A decision rule may be defined as any method which from time to time provides an explicit way for selecting one action from a set of alternative actions available to the decision maker(s).[28] It might also be emphasized that the task of defining the decision rules to tell the participants which organizational structure should be used under a given set of conditions will be assigned to as many participants as possible. In other words, although the organization will use at least one strategy that minimizes individual self-actualization (Structure I), the participants will have the power to decide when this strategy is to be used in their organization. If autocracy is to be used, the use of it will be defined under participative conditions (Structure IV). Control, in a given unity, over its core activities will be in the hands of as many individuals within that unity as possible.

Some research has been published that illustrates, to some degree, the point being made. Leavitt [29] has recently made a similar proposal based on research on communication networks. One network (similar to the pyramidal structure) was most effective for the highly routinized, noninvolving tasks. Another network (similar to a circle) was most effective in terms of criteria of creativity and flexibility and dealing with novel problems. Leavitt concludes, "(I favor the conclusion) that if we want to achieve one kind of goal, then one kind of structure seems feasible. If we want other criteria to govern, then another structure may make sense." [30]

Thompson and Tuden [31] suggest that two major variables in understanding decision making are "beliefs about causation" and "preferences about outcomes." They hypothesize that an organization's activities can be described in terms of decisions that (1) are computational (that is, routine or programmed), (2) require majority judgment, (3) make compromises, and (4) develop by inspiration. For each of these (admittedly pure types) the authors develop a particular organizational structure.

[28] C. West Churchman, *Prediction and Optimal Decision*, Prentice-Hall, New York, 1961, p. 13.
[29] Harold J. Leavitt, "Unhuman Organizations," *Harvard Business Review*, Vol. 40, No. 4, July–August 1962, pp. 90–98.
[30] *Ibid.*, p. 95.
[31] James D. Thompson and Arthur Tuden, "Strategies, Structures, and Processes of Organizational Decision," in *Comparative Studies in Administration*, edited by the same authors, University of Pittsburgh Press, 1959, pp. 195–216.

In the case of the computational, they develop a pyramidal structure. We have done the same. For the decision by majority judgment, they describe a structure that is similar to a *collegium*. This is a structure populated by ". . . wise and knowing men, operating according to constraints or rules which (1) require fidelity to the group's preference hierarchy, (2) require all members to participate in each decision, (3) route pertinent information about causation to each member, (4) give each member equal influence over the final choice, and (5) designate as ultimate choice that alternative favored by the . . . majority." [32] This structure combines aspects of our Structures II, III, and IV. The fact that each has equal power places it in Structure III, and since there must be participation it also includes aspects of Structure IV. However, the fact that "majority rules" places it in Structure II. In terms of our model, the Thompson-Tuden typology may cause some confusion and difficulty if it is applied. For example, if "majority rules" then the "equal power" exists only for the exploration stages. It seems probable that participants may become frustrated if they have equal power to make a point, yet somehow they can be shut off by the majority. This could lead to the politicking so often found in organizations, which leads to pseudo-participation.[33] The probability that this may become the case is increased when we learn that Thompson and Tuden would give the administrator the power to decide which structure should be used.[34] This could easily lead to the power individual controlling the organization by varying the structures as he sees fit.[35] In our model Structure IV must be used in defining the rules and in changing the structures.

Thompson and Tuden suggest that decision by compromise should be resolved by a structure of a *representative body*. Their description of the characteristics of the structure suggest that it may develop the problems that Robert Blake and Herbert Shepard have described. For example, the factions may polarize, there may be the problem of "hero" and "traitor," and so on. (More of this later.) It should be pointed out that Thompson and Tuden do suggest that the members be required to hold as its *top* priority preference the desire to reach agreement. How-

[32] *Ibid.*, p. 200.
[33] See the previously cited work of Blake, Shepard, McGregor, and Argyris (budget study).
[34] Thompson and Tuden, *op. cit.*, pp. 205–206.
[35] I believe the same may be said for Janowitz' differentiation between domination and manipulation. In terms of our model both of Janowitz' categories would be in Structure I. Morris Janowitz, "Changing Patterns of Organizational Authority: The Military Establishment," *Administrative Science* Quarterly, Vol. 3, No. 4, March 1959, pp. 473–494.

ever, as Blake and Shepard have shown, such requirements tend to fall into the background and the "fight aspects" come to the foreground.

Organizational Leadership

We have concluded that an organization can conceivably have several organizational structures, each structure being appropriate for a particular set of decisions. Decision rules would exist to define the conditions under which each structure should be used.

Organizational leadership may also be conceived as a strategy for accomplishing work effectively. We may hypothesize that the leadership used should be consonant with the organizational structure. Since the organizational structure will tend to vary, we may hypothesize that the leadership pattern also will vary. As in organizational structure, leadership may vary from that approximating the left ends to that approximating the right ends of the continua. Each leadership pattern will tend to be associated with a certain set of costs and pay-offs. These should be comparable to the costs and pay-offs associated with an organizational structure that is at the same point along the continua.

Stage I: Reality-Centered Leadership

The first stage in organizational leadership, therefore, is the one in which leadership develops along a whole range of patterns. Also, decision rules are developed to serve as guideposts as to how and when leadership patterns are changed. This has been called *reality-centered* leadership.

If one examines the literature on leadership, there has been a trend indicating that what is considered to be "effective" leadership varies with the situation as well as with the personalities of the participants. For example, directive, firm, "headship" leadership, was considered as most effective. With the onset of the Lewin, Lippit, and White studies, "democratic" leadership became the desired pattern for effective leadership by many practitioners. Democratic leadership was modified by various researchers to "participative," "collaborative," "employee-centered," "group-centered," leadership.

Soon this trend was questioned and the pendulum swung to the position that no one leadership style is to be considered *the* most effective. Each style was probably effective under a given set of conditions. Consequently, effective leaders were those who were able to behave in many different leadership styles depending on the requirements of reality, as they and others perceived it.[36] For example, Parker reports that leadership varied with the needs of the groups.[37] Ross and Hendry also conclude that various leadership styles may be effective under different conditions. Directive leadership may lead to high productivity but low morale and poor commitment to work. Also larger groups seem to tolerate and use authoritarian leadership more effectively than small groups.[38]

The second set of relevant factors are related to the personalities involved. Not all individuals will tend to react in the same manner to the various types of leadership. For example, an increase in the degree of participation will tend to have favorable effects to the extent that (a) the participants are high on the need for independence, and (b) they are low on authoritarianism.[39]

The first step that suggests itself, therefore, is that the executives be assisted to develop reality-centered leadership patterns. When a leader is reality centered, he is able to diagnose a given administrative situation from the point of view of all those involved (including himself). Recalling the concept of the self discussed earlier, we are reminded that diagnosing reality from many different points of view is quite difficult. It requires, among other things, a high degree of self-awareness, awareness of one's impact on others, and awareness of their impact on oneself. It also requires a low degree of defensiveness so that (1) one might admit to one's cognitive field as many different factors as are relevant in the specific administrative situation, and (2) one can differentiate oneself (needs, anxieties, etc.) from the situation, thereby distorting perceptions less or at least being aware of the distortions.[40]

[36] See Chris Argyris, *Personality and Organization*, Harper, New York, 1957, pp. 205–208, and "Organizational Leadership," in L. Petrullo and B. M. Bass (Eds.), *Leadership and Interpersonal Behavior*, Holt, Rinehart and Winston, 1961, pp. 326–354.

[37] Seymour Parker, "Leadership Patterns in a Psychiatric Ward," *Human Relations*, Vol. XI, No. 4, pp. 207–302.

[38] M. G. Ross and C. Hendry, *New Understandings of Leadership*, Association Press, New York, 1957, see pp. 47–72, 81ff.

[39] J. R. P. French, E. Kay, and H. H. Meyer, "A Study of Threat and Participation in an Industrial Performance Appraisal Program," *Behavioral Research Service Report*, General Electric Company, 1962, pp. 118–119. See also the work of Vroom previously cited which suggested that authoritarian individuals react differently to opportunities for participation.

[40] The latter ability is similar to what Rollo May may have defined as being objective (i.e., to be aware of one's subjectivity). For an interesting article regarding the dynamics of "separating" the situation from one's self, see Thomas S. Szasz, "The

Once the administrative situation is understood correctly, the leader behaves appropriately. *But what is appropriate behavior?* The probability is high that different leadership patterns will be appropriate for different situations. For example, under certain conditions "participative" leadership might be most effective. Under other conditions a more directive or a more laissez-faire leadership might be required.

It is, therefore, the responsibility of every executive in the organization that is considering any of these major organizational changes to develop first his competence in several leadership patterns so that he is able to shift from one to another with minimal ambiguity and personal insecurity. The leader will need to have this philosophy of leadership fully internalized. An operational criterion of adequate internalization is that his confidence in the reality-centered leadership is so high that he will not tend to feel insecure or guilty when and if he is questioned about his changing behavior from, for example, being directive to becoming more participative.

Moreover, it will be necessary for the leader to communicate clearly to the subordinates the conditions under which he will tend to behave in each given leadership style. This can be accomplished by developing a set of decision rules that make it operationally clear to the subordinates when he will use each of the different leadership patterns. These requirements in turn assume that it is possible for a leader to vary his leadership style according to the situation in which he exists. This assumption seems congruent with the Jahoda model of mental health since she states that a healthy individual is able, among other things, to perceive reality accurately and to behave in such a way as to facilitate his and others' effectiveness in a given situation. The leader also understands reality requirements that are necessary if his society is to exist. He is not threatened by environmental demands if he feels they are justified. Indeed, it seems that an effective leader is basically a mentally healthy individual.

Stage II: Subordinates and the Leader Control the Decision Rules for the Appropriate Leadership

The second stage is characterized by the leader inviting the subordinates to participate with him in defining the decision rules that will guide in his selection of a leadership pattern to use under specifically defined conditions. The participation in these deliberations would be on the basis that each subordinate and the leader has equal power. The decision rules defined by the group members would become binding when unanimously accepted by the group. Once the group has defined the decision rules, the leader can if he wishes, disband it. Any future modifications could be made by him and communicated to the subordinates.

A natural sequence to this is to offer to the subordinates permanent control over the definition of the decision rules. In giving the control of the decision rules to the subordinates, the leader does not relinquish his freedom to decide how he shall behave in a particular leadership pattern. He still has control over his style of leadership.

Stage III: The Subordinates and the Leader Control the Use of Rewards and Penalties

During the third stage, the leader and the subordinates share equally the control over rewards and penalty. The salaries, promotions, and bonuses are under the control of the entire group. The rewards and penalties cannot be distributed without the authorization of all the individuals involved.

With material rewards such as money and benefits it is possible for the executive committee or the board to define the financial limits within which each department must work. For example, the department may be allotted $100,000 for their salaries. The exact distribution of this money among the managers in the department is the complete responsibility of the managers. In other words, the recommendation is not that the managers tell the organization exactly how much they should earn. The organization is still represented by the broad allocations which set realistic limits for the members of a particular department.

To go further and give the employees the right to define the broad allocations would mean that the employee is given access to rights and responsibilities that are presently legally given to the officers of the organization. This could lead to the employees becoming quasi or real owners. From our point of view, such a step would *not* solve the employees' problems. Indeed it could make them worse. The difficulties inherent in such a move are discussed in Chapter 15.

Stage IV: The Subordinates and the Leader Control the Rules for Membership in the Group and the Make-up of the Group

The final change in leadership is to give the subordinates as well as the formal leader control over the membership and make-up of the group. Research has shown that members value more highly those groups in which membership status is constantly reviewed, and over which they participate and consequently have some control or influence.

Introducing these stages decreases gradually the degree of dependence of the subordinates on the leader. It should decrease the leader centeredness, the rivalry among subordinates for the favor of the leader, and the tendency to evolve scapegoats.[41]

This decrease in turn should increase the probability that the subordinates can express themselves more freely, increase their sense of psychological success, decrease their interpersonal competition and conflict. Such conditions would not only tend to enhance the decision-making processes of the organization but they would also tend to free the formal leader to consider problems of a long-range nature for which previously he could not find the time.

In terms of our model, the participants would experience a greater sense of interdependence with themselves and the whole. This awareness, therefore, of the whole would enlarge. Their capacity to modify their organization's (or department's or group's) internal make-up would increase. Their time perspective would also tend to be enlarged. In other words, as these changes materialize, the individuals will begin to behave in such a way as to bring the organization behaviorally closer to our model of the healthy organization.[42]

It should be pointed out that the analysis assumes that each participant will manifest a minimum degree of conceptual competence and will be able to deal effectively with the cognitive world. Individuals who tend to operate poorly on the cognitive level will tend to have difficulties trying to accomplish some of these suggested changes. Lower-class individuals and those who have lived in underdeveloped areas of our society may well be sociological examples of individuals who have learned a language and concepts that would not tend to help them with the scheme presented here.

It should also be pointed out that these groups will tend to be worse than useless if they are not developed into effective, cohesive units. Effective groups may be described in terms of the model developed earlier. The effectiveness of a group may be hypothesized to increase as the members are able to:

own their ideas, feelings, and values
be *open* about their ideas, feelings, and values

[41] Chris Argyris, *Executive Leadership*, Harper, New York, 1953.
[42] The stages outlined above may be one way to develop a "due process of law" among management personnel. William M. Evan, "Organization Man and Due Process of Law," *American Sociological Review*, Vol. 26, No. 4, August 1961, pp. 540–547.

experiment with new ideas, feelings, and values
and as the group develops viable norms for:
individuality rather than conformity
trust or *risk taking* rather than mistrust
concern for individuals rather than lack of concern
and as the group develops:
effective decision-making processes
less defensive reactions
fewer rivalries and hostilities.

Developing such groups will not be an easy task. As has been suggested elsewhere it may take half or a full decade of concentrated effort to develop effective groups.[43]

One of the crucial problems that will have to be dealt with if small groups are to be effective within the organization is the use of authority. Peabody, in an analysis of various views of authority, shows that it is not a unitary concept.[44] Authority may be described as formal and functional. Formal authority may be divided into "legitimacy" and "position"; functional authority into "competence" and "personal."

Legitimacy derives from the basic source of authority such as "legal order," "social approval," and a "generalized deference toward authority." Position authority derives from "hierarchical office," "formal role," or "formal authority sanctioned by the organization." Competence authority derives from "technical knowledge and skill," "authority of confidence," and "knowledge of performance." Personal authority derives from "knowledge of the human aspect of administration" and "rapport with subordinates."

We suggest that a group will have to come to grips with and "work through" all these dimensions of authority. Each member will have to explore his feelings and reactions to legitimacy and position. The cognitive as well as the interpersonal competence of each member will have to be ascertained and hopefully increased.

One final comment about organizational leadership. Extrapolating from the work on mass communications by Hovland, Janis, and Kelley, we may hypothesize that, other factors being constant, the participants of the organization will tend to resist attempts at mass influence toward change even if the changes are well conceived, if they do not trust those attempting to induce the change. We hypothesize, therefore, that the integrity of the program for reconstructing the organization that we are

[43] Chris Argyris, *Interpersonal Competence and Organizational Effectiveness, op. cit.*
[44] Robert L. Peabody, "Perceptions of Organizational Authority: A Comparative Analysis," *Administrative Science Quarterly*, Vol. 6, No. 4, March 1962, pp. 463–482.

presenting will be judged initially by the participants primarily on the basis of their leaders' behavior. If the participants do not trust their leaders (as well as one another), it is doubtful whether any suggestions that may be offered, no matter how valid, will have a respectable probability of being achieved. Thus organizational leadership will be the foundation on which the rest will be built. If leadership is not effective, we question the probability that the other changes will be effective.

Organizational Staffing
and Job Design

In this chapter we will focus on how to modify the staffing of organizations as well as parts of the technology in order to inhance the opportunity for psychological success and organizational effectiveness.

The Staffing of Organizations

Along with the specialization of work, another fundamental characteristic of organizations is the "optimum" staffing of the system. "Optimum" is difficult to define explicitly, but it usually connotes an adequate enough staff to promote feelings of not being pressured, of work being relatively easy, and of minimum dependence on others. "Optimum" usually means, subjectively, a "fair day's work."

Recent research suggests that a "proper" understaffing could lead to positive results for the individual and the organization. The basic concepts have been developed by Barker in the study of children. However, as we shall see, there exists some empirical evidence to illustrate these concepts in the field of organizational behavior.

Barker has attempted to correlate human behavior with various kinds of "behavior settings" (social systems in our terms) that have the property of coercing different people to behave largely in the same manner once they "enter" them.[1] For example, psychologically different foremen may all behave in a similar manner when they enter the plant manager's office for a budget meeting. Barker suggests that one of the important properties of behavioral settings is their degree of populatedness. Behavior settings will tend to coerce particular behavior when they are "undermanned" but not when they are optimally manned or overmanned. Picture, for example, a baseball game. To be successful it requires the participation of a given number of people. If this number is decreased (up to a point) there will exist "homeostatic mechanisms" to maintain the setting intact so that the game may continue.[2]

Two consequences of this undermanning are that the range in the direction and the strength of the forces acting on the individual participants increases. As Barker points out, there is nothing mysterious about this. "So long as the homeostatic controls maintain the functional level of the setting (system in our terms) the same pattern and strength of forces is distributed among fewer persons."[3] Put in another way, fewer available persons are pressed more strongly to produce the same level of activity.

In comparing behavioral settings in various towns (including across cultures), Barker has found that when behavioral settings are undermanned, there tends to be greater effort and people work harder. Also, individuals tend to experience more difficult, challenging, and important tasks. In addition, each occupant is called upon to fill a greater variety of activities. Individuals tend to see themselves as suitable for previously "inappropriate" tasks. Moreover, the person has to meet and interact with a greater proportion of the total variety of people present. There is also an increasing tolerance for people because now individuals' contributions become much more important. These findings were recently confirmed in a study of small and big schools, in which the sample of students was nearly 2500.[4]

Apparently as a result of such conditions, the individuals tend to experience a greater feeling of responsibility, a greater sense of challenge, and a higher evaluation of their functional importance in the system. The probability increases that they may enhance their feeling of psychological success and their self-esteem. Greater confidence and trust in self and others begins to arise as the challenges are met.

[1] Roger Barker, "Ecology and Motivation," *Nebraska Symposium on Motivation*, University of Nebraska Press, Lincoln, 1960.
[2] Roger Barker, *Big School—Small School*, Midwest Psychological Field Station, University of Kansas, Lawrence, Kansas, 1962.
[3] *Ibid.*, pp. 24–25.
[4] *Ibid.*, Chaps. 4–8.

The effect on the output may vary. Logically, we may expect a lower level of maximal performance. The demands of great versatility, for example, introduce interfering skills. Also, greater effort and longer hours may lead to fatigue. The maximum level of a person's achievement in *any particular* task may be reduced.

These results, however, may not necessarily be as dysfunctional as we might infer at first glance. For example, an individual's performance can be greatly improved if he receives support from others. It is easier, notes Barker, to pitch a superlative ball game if the fielders are excellent. But it should be noted that the individual's maximal performance in any one task may be reduced. This does not necessarily spell difficulties for the organization. It may well be that the effectiveness of an organization does not require maximal skills in any one task, but better than average skills in several tasks. Also, organizational effectiveness may be less a function of what one individual does and more a function of the degree to which the work of many dovetails and supports each other.

There is some empirical work that illustrates some of Barker's views. For example, in the school study cited, Barker predicted that small- and large-school juniors would report different kinds of satisfactions from their experiences in the behavior settings they inhabited. This prediction was confirmed; specifically, juniors from the small schools reported more satisfactions relating to the development of competence, to being challenged, to engaging in important actions, to being involved in group activities, and to achieving moral and cultural values; whereas large-school juniors reported more satisfactions dealing with vicarious enjoyment, with large entity affiliation, with learning about their school's persons and affairs, and with gaining "points" via participation. It was further predicted that these school differences would be causally related to differences in filling important and responsible positions in school settings. This prediction was verified: the satisfactions reported were significantly influenced by the positions the student respondents occupied within settings, and most of the differences between large and small schools in this regard were eliminated when differences in setting position were held constant. The burden of the evidence supports the conclusions that large- and small-school juniors experienced different satisfactions and that these differences were due to differences in the number of students who occupied important, responsible positions.

Students of small schools reported experiencing more attractions and more pressures toward participation in school nonclass activities than students of large schools, and their responses reflected more involvement and more feelings of responsibility. Furthermore, the small schools did not produce such great individual differences in experienced attractions and pressures as did the large school; the small schools contained fewer "outsiders." The findings indicate that the small-school students lived under greater day-by-day attraction, obligation, and external pressure to take active part in the various behavior settings of their schools.

In one study several branch banks [5] were compared with the home office. Each branch bank was a miniature carbon copy of the primary departments of the home office. When the branches were first staffed, they were populated on the bases of predicted work demands. During the heavy work period (the lunch hour and closing time) the branches were undermanned. During the morning and afternoon the branches were optimally manned or (in some cases) overmanned.

It was interesting to note that the attitudes and behavior of the same employees changed as they went from optimally manned to undermanned situations (behavioral settings in Barker's terms). In the undermanned setting, they worked harder, performed their work more effectively even though it was more difficult and complex, cooperated significantly more with those who were "swamped," exhibited more responsibility in seeing that all the work was done, and spoke of the importance of their branch as a whole.

As the branches became more popular and customers increased, the number of hours that the branches were undermanned increased. Yet the commitment, hard work, and sense of responsibility seemed to remain at a level which was much higher than that reported by the employees when they were at the home office or in the early days of the branches when business was slow.

Sweetland and Heythorn present more evidence illustrating some of Barker's predictions. They simulated and studied in great detail an "Air Defense Direction Center." Some of their conclusions were:

The increase in load provoked the elimination of non-essential behavior. Load increases finally caused a pruning of almost all behavior not critical to defending the area. As will be shown; the crews also (as load went up) tended to carry tracks for shorter and shorter times, and also with fewer and fewer reports.

Thus, the increase in load causes a modification of the model of reality made by the crews. At the beginning (under low loads), the crews tended to include everything (penetrating, noise, outbound) in the model. As the

[5] Chris Argyris, *The Organization of a Bank*, Yale Labor and Management Center, 1952.

loads increased, they dropped the non-essentials, still maintaining an accurate replication of the essentials. This one-to-one relationship between important reality and model remained. Rather than yield, they made improvements in their processing techniques (quicker decisions, fewer reports). Our feeling is that an excellent way to measure the importance of a phenomenon to a system is to determine the accuracy of the organization's model of reality with respect to the phenomenon (the greater the accuracy the greater the importance).[6]

We might speculate that one reason the increase in working tempo of a group of factory workers who went from a six- to a five-day week did not increase fatigue, decrease morale, or negatively effect quality and quantity production is that the employees went from an over-manned to an undermanned situation, and that they were rewarded by more free time.[7] Some recent studies that relate lower absenteeism to smaller size may also be related to the same underlying cause.[8] However, we must be careful because it is theoretically possible for a small organization to be overmanned and a large one to be undermanned.

Indirect support from experimental studies comes from the Guetzkow-Dill [9] experiments, which in turn drew from the Heise and Miller [10] and Leavitt [11] studies. Briefly, we may conclude that if a group of individuals is originally constrained to interact in interpersonal systems requiring more than the minimum number of links, they will, if given the opportunity, and if motivated to complete the task, reduce the number of communication links. The individual seems to go toward an undermanned communication system.

Herbert Thelen, as a result of extensive research in small groups, concludes that the optimum challenge to an individual comes in a

[6] Anders Sweetland and William W. Haythorn, "An Analysis of the Decision-Making Functions of a Simulated Air Defense Direction Center," *Behavioral Science*, Vol. 6, No. 2, April 1961.
[7] Einar Thorsrud, *The Forty-Hour Five-Day Week*, European Productivity Agency Union Study, No. 11, Organisation for European Economic Co-operation, Rue Andre Pascal, Paris, 1957.
[8] *Size and Morale*, Action Society Trust, London, 1953. Howard Baumgartel and R. Sobal, "Background and Organizational Factors in Absenteeism," *Personnel Psychology*, Vol. 12, 1959, pp. 431–443. D. Hewitt and J. Parfit, "A Note on Working Morale and Size of Group," *Occupational Psychology*, Vol. 27, 1953, pp. 38–42.
[9] H. Guetzkow and W. R. Dill, "Factors in the Organizational Development of Task-Oriented Groups," *Sociometry*, Vol. 20, 1957, pp. 175–204.
[10] C. A. Heise and G. Miller, "Problem Solving by Small Groups Using Various Communication Nets," *Journal of Abnormal and Social Psychology*, Vol. 46, 1951, pp. 327–336.
[11] H. J. Leavitt, "Some Effects of Certain Communication Patterns on Group Performance," *Journal of Abnormal and Social Psychology*, Vol. 46, 1951, pp. 38–50.

"least-sized" group.[12] Such groups are the *"smallest"* [13] groups in which it is possible to have represented at a functional level all the social and achievement skills required for the particular required activity. Talacchi concludes that the larger the organization, the lower the employee level of satisfaction, and the higher the absenteeism. In his suggestions for designing an organization, Talacchi suggests that "minimizing the number of levels of authority," "reducing the number of departments," divisions, etc., and enlarging the membership of meetings (from departmental to interdepartmental) may tend to develop more effective organizations.[14] All these suggestions, in terms of Barker's concept, would tend to increase the probability of undermanned behavioral settings, which would corroborate his hypothesis.

Indirect support of the proposition that "optimally" undermanned organizations may be correlated with effectiveness may be inferred from research on communication. Miller, for example, has suggested that man is limited in the amount of information that he can receive and cope with effectively.[15] Attneave [16] and Quastler [17] maintain that there can be "channel overload" where accurate reception of the message begins to plateau and fails to increase with further increase in the rate of transmission. Beyond the plateau, the receiver becomes overloaded and reception becomes inaccurate.

"All other things being equal, the greater the number of links in the system, the greater will be the probability of 'noise' in functional connections among organization units. This becomes particularly critical where multiple links to a unit exist so that chances of simultaneous cues being received is great." [18]

In this connection, it is interesting to note that Vroom [19] found that

[12] Herbert Thelen, *Dynamics of Groups at Work*, University of Chicago Press, 1954, pp. 187–188.

[13] Italics are mine.

[14] Sergio Talacchi, "Organization Size, Individual Attitudes, and Behavior: An Empirical Study," *Administrative Science Quarterly*, Vol. 5, No. 3, December 1960, pp. 398–420.

[15] George A. Miller, "The Magical Numbers Seven Plus or Minus Two," *Psychological Review*, Vol. 63, 1956, pp. 81–97.

[16] F. Attneave, "Psychological Application of Information Theory in Psychology" (quoted in Robert Dubin, "Stability of Human Organizations," in Mason Haire (Ed.), *Modern Organization Theory*, Wiley, New York, 1959, p. 228).

[17] H. Quastler (Ed.), *Information Theory in Psychology*, Free Press, Glencoe, Ill., 1955.

[18] Robert Dubin, "Stability of Human Organization," in Mason Haire (Ed.), *Modern Organization Theory*, Wiley, New York, 1959, pp. 218–253. (Footnotes 16 and 17 found in Dubin's work).

[19] Victor H. Vroom, *Some Personality Determinants of the Effects of Participation*, Prentice-Hall, Englewood Cliffs, N.J., 1960.

larger groups tended to favor authoritarian leadership whereas smaller groups favored equalitarian leadership. It may be that as complexity of networks increases, there will be a tendency to "hierarchalize" (as Miller suggests) in order to simplify the problem and (especially in an organization) protect oneself. One way to do this is to prefer that an authoritarian leader take on the responsibilities of the unit.

Perhaps this is enough to suggest that a fruitful area of exploration to increase individual and organization effectiveness is the degree to which an organization and its behavior settings are, with respect to personnel, undermanned, optimally manned, and overmanned. It is the writer's hypothesis that most organizations tend to be optimally manned or overmanned. Much research, however, is needed to test this hypothesis. Basic to such a test would be the need to define more operationally what we mean precisely by these terms. Barker has provided an excellent beginning.

There is another interesting hypothesis that may be related to these concepts. As we have seen, an undermanned organization tends to create stress through the challenges that are created by the undermannedness. The stress, if not too great, can lead to positive results for the individual and the organization.

This raises the interesting question as to whether stress can be created by other means that would lead to enhancing individual and organizational effectiveness. It may be that organizations can develop the kind of stress that leads to positive results just as the stress an individual places on his body when he exercises can lead to positive effects.

In a recent study of fifty corporations, Grusky suggests that the larger firms may well require more frequent changes in top management if they are not to become too stable and rigid. Moreover, if dynamic, aggressive characteristics are associated with entrepreneurship, and if these are necessary (as Grusky suggests), then larger organizations may also tend to have difficulties in developing the characteristics among their executives.[20] This may be one reason why McClelland found that the larger organizations tended to spawn executives with a lower need for achievement.[21]

Recently a study was made comparing "open" and "closed" groups. The latter were stable groups where the membership remained intact throughout the experiment. The former were groups where various degrees of instability were introduced by adding new members, taking away some members, or reintroducing old ones. In all cases, the open

[20] Oscar Grusky, "Corporate Size, Bureaucratization, and Managerial Succession," *American Journal of Sociology*, Vol. LXVII, No. 3, November 1961, pp. 261–269.
[21] David McClelland, *The Achieving Society*, Van Nostrand, Princeton, N.J., 1961, pp. 265ff.

groups did better than the closed groups in originality scores and in production. If we may assume that the changes in manpower created some stress, then we may infer that a certain degree of stress can be correlated with creativity and production.[22, 23]

It would be a tragic mistake for these comments to be interpreted as meaning that indiscriminate speed-up is good for people. It would be self-defeating if organizations were purposely undermanned in order to manipulate the workers to produce more.

An undermanned organization will probably have its predicted effects (1) *if* the tasks available permit individuals to use their important abilities, (2) *if* the employees believe that the undermannedness is legitimate, and (3) *if* they are sharing the fruits of increased productivity. The motive in developing optimally undermanned organizations should be to increase the probability for self-expression, self-responsibility, commitment in individuals, and the flexibility in, and vitality of, the organization. If this is successful, the resulting work should be more deeply satisfying. However, if an organization undermans itself without concomitant enlargement of jobs, increasing mutual influence and control, and deepening its own purpose, it will tend to find that the entire program may backfire.

The Redesign of Jobs

Much imagination and research will be necessary if the tremendous impact of task specialization and managerial controls on the majority of jobs is to be overcome. The magnitude of the task may be sensed by the fact that it is estimated that over 90 per cent of the jobs in the automobile industry can be learned in five days or less. Perhaps more amusing is the report in the newspapers that three chimpanzees have been used effectively in stuffing rubber pillows.[24] Also, one factory has found that certain mental patients are ideal for repetitive assembly work.[25]

Personality theory is one way to begin to think about job design. Individuals have needs and abilities. We may categorize these abilities in terms of motoric (doing), cognitive (knowing), and conative (feeling).

[22] R. C. Ziller, R. B. Behringer, and J. D. Goodchild, "Group Creativity Under Conditions of Success or Failure and Variations in Group Stability," *Journal of Applied Psychology*, Vol. 66, 1962, pp. 43–49.

[23] The study on *Frustration and Regression* by Barker, Lewin, and Dembo, already referred to, also supports the view that mild stress can have a positive influence.

[24] *New York Herald Tribune*, November 11, 1960, p. 3.

[25] *Christian Science Monitor*, February 18, 1960.

Every individual is hypothesized to have a particular range of competence in each of these abilities. The range may be hypothesized to go
from minimum to maximum competence, and it varies from individual to individual and within the same individual at different times of
his development.

The function of scientific management historically has been to define jobs with as few abilities as possible. For example, Louis Davis has
shown that the prevailing practice in designing the content of industrial jobs is to reply on the criterion of minimizing immediate costs,
as indicated by minimum unit operation time. To satisfy the minimum-
cost criterion, skills are specialized to a pattern. Learning time and
variety are minimized; repetitiveness is maximized. This practice leads
to a physiological organization theory, which, in turn, is based on a narrow, if not questionable, set of assumptions about human motivation.[26, 27] Classical organizations tend to use those abilities of individuals that are usually related to the motoric and those that require "minimum competence." The lower one goes down the chain of command
and the more specialized the company becomes, the greater the probability that one will find jobs with minimal use of the cognitive and conative dimensions and almost minimal use of the motoric dimension.

Our position is not that this trend should be completely eliminated.
An organization would probably not exist if some assignment and specialization of word were not made. Every job must have some limits
and no job will probably exist in which the individual is permitted to
have complete freedom to make a significant decision. Jaques describes
the point in his study of the measurement of responsibility.[28]

Every job is limited in some of its aspects, in the sense that complete freedom to use discretion or judgment is definitely not allowed. When we talk
about discretion and judgment, therefore, we are talking about those aspects
of a job in which the person is allowed to choose, and, indeed, required to
choose, from among alternative ways of doing something, as opposed to
those aspects in which he is prohibited from choosing and must follow a
prescribed policy or method.

Stated positively, our position is to suggest that jobs be designed that
emphasize the right ends of the continua. Kilbridge expresses the same

[26] Louis E. Davis, "Job Design and Productivity: A New Approach," *Personnel*, Vol.
33, No. 5, March 1957, pp. 418–430.
[27] James G. March and Herbert A. Simon, *Organizations*, Wiley, New York, 1958,
pp. 12–22.
[28] Elliot Jaques, *Measurement of Responsibility*, Harvard University Press, 1956,
p. 86.

view in another way: "Job enlargement is the expansion of job content to include a wider variety of tasks and to increase the worker's freedom of pace, responsibility for checking quality, and discretion of method.".

One strategy to enlarge the job has been attempted by IBM.[29] If one examines the enlarged jobs, however, one will find that the greatest degree of enlargement is primarily in terms of the motoric dimension. In other words, instead of putting one piece in a typewriter, the man now may put forty pieces together. The jobs were enlarged primarily by increasing the tasks but these new tasks did not present a significantly more challenging job to the employee. If the possibilities for psychological success and organizational effectiveness are to increase, the enlargement of jobs, we hypothesize, must include the rise of significant portions of the cognitive (knowing) and conative (feeling) abilities.

What if jobs are found that cannot be enlarged because of their nature? There are several possible ways in which to cope with this situation. It may be possible to enlarge other aspects of work and offer these to the employees. For example, a significant increase in the use of cognitive and conative dimensions in designing jobs will occur automatically if the recommendations made for leadership and organizational structure already defined are put into practice. Even if the production job of the employee is not significantly enlarged (he may still have to put four bolts in a car, for example) it would be possible for him to experience significant enlargement when he participates in the decision-making processes characteristic of the latter stages of leadership and the third and fourth organizational structures discussed earlier. The participation in a decision-making group dealing with crucial decisions involves emotionally laden experiences. This would tend to require the employee to use and to develop his cognitive and conative abilities. Admittedly, this may mean that an employee may experience significant job enlargement only a few hours a day, or only every several days. However, this enlargement may be more than he is presently experiencing. Moreover, it may be that man does not need to experience himself as a total person and to be psychologically successful all the time. In fact, creative, psychologically successful experiences may well be exhausting. As in eating, one may fill up and have to wait a while before he becomes hungry again. Exactly how much success an individual would need to experience during a given time period must be determined by research.

One example of how the working world can be enlarged without significant changes in technology is the Scanlon Plan, which has already

[29] F. L. W. Richardson, Jr. and Charles Walker, *Human Relations in an Expanding Company*, Labor and Management Center, Yale University, 1948.

been discussed. Membership in the representative, legislative, and appeals procedures of the Glacier Metal Company already outlined could also provide employees important opportunities to utilize their intelligence and their interpersonal abilities, as well as to develop a true feeling of participation in and commitment toward the organization.[30]

Other ways might be found to broaden the opportunities for employee participation. One might be to elect employee representatives and to utilize closed-circuit television so that employees could watch how they are actually being represented and have the opportunity to recall their delegates for discussion and change of instructions. Under such conditions, delegates may tend to take their jobs more seriously. The experiences of being a delegate could also provide an increase in the use of the employees' interpersonal abilities and help to develop their competence in dealing with intergroup problems, which, as Landsberger[31] and Argyris[32] have shown, are commonplace in organizations. For example, in resolving intergroup problems, all members are invited to define the facts of the problem, develop alternatives (not fixed positions), seek common grounds among positions before tackling differences, and increase their participation in problem solving. The participants would become especially involved in understanding the difficulties of evolving effective groups and of such intergroup phenomena of "tractor" and "hero" as first described by Blake.[33] As the participants are able to overcome the tremendous intergroup pressures inherent in formal organizational structure, they should begin to enlarge their experience in, and their perception of, the organization as a whole.[34] Since Blake's original publication, Blake and Mouton[35] have presented empirical evidence to suggest that the basic processes for reducing inter-

[30] Wilfred Brown, *Explorations in Management*, Heinemann, London, 1960.

[31] Henry Landsberger, "The Horizontal Dimension in Bureaucracy," Cornell University, mimeographed, 1958.

[32] Chris Argyris, *Executive Leadership*, Harper, New York, 1954, and *Interpersonal Competence and Organizational Effectiveness, op. cit.*, Chapters 2ff.

[33] Robert Blake, "Psychology and the Crisis of Statesmanship," *American Psychologist*, Vol. 14, No. 2, February 1959, pp. 87–94. See also Irving L. Janis and Daniel Katz, "The Reduction of Intergroup Hostility: Research Problems and Hypotheses," *Conflict Resolution*, Vol. III, No. 1, March 1959, pp. 85–100.

[34] The administrator is no doubt wondering where the time will be found for such meetings. Later I discuss the possibility of industry utilizing the "extra hours" available from a shorter work week (for which they no doubt would pay) to hold such activities.

[35] Robert Blake and Jane S. Mouton, "The Intergroup Dynamics of Win-Lose Conflict and Problem-Solving Collaboration in Union-Management Relations," *Symposium on Intergroup Relations and Leadership*, University of Oklahoma, April 6–8, 1961.

group conflict can be used in resolving labor-management disputes. The model that is presented could provide the basis for significant degrees of job enlargement for employees at the lower levels as well as for management and trade union leaders.

Another way to enlarge jobs, and perhaps the most effective in the long run, is to increase significantly the individual's opportunity to produce as much of the total product as possible.[36] If jobs could be redesigned so that the whole product or a significant subpart of the product could be produced by an individual, progress would certainly be made. Moreover, such a change would set the stage for another important type of job enlargement. Industry has been dominated in its job design by the scientific-management principles of separating the production of a given unit from the evaluation of its quality. It is difficult for an individual to feel responsible for the piece he produces if he *experiences* that he is not responsible. In industries in which the inspector is made responsible for quality, the individual's feelings of responsibility tend to decrease. Also his degree of submissiveness may increase—for in addition to his boss he now has the inspector to worry about.

It is not difficult to see why employees soon lose their feelings of responsibility for the quality of their product. As the employees in plants X and Y state, "Quality is not my responsibility that's the inspector's job." After many years "on the job" it is not uncommon to observe that the sense of a lack of responsibility for quality is soon internalized by the individual and legitimatized on the realistic grounds that if he produced everything well he might create the conditions for the inspector to lose his job!

Wherever possible, therefore, the jobs should be redesigned so that the employee is responsible for quality of the job that he performs. Marks, under Davies, has shown that if such changes could be accompanied with an enlargement of the job so that the employee is responsible for the total product (or as much of the product as possible), then the situation would be healthier.[37]

[36] Some of the more interesting work is being done by Professor Louis Davis and his colleagues. See, for example, Louis E. Davis and Richard Werling, "Job Design Factors," University of California, supported by Dow Chemical Company, 1960. Louis E. Davis, "Toward Theory of Job Design," *Journal of Industrial Engineering*, Vol. 8, No. 5, September 1957. Among the human-relations groups, William F. Whyte, Leonard Sayles, Elliot Chapple, Robert Guest, and Charles Walker have written about the importance of changing the technology to significantly influence lower-level employee attitudes.

[37] Richard Marks, "A Theory of Job Design and Research Findings," International Association of Applied Psychological Proceedings, 13th Congress, Mimeographed, April 1958.

In a recent paper, Kuriloff has attempted to describe some of the structural changes being explored at Non-Linear Systems.[38] In addition to developing an organizational structure that is extremely flat, there is much emphasis on enlarging the job so that an employee not only produces more of the product but he actually inspects it.

For example, the instrument-assembly department is self-contained. It does the whole job from putting complete instruments together from kits of parts to placing components on etched circuit boards, doing the soldering, and so on to running, calibrating, troubleshooting, and repairing the machine, if necessary.[39]

Moreover, the members of the group decide who will do what by mutual consent and decision. "They know each others' strengths and weaknesses and will generally do a far better job of planning when left alone than if directed by some kind of authority." [40]

The capabilities of the people have been developed in two and one-half years to the point where they write their own instructions for assembly, for troubleshooting, for servicing the product. During this period, production has increased 30 per cent. Although the data presented by Kuriloff are anecdotal, they do warrant very careful consideration and study.

A third way to enlarge jobs is to introduce wherever possible the principle of feedback into the organization even down to the assembly line.[41] For example, a very small secretarial pool could be assigned to type letters *written by the employee* working on the line whose product a customer may query or whose product does not meet the promised quality standard. It would be the responsibility of the employee to explain to the customer why he had the trouble that he reported, assuming the fault is traceable to the employee's work and not to some external (to him) factors.

A fourth possible change toward job enlargement would be to permit the employee to participate in defining the quality standards for a product, in designing the jobs, getting their job rates by conducting their own motion and time studies, etc.[42] Such activities would greatly

[38] Arthur H. Kuriloff, "Management by Integration and Self-Control," 15th Annual Industrial Engineering Proceedings, University of California, February 1963, mimeographed.
[39] *Ibid.*, p. 9.
[40] *Ibid.*
[41] I am told the following incident occurred in a large washing machine manufacturing plant. A picture was published of the top of a washing machine, which was made by one individual. By accident, the photograph also included the identification number. Great interest was aroused in the department that makes tops to learn precisely who had manufactured the top.
[42] Gillespie found this was possible in a large organization. James J. Gillespie, *Free Expression in Industry*, Pilot Press, London, 1948.

enlarge the employee's experience of his conative and cognitive (as well as high motoric) abilities. It would also provide the employee with the experience of being truly responsible for the product or that part of the product that he produces. One example in the motion and time study activities is the "work simplification" concept developed by Mogensen. He suggests that the more employees can become responsible for, and have control over, the industrial engineering activities (such as motion and time studies) the more effective the results will tend to be. The role of the industrial engineers, continues Mogensen, would then be to act as consultants or provide whatever technical assistance that the employees seek.[43]

King has conducted some ingenious methods of training operators in a clothing factory. He created learning situations in which the trainee was required to act as a "self-regulating system." She was her own trainer. The operator not only learned more effectively but her supervisor's role was made more creative and productive. Moreover, her job was greatly enlarged during the learning process. In another paper King expands the idea of "self-regulating system" to executive development. The executive becomes responsible for his own development, which leads to a significant enlargement of his job duties.[44]

To be sure these recommendations would be costly to put into operation. However, as a result of some experimental studies in job enlargement, Davis [45] reports "reduced costs . . . as well as gains in productivity and morale." Moreover, Kilbridge,[46] after a systematic study, shows that job enlargement does lead to lower manufacturing costs. He reports, "The argument is based on tangible cost savings only. Improved quality, greater production flexibility, worker satisfaction . . . although important to the argument favoring job enlargement are not needed to establish its desirability in this case." Golembiewski reports that an enlargement of the job plus an increase in responsibility and self-control has led to 40 per cent increase in work performed with only a 10 per cent increase in the work force. Mann and Hoffman, in a study of the jobs in a new automated power plant, found that the jobs had been redesigned in such a way that they were enlarged. Also, each operator rotated jobs, which, in our terms, enlarges his job. The increase in job

[43] H. F. Goodwin, "Work Simplification," *Factory Management and Maintenance,* July 1952, pp. 72–106.
[44] David M. King, "The Operators as a Self-Regulating System," *Economics,* Vol. 2, No. 2, February 1959, pp. 171–179. Also "The Integration of Training Organization and Policy," paper presented to the London Polytechnic Winter Lectures, 1957.
[45] Louis E. Davis, "Job Design and Productivity: A New Approach," *op. cit.,* p. 428.
[46] Maurice D. Kilbridge, "Reduced Costs Through Job Enlargement," *Journal of Business,* University of Chicago, Vol. XXXIII, No. 4, October 1960, p. 362.

enlargement and responsibility apparently increased the degree of job interest and commitment but not necessarily the satisfaction.[47] Mann and Hoffman point out that job satisfaction is different from intrinsic job satisfaction. They have shown that although responsibility and tension increased among the workers, their job interest also increased while their absence rate was halved.[48] Davis and Werling [49] have shown that job enlargement in maintenance and repair work was accompanied by reduced costs, improved quality, and better interpersonal relations.

Guest reports that job enlargement has brought about increased productivity as well as employee satisfaction.[50] Muller-Thym has provided a comprehensive discussion of how changing concepts of job design and job enlargement have achieved unusually good results in terms of achieving a stated objective quickly and efficiently and at the same time raising the degree of commitment, self-responsibility and self-control an employee experiences on the job. The task-force concept is an example of a new concept that has been used effectively. The Germans used it to maintain very high steel production during the war. They established pools of mechanics, engineers, and workers who could be easily assembled into task forces and sent to a bombed plant to put it back into production. The Polaris project was organized as a separate organization, nonfunctional in character, with all the competences necessary to accomplish the objectives regardless of previous loyalties. In this connection, submarine crews have been trained to be able to perform more than one job.[51] Recently, the Sun Oil Company designed a refinery whose work structure was similar to the strategy implied in our concept of effective organization. All the men in the refinery except the accountants and laboratory technicians were part of one single team. They were trained to perform all the different kinds of work, which ranged from crude distillation and catalytic cracking to blending and the shipping of products. The refinery, reports the management, is operating extremely effectively.[52]

[47] Robert T. Golembiewski, "O and M and the Small Group," *Public Administration Review*, Vol. XX, No. 4, Autumn 1960, pp. 205–212.
[48] Floyd C. Mann and Richard Hoffman, *Automation and the Worker*, Henry Holt, New York, 1960, pp. 77–103.
[49] L. E. Davis and R. Werling, "Job Design Factors," *Occupational Psychology*, Vol. 34, 1960, pp. 109–132.
[50] Robert H. Guest, "Job Enlargement: A Revolution in Job Design," *Personnel Administration*, Vol. 20, No. 2, March–April 1957, pp. 9–16.
[51] Bernard Muller-Thym, "Practices in General Management: New Directions for Organizational Practice," American Society of Mechanical Engineers, Paper 60-Wa59, July 18, 1960.
[52] Clarence Thayer, "Remarks of Clarence Thayer," mimeographed, speech before the Society for Advancement of Management, Wilmington, Del., October 14, 1958.

Still another organization has given production employees the opportunity to be salesmen of their products. The men apparently responded enthusiastically with an "enormous amount of pride and responsibility" reported. Moreover, within six months sales rose 26 per cent, and then another 77 per cent a year later. Production rejects and absenteeism dropped to a new low for the industry.[53]

At this point, we report Melman's recent study in which he systematically compared manufacturing plants producing the same products. His findings cut across several of the kinds of changes that we have recommended. They illustrate the importance of increasing employee participation and responsibility. They also illustrate recommendations that we shall make such as changing the locus of control systems and emphasizing responsibility for units of employees rather than individual jobs. He found that plants with working conditions that enlarged worker's jobs and responsibilities and that created settings in which the worker felt a responsibility for the entire subsystem of which he was a part, outproduced (in costs) those organizations with traditional unilateral decision-making structures. Where a worker decision-making structure had been developed to support the management decision-making structure employees manifested high degree of responsibility, not only for internal costs but for the plant's relationships with suppliers. For example, during a strike of some of their suppliers, the workers' representatives visited the other plants to keep their own plant posted and to see what could be done to assure the supply of materials.

Melman concludes:

The worker decision system integrates the work force into a dynamic, organized entity so that they formulate decisions among themselves concerning both internal codes of behavior and the pattern of their relation to the employer. In the workers' code the direction of development is toward unifying the functions of decision-formulating and decision-executing. In this way, the workers' decision system, paralleling that of management, alters the pattern of the worker as the receiver and the executor of decisions, which are made by separate decision-formulating occupations (the management). The workers' decision system is an evolving system which extends the breadth of its decision-making over more aspects of the productive activity of industrial workers, as well as their extra-occupational behavior. The effects of worker decision-making on production are independent of conscious awareness among industrial workers of such effect. Moreover, the operation of the system, the formation of codes and their implementation does not necessarily require an awareness of a "process" for its operation.

Finally, we note that a workers' mutual decision-making system is inter-

[53] *Industrial Relations News*, Vol. X, No. 39, September 24, 1960, p. 1.

dependent with that of the management. The worker decision system, while leading to demands on management, is not a competitor, which usurps the occupations of a managerial kind. The employer has played the dominant role in decision-making on whether and what production shall be carried out. Within the limits of the employer's decision that workers shall be employed to work, the details of the conditions of production (terms of employment) are opened to the effects of the workers' decision-making.[54]

It is interesting to note that under conditions of increased work responsibility, management was freed to focus more on marketing problems (and other problems with the environment). Also the need for foremen was greatly reduced and their work responsibilities became radically changed. Anticipating the next chapter, Melman found that, in the plants with increased worker responsibilities, the formal budgeting procedures and the accompanying paper work greatly decreased. The effectiveness of the control processes increased through face-to-face relationships. Thus, rather than controls becoming less effective, they became more effective, because in a climate of trust and mutual responsibility the fear of face-to-face confrontation is greatly reduced and the impact of face-to-face contacts can be used to their maximum effect.

These changes may be found to be financially unfeasible for certain jobs. But before these suggestions are too readily discarded by the practitioners, they should be considered seriously. No one knows how many millions of dollars are directly or indirectly lost through goldbricking, rate setting, slowdowns, cheating on the job, lying to the motion and time expert, doctoring production figures and quality control samples, poor quality work, and so on. More important, these informal activities serve to increase the gap that the employees and management perceive as existing between them. This in turn tends to increase management's mistrust of the employee, which then increases management pressure. This closes the cycle and sets into motion organizational compulsive defensive behavior. As the defenses become embedded the organization rigidity increases and the degree to which the participants (management and employee) can influence the organization as they might desire decreases.

It should also be pointed out that even if job security and money were not a problem, it is not clear that the employees would respond kindly to these suggestions of job enlargement. In the writer's discussions with the employees at plants X and Y, he gained the impression that they did not favor proposals to increase their opportunity for self-

[54] Seymour Melman, *Decision-Making and Productivity*, Wiley, New York, 1958, p. 92.

responsibility and self-control. Many seemed to have reached the state where noninvolvement, apathy, and disinterest have become, for them, the proper outlooks.

Finally, if recommendations such as these are ever put into effect, the character of job descriptions will also have to be redefined. No longer will a job description be limited to a static description of duties and responsibilities as narrowly applied to the particular job being described. The new job description would include, along with a description of the job, a description of the social system in which the employee will enter if he takes the particular job. The job description will give the employee an idea of the kinds of individuals and the possible interactions he will tend to have, including the informal groups, their rules, pressures, and norms. Also, in order to provide the employee with a more accurate concept of his work which could lead to his developing his own measurements of his effectiveness, job descriptions could also make estimates of (1) costs of serious or typical errors, and effects of others' errors on one's job, (2) absence effect, (3) range of choices permitted, and (4) necessity for understanding other work.[55]

For example, it would certainly be possible, on the basis of our research, to write job descriptions for plants X and Y describing in detail the informal employee culture. The difference between the low- and high-skill culture as well as the difference between those and the office culture could be made explicit. The employee faced with such information will begin to feel that the commitment expected of him is not limited to the narrow confines of his job. He will see that he is being asked to become a member of a culture, to commit a larger part of his self than is usually requested.

Although the core of any given job may be clearly defined, the relationship with other jobs and people (especially on the upper levels of management) would be left relatively unstructured. It is in the area of interrelationships among jobs where individuals can make important modifications to enhance their and the organization's actualization.[56] In the writer's experience as a consultant, wherever detailed studies have been made to define equally detailed job descriptions, nothing has ever been resolved. If individuals disagree as to each others' scope of responsibility, a job description will not tend to solve the problem. Here may be an opportunity for the individuals to meet and discuss the is-

[55] Floyd C. Mann and Lawrence K. Williams, "Some Effects of the Changing Work Environment in the Office," in Sven Lundstedt (Ed.), *Mental Health and the Work Environment*, Foundation for Research on Human Behavior, Ann Arbor, Mich., mimeographed, 1962, pp. 19–20.

[56] Douglas McGregor, *The Human Side of Enterprise*, McGraw-Hill, New York, 1960.

sues. As the degree of trust among the employees increases, the need for job descriptions sharply delineating their job relations with one another may tend to decrease.

These suggestions do not imply that the less regulations that are stipulated in a job description, the better the situation will be. The optimum amount of freedom will have to be calculated for each set of jobs. Realistic regulations, especially in routine jobs, may have a liberating effect on initiative. Under certain conditions failure to establish clear "perimeters of action" may bog down a person in problems that are not central to his interests and may cause him much loss of time and efficiency.[57]

These views may also be valid for the jobs at the lower levels of the managerial ladder. Industry is beginning to realize that it may have made too much of a fetish of the first-line foreman. For example, it has been commonly accepted that one of the key roles of a foreman is to provide a viable link between top management and the employees. The foreman, with his day-to-day contact with the workers, should be able to keep his finger on the employees' pulse. Kahn [58] and Likert [59] have recently cited data suggesting that foremen consistently overestimate the importance that their subordinates attach to economic factors and underestimate the importance to them of the human variables. Moreover, the supervisors consistently underestimate the importance to their subordinates of those dimensions of the job that deal with human factors. Bennis et al.[60] present evidence that a similar problem may exist in hospitals.

In suggesting that there is a lack of effectiveness in foremen along the human dimensions just mentioned, we do not imply that the fault lies "in" the foremen. Indeed, there are much data that suggest the foremen exist in a difficult, tension-full world as "men-in-the-middle." [61] It is difficult to see how foremen can be very effective under these conditions.

---

[57] Elliot Jaques, *op. cit.*, p. 87.
[58] Robert Kahn, "Human Relations on the Shop Floor," in E. M. Hugh-Jones (Ed.), *Human Relations and Modern Management*, North Holland Publishing Co., Amsterdam, Netherlands, 1958, pp. 43–74, and "The Characteristics of a Good Manager—from the Employee's Point of View," National Industrial Conference Board, 1958.
[59] Rensis Likert, *New Patterns of Management*, McGraw-Hill, New York, 1961, pp. 46–52.
[60] Warren Bennis, N. Berkowitz, M. Affinito, and M. Malone, "Authority, Power, and the Ability to Influence," *Human Relations*, Vol. XI, No. 2, 1958, pp. 149–150.
[61] For a review of the literature, see the author's *Personality and Organization*, Harper, New York, 1957, Chap. IV.

It may be that the first-line superior is not, or cannot be, as important as was thought in order to get the job done. It is well known that General Electric has pioneered in experimenting with a "unit manager." The concept of the unit manager is to have available at the lowest level possible an individual who can actually manage and who has authority over all the functions relevant to achieving the objective. The unit manager is given necessary staff help and acts as a "lower-level" general manager. The role of the foreman under these conditions is almost eliminated.

Thus it is not necessarily true that the foreman is necessary to maintain the close human contact between management and the worker. Indeed, Paterson has shown that foremen handle human relations on the shop floor relatively ineffectively.[62] One of the important lessons learned by the staff members of the recent laboratory programs at Esso was how ineffective foremen tended to be in diagnosing and coping with human situations.[63] If this is found to be true throughout industry, then we might predict that with appropriate role enlargement and the inception of the unit-manager concept, the need for the foreman to control and direct employees may be largely eliminated. The control will now reside more "in" the worker as it is dictated by the requirements of the enlarged job (but also checked by the unit manager).

[62] T. T. Paterson, *Glasgow Limited*, Cambridge University Press, England, 1960, pp. 164–166.
[63] Chris Argyris, *Organizational Development: An Inquiry into the Esso Approach*, Research Development, Esso (now Humble Oil), Houston, Tex., July 1960.

Managerial Controls, Rewards and Penalties, and Incentive Systems

We turn from changes in the organizational structure, the staffing, and the design of work to the changes that may help to make control systems more effective. More specifically, we shall attempt to redefine managerial controls such as budgets, reward and penalty systems, and incentive systems in such a way that they begin to approximate the right ends of the continua. Churchmen defines the control process as "the process of deciding when to test for accuracy and what corrective action to take when it is decided that the accuracy requirements are not met." [1]

Elsewhere it has been shown that managerial controls, as presently conceived, tend to create situations in which the employees feel dependent on their superiors and fearful of the staff personnel in charge of the various types of controls.[2] For example, employees and supervisors tend to perceive controls as instruments of punishment, coercive mechanisms to increase constantly and unilaterally the production goals, evaluative techniques that are unfair in that they continually

---

[1] C. West Churchman, *Prediction and Optimal Decision*, Prentice-Hall, Englewood Cliffs, N.J., 1961, p. 128.
[2] Chris Argyris, *Personality and Organization, op. cit.*, pp. 130–139.

accent failures without showing why such failures may be necessary.[3]

These conditions tend to increase the probability of psychological failure and decrease the probability for psychological success Moreover, they tend to create interdepartmental rivalries and hostilities which can lead to competition that consumes much energy and, at the same time, causes the subordinates to defend themselves by becoming centered toward the interests of their own department and forgetting the interests of the organization as a whole. These unintended consequences do not tend to be observed overtly because they are not measured by the instruments. The managerial controls focus on the costs an organization incurs with regard to machines and do not concern themselves with the "human" costs.[4]

Ironically, if budgets are to be effective they must rely heavily on the very people whose behavior they are designed to control. Moreover, many of them are designed and utilized in a manner implying that the employee can be trusted to give accurate information but cannot use it competently.

Gillespie has cited evidence showing that when employees are permitted to control their own behavior, they tend to behave responsibly. He writes:

The example I wish to quote is from a study of a quite ordinary group of craftsmen working in a factory. These craftsmen, twelve in number, were engaged on complex metal work requiring a high degree of skill and they worked in a small shop by themselves in the midst of a large factory. I was assisting the management to organize the various departments in the factory and after considerable economies in six departments, I came to this particular craft shop. To my surprise and righteous horror (sic) I found this group was allowed to:

    a. supply estimates for material and labor costs for inclusion in sales quotation.

    b. say what particular methods should be adopted in the doing of any particular job, and

    c. suggest what times and money rates should be allowed for each job.

The foreman of this shop was also foreman of a larger shop and, in fact, he was not a skilled craftsman. When a new job was to be quoted, the job description was sent to the shop and the men got together and worked out methods, times and prices; the result went back via the foreman to the sales department in order that a quotation could be sent. I was, as said above, sur-

[3] Chris Argyris, Frank Miller, under the direction of S. D. Hoslett, *The Impact of Budgets on People*, Comptrollership Foundation, New York, 1951.
[4] Rensis Likert, *New Patterns of Management*, McGraw-Hill, New York, 1961, pp. 71–76.

prised and horrified at this unplanned, nonspecialized and dishonesty-provoking procedure and set out to improve organization and method. As I went deeper into the study of department economies, I found:

a. The group's estimates were intelligent.

b. The estimates were honest and enabled the men, working consistently at a good speed, to earn a figure LESS THAN THAT COMMON TO SIMILAR SHOPS ON ORGANIZED PIECEWORK.

c. The overhead costs were lower than they would have been if the shop was run on modern lines.

d. There was no group leader in the dominant sense of leadership. One skilled person received the job data and undertook to collect and coordinate the data supplied by members of the group, i.e., the leader was a secretary leader rather than a dominant in group thinking and activity.

e. Leadership shifted from one person to another as the situation required.

f. The group psychic texture I would describe as a mild WE one.

g. Inquiry among the group members showed no evidence of the group having or exhibiting aggressive feelings about other groups in the large factory. Some pity for the other groups engaged on the less skilled varieties of work organized on modern lines was expressed.

h. The foreman who was nominally in charge of his group dubbed it the best group in the factory and the least greedy.

i. The manager of this and many other groups took this group's honesty for granted. "They never trouble me, they do good work, costs are low and profits good, why should I worry?" summed up his expressed attitude.[5]

In the writer's opinion the same may be said for such activities as analysis of plant layout, materials flow, machine requirements, safety programs, and quality control. The question arises, how can more effective control systems be developed?

Unfortunately, almost no research exists on this central question. Gordon has outlined some of the economic and accounting hurdles that must be overcome if effective "responsibility accounting" is to be achieved within the firm.[6]

One of the first writers to question the traditional concepts of internal financial control and to suggest a possible direction for a solution was Villers.[7] He concluded, on the basis of several detailed studies,[8]

[5] James J. Gillespie, *Free Expression in Industry*, Pilot Press, London, 1948, pp. 94–96.

[6] M. M. Gordon, "Economics, Organization Theory, and the Use of Accounting Systems in Administering a Decentralized Company," Graduate School of Industrial Management, Massachusetts Institute of Technology, 1961.

[7] Raymond Villers, "Control and Freedom in a Decentralized Company," *Harvard Business Review*, Vol. 32, No. 2, March–April 1954, pp. 89–96.

[8] Raymond Villers, *The Dynamics of Industrial Management*, Funk and Wagnalls, New York, 1954.

that the way most financial controlling systems operated tended to take away the freedom of the line supervisor to make important decisions and to shoulder the responsibility for the performance.

Villers suggested a centralized planning and control department with no line authority. It would act as a service department; it could not issue orders. Its main function was to translate overall policy decisions into specific assignments. It would not tell each department *how* a certain goal should be reached; it would define *what* should be accomplished and *when*. These assignments, however, should be viewed by the line supervisor as suggestions or proposals, not binding. If, after careful consideration (and assuming proper training) the line supervisor still rejected them, he could ask his superior for the necessary changes.[9] Presumably, only his line superior could order him to carry out a set of objectives with which he disagreed.

Becker and Green [10] have developed a suggested process by which the traditional budgeting process can be made more effective. Instead of the traditional budgeting cycle of imposed budget, performance, comparison of performance with budget, and revised imposed budget, they suggest a much more complicated process beginning with the employees participating in the setting of the budgeting goals. They caution against "pseudo" participation as well as participation in a situation where authoritarian management would unilaterally reject the goals arrived at through meaningful participation.

With valid participation, they predict not only realistic goal setting but also increased employee commitment to these goals as well as increased group cohesiveness. As soon as the performance is obtained, the next step is immediate and honest feedback to the employees. If the performance meets or exceeds the expectation, the level of aspiration will rise and budgets can be revised upwards. If performance is just slightly below budget expectations, budget changes are not necessary, but feedback is necessary so that employees will continue to strive for the goals. If performance is well below the budget, it may be necessary to revise the budget downward. If this is not done, we may predict a decrease in the employees' aspiration level, the budget will be viewed as unattainable and unfair, and the group's cohesiveness could become increased by antimanagement attitudes and behavior.

We should like to describe several other possible strategies, but it

---

[9] Raymond Villers, "Control and Freedom in a Decentralized Company," *op. cit.*, pp. 90–91.

[10] Silwyn Becker and David Green, Jr., "Budgeting and Employee Behavior," *Journal of Business*, University of Chicago, Vol. XXXV, No. 4, October 1962, pp. 392–402.

cannot be too strongly emphasized that none of these strategies has been validated. They are, at best, hunches that need much research to validate.

The first strategy conceives a control group as a consulting organization to provide managerial control services, especially to the upper levels of management. A modification of this practice might be introduced throughout all units of the organization. The objective of the new structure would be to optimize the line and staff freedom to function as effectively as possible. Let us assume that all control instruments have been studied and analyzed to learn precisely (1) what information they obtain, (2) from whom they obtain this information, and (3) what units actively are supposed to be influenceable by the control instrument(s).

Next we should define the following policy. *In any given situation the information collected by any control instrument will be fed back only to the lowest levels of the unit whose activities are evaluated by that particular control instrument.*

For example, in a typical manufacturing department the first-line foremen and *only* the first-line foremen would receive the information on how well their departments are performing on such items as cost, errors, waste, etc. It would be the responsibility of the foremen to use the information as they see fit to correct the situation for which they are accountable. It would also be their responsibility to decide when, and if, to feed back the control information up the line. Finally, the foremen would be administratively free to go to anyone in the organization to receive help, including their superior and, of course, the consulting department. They would probably have to consult with their superior before obtaining the final approval for the consulting aid since such aid would cost the department money. To the extent that the foremen and superior are organized according to Structures III and IV, they as a group will decide whether, or how, much they can afford the help.

Although the consulting unit would keep copies of all the reports made to their "clients," they would not, under any conditions, be permitted to release the reports without the approval of the managers on the lowest rung of the administrative ladder in the department involved. To the extent that the line department is administered with Structures III and IV, the leader would also be included in the decision-making process.

It is important to emphasize that the consulting organization would be under no obligation to "sell" or push its findings to the line management. In fact, we might define a rule that the consultants may not try to sell the line on changing their activities. It is the line's responsibility to consider and institute changes.

At the same time the superiors of the consulting organization may not use the "number of acceptances of the consultants' ideas by the client" as criteria of the consultants' effectiveness to evaluate the consultant. Some possible criteria of the consultant could be:

1. The intellecual and technical competence of the diagnoses that he makes.
2. The organization and clarity of presentation.
3. The degree to which the consultant creates a climate where his resources could be used maximally *at the same time* maximizing the "client's" own self-confidence and initiative in discovering solutions and putting them into action.

The consultants would report administratively to their own line organization. This means that the question of salaries, evaluations, promotions would be their own unit's responsibility. The manner in which these are dealt with would depend on the stage of leadership and organizational strategy with which they operate.

A second strategy would be to place all the employees responsible for managerial controls (for example, budget, quality control, production control employees) under direct line supervision. Presently, as already noted, most employees responsible for some control activity are in a staff relationship to the line and they report to their own professional superior (for example, budget people report to the director of budgeting who in turn reports up the financial ladder).

It may be more effective for the budget man to report to the line supervisor whom he is supposed to help. Under these conditions he would act as a consultant to the line and maintain a professional, confidential relationship with the line. As in the previous case, he could no longer send reports of the line's failures or successes directly to the financial department. The decision as to whether such reports are to be required, and how they are to be routed throughout the organization, would be the responsibility of the relevant line employees.

Unlike the previous case, however, the staff employee under this strategy would be organizationally part of the line group he serves. If the budget employee is dissatisfied with the activities of his "clients" and if he does not seem to be able to influence the clients, he would be free to go to the clients' superior. He may *not*, however, go to the financial department. If this does not meet with the desired results then he has no other recourse open to him. If the budget employee's view is correct, it will not be long before the problem becomes evident. At this point, the top manufacturing executive would be expected to take action with the line personnel.

A third alternative might be to place the responsibility for the design and use of the managerial controls under the control of the people who are to be controlled by these instruments. For example, the employee would be asked to record his own errors, waste, and quality for his own information so that he can compare his output with the goals that he had set for himself. He could send the information daily to a data-processing center which would process his data and send it directly back to him. These individual records could be tabulated into departmental results for production and inventory purposes. A weekly or monthly summary report would be sent to the foremen or committee, depending on the organizational structure being used. However, the decision to make these data available should have been made by the total work group and the management. In an organization in which the participants have developed a high sense of self-responsibility, they would probably want to impose on themselves periodic comparison of their past performance with the expectation of modifying it appropriately. Such sessions would focus on helping the individual to evaluate himself in terms of his own level of aspiration and in terms of the organization's needs.

One might wonder if employees would not misuse the privilege. Some available research leads one to doubt it. When individuals are placed in a world that requires a greater sense of self-responsibility, they tend to respond appropriately. Gibb cites an interesting example in a college situation. An experiment was conducted to learn to what extent students would accept responsibility for their own education. Since the faculty basically mistrusted the students willingness to respond responsibly, they built in all sorts of controls on attendance, data-gathering activities, group sessions, and so on. However, when the students were told that the need for the controls was bred from faculty fear and mistrust based on some previous experience, the students reacted promptly. Controls were reduced to a minimum during a period of seven years. Groups took over direction of their own processes, built in their own attendance norms, reduced absenteeism to nearly zero, generated new instruments, and achieved their tasks more effectively than when they were under control.[11]

But let us assume that this is not true. What can be done to increase

[11] Jack R. Gibb, "Climate for Trust Formation," in Leland P. Bradford, Jack R. Gibb, and Kenneth D. Benne (Eds.), *T-Group Theory and Laboratory Method: Innovation in Re-education*, Wiley, New York, in press.

the probability of success? One possibility is that the employee, his peer group, and his superior could develop jointly a set of criteria by which he could be penalized (including discharged) if he does not meet his objectives. It is conceivable that the leader and the employee could agree, *at the outset*, that an individual who does not meet his own level of aspiration (as long as he is not inhibited by other factors) might be penalized in a particular manner for the first infraction. Later, when and if the infractions do occur, the leader and the subordinate would be obliged to follow their own rules (lay-off, discharge, etc.)

A fourth possibility is to combine suggested strategies one and three or two and three. Under the latter strategy the consulting organization would delegate many of its more routine and less skilled but highly influential control activities to the employees who are being measured and whose work is guided by these control activities. The consultants would continue to perform the more difficult technical tasks and would report to the line organization (as in the second strategy). The former procedure (one and three) would provide for a similar delegation to the employees and a delegation of the more difficult activities to the consultants. The difference is that the consultants would not report to the line but to their own staff organization.

Exactly which one or combination of these alternatives is the most effective will depend on a host of internal organizational variables plus the nature of the environment in which the organization is embedded. Much empirical research must be conducted before any conclusions can be reached. However, the writer's personal preference at the moment would be the combination of delegating as many as possible of the more routine and less difficult control activities to the relevant line employees and to create a separate consulting subunit similar to the one suggested in the first strategy.

Whatever strategy is eventually selected, it should attempt to minimize the extent to which the line conceives of the staff as specialists (1) who are subordinates to the line specialists, (2) who ought to be told what to do by the line, (3) who give advice to the line which the line is free to accept or reject, and (4) who can gather information, coordinate and control the line's subordinates (thereby making the line task easier). To the extent one uses any one or a combination of these factors, the staff will become controlled by the line or the staff will control the subordinates of the top-line management and, in some cases, may even control the top-line management (for example, by selecting the kind of information it sends to the line).

As the first two of these conditions arise within the organization, the staff will tend to view their top-line management in terms of any one or combination of the following ways. Top line management are (1) a source of rewards, (2) who value system, order, uniformity, and (3) who desire that the staff control the lower levels of the line organization. These three conditions lead naturally to the staff's developing a relatively low regard for middle and lower levels of line management. This, in turn, leads the lower levels of line management to view the staff as people who (1) pressure them, (2) try to hurt them, (3) do not care for them, (4) enjoy making their life more difficult, and (5) are, at best, indifferent to their interests.[12]

Reward and Penalty Systems

Briefly, rewards and penalties (wages, benefits, vacations, promotions, disciplinary actions) are, according to Barnard, a basic factor in inducing individuals to work for the organization.[13] They are traditionally assumed to be scarce and should never exceed the available incentive resources of the organization.[14] Clark and Wilson suggest that rewards and penalties can be categorized as material (tangible and usually monetary), solidary (intangible and derived from associating with others in the organization), and purposive (intangible and derived from identifying with the purposes or goals of the organization).

We may consider two kinds of innovations of the reward and penalty system. The first deals with modifying the reward and penalty systems under the conditions that the job will not offer much opportunity for intrinsic satisfaction. The second kind will be relevant when jobs are able to provide opportunity for self-actualization, creative activity—in short where intrinsic satisfaction is possible. The second set of modifications considered are not a substitute for but an addition to the first.

It follows from our model of organizational effectiveness that rewards and penalties should as much as possible be geared to reinforce those human activities that (1) increase the individual's (group's) awareness and responsibility for as much of the total organization as possible, (2) enlarge the experience of interdependence with others and with the whole, and (3) increase the control that the whole has over its own destiny.

Under the present formal strategy the opposite philosophy is em-

[12] See Douglas McGregor, *The Human Side of Enterprise*, McGraw-Hill, New York, 1960.
[13] Chester Barnard, *The Functions of the Executive*, Harvard University Press, 1938, p. 139.
[14] Peter B. Clark and James Q. Wilson, "Incentive Systems: A Theory of Organizations," *Administrative Science Quarterly*, Vol. 6, No. 2, September 1961, pp. 134–135.

phasized. For example, the supervisor is rewarded or penalized depending on his department's performance and not on the performance of other departments (no matter how intimately they are related) or on the performance of the whole. Similarly, the individual production worker is rewarded for how well he performs his job or, in some cases, how well his group performs. This type of reward and penalty system reinforces the employee's view of the company as a series of unrelated parts.

Moreover, as a result of our changing concepts of social welfare, of the impact of the traditional strategy, and finally the increasing mechanization of work, the relation of rewards and penalties to productivity may not be clearly seen or even believed by an increasing number of employees. In a systematic review of wage plans, Behrend concludes that a "fair day's work" is not a factual issue but an ethical issue highly influenced by many subjective factors.[15] Moreover, the concept of wages may be changing in the eyes of the workers. Recent research suggests that workers may view wages as part of management's responsibility for the kind of work world they have created. Wages may be viewed by employees as rewards for willingness to live with increased frustration and dissatisfaction.[16] Finally, McClelland suggests that financial incentives do *not* tend to improve the work of men with high need for achievement, but they are effective for those with low need for achievement.[17]

What can be done about this trend? First, let us focus on the monetary rewards. There is a need for a systematic scheme for wage and salary administration. Most of the wage and salary administrative practices in effect today have left much to be desired. Their limitations have been discussed adequately elsewhere and we need not dwell on them in detail here. Briefly, most of the wage and salary "scales" do not seem to be real scales, the intervals are not intervals and objective measurements neither objective nor measurements.[18]

Simple as it may be to criticize the present schemes, it is difficult to

[15] Hilde Behrend, "A Fair Day's Work," *Scottish Journal of Political Economics,* Vol. VIII, June 1961, pp. 102–118.
[16] Chris Argyris, "The Organization: What Makes It Healthy," *Harvard Business Review,* Vol. 36, No. 6, November–December 1958, pp. 107–116.
[17] David C. McClelland, *The Achieving Society, op. cit.,* p. 235.
[18] Some of the recent books suggesting new horizons for personnel administration are George Strauss and Leonard R. Sayles, *Personnel: The Human Problems of Management,* Prentice-Hall, Englewood Cliffs, N.J., 1960; and William B. Wolf, *The Management of Personnel,* Wadsworth, San Francisco, 1961. On incentive systems see R. Marriott, *Incentive Payment Systems,* Staples Press, London, 1957; and William F. Whyte, *Money and Motivation,* Harper, New York, 1955.

present something to replace them. Unfortunately little or no research has been done in this area, with the exception of the work of Jaques.[19] Along with criticizing the present practices, Jaques has presented a new approach to the establishment of pay differentials. He suggests that there exists an unrecognized system of norms for what constitutes fair payment for any given level of work. After careful examination of nearly one thousand jobs, Jaques concluded that employees share these norms regardless of the type of work they are doing.

The core of the procedure is to establish the level of weight of responsibility in a job. This can be measured by determining the maximum period of time during which the work assigned by a manager requires his subordinate to exercise discretion, judgment, or initiative in his work without that discretion being subject to review by the manager. This measure rigorously excludes all aspects of work prescribed by policies and practices to which the subordinate must conform or be guilty of negligence.

The resulting measure of "time span of discretion" is an objective quantitative measure which, in practice, correlates highly with "importance of job" to the firm and with the level in the hierarchy. Jaques maintains that individuals with different jobs who have the same time span of discretion privately state the same wage or salary bracket to be fair for the work they are doing. Moreover, deviations below the equitable level tend to be accompanied by grievances calling for organized action to remedy the situation. On the other hand, deviations above the equitable level are accompanied with feelings of being well off to feelings of preferential treatment. These findings coincide with our conclusions that one of the most crucial variables in work is the degree of control an individual feels he has over his behavior.

One might begin, as McGregor suggests,[20] by considering rewards that emphasize excellence and responsibility. Most organizations, he suggests, use two kinds of rewards.

1. Those that can be directly tied to objective criteria of accomplishment such as profit and loss. These rewards will necessarily be limited to a few people in the total population if they are administered on an individual basis. Moreover, they will potentially be large enough to have genuine motivational value.

---

[19] Elliot Jaques, *Equitable Payment*, Wiley, New York, 1961, and *Measure of Responsibility*, *op. cit.* Also Elliot Jaques, "Objective Measures for Pay Differentials," *Harvard Business Review*, Vol. 40, No. 1, January–February 1962, pp. 133–138.
[20] Douglas McGregor, *The Human Side of Enterprise*, McGraw-Hill, New York, 1960, pp. 96–98.

2. Those that are administered as "time-service" increments received automatically at intervals so long as performance is not unsatisfactory. Such increments will be small and will have as their chief value the maintenance of equity (on the assumption that time on a job brings some increase in competence and in contribution).

McGregor believes there is value in considering two other kinds of rewards.

1. Merit increases to the small proportion of individuals in a given salary classification whose performance is clearly *outstanding*. These will require only gross differentiations of performance in which the probable error of measurement will be small, and they will also involve large enough salary increments to have genuine motivational value.
2. Group rewards for departmental, divisional, or company-wide achievement of objectively measurable economic results. These would be shared within the group in terms of an equal percentage of base salary.

Regardless of which of the four kinds of rewards are used, they are typically conceived as rewards for accomplishing some end such as producing a product. Another step would be to enlarge the basis of rewards and penalties. An individual would be rewarded not only as a function of his contribution to the organization's goals (for example, producing shoes) but also as a function of his contribution to the organization's two other core activities—the maintenance of the internal system and the adaptation of the organization to the environment at a decreasing human (and material) cost. According to the present formal organizational strategy, only managers tend to be rewarded for contributions to the latter two activities. Employees are hardly ever offered an opportunity to participate in such activities. However, through the change in organizational structure, leadership, and job design described previously, the employee could be provided a greater opportunity for making contributions to all three of the core activities.

How is this to be accomplished? In order to make such a reward and penalty system a reality, the source for rewards and punishments should be enlarged as much as possible. For example, if the foregoing recommendations were put into effect, an employee would no longer be rewarded simply for producing shoes. His participation in Scanlon-type committees, in committees to define the decision rules for the use of the various organization structures, in committees to define criteria for advancement, would be evaluated so that he might be paid in accordance to his contribution in each of these activities. The employees, along with management, would have the responsibility to define what is a contribution and how much each type of contribution would be rewarded. In other words, the employees would be given an opportunity to participate in the criteria that establish their wages.

The decision rules as to how these wages would be paid in a given department could also be under the control of the individuals in that department. The same might be said for the definition of a bonus, if such is available. In this connection it is interesting to note that Hoffman and Maier found that a work group, if given the opportunity to distribute the bonus, can do it in a manner that, to the individual, seems fair and equitable.[21]

Under the new scheme an individual's rewards and penalties will vary daily or weekly depending on the ratio of his actual contribution to the core activities in proportion to his potential for contributing to these core activities. An individual's potential for contributions may be a function of his own limitations and strengths and of the organization's ability to provide increasing opportunities for such contributions. If the individual's personal potential is low, he will not be penalized but his wages will be limited to his personal potentialities. If the opportunity the organization provides the individual for contribution to the core activities is small, the organization must seek modifications to enlarge the opportunity.

Let us see how this might be applied in an organization. An employee who manufactures electronics parts at a piece rate or straight hourly rate may still receive such a compensation. The exact amount would have to be determined for each individual, given the organization's financial situation. He would be paid at a different scale for his contribution to the reduction of waste, errors, etc. He would also be paid, again it may be at a different scale, for his participation in, for example, the Scanlon Plan groups and productivity groups.

The possibility of having three different bases for wage payments may seem clumsy and difficult, if not absurd. Research and experience are needed to answer these possible charges. However, we can say the following in defense of the suggestion. First, the computer technology that is evolving may be adequate to cope with the information-handling problems. Second, the basic philosophy is to apply the principles of (*a*) feedback, (*b*) relating rewards or penalties to actual results and (*c*)

---

[21] Richard L. Hoffman and Norman F. Maier, "The Use of Group Decision to Resolve a Problem of Fairness," *Personnel Psychology*, Vol. 12, No. 4, Winter 1959, pp. 545–559.

relating rewards and penalties to an enlarged conception of "the job." The relay assembler would no longer be able to say that he is being paid simply to assemble relays. He would have to say that his take-home pay is based on activities that are much broader in scope and deeper in responsibility. Under these conditions it would be easier for him to perform such control activities as job simplification or modification because there are built-in rewards for such initiative. Moreover, he may no longer experience "his job" as being a little narrow band of motoric activities whose relatedness to the rest of the department is uncertain and whose relatedness to the entire organization is unknown and unponderable. He is now paid according to his participation in making decisions ranging from defining the decision rules under which the leader selects the appropriate leadership pattern to defining new ways of effective measurement and control, to helping redesign the departmental and organizational structure. These are but a few—very few—of the activities that could become part of every employee's job. And as they do, it is hypothesized that the employee will tend to have an increasing degree of experience of the whole organization, of effective decision making, of striving to decrease the department's, indeed, in some cases, the organization's, defensiveness. Under these conditions one may expect their involvement to increase significantly. An increasing number of their cognitive and emotional abilities and, thus, their more inner needs will tend to be utilized. As the involvement increases and as the deep satisfactions related to being a more fully functioning, participating, self-responsible individual increases, the amount of psychological energy available for productivity will also increase.

On an individual level of analysis the increase in the individual's use of his self (especially the employee's use of his cognitive and conative abilities) could lead to an increase in the probability that he will experience psychological success, which in turn will lead to a greater sense of self-esteem. The increased self-esteem may lead to a decrease in defensiveness. All these results could tend to enhance the individual's "state of mind," which also could increase his psychological energy output, which in turn should lead to a more fully functioning individual and a more effective relationship among the participants. The increase in involvement in his own and other departmental activities will increase the employee's sense of, and commitment to, the total organization.

The second kind of change in rewards and penalties will tend to be appropriate for a work world in which the participants are offered jobs that provide opportunities for challenge, responsibility, and creative work. Recalling the Maslow concept of hierarchy of needs, the second concept of rewards and penalties will probably be best suited for (1) those jobs that require relatively creative activity, and (2) those individuals who emphasize self-actualization needs and not physiological and security needs. At the moment these conditions tend to exist primarily for the upper levels of management, for researchers and some engineers, and some sales people (those selling complex products such as large-scale computers).

Under conditions where learning, responsibility, and internal commitment are valued by the individual and made possible by the organization, rewards and penalties would *not* tend to be used primarily to reward or penalize others in the traditional sense of these words. Rewards and penalties would be given to *confirm* [22] to the individual that others feel as he does. As Bruner suggests, under conditions of self-actualization and learning, success and failure are not experienced as rewards and punishments but as information. "For when the task is his own rather than a matter of matching environmental demands, he becomes his own paymaster in a certain measure. Seeking to gain control over his environment, he can now treat success as indicating that he is on the right track, failure as indicating he is on the wrong track." [23]

Under these conditions the reward does not motivate gratitude toward others as much as deep feelings of emotional satisfaction that others see him to be as successful as he sees himself. Such feelings tend to enhance the employee's own feeling of competence, which, as White has suggested, may be a basic need of man.[24] As the employee's feelings of competence increases, we may hypothesize that his self-confidence and internal commitment may also tend to increase. This in turn may tend to increase his feelings of respect and confidence in his fellow man. Similarly, if penalties are necessary, they will be given to a man who realizes that he has not done well. The penalty confirms to him that others also see him as being as unsuccessful as he sees himself. Penalties under these conditions could, if given appropriately, imply a real trust in the individual's capacity to receive "negative" confirmation without "cracking." To put this another way, the source for motivation to increase learning and work will tend to stem from the individual's competition with his own previously established goals. Under conditions

[22] In the sense that Martin Buber uses the concept of confirmation (Chap. II).
[23] Jerome S. Bruner, "The Act of Discovery." *Harvard Education Review*, Vol. 31, No. 1, Winter 1961, pp. 26–28.
[24] Robert W. White, "Motivation Reconsidered: The Concept of Competence," *Psychological Review*, Vol. LXVI, 1959, pp. 297–333.

of internal commitment and psychological success, the motivation for realistic increases in productivity and achievement is almost limitless.[25]

Finally, rewards would not tend to be given by others to an individual who feels he has not done well even though others believe that he has done quite well. Such behavior could be perceived by the rewardee as "playing favorites" or "flattery," or simply incompetence on the part of the rewarder.

If the rewarder desires to give some rewards in the foregoing situation in order to be consistent, he would first attempt to clarify the different views with the individual involved. If his view develops correctly, he would have helped the one to be rewarded to see for himself how well he has really done. Then a reward can be given because it becomes an act of confirmation.

Similarly, penalties would not tend to be given when the individual to be penalized feels he has done well. Again, the first step is to help the one to be penalized to see for himself how poorly he has done. The *emphasis, in giving rewards and penalties, is to diagnose first in order to confirm.*

We may depict the position that we have taken on rewards and penalties and the act of confirmation as follows. In the column labeled Mr. A, we depict his view of his behavior. In cases 1 and 4 Mr. A believes he had done well and in cases 2 and 3 poorly. In the column labeled Mr. B, we note that he believes Mr. A has done well in 1 and 3 and poorly in 2 and 4.

	Mr. A	*Mr. B*	*Confirmation*
1	+	+	yes
2	−	−	yes
3	−	+	no
4	+	−	no

The process of confirmation occurs in the cases 1 and 2. Under these conditions Mr. B.'s reward (+) or penalty (−) confirms Mr. A's view of the situation. Such rewards and penalties should tend to enhance self-actualization. Mr. B will not tend to reward or penalize Mr. A in cases 3 and 4. He will first diagnose the situation so that he or Mr. A changes his view. Once this is done the signs will change to either two plusses or two minuses. We then revert to the first two cases. We are *not* im-

[25] Kurt Lewin, Tamara Dembo, Leon Festinger, Pauline Sears, "Level of Aspiration," in J. M. V. Hunt (Ed.), *Personality and the Behavior Disorders*, Ronald Press, New York, 1944, pp. 333–378.

plying that rewards or penalties should never be given under conditions 3 (where A feels he has done poorly and B feels that A has done well) or 4 (which is the reverse). We simply maintain that under these conditions rewards and penalties will not tend to reinforce self-responsibility and self-actualization.

There are other conditions which influence the impact that confirmation has upon self-responsibility and self-actualization in human relationships.[26] For example, we may hypothesize that the impact of the process of confirmation will vary as a function of:

1. Whether or not what individual A did was in the direction that he intended. The impact of confirmation will differ if A's acts that are being confirmed are (1) motivated from within or induced by others, (2) if they are related to central or peripheral needs, and (3) if they are related to one or several needs.
2. Whether or not A expected to fail or succeed. Clearly, the impact of the act of confirmation will differ if the individual expected to fail or succeed. The expectation of success or failure, in turn, is a function of the individuals perception of his competence, his freedom to use his competence, and his previous experience of failure and success under similar conditions.[27]

Incentive Systems

Over the last thirty years, there has been a gradual tendency, greatly accelerated since the last war, to reject the idea that incentive payment schemes can, of themselves, provide the motivation that is necessary if production and nonproduction workers are to reach an optimum level of productivity.[28]

There are several reasons for this trend. First, in the past, too much attention has been placed on breaking the job down into short time cycles devoid of variety and interest. Too little attention has been paid to "disincentives" such as weaknesses in the technical organization (e.g., waiting for work and troublesome material).

Second, apparently few administrators realize that incentive systems,

[26] A book that presents an important contribution to understanding the process of confirmation is O. J. Harvey, David E. Hunt, and Harold M. Schroder, *Conceptual Systems and Personality Organization*, Wiley, New York, 1961, Chap. III.

[27] The work of McClelland and his co-workers is relevant in this connection. D. C. McClelland, J. W. Atkinson, R. A. Clark, and E. L. Lowell, *The Achievement Motive*, Appleton-Century-Croft, New York, 1953.

[28] R. Marriott, *Incentive Payment Systems*, Staples Press, London, 1957, p. 202.

as they are presently understood, operate only in the sphere of voluntary effort.[29] Yet most of the work situations have little in them that is related to voluntary effort. Indeed, in most cases, the "felony has been compounded" because incentive systems have been imposed upon workers.[30]

Marriott cites at least five scholars who have suggested that more attention should be paid to the "level of willingness" to work or the "will to work." [31] This has been, and is, our position. We are more interested in asking how we can develop incentive systems that increase the participant's willingness to work.

Incentive systems usually reward the employee for his own production. They assume that the employee is an individual who seeks to maximize his income and who is not significantly affected by group norms.

Whyte and Melman (already quoted) seriously question these assumptions. They bring much evidence to bear on the theory that the individual's production is greatly influenced by group norms, and that incentive systems may create more problems than they solve. The very existence of the rate setter and rate buster implies that norms are operating to restrict production.[32] Whyte suggests that if incentive systems are to exist they should take into account the group norms and values related to production. He argues convincingly that management is not going to make effective changes in incentive systems by assuming that they are to be dealt with on an individual basis. In this connection, it is interesting to note that Glacier Metal has abandoned piece work. According to its chairman, this has led to many positive results, some of which are (1) release of managerial time from concern with bonus to concern with more central production problems, (2) decrease in clerical work, (3) decrease in resistance to change, (4) fuller achievement of production potential, (5) greater freedom to assign operators to various tasks, and (6) decrease in feelings of hostility and suspicion between managers and employee representatives.[33]

Although we agree with Whyte, it should be pointed out that in terms of our concept of individual and organizational effectiveness any pressure on the part of the employees to restrict production, especially

[29] W. Clewes, *The Human Implications of Work Study*, Industrial Welfare Society, London, 1957, p. 5ff.

[30] F. C. Bartlett, "Incentives," *British Journal of Psychology*, Vol. 41, 1950, pp. 122–128.

[31] R. Marriott, *op. cit.*, pp. 198–205.

[32] William F. Whyte, *Money and Motivation, op. cit.*

[33] Wilfred Brown, *Piecework Abandoned*, Heinemann, London, 1962, pp. 66–67.

in jobs that offer greater opportunity for self-actualization, could also act to decrease the freedom the individual experiences to challenge himself and to become more fully functioning. Therefore, under our scheme, the reality of informal group pressures against productivity are no more acceptable than management pressures for increased productivity. Pressure leads to dependence and submissiveness regardless if it is sanctioned by management or the employees.

Of course, if the restriction of output is due to employees' fear of the loss of their jobs if they produce too much, then it is the organization's responsibility to meet the problem realistically. Otherwise, although the restriction of output can lead to employee psychological failure, this failure is in the eyes of the employee a lesser evil than the loss of his job.

Theoretically, if jobs were truly enlarged, if structures, leadership, and controls were changed and incentive systems designed to increase the individual's motivation, incentives for production would be much less necessary. The opportunity to increase one's sense of fulfillment would be rewarding in itself. This does not mean, however, that employees should not receive just wages or their share of the economic pie. Indeed, the foregoing ideas will tend to be valid, if at all, under conditions in which the employees are receiving a wage to satisfy their physiological and security need. The probability of this inequity occurring under the changes that are recommended is low because the employees would have a significant say in the definition of their wages.

Nor would it necessarily be desirable to have an incentive system that rewards individuals who produce with the fewest errors and the least waste. Minimal errors and waste would be a responsibility the employee has to his own self if he is to increase his feeling of essentiality as well as his own sense of self-esteem. He should not be given extra financial rewards for behaving in a responsible manner. Again, this assumes that an individual is now operating under a greatly expanded job where he has some influence over the degree of waste and errors produced. Clearly, the individual cannot be penalized if the waste and errors are the responsibility of the machine or some other external factors.

It is worth emphasizing that employees should receive just wages; that these wages should be related to their contribution to the fulfillment of the core activities; and that they should have a significant degree of participation in the establishment of a concept of just wages.

Some managers may complain that if the employee is given a say over his wages, he would give himself more money than he deserves. This fear may be valid. Employees would tend to overpay themselves not because they are inherently greedy or irresponsible but because employees have learned to develop a "market orientation" in which their sense of worth is measured in terms of how much money they can earn. If employees dominated by a market orientation are given power to determine their wages, it seems reasonable to expect them to over-pay themselves.

One solution may well lie in the direction of helping the individual return to a basic human orientation where his own inner sense of worth is paramount. This situation cannot be achieved by exhortation, semi-therapeutic sessions, or mass communication schemes. It can be reached by instituting the basic changes in the structure, leadership, and con-trols that have been recommended here, that hopefully will tend to place the employee in a world where his return to the human orienta-tion would be required if he is to be rewarded.

Patience is needed and slow progress expected because the employees ironically will probably be the first to resist the changes. The notion that increased quality and opportunity to be more productive should not be rewarded by an incentive system is foreign to their market orientation. It is also threatening to the unions who, by and large, have staked their survival on emphasizing the employees' market orientation.

Evaluating, Hiring, and Terminating Employees[1]

Evaluation Activities[2]

Let us now examine evaluation procedures such as merit ratings and management performance reports. There are many varieties and programs of evaluation activities. In the final analysis, they are activities designed to measure the individual's present development and future potential. In the writer's opinion, at their best they do not provide positive influence for the growth of the subordinate being evaluated. At worst they magnify the subordinate's feelings of dependence and submissiveness and eventually destroy his desire for self-development while requiring increased conformity.

Marriott[3] has reported an exploratory but intensive study of merit-rating practices in three factories. The main objective of these schemes

[1] May we again remind the reader that these chapters are not intended to be reviews of the current scope of practice. Rather they are meant to give some preliminary indications of some of the new directions in policies and practices.
[2] For the best discussion of current practice in the area of performance appraisals, see Thomas L. Whisler and Shirley F. Harper, *Performance Appraisal*, Holt, Rinehart, and Winston, New York, 1962.
[3] R. Marriott, "An Exploratory Study of Merit Rating Payment Systems in Three Factories," *Occupational Psychology*, Vol. 36, No. 4, October 1962, pp. 178–214.

was to provide a financial reward to manual workers based on individual merit. Marriott reports the following conclusions.

1. The majority of the employees were placed in the upper half of the
scale.
2. Training to help foremen realize and correct their "errors of leniency"
was either unavailable or ineffective.
3. Little relation was found between the score level and the amount of
the award.
4. Many anomolies developed which led to schemes that could not
please the employees and management. Some reasons for these manipulations were: [4]
    (*a*) The reductions in frequency and amounts of awards when there
    was a lower demand for the firm's products.
    (*b*) The granting of awards above top rate for "indispensable" men
    and others because of competition for labour.
    (*c*) The adjustment up or down of awards which were not in keep-
    ing with the scale laid down.
    (*d*) The adjustment of maximum awards to fit the existing wage
    structure, or raising them to meet the demands of specific groups
    rather than changing basic rates.
    (*e*) The starting of some newcomers above the minimum award
    rate, and their rapid progress to top rate because of the scarcity of
    workers, particularly in some skilled grades.
    (*f*) The tendency, in some cases, to give identical scores and awards
    to men in groups or on similar work in order "to keep the peace."
    (*g*) Rating on a money basis and fitting the merit points to agree
    with the award made.
    (*h*) The almost complete non-existence of down-rating or reduction
    of accumulated awards.
    (*i*) The granting of special awards to senior individuals or groups
    because the juniors were quickly reaching the same award level.

French, Kay, and Meyer [5] have conducted what is probably the most
thorough evaluation of a performance-appraisal program designed along
the lines of "management by objective." The study was held in a department where the system being used would meet the usual criteria
established for a "good program." Eighty-four management personnel

---

[4] *Ibid.*, pp. 211–212.
[5] John R. P. French, E. Kay, and H. H. Meyer, "A Study of Threat and Participation
in an Industrial Performance Appraisal Program," Behavioral Research Service,
General Electric Company, May 1962.

holding positions representing several different managerial functions and earning $7,000 to $14,000 per year participated in the study.

The subjects were observed during the performance-appraisal session and interviewed during four different time periods ranging from immediately after a session to twelve weeks after the goals had been set.

Briefly, some of the major findings were that the performance-appraisal sessions were frustrating for both principals. The subordinates tended to be frustrated because they discovered that their conception of their performance was less favorable than their superiors' conception. Also, most felt punished because they did not receive as high a salary increase as they felt was justified.

The manager tended to be frustrated because he saw the subordinate as not responding adequately and gratefully for the praise given him. Moreover, every time the manager attempted to point out shortcomings of the subordinate he tended to receive defensive responses from them about 50 per cent of the time. Indeed, "the more areas of needed improvement the manager calls attention to in the interview, the poorer the results he achieves subsequently in terms of constructive goal achievement on the part of the subordinate." [6] A manager could be sure of receiving defensive, nonaccepting reactions from a subordinate to a large percentage of the criticisms of performance he cited in the appraisal discussion.

Returning to the subordinate, the data imply that there might have developed a lack of trust by the subordinate toward the superior. Apparently the "experimental" treatment of "increased participation" did not seem to have the expected effect. One plausible explanation was that the subordinates did not tend to interpret as genuine the superior's attempt at becoming more participative.

One wonders how participation can have its expected effects under conditions where the superior is in constant control over the outcome of the session as well as the subordinate's long-range future in terms of wages, promotions, and so on.

In another example, one executive studied had unusual insight into what factors inhibited or facilitated the subordinate's growth in his company. He would, with equal skill and warmth, help the subordinate to see, as he would put it, "first his strengths and then his weaknesses." Seven of his subordinates were interviewed. In all cases each left the evaluation session with the leader feeling, as one put it, "My heavens this guy is terrific. He helped me to see things about myself that I just didn't realize. He pointed them out very carefully and diplomatically.

⁶ *Ibid.*, p. 115.

Not only do I not dislike him; I think he is great." Such comments are music to staff specialists' ears who usually design these evaluation programs and spend many hours training the superiors to evaluate. It is not unfair to say that the foregoing is an example of an unusual and rare case.

However, the crucial point is that as a result of continued observation and interview it was found that the seven had a new and deeper dependent relationship to their boss. "When I need to get some things cleared up I ask him. I can always count on him to help me to see something new about myself or my relationship with my subordinates." Moreover, none of the *subordinates* of these seven men reported similar feelings when they were being evaluated. In other words, the men were now learning how to learn, how to become increasingly self-sufficient and self-responsible for their growth.

Finally, nine different evaluation sessions that these seven men held with their subordinates (at least one each) were observed. In *all* cases they (unknowingly) communicated to the subordinates their enthusiasm about their own boss. For example, "Now this is the kind of a guy that should and will get ahead. He's terrific. If you ever have the pleasure of working with him you will find him very insightful. I wish I could be like him." If these comments are typical, then we can see one way by which conformity and development into the images of an individual is begun and enhanced.

These data suggest that the interpersonal processes of a typical performance-rating situation may not tend to approximate those implicit in the right ends of the continua. The typical performance-evaluation situation more closely approximates the left ends of the continua in the "mix" model. If the evaluation process is carried out in accordance with the best available advice, the subordinate tends to be controlled, directed, evaluated, and rewarded by the leader. This is not as extreme as it may sound. If we go back to our value model of executive relationships described in Part I, we will note that dependence, mistrust, external commitment, rivalries, and conformity were hypothesized to be "built into" executive systems. It would take a highly skilled individual to overcome these factors with "skillful interviewing." Interestingly, most therapists and counselors resist if not refuse to have authority reporting relationships with those whom they hope to help. They find that such relationships get in the way of establishing a helping relationship. Whisler, in a recent analysis of performance ratings, has arrived at a similar conclusion.[7]

[7] Thomas L. Whisler, "Performance Appraisal and Organizational Man," *Journal of Business*, Vol. 31, No. 1, January 1958, pp. 19–27.

The subordinate tends to become aware of those aspects of himself that the superior and the company feel are important: changes in behavior if they occur are not self-induced, self-motivated. Consequently, the depth and competence of the problem-solving activities of the subordinate are related to, and dependent on, the superior's capacity. It is not difficult to see why many executives, when asked what they desire most to enhance their development, reply, "I want to know where I stand." The emphasis is on what the boss or the company thinks of him, not what he thinks of himself. Such development is more "image" development than self-development.

Image development, in the opinion of the writer, is much more prevalent in organizations than the literature suggests. Unfortunately, the phenomenon has not been studied adequately. However, there are a few studies that support our hypothesis. McCormick and Middaugh [8] and Argyris [9] found that executives reward and promote those who manifest the accepted image of the system. Ward,[10] in a large sample study shows that different images exist for different functions (for example, for manufacturing and finance) and that individuals within these functions are influenced by these images in their selection of effective executive characteristics. Freeman and Taylor [11] support Ward's findings. Schutz has shown that an individual will tend to respect individuals whose needs are consonant with their own; if they are not consonant, the others' needs will not tend to inhibit the expression of their own needs.[12]

According to our model, if the situation is to be remedied, the individual should direct and control (as much as possible) his own evaluation.

Some steps that might be worth trying are:

1. Each individual is officially held accountable for his own development.
2. All individuals jointly with their peers and superiors and under conditions of equal power evolve criteria of growth that are effective and mutually acceptable. One possible set of criteria to be considered

[8] E. J. McCormick and R. W. Middaugh, "The Development of a Tailor-Made Scoring for the How-Supervise? Test," *Personnel Psychology*, Vol. 9, 1956, pp. 27–37.
[9] Chris Argyris, "Human Relations in a Bank," *Harvard Business Review*, Vol. 32, No. 5, September–October 1954, pp. 63–72.
[10] Lewis B. Ward, "Do You Want a Weak Subordinate," *Harvard Business Reveiw*, September–October 1961, pp. 6–26.
[11] G. L. Freeman and E. K. Taylor, *How to Pick Leaders*, Funk and Wagnalls, New York, 1950.
[12] William Schutz, *Procedures for Identifying Persons with Potential for Public School Administrative Positions*, University of California, Berkeley, 1961, pp. 166–168.

could be those of the effective organization that we have presented. The closer the individual's behavior approximates the characteristics of the pure organization, the more effective, the higher quality, the better is his development.

3. The continuous process of striving to approximate the right ends of the continua in our model is the responsibility of the individual.

4. The individual's self-development activities should be available for the inspection of others.

5. Any time the individual's self-development does not seem to be in the direction of approximating the criteria of effective organization, he may be questioned and asked to account for this. Exactly who will do the questioning depends on the nature of the power structure in the organization. If the organization is dominated by the formal strategy, the superior would raise the question. If the organization contains the strategy outlined in Structures III and IV, the peers with whom the individual is interrelated may raise the question.

In these discussions there always arises the problem of the individual who does not wish to go along with these policies. These individuals are difficult to deal with, but much time and effort must be taken because they tend to provide the test, for the *others* in the organization, of the genuineness of the new policies.

We may recall that under our new system, self-development (including the criteria for growth) is defined by and (in latter stages) controlled by the peer group. This means that if the supervisor is unable to understand why a particular subordinate refuses to go along, the problem may be turned over to the entire group. A meeting could be held. The initial objective of the meeting would not be to quiz the individual and force him to go along. On the contrary, the group members could perceive this as an opportunity for them to reexplore their policies and practices. It is probably seldom that they will find a team member who disagrees with the group. He should be treasured and his desire to deviate from the current practice should be sanctioned by the group. If they can help the "deviant" to feel that he is truly accepted and appreciated for his views, they may utilize him to retest and reexplore the existing point of view. Under these conditions the group and the individual may well learn something, and each may modify his own position to the betterment of the individual and the organization. However, if there is a disagreement that is clear and unreconcilable, and if the group has done its best to explore the weaknesses of the present policy (and also protect the deviant), they may reach the point where they have to take appropriate disciplinary action, including, if necessary, asking the individual to leave.

It should also be kept in mind that an individual should, and to the extent that he is self-responsible he would, raise the question of his lack of growth. Since, in the situation being outlined, the individual is rewarded as a function of his *process* of growth, it may be possible for him to make more effective plans to enhance his development or to be able to accept realistic self-limits because the situation is potentially less threatening.

No doubt the practitioner will tend to say it is unrealistic to expect individuals to be self-analytical, to accept that they can no longer progress, and indeed under certain conditions to discharge themselves. Under the traditional formal organizational milieu these expectations would be unrealistic. However, in an organization that approximates, and whose participants truly approximate, our concept of effectiveness, these expectations are hypothesized to be realistic.

Moreover, evidence from counseling and clinical studies shows that as individuals become more aware of themselves, more self-responsible and self-motivated, they tend to increase their own feelings of inner worth and the degree to which they care for themselves and their fellow man.[13] Under these conditions it becomes quite unrealistic for the individual not to try to develop himself and to face reality.

Since the emphasis is now on the processes of growth and, therefore, the relationships among individuals, it may be that there is much less need for an elaborate preplanned, predefined, performance-appraisal program and forms. It is when one emphasizes a uniform *product* or when one worries about making the dimensions for evaluation among individuals comparable and standard that predefined programs are necessary.

What would happen if the first step in a new program was to assign to each individual the responsibility to develop his own program? One would no longer need to worry if the technical details in each program were the same. Focusing on interpersonal relationships for self-growth should tend to make it mandatory that the individuals be given freedom for, and responsibility to, define them the way they feel they will grow most effectively.

Under the new scheme, individuals would not be placed in competition with one another via the standardized merit-rating programs. If the individual competes "against" anyone, it is his own level of aspira-

[13] See especially the work of Carl Rogers and his students.

tion. We are inferring from the level of aspiration studies quoted before that the healthier the individual, the more realistic and effective is this self-stimulation through "self-competition."

Hiring New Employees

The hiring of new people for any level can provide another important experience for employees to participate in decisions that deeply affect them. One possible experiment would be: The new employee would be actually asked to consider his new job as a new culture with as compelling a set of norms and values as any other culture. The prospective employees could be placed in a room for "orientation purposes." What would occur if the company orientation changed from telling people what is expected of them to diagnosing to see if they are capable of becoming responsible members of the plant culture and of striving toward individual-organizational health. The company representative would attempt to diagnose the predispositions of the employees, their level of aspiration, their probable quality of, and capacity for, commitment. In a company that was truly aspiring to provide employees as much self-actualization as possible, the emphasis would be to find employees who desire to work in such a world.

For example, in one experiment, about fifteen employees were interviewed under experimental conditions similar to the foregoing for fifteen different jobs. The company representative began by describing the history of the company, trying to stress the social characteristics or the "organizational charter" of the company. He received the usual nods and comments of appreciation from the employees.

To their surprise, however, he then asked to learn about them. "Now that I have given you some idea about us, I am interested to learn something about you. What, for example, do you seek from a job?"

Mr. A: I hear you pay $3.40 for skilled welders. Mister if you'll give me $3.40 for welding, I'll be very happy.

P. R.: Is this all you wish?

Mr. A: Yeah, well what else is there?

P. R.: I am not saying there must be something more for you. I am trying to understand what you wish from a job.

Mr. A: Well, I can't think of anything else. (Silence.) Well, of course, there are the benefits. But I didn't mention those because they are so obvious.

The personnel representative guided the group discussion until he had on the blackboard a composite future of the predispositions of the employees. They amounted to high wages, high job security, togetherness, control, and noninvolvement. If these employees could have these predispositions fulfilled, they would in return produce at the company's standard.

In the next two sessions the personnel representative tried to show what he felt the impact of such predispositions would be on the social system of the plant. He pointed out, for example, that although the company would surely receive the production it wanted, it would also rate low on all the dimensions of organizational health because they (the prospective employees) seemed to feel no need to experience the whole organization, to take on authority, to participate in and work toward improving the organization problem-solving processes.

The prospective employees agreed to analysis but as one said, "What the hell do you expect from us? These are the damned craziest meetings that I have ever been to. Nobody has even asked these questions before. Usually all they want to know is if I'm satisfied with the job, my wages, and benefits." The personnel representative replied that he could certainly understand that he was causing confusion. His objective, however, was to communicate the most effective way possible that this particular organization aspired to a different commitment on the part of all the participants.

"But why," asked another prospective employee, "do you want this greater commitment? Why not pay us, get our production, and leave us alone?" The personnel representative replied that the participants in the organization were trying to evolve satisfactory answers to that most difficult question. He had some that he wanted to offer at this time. However, he emphasized that no one was unalterably committed to them, and the company (meaning all the employees and management who participated in evolving the answers) was open to suggestions. In fact, one criterion that they would use to hire and later upgrade people would be the extent to which the individual raised questions about the organization as a whole. The personnel representative then continued by outlining the company's notion of a healthy organization. After three two-hour sessions, these employees had a significant experience in which they realized that the company's "organizational charter" was different.

The next step (although it did not occur) in the process would be for the personnel representative to describe the social system of the total organization. He would strive to present a living model of the world in which the employees were asked to become members. He also could lead a discussion regarding the differences between the requirements of the present social system and the model of organizational health discussed previously. Finally, he could ask for any help from them to initiate processes to modify the system in order to enhance its health. (In this company such initiation of action would come from within the employee group. Also, such activity would be financially rewarded.)

Before the company orientation ended the personnel representative would try to make clear the high standards for entrance requirements. He would point out that once the employees were members they would no longer be evaluated by anyone else as long as their behavior met the standards. The standards in turn would be defined jointly by employees and managers. He would caution them to fully explore these standards with him because once accepted, they would be bound by them. He would also point out the freedom that any group would have to initiate action to modify these standards.

The next step would be for the employees to be interviewed by a representative group of the department in which they desire to work. These discussions will focus on the requirements of the job plus the uniqueness of that particular subculture. The final hiring of employees would be done by the group, with the incoming employees having the right to vote.[14]

Termination of Employees

The processes for termination could be initiated by an individual or groups assigned such responsibility. For example, the line supervisor of the employee could raise the question about the employee's capacity to meet the standards that he accepted upon entrance. The employee's own peers could also raise the same question under the more advanced stage of organization.

Anyone who is to be terminated must have the opportunity to participate in all the discussions involving his termination. If any discussions are held without his being present, the others could be disciplined —indeed under certain conditions terminated—for actions. The final note for termination will include the employee being considered for separation. Exactly who else participates in the process depends on the make-up of the organization at the time of separation. If its struc-

[14] The same process could be done for individual hiring procedures. The schedule of questions used on our research program, modified appropriately, could provide a beginning point.

ture is still primarily one of the pyramidal strategy, the superior and the employee will be involved. If the structure approximates the pure organization, the "superior" plus a representative group of the relevant employees would be involved. An appeals mechanism may also be developed. It could be "built into" the structure as it is in Glacier Metal, or it could be placed "outside" as in the case of the Inspector General in the Armed Services.[15]

[15] For an interesting discussion, see William M. Evan, "Due Process of Law in Military and Industrial Organizations," *Administrative Science Quarterly*, Vol. 7, No. 2, September 1962, pp. 187–207.

Chapter 13 ⌧⌧⌧⌧⌧⌧⌧⌧⌧⌧⌧⌧⌧⌧⌧⌧⌧⌧⌧⌧⌧⌧⌧⌧⌧⌧⌧⌧⌧⌧⌧⌧⌧⌧⌧⌧⌧⌧

The Organization of the Future:
A Summary View

In the past several chapters we have been brainstorming about possible ways to redesign organizations. If these ideas seem plausible and worth exploring seriously, our mission has more than succeeded. If, in addition, the views seem disconnected, with some discussed more fully than others, and do not form an integrated whole, the state of the writer's thinking has also been communicated. It would be good if an organized picture could be presented. To do so would imply not only that we have adequate insight into the parts of the "new" organization but, more important, that we know how they should be interrelated. Such knowledge requires extensive, but as yet nonexistent, empirical research, aimed at discovering the proper fit among the parts for a given set of conditions.*

One conclusion, however, should be evident by now. The pyramidal structure has *not* been overthrown. It has simply been relegated to a more realistic position in terms of its potential. We hope we have shown that the organizations of the future can grow beyond the pyramidal structure. It cannot be too strongly emphasized, however, that we

* A promising start may be found in William M. Evan, "Indices of the Hierarchical Structure of Industrial Organization," *Management Science*, Vol. 9, No. 3, April 1963, pp. 468–477.

are not able, without empirical research, to define the rate, direction, scope, and quality of the growth.

If we may keep in mind that our effort is for the sake of clarity and discussion, it might be useful to attempt a composite picture that *summarizes* some of the basic properties of the organization of the future. The objective is *not* to give a "definitive" view of what organization ought to be. The objective is hopefully to highlight some of the directions that seem fruitful.

The first conclusion is that the management in the organization of the future will give much more thought to its basic values and planning as to how they may be implemented. This does *not* mean, for example, that a business organization will spend more time pondering whether it should strive to make a profit. As long as our economic system does not change this will probably continue to be accepted as an important objective. The pondering will be more in terms of the other two core activities as well as their relationship to the objective. What kind of organization does it intend to be? What will its internal make-up look like? How does it intend to adapt to, and become integrated with, the environment? What influences should it attempt to change the environment? *

Assuming that human energy is still a major resource for the organization, we predict that the following changes will tend to become more dominant.

First, the values about effective organizational relationships will be expanded and deepened. In addition to achieving of the objective(s), the values will be expanded to include the development of a viable internal system capable of adapting to the external environment. The emotionality and interpersonal competence relevant to achieving these three core activities will now be as important as the values of rationality and intellectual competence.

The concept of directive authority or power will be expanded to include the influence of individuals through rewards and penalties that minimize dependence, through internal commitment, and the process of confirmation. The "old" values regarding influence will still be maintained to be used for the appropriate conditions. The "new" values regarding influence will be added to, not substituted for, the old.

Such an organization will tend to require individuals with somewhat

---

* One of the most innovative attempts in industry to begin to truly tackle these questions may be found in the work of John Paul Jones and his group at Union Carbide Corp. See John Paul Jones, "People—The Independent Variable," in Mason Haire (Ed.), *Organization Theory in Industrial Practice*, Wiley, New York, 1962, pp. 48–55.

different "needs," values, or predispositions, than we have suggested is true now. This change is especially necessary at lower levels. Briefly, the organization will require people who are not threatened by, but actually value, psychological success, self-esteem, self-responsibility, and internal commitment. This may well be a most difficult requirement to meet. As we have suggested, striving for psychological health is probably the most painful, tiring, exhausting, and yet need-fulfilling and exhilarating of human activities. Our concern is that the society, through its evolving social norms and political directions designed to support these norms, may indeed produce mostly individuals who simultaneously value and fear growth and who strive for security and safety.

But to develop such human beings in our society and then bring them into the present organizational milieu would be worse than ineffective; it could be tragic for the individual and the organization. And, if enough individuals and organizations are involved, the tragedy could include the nation. Human beings who have gone through the somewhat painful reeducation to value growth and those who have only experienced such development will tend to find the present organizational structures not only frustrating but discouraging.

We suggest that the organization of the future will also strive to enlarge the jobs. The enlargement will not tend to be limited to the "doing" or "motor" abilities. It will include expanded use of the individual's intellectual and interpersonal abilities. Wherever possible the jobs will be redesigned to include responsibility for larger and larger meaningful segments of the product and for its quality.

In addition to, and coming before, the redesigning (where such is not possible), jobs will tend to be enlarged by requiring the individuals to become concerned for the health of the organization. This concern will not be relegated to the suggestion box or to a program dreamed up to "instill new spirit."

The concern, if it is to be genuine, will need to become possible through actual changes in the organization's policies and practices. Thus employees (at all levels) may meet in small groups to constantly diagnose organizational strengths and weaknesses. One model might be the Scanlon plan. The absence of adequate time, which has been one of the major blocks to such activities, will become less of a barrier as the physical work week is shortened. The new time could be used with much profit on organizational diagnosis and the implementation of new ideas.

In addition to the enlargement of jobs, the same will be done for the organizational structure. The pyramidal structure will now exist side by side with several other structures. Each will serve a specific and already defined set of purposes. There will be a set of "decision rules" to make explicit the conditions under which each structure will tend to be most effective as well as the processes and procedures by which one may go from one structure to another.

Leadership will also be expanded. As in the case of the structures, varying patterns of leadership will exist to be used under specific conditions. Again, there will be a set of decision rules to guide the participants in when and how to use each leadership style. We say participants because in the organization of the future participants will tend to be required to accept increasing amounts of responsibility and therefore authority.

Closely related to the expansion of structures and leadership is the contraction or undermannedness in the staffing of the organization. This should tend to lead to "behavioral settings" in which the participants will be able to experience an expansion of their feelings of responsibility, importance, and commitment. In the past one important reason for overmanning the organization was to guarantee that no one became upset, because if he did the system would not be able to help him express it or to deal with it fairly in terms of his or the organization's interests. As emotionality becomes relevant and interpersonal competence increases, the fears, anxieties, and mistrusts that understandably exist in the very difficult area of "defining jobs" may tend to decrease *or* at least be worked out. If we are correct, it should now be much less necessary (1) to hide mistrust by adding another person, (2) to fear rejection by keeping on an incompetent individual, and (3) to sanction insecurity in those occupying power positions by not permitting "incompetence" to be openly discussed and defined. Needless to say, the entire area of optimally undermanning organizations requires much research. Above all, however, it requires a management and employees deeply committed to human growth, respecting one another, and trusting each other to the point that the fears and anxieties obviously inherent in this area can be openly worked through.

As trust increases the climate should tend to be ripe for some major changes in the controls, reward and penalty, and incentive systems. Controls will become much less instruments to "check up on," "change unilaterally," and "discipline appropriately" the subordinates' behavior. Controls will change to instruments of opportunity for increased self-responsibility and psychological success. Information will be collected to guide the individuals in achieving the work. The information collected "on" an individual will be collected "by" him and evaluated by him, and he will take the appropriate action. The attitude that will hopefully be developed is one of using managerial controls to learn something new about one's effort. Under these conditions, it is hoped that the information will not tend to be perceived as communicating whether or not a person has failed or succeeded but as information on how well he is doing.

The reader may conclude that the foregoing is quite idealistic. We would agree that it is in the present world. But if the recent research about personality and learning is valid, our position has a theoretical basis. Individuals who have a high degree of self-esteem, internal commitment, and self-responsibility will tend to see "controls" as information about their behavior, and their self-esteem will tend to drive them to further *realistic* heights without the need for external rewards or penalties.

Rewards and penalties, therefore, will also tend to be modified. There will still be the more traditional rewards and penalties, especially to the degree that (1) the foregoing changes are not possible, (2) the people's physiological and security needs are not fulfilled, (3) the individuals are psychologically threatened by growth and self-responsibility.

However, as the structures, leadership, jobs, and controls become expanded in the direction that we suggest, the opportunity for psychological success on the job should tend to increase. Psychological success is intrinsically rewarding. Herein will be a rich source of energy to be tapped. Effort that succeeds in getting a job done and enhancing individual self-esteem will tend to be realistically increased.

This does not mean that the intrinsic rewards of self-actualization are substituted for the traditional rewards and penalties. These are different phenomena and should be kept separate. Needless to say, an individual who is gaining increased psychological success but who feels he is being cheated by the organization will tend to be at once more accurate in his diagnoses of the situation in which he exists, more patient in his adaptive reaction, and more ruthless if the reaction does not work. Such an individual will also tend to be potentially more able to see (if it is true) that the organization is spending more money in order to make many of the changes that we are suggesting.

If research eventually leads us to conclude that the foregoing has some element of being valid and useful the task will have just begun. It will take many years to even begin to approach fulfillment. And, in our opinion, this is not disturbing. It may provide our society with a challenge with which to grapple and to gain deep feelings of success.

We do not believe that the problems would be solved by changing the ownership of the organizations. Churches, scout troups, schools, trade unions, governmental agencies, all have to some degree the kinds of problems that we have explored. Thus ownership does not seem to be a crucial variable as long as the basic security and physiological needs are satisfied. Indeed, under these conditions we suggest that those who require that the worker own the impoverished work world in which he exists presently may well be adding insult to injury. It is as if one were to say to the worker "It is true your work tends to be dull, boring, monotonous, dirty, nonchallenging, routine, and dissatisfying. But, I'll *help* you by calling *you* responsible for these conditions." This is not helping the worker. It is "fixing" him and "fixing" him good. Workers, we predict, at best will accept such "ownership" with apathy. At worst they may resent the implication that they now must like this world because they own it. Indeed we predict that if ownership (or significantly increased material rewards) does suddenly lead them to truly like it, they may be—or are on their way to being—sick. There is informal evidence available from studies in England, Poland, and Russia to show that the transfer of the ownership of the organization from private to public has meant very little change in terms of every-day problems faced by the people in the organizations. These experiences also suggest another important problem under these conditions is that employees do not tend to perceive the ownership as being "real." The connection between themselves and their government is so distant that feelings of ownership are not experienced.

Let us take Russia as one illustration. Weber long ago pointed out that that there was little difference between socialistic and capitalistic bureaucratic structures. A Russian factory should manifest human problems similar to those in a United States factory.[1] Berliner's analysis supports this view as far as internal organizational activities are concerned.[2] Mead's analysis also corroborates this point of view.[3]

For example, the following paragraph is from Mead's analysis of Soviet theory of organization. The paragraph is quoted verbatim. All the phrases that would tend to identify it as describing a Soviet organization are in parentheses. The remainder of the paragraph could serve as an excellent description of American organizational theory. Indeed, over a period of time, the writer has read this paragraph, modified as suggested, to more than one thousand executives. An overwhelming number have identified it as a valid description of American theory. The only hesitation we have observed is depicted by the statement, "Well, it is a bit strong, I wouldn't have written it that way, but it does have the basic essentials of American management theory." Another difference is that some executives (and Mead would agree [4]) suggest that

---

[1] Alvin Gouldner (Ed.), *Studies in Leadership*, Harper, New York, 1950, pp. 58–60.
[2] Joseph S. Berliner, *Factory and Manager in the U.S.S.R.*, Harvard University Press, 1957.
[3] Margaret Mead, *Soviet Attitudes Toward Authority*, Rand Series, McGraw-Hill, New York, 1951, pp. 35–36.
[4] *Ibid.*

a man's business role is only one part of his personality, one role among many. Presumably in Russia greater commitment to work may be required.

(Soviet) theories of industrial organization insist that organization is something which can be imposed upon a group of individuals, each of whom will be totally involved in the particular role he has to play, whether that of worker, foreman, or manager. This means that not only the particular parts of the personality needed for the particular task, but also all the other always present and contradictory elements in the personality are regarded as present. (Then in accordance with Bolshevik demands), organizational theory also insists that each individual must be presented with clear-cut goals and responsibilities. Clear-cut responsibilities are necessarily limited responsibilities, involving carefully defined lines of command and subordination. Thus (Soviet) organizational theory and practice struggle continually to devise an organizational chart which will define and limit responsibility. But within such an organzational scheme, the worker is expected to respond, not with a careful delineated measured response to the particular demands of his job, but with total devotion and spontaneity.[5]

But if the organization has responsibilities so does the individual. He too dismisses his responsibilities at the risk of his own mental health as well as the survival of the organization and his society. It will not tend to be easy to strive toward psychological success. It will be even more difficult to live through the agonizing transition period where much experimentation will be needed. Many individuals will find the challenge frightening; some will find it impossible. All these problems will have to be faced. No doubt there will be a wide range of differences regarding the extent to which these changes can be instituted. Consequently, there will be room for many of the individual differences that will exist among our population.[6]

[5] *Ibid.*
[6] One may wonder, given the present-day pressures within most organizations, when would time be found to begin to institute the changes (assuming we knew what they would be). This is an extremely difficult and knotty problem. However, there is one possibility to be considered. If the work week is shortened and if organizations are required to maintain their level of wages, then why cannot they use the free days to provide opportunities for workers and managers to tackle the long task that lies ahead.

PART IV

Using the Model to Explore
Other Studies

One of the central questions at the boundaries of sociology and psychology is the use of each discipline by the researchers of the other. There are psychologists who tend to ignore completely the sociological variables and sociologists who ignore the psychological ones.

Apart from the fact that each researcher has a right to choose the limits of his research, the limitation of his human finiteness is imposed on any investigator. He cannot do everything. Legitimate as these reasons seem, organizations are multidimensional and, therefore, a *theory* of organization must take into account all the relevant levels. We shall discuss some of the problems that arise when the interrelationships between the psychological and sociological levels of analyses are not considered as adequately as they might be.

The Need for Integrating the Sociological and
Psychological Levels of Analyses

One way to conduct studies is to find organizations whose profiles (in terms of our model) vary significantly. One organization's activities could be at the left ends of the continua and another's at the right. After describing the organizational characteristics we could observe the individuals' behavior and ask them to give us their attitudes, values, and so on. We would then be able to suggest that certain values and attitudes seem to be correlated with organizations whose make-up matches the left ends of the continua and another set (or a similar one if this is what is discovered) is correlated with the right ends of the continua.

This is typically the attack of many of the "sociologically" oriented organizational studies. Such research leads to important descriptive studies of organizational behavior.

There are two limitations related to this type of research which will be illustrated by the use of some examples. The first is that contributions made to basic theory will tend to be unnecessarily limited. Second, they will tend to provide incomplete evidence. To the extent that they do, they will not tend to be particularly helpful to the pracitioner.

Let us begin with the problem of contributing to theory. One sign of a maturing theory is that it can be used to derive hypotheses that can be empirically tested. This means that the more one can derive hypotheses from a set of interrelated concepts, the more effective is the conceptual scheme. Since more effective conceptual schemes are valued, there should be a predisposition on the part of the researcher, whenever possible, to develop a conceptual scheme from which to derive his hypotheses. It is our contention that in the following studies there was adequate literature and conceptual scaffolding available to have permitted an integration of the empirical hypotheses to a theory. We suggest that an antipsychological bias acted to prevent the writers from doing so.

Recently Vinter and Janowitz [1] published a report on juvenile correctional institutions which is not only a major contribution to sociologically oriented organization theory but could be of help to the practitioner. Street,[2] who worked under Janowitz, completed a thesis that seemed to be part of the larger project.[2a]

[1] Robert D. Vinter and Morris Janowitz, *The Comparative Study of Juvenile Correctional Institutions*, A Research Report, University of Michigan, 1961.
[2] David P. Street, *Inmate Social Organization: A Comparative Study of Juvenile Correctional Institutions*, University of Michigan, Department of Sociology, 1962.
[2a] A word seems appropriate to help explain the research selected for discussion in the next section. Several years ago, I had the opportunity to visit with Professor Morris Janowitz to discuss organizational theory and behavior. Among the many points he made, three were relevant to this section. Professor Janowitz insisted that good research draws from and adds to theory and good theory contains a minimum number of categories. On these two points we agreed.

Then Professor Janowitz stated (a position some sociologists take) that the psychological dimension is unnecessary in understanding organizational behavior.

Let us begin by examining the Street study. His theoretical view and methodology is highly consonant with, indeed he draws heavily from, the Vinter-Janowitz study. Street systematically compared inmate and staff attitudes as well as their behavior in six different institutions. Two of these institutions conceived their goals as being "custodial" (to protect the community from the "dangerous," "sick" inmates); two conceived their goals as being "treatment" (to supply service—e.g., therapy and counseling to help the inmates develop more constructive attitudes and values); and somewhere in between, there were two "training" institutions who saw their goals mainly as those of providing educational, vocational, and other types of training.

It was reasoned that the differences in organizational goals would lead to different internal formal institutional systems (conceptualized primarily in terms of gratifications and deprivations, and patterns of control and authority) which in turn would lead to different attitudes on the part of the inmates as well as different "informal inmate systems and leadership."

Let us first emphasize that the questions we wish to raise are intended in no way to reflect negatively on the results of the study. Given the objectives that were defined (namely to conduct an empirical study), the product is an excellent one. Our purpose is to raise questions about the study that seem to go beyond the writer's objectives.

Street, after some preliminary discussion, begins to develop some hypotheses about the inmates' reactions and perceptions under the varying types of institutions.

He begins (page 31) by stating:

1. Differences in the balance of gratification and deprivation—compared to the custodial institutions, the treatment institutions put much less emphasis upon techniques of degradation, the use of powerful sanctions, and denial of impulse gratifications, and place greater stress on providing incentives and objectives and experiences *which are* desired by the inmates. [The italics are mine.]
2. Differences in patterns of control and authority—compared to the cus-

---

Moreover, having read my work (including an earlier version of this book), he concluded that the type of "equilibrium psychological theory" (as he described my view) was not very relevant.

Try hard as I may, I was unable to get Professor Janowitz to be specific in his views. Finally, in order to pin him down, I asked him for an example of some work which he believed illustrated his view that the psychological dimension was not relevant. He gave me Street's thesis. While reading Street's thesis I learned of the Janowitz-Vinter manuscript which, for some reasons (presumably out of modesty), was not mentioned by Janowitz. I wrote to Vinter and obtained a copy.

todial environment, the treatment environment places less importance on surveillance, control over inmate association, proscriptive rules and the protection of social distance between staff and inmates and *lays greater emphasis upon the use of manipulation rather than domination and the attempt to legitimize the organization's authority structure.*

The words in italics are meant to point up the first question that we wish to ask. It is hypothesized (in point one) that inmates would tend to desire the experience in the treatment institutions. Why should this be so? No data are presented that suggest that the inmates might desire the conditions more typical of the treatment institutions. But, more important in our view, there is nothing in the theory that would suggest the hypothesis. Similarly, it is implied above and made explicit later, that the emphasis on manipulation rather than domination will tend to lead to more "positive attitudes" and "cooperation" on the part of the inmates.

Let it be clear that we would tend to agree with the hypotheses. There is no quarrel with them. Nor is there any quarrel with a scholar defining some hypotheses intuitively based on some set of experiences or a priori thinking. Our objective is to focus on the potential contribution to long-range theory building. Someday it will be necessary, if a theory is to be more fully developed, for these (in our opinion) valid hypotheses to be "derived" from or somehow related to the theory. This will not be possible, we suggest, until a psychological model of the needs of the inmates is made explicit.

To put this another way, Street has developed in his model of organizations the demands that each places on the inmates. For example, he writes:

1. Control is exercised over a greater realm of inmate activities in custodial organizations than in treatment institutions. The custodial daily round of life tends to be one of repetitive scheduling, constant surveillance, routinization, and the performance of activities in the company of large groups of other inmates.
2. The control of inmate behavior in custodial organizations more greatly restricts the inmates' freedom with regard to what previously were minor and personal activities, for example, when to brush one's teeth.
3. Custodial organizations generally make greater use of practices involving degradation, including rituals of depersonalization at the occasion of the inmate's entry to the organization and continuing with rituals of deference throughout his stay.
4. The number and range of incentives or rewards given to inmates is smaller in the custodial organizations, and those few which are made available

tend to be reduced to *not* being disciplined and to *not* suffering an increased stay before release. In treatment institutions, although release from the organization may not be held out conspicuously as a reward, a large number of other rewards, for example, frequent home visits and praise from the counselor, are provided.

5. In custodial organizations, the staff generally reward overt conformity to the institutional rules, with little concern for intra-psychic or character change. In treatment organizations, the rewarded behavior is more often that which seems to the staff to be indicative of such internal change, a conclusion which may be inferred from the inmate's verbal behavior more than from his overt activities.

6. Negative sanctions are more extensive and severe in the custodial institutions, at least with regard to explicit sanctions such as the use of corporal punishment and isolation rooms. The difference in severity is not so clear with regard to sanctions which are connected with delaying the release date through the application of explicit rules (used more often in the custodial institutions), and those which accomplish the same through counseling, in which the misbehavior is defined as evidence of the inmate's "unreadiness" to return home (used more often in treatment institutions).

7. Official rules for inmate behavior tends to be more proscriptive in the custodial organizations and more prescriptive in the treatment oriented institutions.

8. Authority relations in custodial institutions primarily involve domination and a formal emphasis on obedience, while those in treatment institutions involved informal means of manipulation and persuasion. (pp. 29 and 30)

These organizational "requirements" are conceptually related to the goals of the organization. All this is eminently sound and valid. Our point is that it is not possible to derive from this theoretical scaffolding the hypotheses, for example (which are stated and later validated), that the custodial institutions will have a different impact on the inmates than will the treatment institutions. In order for these hypotheses to be derived from a theoretical framework, one would need to have a model of the needs or predispositions of the inmates.

For example, if we assume theoretically (or for that matter establish empirically) that the inmates aspire toward what Jahoda calls dimensions of "positive mental health," we can "derive" the foregoing hypothesis knowing (as we do) the nature of the organizations (custodial and treatment). Thus, if the inmates aspired toward increased control over their institutional life, independence, and a degree of self-esteem, the custodial institution would be much more frustrating than the treatment institution. The result of frustration could then be shown to lead to the "negative" attitudes that the author found in the custodial institutions.

The same reasoning seems valid for other hypotheses. For example, "We expect that the use of extensive and severe measures of control, deprivation, and degradation which substantially limit the available supply of rewards will set the stage for retaliatory or compensatory development of a system for obtaining (other kinds of rewards)." (p. 46)

Why should one expect these consequences? There is little question but that they are probably correct. But such an expectation does not flow from one's sociologically oriented theory. It requires the addition of a theory of personality. For example, one might find highly masochistic, dependent ridden, authority subservient, youngsters with a deep sense of psychological failure who might react negatively to the "positive" treatment milieu and positively to the "negative" custodial milieu.[3]

Again, "the inmate group is more likely to take on such political functions and structures, particularly those connected with illicit goods, in the rigorous environment of the custodial institution. In the treatment organization, *because deprivations are low*, and mutual aid less necessary, such an ameliorative system would tend to lose its market." (p. 47)

How is it possible to conceive of a low deprivation without some model of the human personality? How will one judge when a deprivation is a deprivation, not to say whether it is low or not, without some concept of human personality? Moreover, the writer could find nothing in the theory as presented that would lead one to derive the hypothesis just stated.

"We anticipate that the treatment group will be organized more voluntaristically, built up around friendship patterns. Staff will give much freer reign to inmate association, *with the result that levels* of primary group integration and feelings and norms of group solidarity may be greater than in the custodial places." (pp. 51–52)

Why is there the expectation that the treatment group will behave in this manner and why the hypothesis that it will have these effects on the primary group? Again, implicit in the hypothesis is a theory about people that is not made explicit.

To put this another way, Street's study and the Vinter and Janowitz studies actually have implicit in them a model of the needs of the inmates. They implicitly "correlate" this model with the model of the custodial and the treatment organizations and predict the differential reactions of the inmates. Our attempt here is to suggest that the personality model be made explicit and related to the conceptual apparatus.

[3] There has been some research (for example, the already quoted study by Hartman) that Germans may develop personality needs which are more congruent with authoritarian organizations. If so, Street's hypotheses about outcome would not be valid.

One does not have to look too far for the model of personality that we suggest is implicit. For example, Street does provide us with some insights into two models about "human nature" that staffs of the custodial and treatment institutions hold. The staff of the treatment institution, for example, tends to believe that (1) the inmates can be rehabilitated, and (2) an adult can have trusting and close relationships with inmates. (p. 36)

The philosophy of their organization or, to use sociological terms, the organizational goals, are an outgrowth, we suggest, from the staff's concepts about the inmates plus their view of how the inmates are best helped. These concepts are *partially* rooted in psychological theory. For example, to state that people have the potential to develop trusting relationships, to grow in "mature" or "adult" directions, or that people are unable to trust and to strive toward maturity is to utilize psychological concepts. Here we find an intimate relationship between the psychological and the sociological levels. Each institution is composed of staffs that hold different concepts of the needs and potentialities of the inmates. They develop goals and environments (sociological level) that mirror these concepts. Once the goals and environment are created, they feed back to coerce different staff members in the same institution to behave in the same ways.

The point we are making is that it is senseless to insist that the psychological *or* sociological levels of analysis are adequate to understand the total problem. Both are needed.[4]

The sociological reader may point out that in our analyses we assume that the organizational goals and internal environments are evolved from the staff's concept of the psychological status of the inmates. It appears that we begin with the psychological level (the staff's view of the inmates), go to the sociological level (the objective of the organization), and then go back to the psychological level (the treatment of the clients). We have no objections to changing the order and beginning with the sociological level if certain questions can be answered. We began with the individual level simply because we know of no institution that is born "full blown" with its goals and internal environment ready to operate. Somehow, these goals must have been stated. If not, how are they to be explained? Perhaps those who incorporated or designed the institutions defined the objectives. Or, perhaps the present management has evolved its own concept of what the objectives should be. The difficulty in assuming that they are "given" or already there,

[4] For an interesting and philosophical attempt to integrate the individual and the sociological levels of analysis, see Edward A. Fryakian, *Sociologism and Existentialism*, Prentice-Hall, Englewood Cliffs, N.J., 1962.

as we shall see, becomes evident when those holding such a view attempt to change the organization. Moreover, since the same kinds of institutions (in this case, juvenile institutions) have different administrative goals, internal environments, and so on, but are embedded in the same societal matrix, this suggests that all the causal factors that are operating are not in the societal environment.

If we accept the importance as well as the discreteness of the psychological and sociological levels of analysis, we need conceptual ladders by which to climb up and down each level. One possible ladder is the "mix" model that we have presented. Since the dimensions have been shown to have relevance to both levels of analysis, it is possible (as we have done in previous sections) to relate individual and organizational dimensions.

If we coordinate each of these organizational types to our "mix" model and *if* we assume that the inmates aspire (psychologically) to the right ends of the continua, it is possible to develop a priori the hypotheses that have been stated. We expect (theoretically) that since there is hypothesized to be a congruency between the needs of the inmates and the goals of the organization (in the case of the treatment organization), we should find the cooperative, positive attitudes and the low desire to leave that actually were found.

Similarly, if the inmates are predisposed toward being treated as "mature" individuals, we may predict the negative consequences that were actually found in the custodial institutions.

To summarize up to this point:

1. Organizational theory will eventually have to include the psychological and the sociological levels of analysis. Each of these is a discrete level with its own uniqueness. However, the discreteness cannot be fully understood without relating it to the other levels.
2. In one well-conceived and executed sociological study, the hypotheses developed were postulated, so to speak, on the basis of previous work done and on assumptions held by the staff of the institutions. They were not related to a theory.
3. The inclusion of a psychological dimension, we suggest, would provide the missing link from the hypotheses to the conceptual scheme.
4. Finally, the employment of the model of organizational health helps us to develop, theoretically, predictions that are consonant with those that Street developed intuitively.

Let us now turn to the Vinter-Janowitz study, which seems to be the parent study for Street's work. We will use it to illustrate the difficulties encountered when this approach is used to help or to attempt to change practitioners.

In this study we find two other problems arising from a theory that does not tend to include the psychological level in its structure. These problems probably would not come to the forefront without the authors' willingness to attempt to apply some of their work in addition to their desire to conduct more basic research. If the questions that we raise are valid, they illustrate the important influence of applied research to help correct and enlarge basic theory.

The authors define delinquency on two levels. Psychologically, it is the inability to internalize and accept desirable social norms and values because of the failure of personal controls. Sociologically, delinquency is the inability of community systems to enforce appropriate rules because of the failure of social controls.

If a practitioner attempting to help a delinquent were to focus primarily on the psychological dimension, his attempts would probably meet with frustration, because even if he helped the delinquent to achieve personal control, the client would have difficulty maintaining it if simultaneously there existed a breakdown of societal controls or controls that did not reinforce the new psychological learnings developed by the client.

Similarly, the use of the sociological level of analysis alone would be frustrating. A society with adequate social controls would tend to have little positive impact on an individual whose personal control mechanisms are not effective. The authors' data suggest another difficulty to one operating primarily on the sociological level of analysis. Utilizing their own definitions and focusing on the institution as the unit of analysis, the authors found that the custodial and the treatment institutions were about equally successful in establishing social (organization) controls over the clients. (Indeed, in some dimensions the custodial institutions were even more effective than the treatment.) The frustrating point, however, for the practitioner would be that he would be forced to conclude that (almost) diametrically opposed (in goals, internal environments, conceptions of delinquency) institutions were equally "effective."

The difficulty involved in this primarily sociological approach can be expanded further by examining the change process used by the authors to influence the institutions to change. Their theory is of the organizational-goal variety. It emphasizes the central role of organizational goals or objectives in influencing the nature of the internal organization as well as the attitudes of the executives. staff, and clients. Like the theory of the "scientific-management school" (a view which many bureaucratic theorists of the sociological bias have in their writings), it places great stress on intellectual rationality, goal definition, control, direction, and organizational rewards and penalties that support the goals and the rationality while deemphasizing the role of internal interpersonal relationships and emotionality.

Their strategy for change tends to follow from their theoretical bias. Thus we find that the change process used was to attempt to influence the heads of the institutions. The rationale was that "the key to organizational effectiveness in our view is executive leadership," [5] because it is primarily responsible for the organization's objectives. This theory assumes, as the authors hypothesize, "a high consistency between executive perspectives and institutional goals." [6] This assumption has not only been questioned by previous organizational research,[7] but it is questioned by the authors' data. They did not find a one-to-one relationship, for example, between the executives' goal and perspectives and the staff's views of their organization's objectives.[8]

The change process emphasized the rational and deemphasized the emotional dimensions. Thus the seminar was primarily one in which the researchers presented their data, clarified questions, posed intellectual challenges, and supplied the executives with cognitive maps that helped them to see their institutions in new ways.

If one conceptualizes the executive seminars as an organization, one may infer that the researchers tended to develop more of a custodial than a treatment type of "change organization." The emphasis on rationality, on hypothesizing change based on feeding back information to the people with admittedly different views and perspectives, seems to imply a rather simple and undifferentiated view of the problem of unfreezing the clients. The character of the feedback session as described was one of a class room where the experts were in control defining the agenda, clarifying the research results, and so on. The sessions were designed to help the executives to overcome what the researchers called a "deficit of information," an assumption consonant to one that was held by the staff in the custodial organization, namely, that delinquents lacked the "proper" information.[9]

[5] Vinter and Janowitz, *op. cit.*, p. 42.
[6] *Ibid.*, p. 63.
[7] See, for example, the study by Thomas Whisler, already noted, and Chap. V in the author's *Personality and Organization*, *op. cit.*
[8] Vinter and Janowitz, *op. cit.*, p. 201.
[9] For literature that describes the difficulties involved in such a simplified view of organizational change, see R. Lippitt, J. Watson, and B. Wesley, *The Dynamics of Planned Change*, Harcourt, Brace, New York, 1958; Warren Bennis, Kenneth Benne,

The feedback of information, the researchers state, led many of the executives to realize that they really did not know their institutions well. Moreover, the authors continue, the new awarenesses tended to threaten the executives because they began to realize that they were not as competent as they had thought.[10] As far as one can tell, nothing was done by the researchers to help the executives with their resulting feelings of decreasing worth and administrative incompetence other than to insist that they (the researchers) were not implying that this was bad and at the same time to encourage further analysis, which by the researchers' admission would probably lead to new surprises for the executives and, if they took them seriously, new feelings of incompetence and failure.

Moreover, the writers state that after the feedback of their data, "one executive crashed his fist on the table and angrily exclaimed that he would not tolerate such sentiments among his staff; another was observed, after the session, bracing his staff driver against the wall and demanding to know how he felt about the institution and its purposes." [11] The writers then continue to enlighten the reader as to *how* all this comes about by saying that the executives first became defensive then moved on "toward sharing experiences about ways for coping with such conditions," and finally "out of this discussion emerged a more clear and forthright recognition of internal (problems)."

Initial responses to these findings included attempts to minimize their implications as a "play on words" (i.e., the meaning of questionnaire wording), or to redefine executive-staff discrepancies as showing how advanced was the leadership of administrators. These attempts were abortive and discussion soon moved toward sharing of experience about ways for coping with such conditions. Out of this discussion emerged a more clear and forthright recognition of internal problematic conditions and the ineffectiveness of existing executive approaches to these difficulties.[12]

Another example of the emphasis on the cognitive and the deemphasis of emotionality occurred when the researchers realized that the executives were beginning to use the data to establish a rank order of institutions which they (researchers) felt was not supported by the data. "It

and Robert Chin, *The Planning of Change*, Holt, Rinehart, and Winston, New York, 1961; R. N. Adams and J. J. Preiss, *Human Organization Research*, Dorsey Press, Homewood, Ill., 1960; Chris Argyris, "Explorations in Consulting-Client Relationships," *Human Organization*, Vol. 20, No. 3, 1961, pp. 121–133.

[10] Vinter and Janowitz, *op. cit.*, p. 595.
[11] *Ibid.*, p. 621.
[12] *Ibid.*, p. 602.

appeared self-serving and largely a projection of prevailing beliefs and ideologies," and "it carried with it evaluate connotations not based upon but relevant to criteria of effectiveness," and, finally, "premature acceptance of any ranking order would have prejudged and impeded the aims of comparative research."

How was this defensive reaction on the part of the executives handled?

The authors reply, "The initial ranking system was dissipated only gradually and *primarily through the introduction of more and more findings* which challenged its basic premises." [13] (The italics are mine.) This concept of the change process would not have tended to exist for the researchers if they had applied their theoretical bases to their own behavior. They imply that the more therapeutic or treatment orientation will probably be more effective in dealing with client change. Would it not have been helpful if they had utilized some of the attributes of the "treatment" orientation in helping their clients?

How successful was the change process? In terms of changing the delinquents, not at all effective. We would tend to agree with the authors, however, that a fair test was not made since it probably takes months for changes to trickle down the organization. However, in the case of the executives who were the main focus of the change process, only the executives who were more treatment-oriented tended to profit from the seminars. Such results would be predictable since the objectives of the seminar were probably not as threatening to these executives as they were to the custodial-oriented executives. The treatment-oriented executives were, as the authors point out, more amenable to, and less threatened by, the data (even though the data, at times, surprised them). Interestingly enough, the executives who profited most were the ones who, because of previous commitment, tended to operate on both the emotional and rational levels.

In retrospect, two points are being made. First, a plea for the recognition of the multidisciplinary nature of organizational behavior. The counterargument is acknowledged. Researchers (including the writer) are limited; they cannot study everything. Nor need they study everything. Each researcher has the right to focus on whatever level of inquiry that he desires. Nevertheless, it may not be unfair to ask researchers to at least note the areas relevant to the questions being studied that they are not going to discuss.

However, the issue discussed above is a much more specific one. In the cases of the Street, Vinter, and Janowitz research, hypotheses are defined which deal centrally with personality factors. The contention is that some of the major hypotheses cannot be explained without some

[13] *Ibid.,* p. 607.

model of the human personality. How else is one to explain why it is hypothesized that inmates would tend to feel one way about treatment versus custodial organizations? Some model is needed be it psychological or sociological.*

A Reexamination of "Total Institutions"

Goffman has presented an interesting and systematic study of the "total institution." [14] He defines total institutions as those in which (1) "all aspects of life are conducted in the same place and under the same single authority, (2) each phase of the member's daily activity will be carried out in the immediate company of a large batch of others, all of whom are treated alike and required to do the same thing together, (3) all phases of the day's activities are tightly scheduled . . . , and the contents of the various enforced activities are brought together as parts of a single overall rational plan. . . ." [15] Goffman then cites examples of homes for the blind, the aged, orphans, tuberculosis sanatoriums, mental hospitals, jails, penitentiaries, prisoners of war camps, boarding schools, work camps, and abbeys.

To the writer's knowledge all these organizations tend to have formal structures and activities that approximate the left ends of the continua of our mix model. As such we predict that they would manifest certain characteristics. We find that the majority of the characteristics that Goffman cites of total institutions are consonant with those hypothesized on the left end of the continua. Thus it may be that many of the characteristics that Goffman hypothesizes to be a function of the "totalness" of the system are more a function of the internal structure of the system.

Let us take some examples. Goffman suggests that "inmates" see the "staff" in terms of narrow hostile stereotypes, and the staff often sees the inmates as bitter, secretive, untrustworthy, and lazy. The staff tends to feel superior and righteous, the inmates inferior, weak, blameworthy, and guilty. Social mobility between the two strata is grossly restricted.

Recalling our analysis in the early chapters, we find that the foregoing tends to be true for industrial organizations. The hostility be-

---

* An analogy might be the perceptual psychologists who, when they are unable to explain perceptual phenomena physiologically, attempt to develop psychological models to explain their data.

[14] Irving Goffman, "The Characteristics of Total Institutions," in Amitai Etzioni (Ed.), *Complex Organizations*, Holt, Rinehart, and Winston, New York, 1961, pp. 312–340.

[15] *Ibid.*, p. 314.

tween the two groups, we have suggested, is more due to the dependence and submissiveness obtained by the staff over the inmates by using control, authority, disciplinary policies, and "appropriate" rewards and penalties. As McGregor, Roethlisberger, and Katz have shown, these ways of dealing with individuals are legitimatized by the "staff" by assuming and believing that the workers (inmates) are lazy and not to be trusted.

On the other hand, social mobility and the freedom to spend one's money as one wishes and to choose one's own recreational activities tend to exist in industrial organizations, but do not exist (as Goffman suggests) in total institutions. The reasons for this, however, are clearly related to Goffman's three factors, previously listed, that define a total institution and, in our terms, differentiate it from the pyramidal structure.

The boredom at work, the repetitiveness and seemingly uselessness of work have already been documented in the industrial organization. The changes in "moral career" also occur for a lower-level worker. As Bakke, Chinoy, Fromm, and Friedman have pointed out, the worker learns to face the plant realities of life once he enters a plant. In a recent study several ministers worked on assembly lines in Detroit. In their journals is an eloquent documentation as to how they found their moral character deeply influenced by their work world and the people who became significant in their life. For example, some found themselves swearing, lying, cheating, hating, goldbricking, and consciously producing poor work.[16]

Similarly, in an industrial plant we will find the "stripping process" with "mortification of the self." How else can we explain the comments of workers describing themselves as "there is not much to me," "I'd rather dig ditches than this," and "any dumb guy can do this work." Moreover, we have provided documentation for the "situational withdrawal" cited by Goffman as the apathy, indifference, and rebellious adaptation.

The echelon system of authority, which is directed toward aspects other than work such as dress, department, social intercourse, that Goffman cites is certainly known in industry, especially by the managers.[17] The same may be said for the existence of a "privilege system" containing "house rules," "rewards," and "release binge fantasy." For example, there is the work of Dalton, Whyte, and Roy on the rate busters, rate setters, and the informal rules and regulations of the groups. Also, there is the example of the informal rewards and penalties such as "binging" in the bank wiring room in the Hawthorne experiments. Also,

[16] Personal communication from Detroit Area Study.
[17] William H. Whyte, *The Organization Man*, Simon & Schuster, New York, 1956.

referring again to Chinoy and Blum's work, we find ample evidence of workers with all sorts of fantasies of what they are going to do when they "get out of here." Dalton's work, already cited, on informal management practices describes many of these phenomena on the managerial level. Finally, as we have shown, the human-relations literature is full of examples of the privilege and authority systems, the "house rules," and so on, developed by management to control the employees.

To summarize, by using the model and assuming that the total institutions as defined by Goffman have formal organizational structure, we predict that many of the characteristics cited by Goffman to be characteristic primarily of total institutions are also characteristic of institutions that are *not* total organizations by Goffman's terms.

A Reexamination of the "Who Benefits" Typology

We may raise a similar kind of question with the typology of organizations recently developed by Blau and Scott.[18] Briefly, they have categorized organizations according to "who benefits." In their view four groups benefit. They are (1) the rank and file, (2) the owners or managers, (3) the clients (customers), and (4) the public at large.[19] Four types of organizations result from the application of this criterion: (1) "mutual-benefit associations," (2) "business concerns," (3) "service concerns," and (4) "commonweal organizations."

Blau and Scott suggest that each type of organization has special problems caused by the differences in terms of their criterion "who benefits." For example, the crucial problem in mutual-benefit associations is that of providing participation and control by the membership; in the business concern, it is to maximize efficiency; in service organizations, the conflict is between professional service to clients and administrative procedures; and in commonweal organizations, it is the development of democratic mechanisms whereby they can be externally controlled by the public.

Comparing these predictions with those that could be made by using our framework, we find that the differences cited by Blau and Scott are erased. For example, we suggest that a crucial problem for any organization is to provide participation and control by members, to maximize efficiency, and to resolve the internal conflicts between "clients" and administrative procedures.

[18] Peter Blau and Richard W. Scott, *Formal Organizations*, Chandler, San Francisco, 1962, p. 42.
[19] *Ibid.*, p. 43.

Recalling the literature, there was evidence to illustrate our view. One of the major themes of Likert's and Bass's massive reviews of the literature is that business organizations are increasingly striving to increase the participants' control over the activities of the organization. The Scanlon Plan, job enlargement, middle management board, productivity committees, and labor and management committees are but a few empirical examples to illustrate the point. Also, in the literature much is written about the conflict between professional service to clients and administrative procedures. The clients may be "internal" (as in large corporations with "internal consultants") but the problems are the same.[20]

Blau and Scott suggest that mutual-benefit associations are plagued with problems of "membership apathy." Yet we have already cited this as a central problem of many modern industrial organizations. Their contention that business strives to maximize efficiency to the point where it is not limited by other factors is not fully supported in the literature. The works of Eells, quoted previously, and Anthony are but two examples that suggest this is not necessarily true. Large corporations today are consciously spending money and permitting costs that cannot be shown to be directly related to the product. This is true ranging from the more socially conscious programs such as community relations, college aid, and summer internships, to those internal administrative factors such as goldbricking, rate setting, and feather bedding.

We are simply suggesting that all of Blau's and Scott's characteristics seem to be true (in varying degrees) for all industrial organizations. Moreover, we suggest that they would become even more applicable as organizations strive toward the states characterized by the mix model as effective organization.

A Reexamination of Weber's Definition of Bureaucracy

Another example of the use of the model is to study different predictions made by Weber and compare them with those that we might make. For example, Weber defines bureaucracies as organizations having a high degree of (1) specialization, (2) chain of command, (3) formal rules and regulations, (4) impersonal relations, and (5) carrier potentialities for individuals. Such organizations approximate the unhealthy (axiologically not-good) organization. Assuming this for the moment, we may derive certain predictions about the consequences

[20] See, for example, Douglas McGregor, *The Human Side of Enterprise*, McGraw-Hill, New York, 1960.

of bureaucratization that are somewhat different and more differentiated from those that Blau and Scott suggest for Weber's analysis.

For example, Weber hypothesizes that (1) specialization leads to expertness, (2) authority structure and the existence of formal rules are assumed to make vital contributions to the coordination of activities, and (3) detachment is held to increase rationality.

Our analysis leads us to conclude that these hypotheses are only partially true. Thus we have suggested that extreme specialization at the lower levels leads to such fractionated work that it tends to lead to psychological difficulties. This in turn tends to prevent individuals from becoming more expert in their field. Boredom, frustration, and alienation eventually set in, and these in turn tend to prevent the development of further expertise. Indeed, individuals have been found to counter the trend of specialization by "adding" to their jobs so that they perform much more "generalized" work than is intended. Similar trends are observable at the upper levels of management where specialization has led to expertness in a specific field. There has been an increasing development of a more generalized function commonly called "general management." "General management" seems to have arisen due to the fact that the organization has developed so many unintended consequences (mostly human) that "generalists" became necessary.

This leads us to examine the next hypothesis. There is no doubt that, as Weber suggests, authority makes vital contributions to coordination. We have, however, indicated that authority can also tend to make a number of "dysfunctional" contributions to coordination. Finally, Weber's hypothesis that detachment may lead to increased rationality seems plausible. However, given our viewpoint, we suggest that there comes a point where detachment becomes an emotional phenomenon that significantly influences rationality. It has been shown elsewhere, for example, that "bureaucratic detachment" among top management has led to increased mistrust, lack of confidence, and lack of understanding between the workers and management as well as among executives. They tend to adapt to the former problem by developing a myriad of personnel and psuedo-human-relations programs.[21] The dissonance among executives seems to be coped with by emphasizing rationality even more, thereby "guaranteeing" that the emotional components will not tend to be expressed. Executives learn "not to get emotional," and "to keep feelings out of logical discussions."[22]

[21] Chris Argyris, *Personality and Organization, op. cit.*, Chap. V.
[22] See Chapter 3 in this book.

Organizational Pseudo-effectiveness and Individual Pseudo-health

In this chapter we intend to explore, in a very preliminary manner, some insights that are possible by relating our concepts of organizational effectiveness and pseudo-effectiveness to individual health and pseudo-health.

We have suggested that on a theoretical level the concepts of effective organization and individual positive mental health are congruent. The question arises: can we show that such a relationship exists empirically? For example, if we were to find an actual organization that fulfills the criteria of effectiveness, would the individuals in it also tend to be psychologically healthy? We would expect this would be true if the individuals can be assumed to be influenced psychologically by the work world in which they exist (and if the outside environment is, at least, benign).

Unfortunately, no empirical data are available to check this prediction. However, we do have some data to explore another aspect of the question. In a previous chapter we said that plant X is characterized by a state of pseudo-effectiveness (unrecognized disorder).[1] We also stated that this organization's activities approximate the characteristics of

[1] The original study was published by the writer as *Understanding Organizational Behavior*, Dorsey Press, Homewood, Ill., 1960.

what we defined as organizational ineffectiveness. The ineffectiveness became manifest when the organization was placed under stress.

It would be interesting to speculate whether an organization experiencing pseudo-effectiveness may also influence individuals to experience a state of psychological pseudo-health. On theoretical grounds the answer would seem to be affirmative. If individuals are required to behave according to the values of the unhealthy organization and if they internalize these values (and if the environment is benign), over a period of time we might speculate that their own personalities may begin to mirror the state of pseudo-health characterized by the organization.

To test this hypothesis we would require extensive longitudinal studies. We also would need to develop operational criteria to measure the degree of internalization as well as its impact through time on the process of internalization and finally the "radiation" effect on the remaining areas of the individual's life activities. The latter would be important because even if we could demonstrate that the individual was influenced toward a psychological state of pseudo-health by the organization, he might be capable of containing and limiting this state to the time that he is actually working. Unfortunately, we are not able to meet these requirements now.

We have, however, some very crude data by which to explore this problem in a very preliminary manner. During the study of plant X we developed data about the self-concepts of the individuals. The data, unfortunately, were at relatively surface levels of analysis. They lacked the clinical depth required for systematic analysis. There is another limitation to the forthcoming analysis. Even if we do find some correlation between the individual's and the organization's state of well-being, we are still left to determine whether the causal relationship runs from the organization to the individual, vice versa, or (as is probably true) both ways. Our data simply are not adequate to cope with this question.

One more preliminary point. In order to study psychological pseudo-health, we must have some concept of psychological health. For the sake of exploration, we will again utilize the concept of positive mental health by Jahoda.[2] Pseudo-health will tend to exist in the individual if, on the surface, he reports no illness or uncomfortableness, yet upon closer examination it is found that he deviates from the Jahoda dimensions of positive mental health.

The first step is to establish whether individuals feel any uncomfort-

[2] Marie Jahoda, *Positive Mental Health*, Basic Books, New York, 1958. We again remind the reader that we realize the Jahoda dimensions have yet to be validated.

ableness. The data indicate that the employees reported extremely high satisfaction. Over 95 per cent liked their jobs, the organization, and the people in it. Another measure is the number of individuals whose self-actualizing score is high (arbitrarily defined as seventy and above). In plant X, we find that over 90 per cent of the self-actualizing scores in both the high- and low-skill departments are over seventy.[3] We may conclude, therefore, that the individuals view their world as being a relatively satisfying one with minimal feelings of disease and, of course, almost no reports of disorder.

Let us now turn to a brief comparison of the available data about the individuals with the Jahoda dimensions. Again we must keep in mind that the empirical data originally had not been collected to understand these dimensions; consequently, they are not as systematic as we would desire.[4]

1. The first dimension is that the individual's self-concept is rich and differentiated. It "contains an image of all important aspects of the person." It includes ". . . a successful synthesis by the individual of all that he has been and done, with all he wants to be and do with all that he should and is able to do . . ."

The data suggest that 91 per cent of the low-skill employees describe themselves as psychologically simplified and psychologically impoverished.[5] Many (over 70 per cent) were visibly surprised to be asked anything about their self-concept. (The question regarding their self-concept was not direct.) "You mean, you want to talk about me? (Laughs.) That's a funny one. No one ever asked me that kind of question before. (Silence.) Honestly, I don't know how to answer that. There isn't very much to me I just do . . . job day in, day out."

Another aspect of the same question is the respondent's perception of his strengths, limitations, and growth potential. Apparently, being asked to discuss their growth potential and limitations is for them even more surprising. The low-skill employees are more surprised and bewildered than the high-skill employees. Although all respondents report that they

[3] Chris Argyris, *Understanding Organizational Behavior, op. cit.,* pp. 104–114; see p. 111 for the scores.

[4] Nor are the data presented in their entirety. Those who wish further information are referred to footnote 3 above.

[5] The data refer to the individual's perception of self while in the organization. No claim is made that these findings are generalizable to the total life of the employee. The N's are as follows:

Plant X

HS = 30

LS = 90

are honestly and sincerely willing to discuss these subjects, most (90 per cent) find it difficult because as one states it, "Honestly, I've never given a moment's thought to that. I've been working here nineteen years and the only thing I really think about is my pay!"

The high-skill employees, on the other hand, speak quite freely in positive terms about their many technical abilities (70 per cent). They point out that they aspire to high-quality work in the different jobs that they perform. They speak with pride about their capacity to perform several highly skilled jobs.

A somewhat different picture appears when we focus on *interpersonal* abilities. In the majority of cases the low-skilled and high-skilled employees find it difficult to discuss whether they have, and to what extent they use, interpersonal abilities. When questioned, they usually reply that these abilities are unimportant or that they are used very infrequently while at work. Both the low-skill and high-skill employees emphasize that they spend most of their time working "on their machine" or "at the bench" and have "little time to talk" or even "yak, yak, with the boys."

Our observations confirm their reports. The overwhelming portion of the low-skill and high-skill employees' time while at work is spent interacting with a machine or producing a product by hand We find very few cohesive groups within, and even fewer outside, the plant. Data to shed light on this phenomenon are presented in a subsequent section. Suffice to say at this point that the observations suggest that employees do not interact frequently with one another. When they do, the interactions are fleeting and skin-surfaced.

The employees' descriptions of their "off-the-job" activities suggest a similarly "impoverished" interpersonal world. Seventy-two per cent of the high-skill and low-skill employees spend the majority of their time looking at "T.V.," "reading a paper," "drinking beer," "doing jobs around the house," and once in a while "going to a movie with the wife" (never more than once a week). Another 20 per cent, who are mostly highly skilled employees, spend time working in their shop on hobbies (for example, cabinet making, carpentry, radios).

2. The "correctness" of the fit of the more manifest aspects of the self-concept with the reality of the total organization seems to be quite high. The low-skill employees do live in a world in which they rarely use any motor or cognitive abilities. They perceive their jobs as nonchallenging, routine, and dull (77 per cent). Over 75 per cent of the low-skill employees report that their jobs require no abilities other than physical stamina. If a low-skill employee limits his description to that

part of his self that is related to, or required by, his job, then it seems that he is being quite reality centered when he states, "There's not much of me used in this job."

The high-skilled employees seem to be equally reality centered. They characterize their jobs as being challenging, with plenty of variety (85 per cent). Nearly 70 per cent report that their jobs require many technical abilities and high quality standards. However, they too are in a work world in which their interpersonal skills are seldom required.

3. Positive mental health implies that the individual "accept himself including his shortcomings," and that he "accept his own human nature with all its discrepancies from the real image without feeling real concern." [6]

Our data suggest that the majority of the employees accept, at least overtly, their "simplified" selves. They seem to express little dissatisfaction with work situations requiring no technical or interpersonal abilities (for low-skill employees) and only technical but no interpersonal abilities (for high-skill employees). One employee's comment illustrates the majority feeling when he states: "After all, mister, that's true wherever you go. Most jobs are so set up that any nitwit can do them. Why get teed off about that."

However, when *both* the low- and high-skill employees (in plants X and Y) are asked about their perceived interpersonal competence (as differentiated from their technical competence) less than 10 per cent respond with a sense of positive regard. The majority of the employees prefer skin-surface interpersonal contacts. For example, the majority in both plants (90 per cent) describe friendly employees as employees "who you hardly ever see and leave you alone." Over 90 per cent of the high- and low-skill employees in both plants describe the management as being "friendly," "warm," and "kind" because "they leave you alone and you hardly ever see them."

4. A sense of identity is another crucial dimension of mental health. The ego identity increasingly becomes more clear, more consistent and free from transient influences. "It becomes increasingly determined by accumulated personal experience." [7] The distinguishing mark of this aspect as compared to self-acceptance is its cognitive emphasis on clarity of self-image.[8]

It is difficult to know exactly what evidence to cite for this dimension. The data suggest, for example, that the majority of the employees who are with the plants for three years or more seem to resign themselves

[6] Argyris, *op. cit.*, p. 28.
[7] *Ibid.*, pp. 29–30.
[8] *Ibid.*

to their particular world. The ego, as represented by the respondents, seems to be consistent with the requirements of the work world, which are very few. This implies that the employees' behavior is highly influenced by the accumulated experience in their respective plants.

If the concept means that the healthy individual identifies with his environment in the sense that he develops a strong anchor (sense of identity) in order to maintain self-stability in a world full of pushes and pulls, then the low-skill and high-skill employees may be clearly described as having a high sense of identity with the organization. Nothing is said about the quality of the identity. To use the anchor analogy, I believe that the anchor is holding down a relatively small ship (simplified self) and is dropped into very shallow water (the organization). Although this is conjecture, the data cited about the individual's perception of the requirements of his job do lend some credence to the organization's aspects of this hypothesis. Moreover, we note that in both plants at least 95 per cent of the low-skill and high-skill employees report that they make no important decisions while at work. An almost similar percentage in X and about 70 per cent in Y add that they prefer this situation to one in which they might be required to make important decisions and to have some responsibility.

However, it may be that the sense of identity more properly refers to the individual's continuous, relatively unchanging awareness of himself in all his complexity and potentiality. The person with a sense of identity is aware of his basic spontaneous aspirations but continually strives to move toward these aspirations and interests. He is able to build on his accumulated personal experience without having to deny part of it in order, for example, to tolerate a routine low-skilled job.

Keeping in mind the restricted nature of our data, we have not found many employees who manifest such feelings. They are rather more identified with (incorporated in) the social system in the sense that an apathetic, noninvolved individual tends to take on the coloration of whatever influential setting he happens to exist in. However, this conclusion is also an inference because the psychodynamic processes involved in the employees' identification with the social system have not been studied.

5. All the data available point to a lack of "growth motivation." The emphasis of the employees is on psychosocial safety, skin-surface relationships, security, and a nonchanging, structured, highly predictable world. Maslow calls this situation "deficiency motivation" and Herzberg, "hygienic orientation." Over 90 per cent of the employees in both plants report little or no interest in developing a "mission" or a "sense of commitment" to tension-producing, but challenging experiences.

They would prefer their world to be predictable, secure, and unchanging. The low-skill employees (85 per cent) prefer dull, routine, non-challenging, repetitive jobs because that guarantees "making a good day's pay" and "after all, that's the only reason why we're working."

The high-skill employees (75 per cent) prefer work with some challenge and variety and work that requires standards of high quality. However, the overwhelming majority would give up these aspirations if they inhibited their making a fair day's pay. Evidence for this is found in the reaction of thirty of the highest skilled employees whose jobs were greatly "deskilled" without any warning. Within one day *all* the high-skill employees accepted the change, they report, primarily because it meant increased earnings.

Still another indication of growth motivation may be the degree to which the employee actively seeks to modify his work in order that it might become more interesting. As we might expect, the degree of freedom to change the work is almost zero. Jobs are set by engineers, and they may not be changed.

However, within the existing job an employee may make modifications ranging from a simple change of pace to a major change in the work process (usually kept hidden from management). Since low-skill jobs are highly controlled by the machine, it is understandable to learn that most of the low-skill employees report almost no opportunity to vary their job in any way. The high-skill employees, however, report a somewhat greater freedom which they see as decreasing in the future. Most use the freedom to make the work *easier*, less challenging. Only two high-skill (and no low-skill) employees report that they actively think how their job cauld be modified so that it could be made more effective and at the same time more challenging to themselves as human beings. The majority in both groups (over 95 per cent) report that they are not expected to worry about their jobs, or even the company. "That's management's worry."

Finally, we note that only 3 per cent in one plant and 2 per cent in the other joined the firm with the hope that they would be able to advance themselves. Only an additional 23 per cent and 30 per cent report that they joined to learn some skilled trade. The remainder of the employees report that they had no aspiration when they first joined except "to earn a living."

To summarize, both groups manifest a desire to work, to keep active. The low-skill employees' aspirations seem to stop there. There is little evidence that they desire anything from their work except to be left alone by management, to make money, to have a secure job, and to experience human relationships which are not personal. The high-skill employees' aspirations seem to go a little beyond this, in that they desire more than to work; they desire to experience challenging, varied work. However, they are willing (and do) give up these aspirations if they threaten the earning of a "just" living.

6. Investment in living is related to the individual's "range and quality of his concern with other people, and the things of this world . . . ," his "dedication to existence of profound and complete participation in living," and finally his "deep concern for others and . . . his striving on satisfying his own needs." [9]

If anything characterizes the low-skill and high-skill employees it seems to be an almost total focus on their strivings to satisfy their own material needs. The most important concern is to "make a buck." Almost no concern is expressed about being in a relationship of "oneness" with others about "participation in living," and about "a deep concern for others." In fact, the predispositions of togetherness (one of the four most potent predispositions) and aloneness emphasize the degree to which the employees do not feel themselves to be part of a group or to care for others.

They (70 per cent) speak continually of "playing it cool" and "being friendly with people so that they leave you alone." "None of this getting personal stuff for me," adds another, "I'm here to make a buck and that's it."

7. It is important for the individual to have a philosophy of life that unifies such conflicting tendencies as the desire to lose oneself in the things of the world and self-objectification (that is, looking at one's self with detachment). This implies the possession of long-range goals regarded as central to one's personal existence.

If we conceive of a unifying outlook on life as being integrated around a set of values and aspirations and involving long-term goals, the available data do not suggest that the employees in X and Y manifest such a philosophy.

The employees do speak, however, of a philosophy of life while at work which at least helps them to rationalize their job situation. This philosophy of life has four major parts: the emphasis on money and job security, to be left alone, to have control over one's immediate job, and to have skin-surface relationships with others. By far the most important is the money and job security. The emphasis on what one is worth in terms of dollars and cents leads the individual employee to continuously think of himself, and especially his skills, as something to be bought and sold. It is an example of the "market orientation" discussed by Fromm.

[9] *Ibid.*, pp. 34–35.

Moreover, there is a conscious deemphasis of human factors (for example, rich interpersonal relationships, challenging work, developing and increasing a sense of responsibility) and a concomitant emphasis on wages, job security, benefits, and other material factors.

The central goals are rather simple and basic. They involve keeping their family and themselves alive, in good health, and adequately housed, clothed, and fed. Education for the children also ranks high. All these require money and again we see more reason for the emphasis on material factors. Consequently, most goals of the employees are short-range ones focusing on the everyday necessities of living.[10]

8. The next dimension is concerned with the degree to which the individual is self-directed and self-controlled, his degree of self-respect, his growing independence from immediate stimuli, and finally the degree to which his behavior is not determined by external factors alone, but dictated also from within.

One of the major predispositions mentioned by 95 per cent of the employees is the need to direct and regulate one's own immediate job. This predisposition is clearly illustrated, for example, in the employees' discussion of the importance of the kitty. Nearly 95 per cent describe the kitty as crucial because it gives them some degree of control of their own immediate job and the earnings obtained on the job. The foregoing data imply that there is a need for self-regulation.

However, the matter is somewhat more complex. We must conclude that the employees prefer to direct themselves *if* management is willing to take the responsibility to define the objectives, requirements, and obligations of the jobs. Thus, although they desire to be self-regulative, 65 per cent prefer to be directed, while over 88 per cent prefer not to have any responsibilities associated with their jobs.[11]

9. Independence means the ability to conform to the behavioral norms of the society by remaining free to choose whether to conform or not, free to depend on their own potentialities and latent resources for their own development and continued growth. Another way of stating it is "to organize . . . the objects and the events of his world to bring them under his own jurisdiction and government." [12]

The pressure to conform to the formal and informal norms in plant X is quite great. In fact, the objective of plant X's social system is to coerce a particular range of behavior so that the system produces a product at a particular cost.

[10] *Ibid.*, pp. 39–40.

[11] The employees, we must remember, exist in an organization whose very function is to prevent them from becoming independent of the stimuli created by management.

[12] Argyris, *op. cit.*, pp. 47–48.

The employees (once they accept employment) report that they feel they have little freedom as to whether they shall conform or not. For example, when their cherished kitty is destroyed, they submit and conform. The same is true when some of the most skilled jobs are deskilled without warning, and without any participation on the part of the employees.

10. Adequacy of interpersonal relations is related to the degree to which the individual "has positive effective relationships," "promotes another's welfare," "works with another for mutual benefit." [13]

As has already been pointed out, the majority of the employees prefer skin-surfaced relationships in which they are psychologically separated from others. Dirty jokes, sports, and weather are frequent topics of discussion. Most employees prefer to see themselves as individual entrepreneurs working alone each day to earn a certain amount of money. Not only is little thought given to promoting other employees' welfare, but many employees actually are afraid that they might be asked to help a friend. This is one reason why many of them prefer not to make friends (70 per cent). We also note that 65 per cent in plant X and over 80 per cent in plant Y report that they have no personal friends at work. Finally, we note that nearly 50 per cent of the high-skill and low-skill employees in X prefer to work completely alone.

Further insight into the quality of interpersonal relationships is obtained when we note that over 80 per cent of the employees describe an effective foreman as one who leaves the employees alone and seldom talks to them. The employees desire the same quality in their fellow workers.

Unfortunately, the available data about the outside activities are so meager that they are not suggestive. The employees did report a relatively simple and impoverished outside life. We are encouraged, however, to consider these conclusions for the sake of illustration because they are supported (indirectly) by the French and Kornhauser data on employee mental health, and by the work of Bakke, Hollingshead, Chinoy, Blum, and Berger (to mention a few) regarding the leisure activities of employees. It may be relevant, therefore, to hypothesize that the employees in plant X may manifest a state of well-being which could cover up an incipient disorder.[14]

[13] *Ibid.*, pp. 58–59.

[14] The writer cannot help but take a tangent for a moment. If the above is valid, what can be the meaning of the replies given by employees in questionnaires to such questions as "Overall, would you say that you are satisfied with your job?" Psychological research suggests that satisfaction is fundamentally a function of a consonance between the individual's expectations or needs and the degree to which these are satisfied. If one has a low level of aspiration, if one expects to perform

Summary

Although it is impossible to develop meaningful measurements from the data, it is fair to suggest that in eight dimensions of positive mental health (richness of self, self-acceptance, growth motivation, investment in living, unifying outlook on life, regulation from within, independence, and adequacy of interpersonal relations), the employees in plants X and Y would tend to score low or are headed in a direction away from positive mental health.

In two dimensions, correctness of self and identity, they would score much higher or are headed in the direction of positive mental health. However, let us examine the meaning of each score. In the first dimension it means that they have developed a relatively realistic self-concept which is impoverished ("that there isn't much to me"). In the second dimension, they are strongly identified with what, in their own eyes, is a relatively impoverished world. We might infer that having high scores on these two dimensions may be one important reason why the employees can live in relatively internal equilibrium with the low score in the other dimensions. Thus, although the high scores are high along two relatively impoverished dimensions, this fact may prevent the mental health from becoming worse.

Keeping in mind the limitations of the data, it seems plausible to suggest that a correlation may exist between organizational pseudo-effectiveness and individual pseudo-health.

dirty, uncomfortable, routine, and boring work, and this is in fact what he finds, then he will not tend to be dissatisfied.

Moreover, as we have learned above, employees after a while learn the "hard facts of life" and adapt by lowering their level of aspiration and expecting routine boring work. Also, as we have shown elsewhere, the employees soon learn to value money and other material factors such as benefits. Under these conditions emyloyees will tend to report satisfaction as long as they are earning what in their opinion are fair wages and have good benefits and job security. (Anne Anastasi and John P. Foley, Jr., *Differential Psychology*, MacMillan, New York, 1949, p. 802.) Compounding this problem are the findings that we reported earlier, to the effect that lower-class individuals tend to grow up in a world where verbal competence is not particularly rewarded. This may tend to make many of the questionnaires and similar measuring instruments somewhat threatening. Anastasi and Foley, in a review of the literature, conclude that one may "detect" a tendency for status differences to be more conspicuous in the more highly verbal type of tests. They point out, however, that in the tests of mechanical ability this trend is by no means confirmed. In one study the highest mean (for mechanical ability) was obtained by the lowest social group.

Some Thoughts on the Mechanisms Relating Individual and Organizational Pseudo-health

The next question that arises is why does the correlation exist? Perhaps the organizational pseudo-health may "infect" the individual? Or is the reverse the case? If it is the former then, somehow, the apparent unawareness on the part of the organization of its increasing ineffectiveness is hypothesized to lead the individual to becoming "blind" in the same manner, but not necessarily to the same degree or at the same level.

By what mechanisms does organizational pseudo-effectiveness facilitate individual pseudo-health and vice versa?

Unfortunately, research shedding direct or indirect light on the question is not available. Keeping in the spirit of this work, however, some tentative hypotheses will be developed about the mechanisms involved. We begin with the following assumptions.

1. All individuals have a history of striving to develop their personalities in some direction before entering the organization.
2. Some will tend to develop in such a way that the requirements of the organization will tend to be consonant with their needs.
3. Others will tend to find a degree of incongruence between their needs and the organization's demands. It is our hypothesis that most lower-level employees tend to find themselves (in varying degrees) in this situation. This hypothesis seems plausible because of the work of such men as Bakke, Chinoy, Blum, Purcell, Whyte, Roy, McGregor, Herzberg, Likert, Kahn, Hollingshead, Katz, Walker, and Guest (already quoted), to mention but a few. They all cite evidence of employees with varying levels of education and from different social classes suggesting that their work is monotonous and nonchallenging. Two typical comments come from two low-skill employees, one a grammar school graduate, and one a high school graduate, in plants X and Y. The first describes his job as: "There ain't much to this job. Any stupid guy can do it." The second states, "I'd rather dig ditches! At least I would be out in the fresh air." We suggest that the very job given to most lower-level employees, the technology that pervades the organization, and the managerial controls that exist, tend to create a working world which is different from what they would tend to prefer.
4. The gap between expectations about the abilities one may use and

those one actually uses closes as one moves up the skill ladder. However, as we have already suggested, another dimension becomes more prominent. It is the administrative structure and managerial controls with the dependence, submissiveness, and lack of control that they tend to create in one's work life. This second factor compounds the difficulties for the lower levels and acts, in varying degree (depending on the organization) to create some difficulties at all the other levels (with the difficulty theoretically being least at the top).

5. Drawing from the work of Bakke, Kahn, Weiss, and Maslow, already cited, we assume that man has a strong set of needs influencing him to work. They range from the basic desire to provide physiological and creature comforts for his family to maintaining some semblance of self-esteem.

6. We also have hypothesized that the problems that we have suggested exist (in varying degrees) for all formal organizations. Thus we may conclude that upon entrance a worker (skilled and nonskilled) is faced with a problem of changing his attitudes and adapting to reality. To be sure, the degree of change necessary will vary and can best be ascertained by empirical research (college graduates face it as well as individuals at the lower levels).[15]

7. This will tend to lead the employees to change their values and attitudes in order to adapt to, and remain within, the organization. This process may be conceptualized as a "re-education" of one's self.

The appropriate model, therefore, of how the organization influences the individual, causing him to change his values, may be related to what Lewin [16] has called "re-education" and more recently Schein [17] has called "coercive persuasion." We hypothesize that this model should hold for any type of organizational influence, whether in the direction of health, illness, or pseudo-health. Our focus, however, will be on pseudo-health.

Lewin viewed influence to change behavior and attitudes as a dynamic process resulting from the forces toward change overcoming the forces against change. Broadly speaking, the individual strives to change if he perceives that in doing so he increases the probability of enhancing the stability and internal integration of his self-concept.[18]

Coercive persuasion, suggests Schein, tends to occur over time and

[15] William Dill, Thomas L. Hilton, and Walter R. Reitman, *The New Managers*, Prentice-Hall, Englewood Cliffs, N.J., 1962.

[16] Kurt Lewin, "Frontiers in Group Dynamics: Concept Method and Reality in Social Science," *Human Relations*, Vol. 1, 1947, pp. 5–42.

[17] Edgar H. Schein, *Coercive Persuasion*, W. W. Norton, New York, 1961.

[18] *Ibid.*, pp. 119–128.

has several successive but overlapping stages. They are (1) "unfreezing" from the "old state," that is, the old equilibrium of forces, (2) changing toward a new "state" ("seeing the light," "having insight," "seeing the merit of the new ideas"), and (3) "refreezing" to the new state by receiving internal and external support for the new values.

The first period of an individual's working life is usually spent in training for the job and "learning the ropes." The "unfreezing" of the old values and attitudes probably does *not* tend to begin at this early stage. We hypothesize that during the early period the individual may find work frustrating but challenging, and he may be full of concern about "making out" financially. For example, we have found that girls learning to use semiautomatic bookkeeping machines initially found the work frustrating but challenging. During the learning period they were rarely absent even though they were frustrated more than they were ever to be again on that job.

Once the learning period was over, the job became monotonous and boring to the point that day-dreaming, singing (individually and in groups), etc., were commonly observed activities, and absenteeism and turnover increased several hundred per cent.[19] The molecular nature of the work now became obvious and stood out as the main characteristic of work. Thus the first major set of factors that induces the individual to begin to "unfreeze" are the technological ones that define his work world.

The second set of factors, as we have already suggested, are related to the administrative structure in which the individual is embedded. Not only will he tend to use few of his abilities, but he will also tend to experience a minimum degree of control over his working world (including whether or not he is to continue working, to receive wages, etc.). As McGregor and this writer have suggested, this degree of dependency and lack of control over one's life is reminiscent of childhood. Such conditions may tend to arouse guilt feelings as well as feelings of "wanting to do something about it."

At this point the worker may have reached the stage that Schein has called the "precipitation of an identity crisis as a result of an intensive unfreezing process." [20]

The next stage is to develop new values and beliefs in order to make this new world an acceptable one to the self. The difficulty lies in the fact that the number of such available values and beliefs is sharply limited.

[19] Chris Argyris, *Organization of a Bank*, Labor and Management Center, Yale University, 1952.
[20] Edgar H. Schein, *Coercive Persuasion, op. cit.*, p. 131.

The employees, according to Schein, should then be observed to:

1. search for information to find acceptable beliefs about the self.
2. find an "other" whose "identity" is acceptable (i.e., his beliefs about himself are accepted as correct by other employees).
3. identify with the "other."
4. accept things this "other" says.[21]

Let us assume that our hypothetical employee is in a new plant full of employees who are also new to work. Drawing on the data from plants X and Y and Part I, we may develop the following sets of hypotheses.

Since there is a need to work, for financial and psychological reasons, the individual will attempt to adapt in some manner that does not cause him to be fired or endanger the level of his wages. The exact methods for adaptation will vary with each organization. We will focus on organizations similar to plants X and Y.

1. One step the employee may take is to begin to change his conception of himself. For example, we have seen that employees in plants X and Y simplified their selves, *decreased* their view of their worth, their estimation of their capacity to grow, and their desire for psychological success. They tended to *increase* the value of material rewards such as money and benefits, the importance of what they produced, the technical skills they had, and the length of work experience. In short, the employees began to alter their selves in the direction of what Fromm has called the "market orientation."

This could be the kind of factor that led to employees who seemed to lack a sense of identity that focused on their human potentialities, who had a low growth motivation and a low need for independence as well as a low concern for their fellow workers.

We suggest, therefore, that due to the pervasiveness of technology and the administrative structure, the employees who decided to remain began the change process by changing their own views about themselves and the world around them. To put it extremely, they saw no other alternative since they could not leave and they wanted to work.

Once these values were developed individually, the employees sought "others" who held similar values and who could help them to "refreeze" these new values. As the acceptance and public acknowledgment of these values increased, they began to act as norms in the workers' world. It is at this point that these norms infiltrated the world of the employee outside the plant and led to (but were not the only causes of) the low level of aspiration and the apathy that researchers have found throughout the employees' life.

Let us explore this more fully. For the sake of illustration, let us as-

[21] *Ibid.*, p. 132.

sume that pseudo-health is internalized by employees. We may then hypothesize that it can "infect" and be passed on to the children. This means that the children will have various degrees of the same states of pseudo-health "injected" into them. If this occurs, then the parents help to develop within the children a self-concept that goes in the direction of an unhealthy organization. For example, we should find that the lower-class working children will tend to (1) have personalities that are relatively "simplified," (2) not be aware of all the parts, especially those that the clinician categorizes as deeper and leading toward self-actualization, (3) have a relatively less effective problem-solving competence due to low interpersonal competence, lack of awareness of total self, etc., (4) express fear of challenges and responsibilities which in turn may develop within them a compulsive striving to maintain these defenses, less they be threatened, and finally, (5) shorten their time perspective (in order to protect themselves from experiencing failure by dealing with problems and challenges which they are unable to cope with effectively).

This in turn will reduce the chance their children have to develop their own psychological destinies. We might argue that this is realistic since the children will tend to have a limited destiny. The other side of the argument is that such a view is at once realistic and reinforcing to the present state of affairs. (Moreover, we may hypothesize that an organization may develop difficulties primarily populated by such predispositions.)

Once this process is activated, the next generation of employees will tend to have less of a problem in reeducation because, due to their family upbringing as well as their social class values, they will tend to be developed closer to the situation that they will find at work.

2. Since organizations in a free society are also open to some manipulation, the second step was for the employees to change aspects of their work world without jeopardizing their position. This leads to the informal activities that we have already discussed. Absenteeism and turnover become institutionalized as do trade unions, apathy, goldbricking, rate setting, increased emphasis on material factors, and alienation.

This step begins the process of refreezing. The employees now have support from their fellow employees regarding their new conception of themselves as well as the new values toward work. Interestingly, the informal activities, with the exception to be mentioned, do not tend to act to increase the individual's self-esteem. Apathy and noninvolvement do not tend to lead to positive mental health, but neither would a high degree of ambition and involvement. The point is that most of the employees in the foregoing situation have a choice between two "evils."

The informal activities do tend to provide the worker with a feeling of some power (especially the trade union, slow downs, rate setting, etc.). This may tend to ameliorate the feelings of guilt and dependence to which we have already referred.

Incidentally, personnel programs, viewed from this light, may act as guideposts to the employees as to how far they can go in their informal activities and what processes they should use in institutionalizing them. Thus, in plants X and Y where the philosophy of personnel had been "to keep workers happy" and "not to rock the boat," the employees tended to choose less aggressive modes of adaptation and to achieve a lower degree of control than employees in organizations with a more militant personnel policy.

With the workers developing a self-concept dominated by "non-growth" motivation, a simplified self, and minimal concern for the expansion of their and others' selves, they will not tend to be aware of the cues that would suggest to them that they are heading in the direction of illness (on the individual level). Such factors would threaten the "new" simplified self. The new self, therefore, actually directs the individual toward behavior that is consonant with the continua that are away from individual health (for example, to be controlled and directed by others, to have a short time perspective, to be apathetic and indifferent, etc.).

But if, as we have hypothesized, individuals have had to see these aspirations as their only relatively safe choice, they will tend to value them. Moreover, they will tend to be supported by most of the employee informal systems as well as by a substantial portion of the managerial personnel programs. Under these conditions the individual may tend to become "blind" to behavior and values that approximate the healthy ends of our continua. Once this occurs we have the beginnings of individual pseudo-health.

In closing it is important to emphasize that the preceding analysis is hypothesized to be valid under these limited conditions: (1) the requirements of the organization inducing individuals toward individual illness are not extreme; (2) the individuals wish to remain within the organization; and (3) they have some influence over the organization to modify it if, and as, it is necessary.

A Note on Essentiality, Interdependence of Parts, and Organizational Growth

Implicit in this conception of organization is that all organisms seem to manifest three kinds of activities. We shall refer to these activities as the *organizational core activities* or simply *core activities*. The core activities are (1) achieving objectives, (2) maintaining the internal system, and (3) adapting to the external environment.

The core activities are in turn composed of many subactivities, all with the purpose of contributing to their respective core activity. Since people or combinations of people are to be assigned to perform these activities, they must be defined in behavioral terms. These sequences of behavior may be called *functions*. Functions, therefore, may be defined as sequences of behavior which lead to necessary and intended consequences.[1]

The intended consequence (purpose) of each function is to contribute to the successful operation of the core activities (that is, achieving the objectives, maintaining the internal system, and adapting to the environment).

Also, because people are finite in their capacities, the functions must be "chopped up" into manageable units. These units have been called

[1] As we shall see in a moment, this does not preclude functions arising out of a response to unintended consequences.

roles or jobs. Roles or jobs are usually combined into larger units, typically labeled sections, departments, divisions, and so on.

Whether one conceptualizes the organization in terms of functions, jobs, or sections, we may say that subsystems are created and each assigned (whole or part) responsibility for the continued successful operation of a particular function. These subsystems *contribute* to the core activities by *supplying* one or more essential functions. Their degree of essentiality to the organization is related to how much they contribute to the core activities. Their contribution may vary, and thus their degree of essentiality may vary. However, since every function has some degree of essentiality, so does each subsystem.

Each subsystem may also be conceptualized as receiving appropriate help from the other subsystems so that it may continue to perform its function. This activity may be described as *drawing from* other subsystems of the whole. We, therefore, conceive of an *organic* part as an integrated set of activities which (1) contributes a particular (set of) function(s) which in turn contribute to the whole, (2) draws from other parts in order to maintain itself and to continue performing its set of activities, and (3) contributes to other parts so that they maintain their discreteness and continue their work.

The *interdependence of parts* is a function of the degree to which they draw from each other. The more a part draws from any given part, the more it is dependent on those other parts. The less a part draws from any given part, the less it is dependent on the other parts. Thus every part may be considered in terms of its essentiality to the whole, its dependence on other parts, and their dependence on it. The more a part contributes to the whole and to the other parts, the more *central* it is to the organization. The less a part contributes to the whole and to the other parts, the less central it is to the organization.

The impact of the parts on the whole may also vary as a function of their relevance to the core activities. For example, a central part related to maintaining the system to the external environment may be less central than a more peripheral part related to adapting to the environment when the organization is under attack from the environment. To put this another way, parts may have a *planned centrality* which is characteristic of the whole system in a steady state. The planned centrality may be temporarily modified if for some reason the steady state is upset. The temporary centrality which is in response to the momentary disruption of the steady state may be called a *spontaneous centrality*. (Organizations may develop planned strategies as to how the system may shift from its planned centrality to a spontaneous centrality.)

An example may be an organization whose management has never considered its manufacturing department as being a central part. This second-class status then leads to many inequities which eventually lead the employees to attempt to unionize. If this company desired not to be unionized, we may predict that the manufacturing department will become temporarily central in the organization. Or an organization that has been coasting along because of competitors may suddenly place new emphasis on research and development if its product may become obsolete.

The planned centrality may also be altered on a more permanent basis. For example, it is well known that a large communications utility has recently decided to make marketing a central department throughout its entire organization.

The more central (planned or spontaneous) a part, the greater the scope, speed, and length of impact on the other parts surrounding it and on the core activities as a whole. Peripheral parts, no matter how peripheral, have some impact on the core activities. Otherwise they would not be organic parts.

Parts may also perform activities to protect themselves from disequilibrium of other parts. The more central the parts, the more important the functioning of these protective activities to the whole. These protective activities may be "defensive" in that they parry or block dangerous influences from other parts, or "offensive" in that they continually seek to discover potential difficulties before they influence the part. Finally, the relationships among parts may vary in terms of the degree to which they facilitate and inhibit each other. For example, in recent years it has become fashionable in electronic firms to establish "product test" departments to "check" on the quality of a finished product. Unfortunately, this tends to create a situation where manufacturing and engineering feel that the "product test department" is out to "get them." A more well-known example is the internal audit department in a bank. It tends to be perceived as having a mission that is incongruent with the other departments.

This discussion has focused primarily on the planned aspects of interdependence or those parts that can be predicted and understood in terms of necessary deviation from the original plan. There may be cases, however, where parts arise spontaneously that do not seem to be related to any plan or consequences of such a plan. The part indeed seems to be unintended from everyone's point of view. It seems to be a spontaneous growth resulting from or responding apparently to nothing. Such parts have been reported within organizations on the individual and departmental level. For example, the organization is unable to explain why some people were hired, why they are kept, and why their function is relevant. The same has been reported from time to time in large, bureaucratic departments.

It may be that what we diagnosed as "spontaneous" growth is really not spontaneous. If we understood the factors at the time the part developed, the helping and receiving functions that it provided would be clear. Our position is simply the acceptance of determinism, one of the most fundamental assumptions in most sciences. We hypothesize that no part "just develops." In an organization every part plays some important role. It is our task to search until this role is discovered.

Organic parts exist at various levels of analysis. For example, an organization may be composed of organic parts A, B, and C. Each of these parts may have their own organic parts (a, a, a), (b, b, b), and (c, c, c). The small-letter parts are organic to the large-letter parts and those in turn are organic to the whole. Thus small-letter parts can only influence the whole through their respective large-letter parts.

The number of parts of the whole may be conceptualized in a number of ways. One is in terms of the number of discrete functions and not the number of subunities performing each function. Two ears are one part because the part is the function of hearing. Similarly, four identical departments, all producing the same product, are one part, namely, the manufacturing function. However, four departments, each producing different parts of the same product, are conceptualized a separate subpart of the larger function (in this case, manufacturing). Thus the number of people performing a particular function is a different question from the number of functions that constitute the whole.

Up to this point we have emphasized that organic parts perform functions without which the whole cannot exist, and without the whole the parts cannot survive. Thus there is a state of mutual dependence among the parts and between the parts and the whole.[2]

Organizational Growth

Let us see how these general conceptions might be used to help us to understand organizational growth and organizational stress. At its most general level, growth tends to be viewed as some increase of some aspect of the organization. Biologically, growth tends to be internally rooted but influenced environmentally. As far as we can tell, growth is not a necessary property of social organization in the same strict sense that growth is a part of the "genetic" nature of biological organisms.

[2] Lawrence K. Frank, "Genetic Psychology and Its Prospects," *American Journal of Orthopsychiatry*, Vol. XXI, No. 2, July 1951, No. 3, pp. 506–522.

There are no factors such as "genes" within the social organization that guarantee its growth, much less define the probable sizes and forms that it must take. Some writers have suggested that organizations must grow, for example, "to make optimal use of communication channels." Thus there is a size below which the organization is not using its full potential and above which its potential is overused. Other writers have suggested that the size of the organization is related to the problem of the organization becoming integrated with the environment.

It is our hypothesis that growth in a social organization is related to the development of the "proper form" that is necessary to fulfill the three core activities of (1) achieving the objective(s), (2) maintaining the internal system, and (3) adapting to the external environment.[3] "Proper form" may be conceived in terms of the quality and quantity of interdependence. That is, the "proper form" is that patterning or combination of "contributing to" and "drawing from" processes that will tend to lead to the "best possible" expression of the core activities. (Our concept of "best possible" is discussed in more detail in Chapter 7.) The "best possible" expression of the "proper form," in turn, will tend to depend not only on the nature of the three core activities but also on the degree to which the organization has chosen to express each of these activities.

For example, illustrating the core activity of adapting to the environment, Kaufman suggests that if we assume that organizations are continually faced with various degrees and complexities of uncertainty, we may hypothesize that they may respond to uncertainty by increasing their self-containment and by centralizing.[4]

The most frequent mode of increasing self-containment, according to Kaufman, is for organizations to expand their boundaries. Expansion "has the effect of bringing the origins of the required resources into the network of incentives, coordination . . . so that the flow of resources . . . is now much more heavily influenced by the organization . . . the expanded organization is more self-contained in the sense that it fills more of its own basic needs from within its new boundaries."[5]

Our hypothesis about growth is not new. Biologists seem to have suggested this position long ago. For example, Waddington has stated, ". . . each definite form assumed by an organ must be considered as

[3] For an excellent article on social systems and social organization, see Everett E. Hagen, "Analytical Models in the Study of Social Systems," *American Journal of Sociology*, Vol. LXVII, No. 2, September, 1961, pp. 144–151.
[4] Herbert Kaufman, "Why Organizations Behave as They Do: An Outline of a Theory," in *Administrative Theory Symposium*, University of Texas, Austin, March 1961, pp. 37–72.
[5] *Ibid.*, p. 55.

representing an equilibrium between several opposing and interacting forces. The whole sequence of shapes during the development of an organ is a series of such equilibria." [6] Thompson suggests that, "in an organism, great or small, it is not merely the nature of the motions of living substance which we must interpret in terms of force, . . . but also the *conformation* of the organism itself, whose permanence or equilibrium is explained by the interaction or balance of forces. . . ." [7]

Exactly how the parts interact with one another to create a social organization is still one of the important unanswered questions. Nor do we know much about the laws that govern organizational growth. We may or may not find that, as in living biological organizations, growth of the individual parts occurs at decidedly different rates, that maximum rate in different parts is reached at different times in the life cycle, and that extreme over- or underproduction of parts may stimulate or retard growth. [8]

Unfortunately there is very little research available on organizational growth. Most of the existing research has been conducted in formal organizations. But these represent only one kind of social organizations. There is no known (to the writer) theory or empirical evidence suggesting that organizations must be created as pyramidal structures. There may be other "genes" that man can plant to grow different kinds of organizations. Our discussion of growth, therefore, should be able to consider conceptually other structures or organizational strategies.

Typically, growth in initially and predominantly formal organizations has been studied in terms of the number of people, the number of departments, and capital assets, whose form will tend to be guided by such "managerial principles" as "chain of command," "unity of direction," "span of control," and "specialization of tasks." Once these are used as the guideposts for understanding growth, then Ross's analysis of the factors that tend to limit the growth of firms is relevant: [9]

(a) That co-ordination must be the act of a single centre and, therefore, the principle of division of labour cannot be applied to this task.

(b) That the supply of co-ordinating ability available to the firm thus cannot be expanded along with an increase in the supply of other factors.

---

[6] C. H. Waddington, *Organisers and Genes*, Cambridge University Press, Cambridge, England, 1940, pp. 128–129.

[7] D'Arey W. Thompson, *On Growth and Form*, Cambridge University Press, Cambridge, England, 1961, p. 11.

[8] Charles Wilson Green, "Psychological Factors Regulating Normal and Pathological Growth," in *Growth*, Yale University Press, 1928, pp. 149–150.

[9] M. G. Ross, "Management and the Size of the Firm," *Review of Economic Studies*, Vol. 19, No. 48, 1950–51, W. P. Griffith, London, p. 148.

(c) That the supreme co-ordinating authority must have knowledge of the detail of problems as a condition of their solution. Thus the larger the field in which co-ordination is attempted the greater must be the knowledge possessed by the co-ordinators.

(d) That every increase in size beyond a certain point can be achieved only by lengthening the scalar chain of authority, thus increasing costs of co-ordination which at some point must exceed the declining economies in this and other spheres.

(e) That the scalar chain of authority cannot be indefinitely extended.

Recalling Part I we agree that these factors do tend to limit growth in a *pyramidal organization*. For example, we have shown that pyramidal organizations can spawn internal conflicts, apathy, goldbricking, etc. (at least at the lower levels), and mistrust, conformity, and organizational defensiveness (at the upper levels). Under such conditions co-ordination may have to be centralized, the freedom to coordinate restricted, the information flowing primarily up to the top.

It is interesting to note, and it suggests a preview of our viewpoint, that Ross concludes that the pyramidal organization can be helped to grow more with decentralization. Decentralization may be conceived of as fundamentally a shift in the kind of interdependence of parts. Parts that were peripheral now become central. Also the degree of interdependence becomes more complex because there is a greater degree of activity among the parts where they are "feeding upon" and "drawing from" each other. But as we also hope to suggest, in considering organizational growth, one need not be limited to the possible flexibility of pyramidal organizations. We maintain that there are other forms of organizations which, if considered, would greatly enlarge the scope of an organization's flexibility and its freedom to change itself.

A second problem in understanding growth is related to the unit one chooses as the basis of study. Mason Haire, for example, has chosen people as the unit by which to study size.[10] He is able to show, through careful research, that certain organizations seem to grow in accordance with known biological laws of growth.

Scott [11] and Leavitt [12] have criticized him on the grounds that people are not the proper unit. Computers, for example, may replace individuals

[10] Mason Haire, "Biological Models and Empirical Histories of the Growth of Organization," in Mason Haire (Ed.), *Modern Organization Theory*, Wiley, New York, 1959, pp. 277–283.

[11] William G. Scott, *Human Relations in Management*, Irwin, Homewood, Ill., 1962, p. 159.

[12] Harold J. Leavitt, "Management According to Task: Organizational Differentiation," *Management International*, Vol. 1, January–February 1962, p. 18.

and the organization can still grow. Their argument points up the limitations involved in selecting a unit, but is not as damaging as they imply. For example, one could simply decide to calculate how many people each machine is replacing and continue on with the original models.

Leavitt suggests that the proper unit is a "task" or "action unit." Unfortunately the "size" of the task action unit is not defined. It is one job, five jobs all performing the same work, a department? In our view all these would be valid units and would lead to interesting insights.

The choice of the unit depends on the theory one holds. For example, in our case we might begin by focusing on what we have defined as "functions" irrespective of how many people, departments, and machines perform them. It would be consistent with our view to study the mechanisms by which each function "draws from," and "provides help to," other functions. Growth could then be defined in terms of the change in number and quality of (*a*) the functions as well as (*b*) the mechanisms of "drawing from" and "giving help to" other functions. Included in such a study would be the degree of congruence among functions (that is, the degree to which they facilitate or inhibit each other).

Another interrelated approach would be to study the shifts, if any, of the degree of centrality and peripherality of parts. It may be that growth in social organization is not limited to the addition of parts but the shifting of the parts into a "better" or more "efficient" whole. Such a study would require some independent criterion of "better." This approach would focus on the different levels of parts such as people, groups, and departments. It would study how the changes within, and the shifts among, the parts influence each other and the whole.

To summarize, let us limit ourselves to the generalization that growth in a social organization is related to the development of the "proper form" to achieve the three organizational core activities of (1) achieving the objective(s), (2) maintaining the internal system, and (3) adapting to the external environment.

Name Index

Adams, R. N., 291
Affinto, M., 239
Allport, Gordon W., 4, 5, 21, 37
Anastasi, Anne, 308
Anderson, Harold H., 162
Angel, Ernest, 21
Argyle, Michael, 60
As, Dagfinn, 15
Atkinson, J. W., 257
Attneave, F., 226
Avery, R. W., 18

Bakke, E. W., 8, 35, 75, 80, 124, 140, 152, 173
Baldamus, W., 52, 71
Banks, Olive, 82
Barker, Roger, 4, 222, 228
Barnard, Chester, 249
Barnes, Louis, 182
Bartlett, F. C., 258
Bass, Bernard, 167, 170, 179, 203, 215
Bates, F. L., 177
Bateson, G., 22
Baumgartel, Howard, 225
Becker, Silwyn, 244
Beckner, Morton, 122
Behrend, Hilde, 250
Behringer, R. B., 228
Bell, D., 76
Bendix, Reinhard, 74, 79
Benne, Kenneth D., 247, 290
Bennis, Warren, 8, 67, 136, 182, 239, 290
Berelson, B., 87, 170
Berger, Bennett, 74, 77, 78

Berkowitz, N., 239
Berliner, Joseph S., 277
Bertallanfy, Ludwig, 12
Bettelheim, Bruno, 5
Bidwell, Alvin C., 202
Blake, Robert, 11, 182, 184, 202, 213, 231
Blau, Peter, 9, 176, 295
Blauner, Robert, 41, 52, 66
Blum, F. H., 75
Bradford, Leland, 247
Broom, Leonard, 8
Brown, Wilfred, 10, 171, 194, 203, 204, 208, 211, 231, 258
Bruner, Jerome, 5, 255
Buber, Martin, 28, 255
Burgess, Eugene, 16, 17
Burns, Tom, 169, 182, 184

Cannon, Walter B., 122
Caplow, Theodore, 124
Capwell, Doral F., 75
Carlson, R. O., 18
Carnarius, Stanley E., 50, 51, 83
Cartwright, Dorwin, 7, 96
Cattell, R. B., 167
Chamberlain, Neil W., 180
Chapple, Elliot, 232
Chin, Robert, 291
Chinoy, E., 74, 79
Churchman, C. West, 212, 241
Clark, James V., 136
Clark, Peter B., 249
Clark, R. A., 257
Clewes, W., 258

Subject Index